GO MATH!

Volume 1

Made in the United States
Text printed on 100% recycled paper

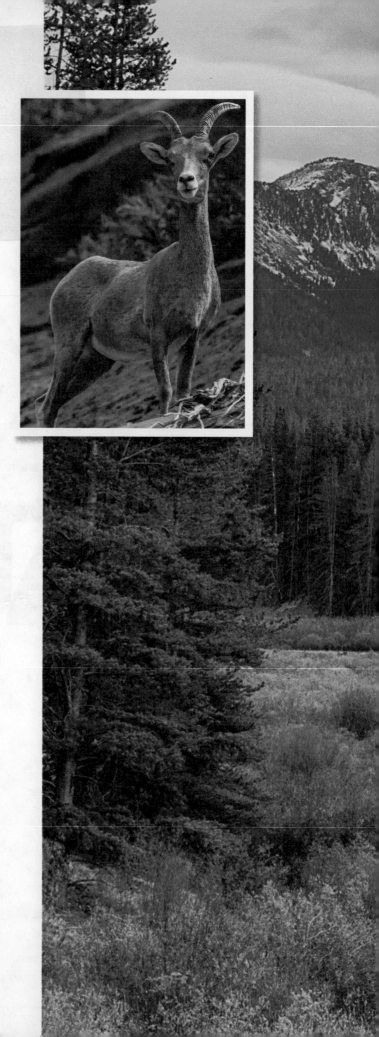

Printed in the U.S.A.

ISBN 978-0-544-43279-6

4 5 6 7 8 9 10 0868 22 21 20 19 18 17 16 15

4500529369 B C D E F G

Dear Students and Families,

Welcome to **Go Math!**, Grade 5! In this exciting mathematics program, there are hands-on activities to do and real-world problems to solve. Best of all, you will write your ideas and answers right in your book. In **Go Math!**, writing and drawing on the pages helps you think deeply about what you are learning, and you will really understand math!

By the way, all of the pages in your **Go Math!** book are made using recycled paper. We wanted you to know that you can Go Green with **Go Math!**

Sincerely,

The Authors

Made in the United States
Text printed on 100% recycled paper

Authors

Juli K. Dixon, Ph.D.
Professor, Mathematics Education
University of Central Florida
Orlando, Florida

Edward B. Burger, Ph.D.
President, Southwestern University
Georgetown, Texas

Steven J. Leinwand
Principal Research Analyst
American Institutes for Research (AIR)
Washington, D.C.

Contributor

Rena Petrello
Professor, Mathematics
Moorpark College
Moorpark, CA

Matthew R. Larson, Ph.D.
K-12 Curriculum Specialist for Mathematics
Lincoln Public Schools
Lincoln, Nebraska

Martha E. Sandoval-Martinez
Math Instructor
El Camino College
Torrance, California

English Language Learners Consultant

Elizabeth Jiménez
CEO, GEMAS Consulting
Professional Expert on English Learner Education
Bilingual Education and Dual Language
Pomona, California

VOLUME 1

Fluency with Whole Numbers and Decimals

Critical Area Extending division to 2-digit divisors, integrating decimal fractions into the place value system and developing understanding of operations with decimals to hundredths, and developing fluency with whole number and decimal operations

Place Value, Multiplication, and Expressions 3

Domains Operations and Algebraic Thinking
Number and Operations in Base Ten

COMMON CORE STATE STANDARDS
5.OA.A.1, 5.OA.A.2, 5.NBT.A.1, 5.NBT.A.2, 5.NBT.B.5, 5.NBT.B.6

GO DIGITAL

Go online! Your math lessons are interactive. Use *i*Tools, Animated Math Models, the Multimedia eGlossary, and more.

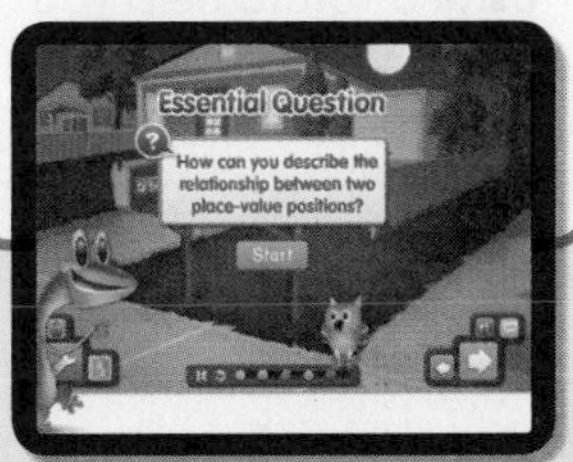

Chapter 1 Overview

In this chapter, you will explore and discover answers to the following **Essential Questions**:

- How can you use place value, multiplication, and expressions to represent and solve problems?
- How can you read, write, and represent whole numbers through millions?
- How can you use properties and multiplication to solve problems?
- How can you use expressions to represent and solve a problem?

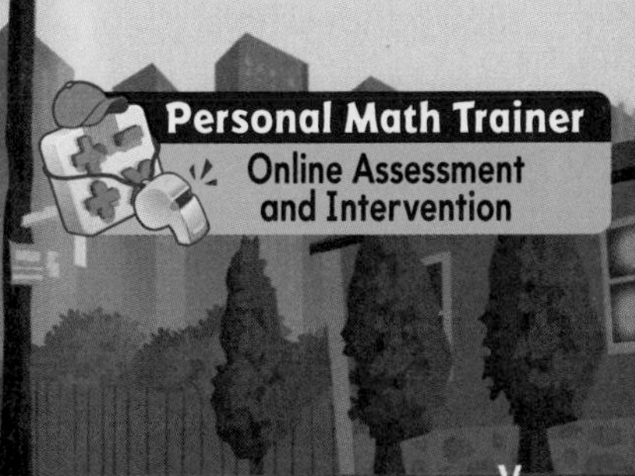

Chapter 2 Overview

In this chapter, you will explore and discover answers to the following **Essential Questions**:

- How can you divide whole numbers?
- What strategies have you used to place the first digit in the quotient?
- How can you use estimation to help you divide?
- How do you know when to use division to solve a problem?

Practice and Homework

Lesson Check and Spiral Review in every lesson

Chapter 3 Overview

In this chapter, you will explore and discover answers to the following **Essential Questions**:

- How can you add and subtract decimals?
- What methods can you use to find decimal sums and differences?
- How does using place value help you add and subtract decimals?

2 Divide Whole Numbers 85

Domains Number and Operations in Base Ten
Number and Operations–Fractions

COMMON CORE STATE STANDARDS
5.NBT.B.6, 5.NF.B.3

3 Add and Subtract Decimals 149

Domain Number and Operations in Base Ten

COMMON CORE STATE STANDARDS
5.NBT.A.1, 5.NBT.A.3a, 5.NBT.A.3b, 5.NBT.A.4, 5.NBT.B.7

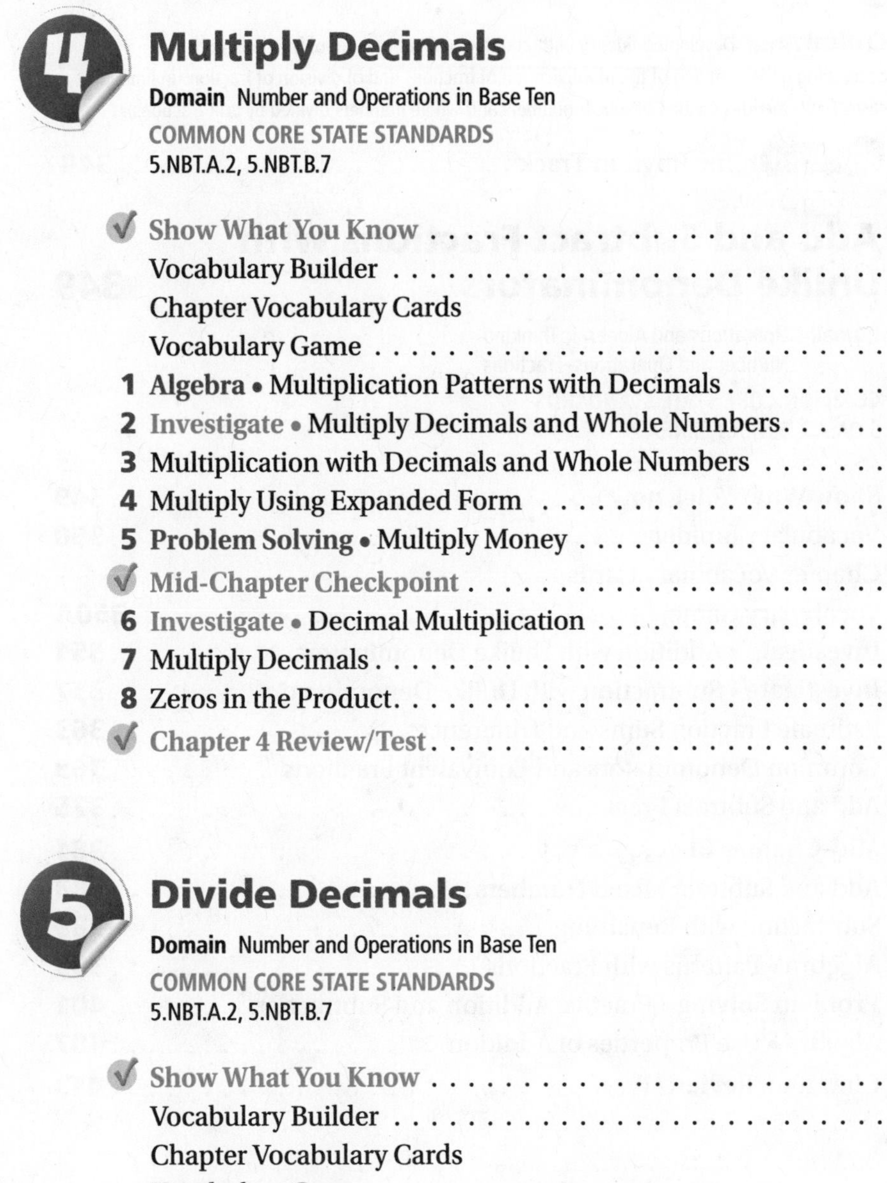

4 Multiply Decimals 231

Domain Number and Operations in Base Ten

COMMON CORE STATE STANDARDS

5.NBT.A.2, 5.NBT.B.7

Chapter 4 Overview

In this chapter, you will explore and discover answers to the following **Essential Questions**:

- How can you solve decimal multiplication problems?
- How is multiplying with decimals similar to multiplying with whole numbers?
- How can patterns, models, and drawings help you solve decimal multiplication problems?
- How do you know where to place a decimal point in a product?
- How do you know the correct number of decimal places in a product?

5 Divide Decimals 289

Domain Number and Operations in Base Ten

COMMON CORE STATE STANDARDS

5.NBT.A.2, 5.NBT.B.7

Chapter 5 Overview

In this chapter, you will explore and discover answers to the following **Essential Questions**:

- How can you solve decimal division problems?
- How is dividing with decimals similar to dividing with whole numbers?
- How can patterns, models, and drawings help you solve decimal division problems?
- How do you know where to place a decimal point in a quotient?
- How do you know the correct number of decimal places in a quotient?

Critical Area

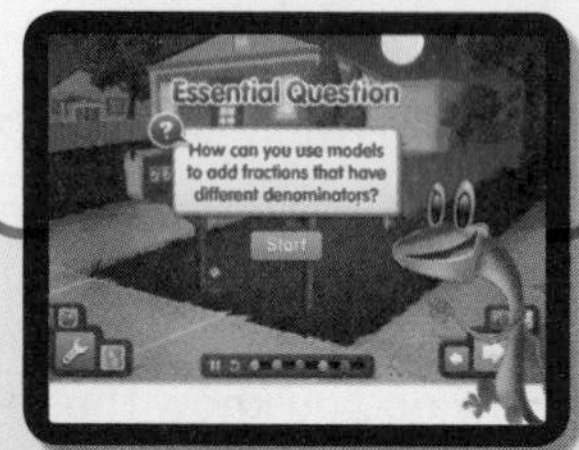

Go online! Your math lessons are interactive. Use *i*Tools, Animated Math Models, the Multimedia eGlossary, and more.

Chapter 6 Overview

In this chapter, you will explore and discover answers to the following **Essential Questions**:

- How can you add and subtract fractions with unlike denominators?
- How do models help you find sums and differences of fractions?
- When you add and subtract fractions, when do you use the least common denominator?

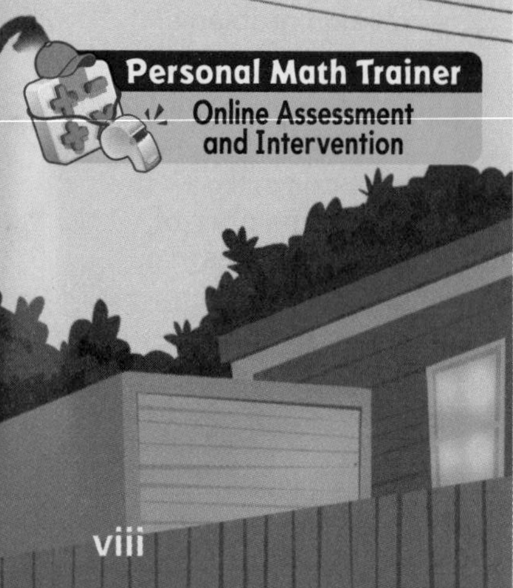

VOLUME 2

Operations with Fractions

Critical Area Developing fluency with addition and subtraction of fractions, and developing understanding of the multiplication of fractions and of division of fractions in limited cases (unit fractions divided by whole numbers and whole numbers divided by unit fractions)

6 Add and Subtract Fractions with Unlike Denominators 349

Domains Operations and Algebraic Thinking
Number and Operations–Fractions

COMMON CORE STATE STANDARDS
5.OA.A.2, 5.NF.A.1, 5.NF.A.2

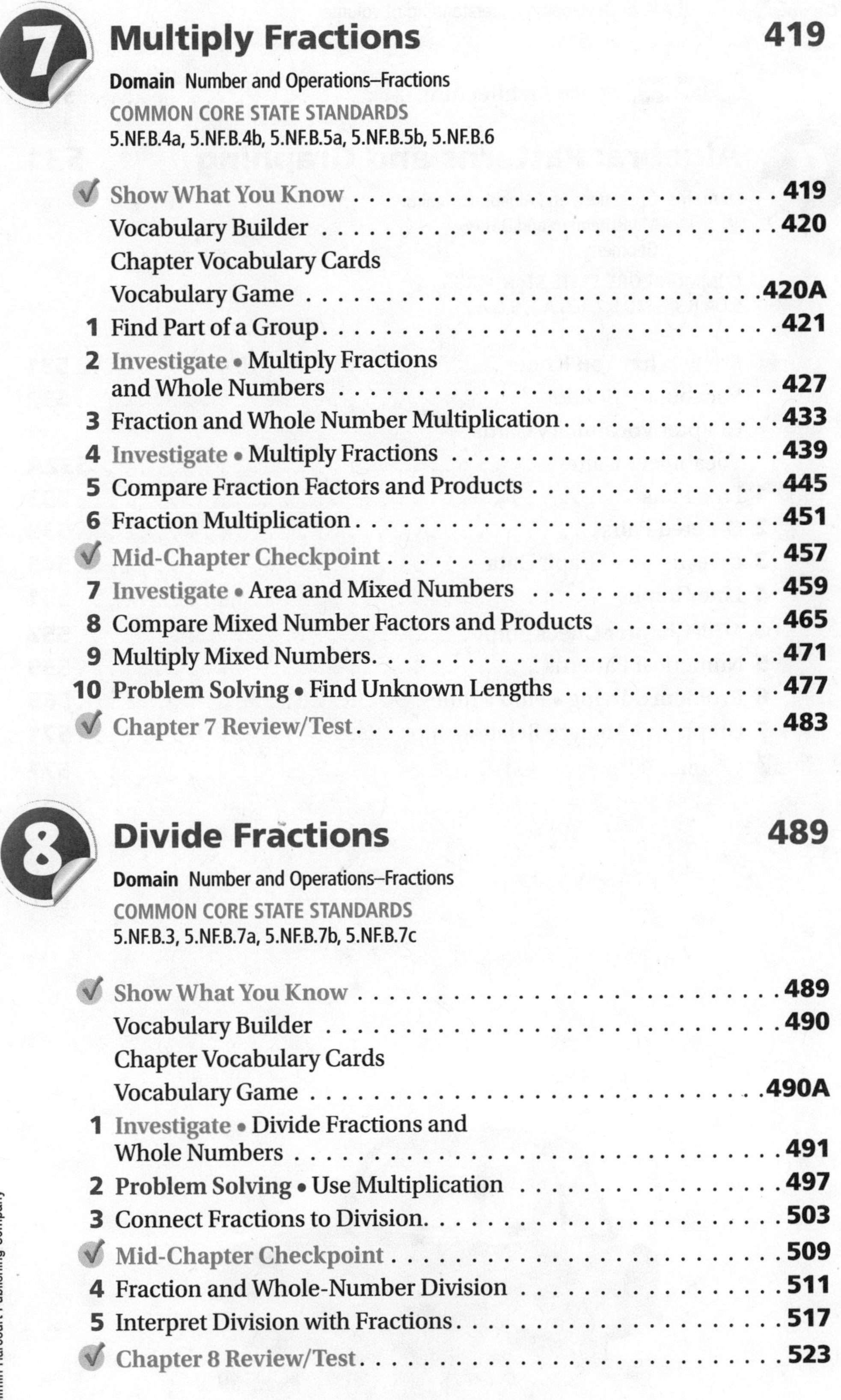

7 Multiply Fractions 419

Domain Number and Operations–Fractions

COMMON CORE STATE STANDARDS
5.NF.B.4a, 5.NF.B.4b, 5.NF.B.5a, 5.NF.B.5b, 5.NF.B.6

8 Divide Fractions 489

Domain Number and Operations–Fractions

COMMON CORE STATE STANDARDS
5.NF.B.3, 5.NF.B.7a, 5.NF.B.7b, 5.NF.B.7c

Chapter 7 Overview

In this chapter, you will explore and discover answers to the following **Essential Questions**:

- How do you multiply fractions?
- How can you model fraction multiplication?
- How can you compare fraction factors and products?

Practice and Homework

Lesson Check and Spiral Review in every lesson

Chapter 8 Overview

In this chapter, you will explore and discover answers to the following **Essential Questions**:

- What strategies can you use to solve division problems involving fractions?
- What is the relationship between multiplication and division, and how can you use it to solve division problems?
- How can you use fractions, diagrams, equations, and story problems to represent division?
- When you divide a whole number by a fraction or a fraction by a whole number, how do the dividend, the divisor, and the quotient compare?

Critical Area

Geometry and Measurement

Critical Area Developing understanding of volume

Go online! Your math lessons are interactive. Use *i*Tools, Animated Math Models, the Multimedia eGlossary, and more.

Chapter 9 Overview

In this chapter, you will explore and discover answers to the following **Essential Questions**:

- How can you use line plots, coordinate grids, and patterns to help you graph and interpret data?
- How can a line plot help you find an average with data given in fractions?
- How can a coordinate grid help you interpret experimental and real-world data?
- How can you write and graph ordered pairs on a coordinate grid using two numerical patterns?

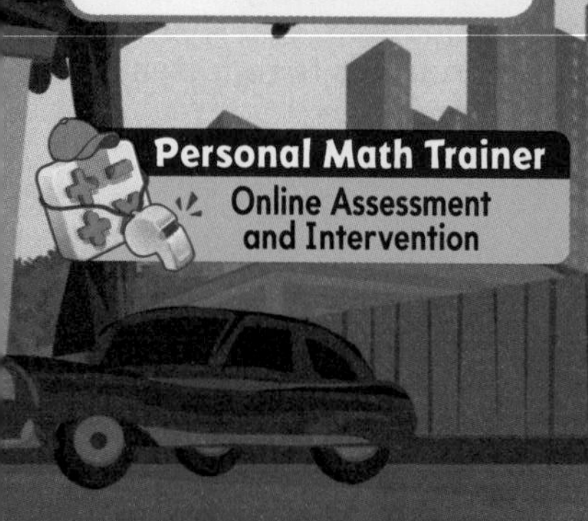

Personal Math Trainer
Online Assessment and Intervention

Convert Units of Measure 583

Domain Measurement and Data

COMMON CORE STATE STANDARD
5.MD.A.1

Chapter 10 Overview

In this chapter, you will explore and discover answers to the following **Essential Questions**:

- What strategies can you use to compare and convert measurements?
- How can you decide whether to multiply or divide when you are converting measurements?
- How can you organize your solution when you are solving a multistep measurement problem?
- How is converting metric measurements different from converting customary measurements?

Practice and Homework

Lesson Check and Spiral Review in every lesson

Chapter 11 Overview

In this chapter, you will explore and discover answers to the following **Essential Questions**:

- How do unit cubes help you build solid figures and understand the volume of a rectangular prism?
- How can you identify, describe, and classify three-dimensional figures?
- How can you find the volume of a rectangular prism?

Critical Area

Fluency with Whole Numbers and Decimals

CRITICAL AREA Extending division to 2-digit divisors, integrating decimal fractions into the place value system and developing understanding of operations with decimals to hundredths, and developing fluency with whole number and decimal operations

Chef preparing lunch in a restaurant

In the Chef's Kitchen

Restaurant chefs estimate the amount of food they need to buy based on how many diners they expect. They usually use recipes that make enough to serve large numbers of people.

Get Started

Although apples can grow in any of the 50 states, Pennsylvania is one of the top apple-producing states. The ingredients at the right are needed to make 100 servings of Apple Dumplings. Suppose you and a partner want to make this recipe for 25 friends. Adjust the amount of each ingredient to make just 25 servings.

Important Facts

Apple Dumplings (100 servings)

- 100 baking apples
- 72 tablespoons sugar ($4\frac{1}{2}$ cups)
- 14 cups all-purpose flour
- 6 teaspoons baking powder
- 24 eggs
- 80 tablespoons butter (10 sticks of butter)
- 50 tablespoons chopped walnuts ($3\frac{1}{8}$ cups)

Apple Dumplings (25 servings)

Completed by ______________________

Place Value, Multiplication, and Expressions

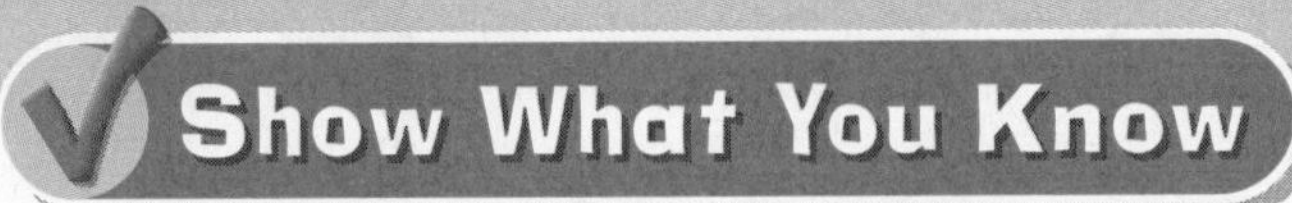

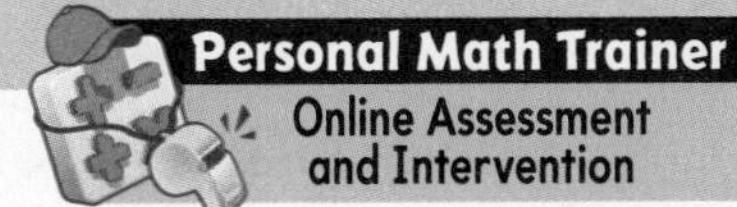

Check your understanding of important skills.

Name ______________________________

Place Value **Write the value of each digit for the given number.** (4.NBT.A.1)

1. 2,904

2 __________

9 __________

0 __________

4 __________

2. 6,423

6 __________

4 __________

2 __________

3 __________

Regroup Through Thousands **Regroup. Write the missing numbers.** (4.NBT.A.1)

3. 40 tens = ______ hundreds

4. 60 hundreds = ______ thousands

5. ______ tens 15 ones = 6 tens 5 ones

6. 18 tens 20 ones = ______ hundreds

Missing Factors **Find the missing factor.** (3.OA.A.4)

7. 4 × ______ = 24

8. 6 × ______ = 48

9. ______ × 9 = 63

Use the clues at the right to find the 7-digit number. What is the number?

Clues

- This 7-digit number is 8,920,000 when rounded to the nearest ten thousand.
- The digits in the tens and hundreds places are the least and same value.
- The value of the thousands digit is double that of the ten thousands digit.
- The sum of all its digits is 24.

Vocabulary Builder

▶ Visualize It

Sort the review words into the Venn diagram.

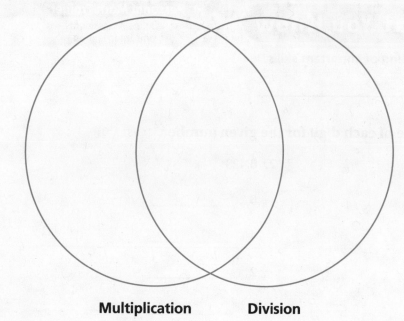

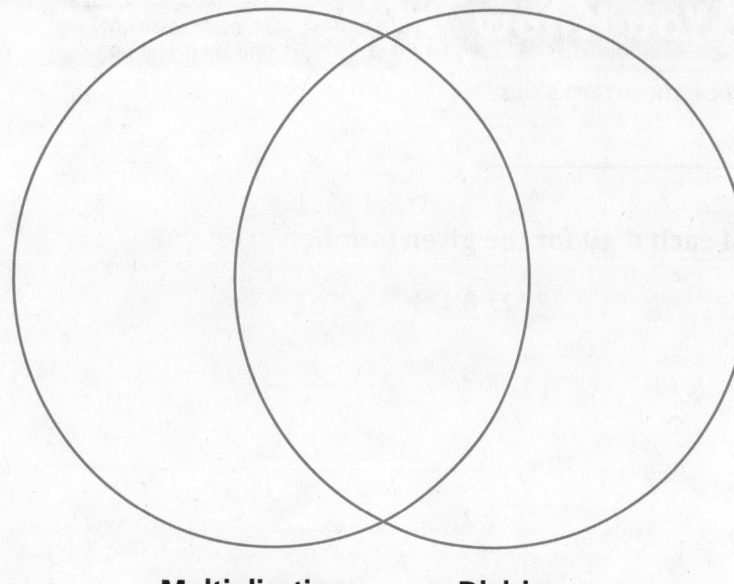

Review Words

- ✓ estimate
- ✓ factor
- ✓ multiply
- ✓ place value
- ✓ product
- ✓ quotient

Preview Words

- base
- Distributive Property
- evaluate
- exponent
- inverse operations
- numerical expression
- order of operations
- period

▶ Understand Vocabulary

Write the preview words that answer the question "What am I?"

1. I am a group of 3 digits separated by commas in a multidigit number. ____________________

2. I am a mathematical phrase that has numbers and operation signs but no equal sign. ____________________

3. I am operations that undo each other, like multiplication and division. ____________________

4. I am the property that states that multiplying a sum by a number is the same as multiplying each addend in the sum by the number and then adding the products. ____________________

5. I am a number that tells how many times the base is used as a factor. ____________________

GO DIGITAL
- Interactive Student Edition
- Multimedia eGlossary

Chapter 1 Vocabulary

base

base

1

Distributive Property

propiedad distributiva

17

evaluate

evaluar

24

exponent

exponente

26

inverse operations

operaciones inversas

32

numerical expression

expresión numérica

43

order of operations

orden de las operaciones

44

period

período

49

The property which states that multiplying a sum by a number is the same as multiplying each addend in the sum by the number and then adding the products

Example: $3 \times (4 + 2) = (3 \times 4) + (3 \times 2)$

$(3 \times 6) = 12 + 6$

$18 = 18$

(arithmetic) A number used as a repeated factor

Example: $8^3 = 8 \times 8 \times 8$

base

(geometry) In two dimensions, one side of a triangle or parallelogram that is used to help find the area. In three dimensions, a plane figure, usually a polygon or circle, by which a three-dimensional figure is measured or named

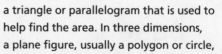

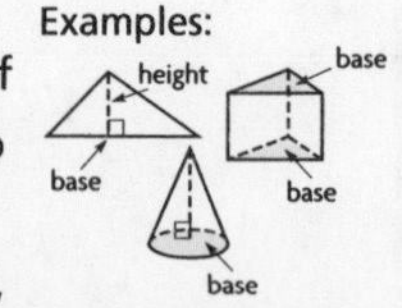

A number that shows how many times the base is used as a factor

exponent

Example: $10^3 = 10 \times 10 \times 10$

To find the value of a numerical or algebraic expression

A mathematical phrase that uses only numbers and operation signs

Example: $(4 + 6) \div 5$

Opposite operations, or operations that undo each other, such as addition and subtraction or multiplication and division

Examples:

$6 + 3 = 9$
$9 - 6 = 3$

$5 \times 2 = 10$
$10 \div 2 = 5$

Each group of three digits separated by commas in a multi-digit number

Periods

MILLIONS			THOUSANDS			ONES		
Hundreds	Tens	Ones	Hundreds	Tens	Ones	Hundreds	Tens	Ones
		1,	3	9	2,	0	0	0

A special set of rules which gives the order in which calculations are done in an expression

Game

Going to London, England

Word Box
- base
- Distributive Property
- evaluate
- exponent
- inverse operations
- numerical expression
- order of operations
- period

For 2 to 4 players

Materials

- playing pieces: 3 of each color per player: red, blue, green, and yellow
- 1 number cube

How to Play

1. Put your 3 playing pieces in the START circle of the same color.
2. To get a playing piece out of START, you must toss a 6.
   - If you toss a 6, move 1 of your playing pieces to the same-colored circle on the path.
   - If you do not toss a 6, wait until your next turn.
3. Once you have a playing piece on the path, toss the number cube to take a turn. Move the playing piece that many tan spaces. You must get all three of your playing pieces on the path.
4. If you land on a space with a question, answer it. If you are correct, move ahead 1 space.
5. To reach FINISH move your playing pieces along the path that is the same color as your playing piece. The first player to get all three playing pieces on FINISH wins.

Game

Is this solution correct? Why or why not? $36 - (8 \times 2) = 56$.

Use the order of operations to evaluate the expression: $6 + [(12 - 3) + (11 - 8)]$.

How can you write this number in two other forms: $(8 \times 1000) + (9 \times 100) + (9 \times 1)$

What is the base in 10^3?

FINISH

What is an *exponent*?

Name two inverse operations.

START

Write an expression: 48 cards are divided evenly among 6 friends.

Fill in the blanks: $7 \times 52 = (7 \times 50) + (\_\_ \times \_\_)$?

In the order of operations, which comes first: adding or dividing?

Fill in the blank: If 108 ÷ 9 = 12, then 9 × 12 = ___.

START

LONDON ROME I ♥ NY PARIS

What does the Distributive Property say?

Use the Distributive Property to rewrite 4 × 39.

FINISH

Fill in the missing exponent: 10,000 = 10__

What does it mean to *evaluate an expression*?

Write an expression: Kim has 12 pencils. She gives 10 to classmates.

Explain how to evaluate the expression (7 − 3) × 6.

START

Image Credits: (bg) ©c/Fotolia; (tl), (tr) ©Stockdisc/Getty Images; (bl) ©Markus Gann/Shutterstock; (br) ©Thinkstock Images/Jupiterimages/Getty Images

The Write Way

Reflect

Choose one idea. Write about it.

- Explain how to use the Distributive Property to complete this equation.
  6 × (40 + 5) = (6 × _____) + (_____ × _____)
- Use the words *base* and *exponent* to tell how to rewrite this expression in exponent form.
  10 × 10 × 10 × 10
- Write two sentences to match this numerical expression: 7 × $3.
- Which solution uses the order of operations correctly? Explain how you know.
  Solution A: 8 × 1 + 3 × 2 = 8 × 4 × 2 = 64
  Solution B: 8 × 1 + 3 × 2 = 8 + 6 = 14

Name ___________________________

Place Value and Patterns

Essential Question How can you describe the relationship between two place-value positions?

Common Core **Number and Operations in Base Ten—5.NBT.A.1**
MATHEMATICAL PRACTICES
MP2, MP5, MP7

Investigate

Materials ■ base-ten blocks

You can use base-ten blocks to understand the relationships among place-value positions. Use a large cube for 1,000, a flat for 100, a long for 10, and a small cube for 1.

Number	1,000	100	10	1
Model				
Description	large cube	flat	long	small cube

Complete the comparisons below to describe the relationship from one place-value position to the next place-value position.

A. • Look at the long and compare it to the small cube.

The long is ______ times as much as the small cube.

• Look at the flat and compare it to the long.

The flat is ______ times as much as the long.

• Look at the large cube and compare it to the flat.

The large cube is ______ times as much as the flat.

B. • Look at the flat and compare it to the large cube.

The flat is ______ of the large cube.

• Look at the long and compare it to the flat.

The long is ______ of the flat.

• Look at the small cube and compare it to the long.

The small cube is ______ of the long.

Math Talk MATHEMATICAL PRACTICES 5

Use Tools How many times as much is the flat compared to the small cube? the large cube to the small cube? Explain.

Draw Conclusions

1. MATHEMATICAL PRACTICE 7 **Look for a Pattern** Describe the pattern you see when you move from a lesser place-value position to the next greater place-value position.

____

____

____

2. MATHEMATICAL PRACTICE 7 **Look for a Pattern** Describe the pattern you see when you move from a greater place-value position to the next lesser place-value position.

____

____

____

Make Connections

You can use your understanding of place-value patterns and a place-value chart to write numbers that are 10 times as much as or $\frac{1}{10}$ of any given number.

Hundred Thousands	Ten Thousands	One Thousands	Hundreds	Tens	Ones
			3	0	0
		?	300	?	

10 times as much as $\frac{1}{10}$ of

______ is 10 times as much as 300.

______ is $\frac{1}{10}$ of 300.

Use the steps below to complete the table.

STEP 1 Write the given number in a place-value chart.

STEP 2 Use the place-value chart to write a number that is 10 times as much as the given number.

STEP 3 Use the place-value chart to write a number that is $\frac{1}{10}$ of the given number.

Number	10 times as much as	$\frac{1}{10}$ of
10		
70		
9,000		

Name ______________________________

Complete the sentence.

1. 500 is 10 times as much as ____________.

2. 20,000 is $\frac{1}{10}$ of ____________.

3. 900 is $\frac{1}{10}$ of ____________.

4. 600 is 10 times as much as ____________.

On Your Own

Use place-value patterns to complete the table.

Number	10 times as much as	$\frac{1}{10}$ of
5. 10		
6. 3,000		
7. 800		
8. 50		

Number	10 times as much as	$\frac{1}{10}$ of
9. 500		
10. 90		
11. 6,000		
12. 200		

THINKSMARTER **Complete the sentence with 100 or 1,000.**

13. 200 is ____________ times as much as 2.

14. 4,000 is ____________ times as much as 4.

15. 700,000 is ____________ times as much as 700.

16. 600 is ____________ times as much as 6.

Problem Solving • Applications

17. WRITE Math Explain how you can use place-value patterns to describe how 50 and 5,000 compare.

____

____

18. MATHEMATICAL PRACTICE 2 Use Reasoning 30,000 is ____________ times as much as 30.

So, ____________ is 10 times as much as 3,000.

THINK SMARTER Sense or Nonsense?

19. Mark and Robyn used base-ten blocks to show that 200 is 100 times as much as 2. Whose model makes sense? Whose model is nonsense? Explain your reasoning.

Mark's Work

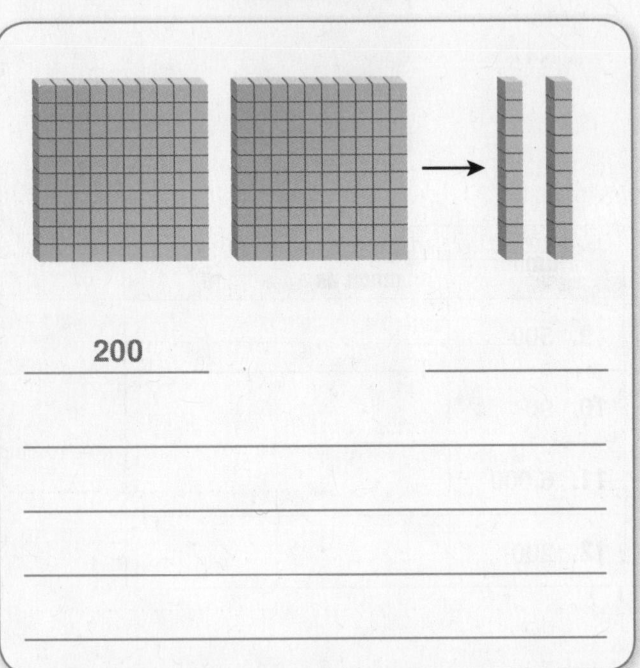

Robyn's Work

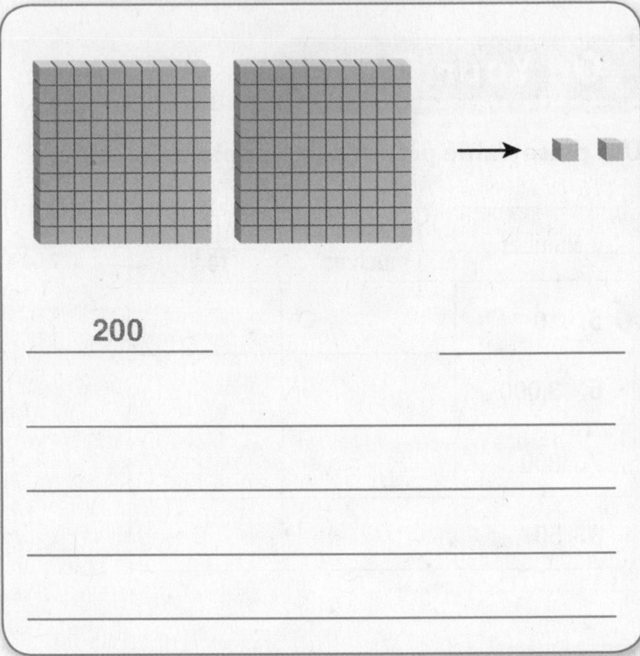

20. GO DEEPER Explain how you would help Mark understand why he should have used small cubes instead of longs.

21. THINK SMARTER For 21a–21c, choose True or False for each sentence.

21a. 600 is $\frac{1}{10}$ of 6,000. ○ True ○ False

21b. 67 is $\frac{1}{10}$ of 6,700. ○ True ○ False

21c. 1,400 is 10 times as much as 140. ○ True ○ False

Name ______________________________

Place Value and Patterns

Common Core **COMMON CORE STANDARD—5.NBT.A.1**
Understand the place value system.

Complete the sentence.

1. 40,000 is 10 times as much as 4,000.

2. 90 is $\frac{1}{10}$ of __________.

3. 800 is 10 times as much as __________.

4. 5,000 is $\frac{1}{10}$ of __________.

Use place-value patterns to complete the table.

Number	10 times as much as	$\frac{1}{10}$ of
5. 100		
6. 7,000		
7. 80		

Number	10 times as much as	$\frac{1}{10}$ of
8. 2,000		
9. 400		
10. 60		

Problem Solving Real World

11. The Eatery Restaurant has 200 tables. On a recent evening, there were reservations for $\frac{1}{10}$ of the tables. How many tables were reserved?

____

12. Mr. Wilson has $3,000 in his bank account. Ms. Nelson has 10 times as much money in her bank account as Mr. Wilson has in his bank account. How much money does Ms. Nelson have in her bank account?

____

13. WRITE Math Write a number that has four digits with the same number in all places, such as 4,444. Circle the digit with the greatest value. Underline the digit with the least value. Explain.

____

____

____

Lesson Check (5.NBT.A.1)

1. What is 10 times as much as 700?

2. What is $\frac{1}{10}$ of 3,000?

Spiral Review (Reviews 4.OA.A.3, 4.NBT.A.2, 4.NBT.B.5, 4.MD.A.3)

3. Risa is sewing a ribbon around the sides of a square blanket. Each side of the blanket is 72 inches long. How many inches of ribbon will Risa need?

4. What is the value of n?

$9 \times 27 + 2 \times 31 - 28 = n$

5. What is the best estimate for the product of 289 and 7?

6. Arrange the following numbers in order from greatest to least: 7,361; 7,136; 7,613

FOR MORE PRACTICE GO TO THE Personal Math Trainer

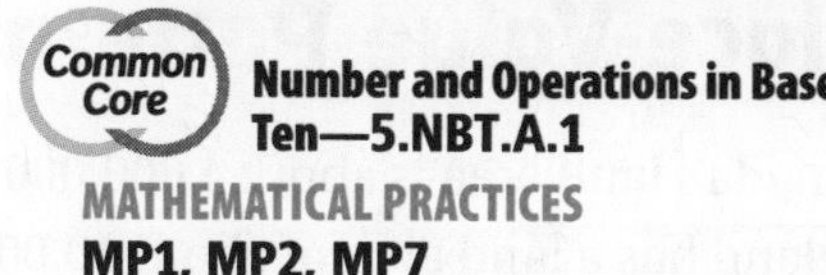

Name ___________________________

Place Value of Whole Numbers

Essential Question How do you read, write, and represent whole numbers through hundred millions?

Number and Operations in Base Ten—5.NBT.A.1

MATHEMATICAL PRACTICES
MP1, MP2, MP7

Unlock the Problem

The diameter of the sun is 1,392,000 kilometers. To understand this distance, you need to understand the place value of each digit in 1,392,000.

A place-value chart contains periods. In numbers a **period** is a group of three digits separated by commas in a multidigit number. The millions period is left of the thousands period. One million is 1,000 thousands and is written as 1,000,000.

Periods

MILLIONS			THOUSANDS			ONES		
Hundreds	Tens	Ones	Hundreds	Tens	Ones	Hundreds	Tens	Ones
		1,	3	9	2,	0	0	0
		1 × 1,000,000	3 × 100,000	9 × 10,000	2 × 1,000	0 × 100	0 × 10	0 × 1
		1,000,000	300,000	90,000	2,000	0	0	0

The place value of the digit 1 in 1,392,000 is millions. The value of 1 in 1,392,000 is 1 × 1,000,000 = 1,000,000.

Math Idea

When writing a number in expanded form, if no digits appear in a place value, it is not necessary to include them in the expression.

Standard Form: 1,392,000
Word Form: one million, three hundred ninety-two thousand
Expanded Form:
(1 × 1,000,000) + (3 × 100,000) + (9 × 10,000) + (2 × 1,000)

Try This! **Use place value to read and write numbers.**

Standard Form: 582,030

Word Form: five hundred eighty-two ____________, ____________

Expanded Form: (5 × 100,000) + (________ × ________) + (2 × 1,000) + (________ × ________)

- The average distance from Jupiter to the sun is four hundred eighty-three million, six hundred thousand miles. Write the number that shows this distance in miles. ____________________

Place-Value Patterns

Canada's land area is about 4,000,000 square miles.
Iceland has a land area of about 40,000 square miles.
Compare the two areas.

Example 1 Use a place-value chart.

STEP 1 Write the numbers in a place-value chart.

MILLIONS			THOUSANDS			ONES		
Hundreds	Tens	Ones	Hundreds	Tens	Ones	Hundreds	Tens	Ones

____

STEP 2

Count the number of whole number place-value positions.

4,000,000 has _______ more whole number places than 40,000.

Think: 2 more places is 10 × 10, or 100.

4,000,000 is _______ times as much as 40,000.

So, Canada's estimated land area is _______ times as much as Iceland's estimated land area.

Remember

The value of each place is 10 times as much as the value of the next place to its right or $\frac{1}{10}$ of the value of the next place to its left.

You can use place-value patterns to rename a number.

Example 2 Use place-value patterns.

Rename 40,000 using other place values.

40,000	4 ten thousands	4 × 10,000
40,000	_____ thousands	_____ × 1,000
40,000	______________	______________

Name ___________________________________

Share and Show MATH BOARD

1. Complete the place-value chart to find the value of each digit.

MILLIONS			THOUSANDS			ONES		
Hundreds	Tens	Ones	Hundreds	Tens	Ones	Hundreds	Tens	Ones
		7,	3	3	3,	8	2	0
		7 × 1,000,000	3 × ______	3 × 10,000	___ × 1,000	8 × 100	______	0 × 1
		______	______	30,000	3,000	______	20	0

Write the value of the underlined digit.

2. 1,574,833 ______

3. 598,102 ______

4. 7,093,455 ______

5. 301,256,878 ______

Write the number in two other forms.

6. (8 × 100,000) + (4 × 1,000) + (6 × 1)

______

______

7. seven million, twenty thousand, thirty-two

______

______

On Your Own

Write the value of the underlined digit.

8. 849,567,043 ______

9. 9,422,850 ______

10. 96,283 ______

11. 498,354,021 ______

Write the number in two other forms.

12. 345,000

______

______

______

13. 119,000,003

______

______

______

14. GO DEEPER Consider the numbers 4,205,176 and 4,008. What is the difference in the values of the digit 4 in each number?

______

Problem Solving • Applications

Use the table for 15–16.

Average Distance from the Sun (in thousands of km)			
Mercury	57,910	Jupiter	778,400
Venus	108,200	Saturn	1,427,000
Earth	149,600	Uranus	2,871,000
Mars	227,900	Neptune	4,498,000

15. Which planet is about 10 times as far as Earth is from the Sun?

______

16. MATHEMATICAL PRACTICE 1 **Analyze Relationships** Which planet is about $\frac{1}{10}$ of the distance Uranus is from the Sun?

______

17. THINK SMARTER **What's the Error?** Matt wrote the number four million, three hundred five thousand, seven hundred sixty-two as 4,350,762. Describe and correct his error.

______

______

18. GO DEEPER Explain how you know that the values of the digit 5 in the numbers 150,000 and 100,500 are not the same.

______

______

______

______

______

WRITE Math • Show Your Work

19. THINK SMARTER Select other ways to write 400,562. Mark all that apply.

Ⓐ $(4 \times 100{,}000) + (50 \times 100) + (6 \times 10) + (2 \times 1)$

Ⓑ four hundred thousand, five hundred sixty-two

Ⓒ $(4 \times 100{,}000) + (5 \times 100) + (6 \times 10) + (2 \times 1)$

Ⓓ four hundred, five hundred sixty-two

Name ______________________________

Place Value of Whole Numbers

COMMON CORE STANDARD—5.NBT.A.1
Understand the place value system.

Write the value of the underlined digit.

1. $5,1\underline{6}5,874$ — 60,000

2. $2\underline{8}1,480,100$ ______

3. $7,\underline{2}70$ ______

4. $8\underline{9},170,326$ ______

5. $\underline{7},050,423$ ______

6. $6\underline{4}6,950$ ______

7. $37,\underline{1}23,745$ ______

8. $\underline{3}15,421,732$ ______

Write the number in two other forms.

9. 15,409

______

______

10. 100,203

______

______

Problem Solving Real World

11. The U.S. Census Bureau has a population clock on the Internet. On a recent day, the United States population was listed as 310,763,136. Write this number in word form.

______

______

______

12. In 2008, the population of 10- to 14-year-olds in the United States was 20,484,163. Write this number in expanded form.

______

______

______

______

13. WRITE ▸ *Math* Write *Standard Form, Expanded Form,* and *Word Form* at the top of the page. Write five numbers that are at least 8 digits long under Standard Form. Write the expanded form and the word form for each number under the appropriate heading.

Lesson Check (5.NBT.A.1)

1. A movie cost $3,254,107 to produce. What digit is in the hundred thousands place?

2. What is the standard form of two hundred ten million, sixty-four thousand, fifty?

Spiral Review (Reviews 4.OA.C.5, 4.NBT.B.6, 4.G.A.2, 4.G.A.3)

3. If the pattern below continues, what number likely comes next?

   9, 12, 15, 18, 21, ?

4. Find the quotient and remainder for $52 \div 8$.

5. How many pairs of parallel sides does the trapezoid below have?

6. How many lines of symmetry does the figure below appear to have?

FOR MORE PRACTICE GO TO THE **Personal Math Trainer**

Name ______________________

Properties

Essential Question How can you use properties of operations to solve problems?

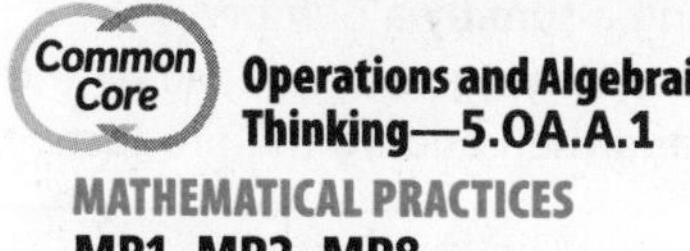

You can use the properties of operations to help you evaluate numerical expressions more easily.

Properties of Addition

Commutative Property of Addition If the order of addends changes, the sum stays the same.	12 + 7 = 7 + 12
Associative Property of Addition If the grouping of addends changes, the sum stays the same.	5 + (8 + 14) = (5 + 8) + 14
Identity Property of Addition The sum of any number and 0 is that number.	13 + 0 = 13

Properties of Multiplication

Commutative Property of Multiplication If the order of factors changes, the product stays the same.	$4 \times 9 = 9 \times 4$
Associative Property of Multiplication If the grouping of factors changes, the product stays the same.	$11 \times (3 \times 6) = (11 \times 3) \times 6$
Identity Property of Multiplication The product of any number and 1 is that number.	$4 \times 1 = 4$

Unlock the Problem

The table shows the number of bones in several parts of the human body. What is the total number of bones in the ribs, the skull, and the spine?

Part	Number of Bones
Ankle	7
Ribs	24
Skull	28
Spine	26

To find the sum of addends using mental math, you can use the Commutative and Associative Properties.

Use properties to find 24 + 28 + 26.

24 + 28 + 26 = 28 + ______ + 26 Use the ______________ Property to reorder the addends.

= 28 + (24 + ______) Use the ______________ Property to group the addends.

= 28 + ______ Use mental math to add.

= ______

So, there are ______ bones in the ribs, the skull, and the spine.

MATHEMATICAL PRACTICES 8

Generalize Explain why grouping 24 and 26 makes the problem easier to solve.

Distributive Property

Multiplying a sum by a number is the same as multiplying each addend by the number and then adding the products.	$5 \times (7 + 9) = (5 \times 7) + (5 \times 9)$

The Distributive Property can also be used with multiplication and subtraction. For example, $2 \times (10 - 8) = (2 \times 10) - (2 \times 8)$.

Example 1 Use the Distributive Property to find the product.

One Way Use addition.

$8 \times 59 = 8 \times (\_\_\_\_ + 9)$	Use a multiple of 10 to write 59 as a sum.
$= (\_\_\_\_ \times 50) + (8 \times \_\_\_\_)$	Use the Distributive Property.
$= \_\_\_\_ + \_\_\_\_$	Use mental math to multiply.
$= \_\_\_\_$	Use mental math to add.

Another Way Use subtraction.

$8 \times 59 = 8 \times (\_\_\_\_ - 1)$	Use a multiple of 10 to write 59 as a difference.
$= (\_\_\_\_ \times 60) - (8 \times \_\_\_\_)$	Use the Distributive Property.
$= \_\_\_\_ - \_\_\_\_$	Use mental math to multiply.
$= \_\_\_\_$	Use mental math to subtract.

Example 2 Complete the equation, and tell which property you used.

A $23 \times \_\_\_\_ = 23$

Think: A number times 1 is equal to itself.

Property: ________________

____

B $47 \times 15 = 15 \times \_\_\_\_$

Think: Changing the order of factors does not change the product.

Property: ________________

____

MATHEMATICAL PRACTICES 1

Describe how to use the Distributive Property to find the product 3×299.

Name ______________________________

Share and Show MATH BOARD

1. Use properties to find $4 \times 23 \times 25$.

$23 \times$ ______ $\times 25$ ______________ Property of Multiplication

$23 \times ($______ $\times$ ______$)$ ______________ Property of Multiplication

$23 \times$ ______

______

Use properties to find the sum or product.

2. $89 + 27 + 11$

3. 9×52

4. $107 + 0 + 39 + 13$

Complete the equation, and tell which property you used.

5. $9 \times (30 + 7) = (9 \times$ ______$) + (9 \times 7)$

6. $0 +$ ______ $= 47$

MATHEMATICAL PRACTICES 1

Describe how you can use properties to solve problems more easily.

On Your Own

Practice: Copy and Solve **Use properties to find the sum or product.**

7. 3×78

8. $4 \times 60 \times 5$

9. $21 + 25 + 39 + 5$

Complete the equation, and tell which property you used.

10. $11 + (19 + 6) = (11 +$ ______$) + 6$

11. $25 + 14 =$ ______ $+ 25$

12. MATHEMATICAL PRACTICE 3 **Apply** Show how you can use the Distributive Property to rewrite and find $(32 \times 6) + (32 \times 4)$.

Problem Solving • Applications

13. GO DEEPER Three friends' meals at a restaurant cost \$13, \$14, and \$11. Use parentheses to write two different expressions to show how much the friends spent in all. Which property does your pair of expressions demonstrate?

____

____

14. MATHEMATICAL PRACTICE 2 **Use Reasoning** Jacob is designing an aquarium for a doctor's office. He plans to buy 6 red blond guppies, 1 blue neon guppy, and 1 yellow guppy. The table shows the price list for the guppies. How much will the guppies for the aquarium cost?

____

Fancy Guppy Prices	
Blue neon	\$11
Red blond	\$22
Sunrise	\$18
Yellow	\$19

15. Sylvia bought 8 tickets to a concert. Each ticket costs \$18. To find the total cost in dollars, she added the product 8×10 to the product 8×8, for a total of 144. Which property did Sylvia use?

____

WRITE Math • Show Your Work

16. THINK SMARTER **Sense or Nonsense?** Julie wrote $(15 - 6) - 3 = 15 - (6 - 3)$. Is Julie's equation sense or nonsense? Do you think the Associative Property works for subtraction? Explain.

____

____

____

17. THINK SMARTER Find the property that each equation shows.

$14 \times (4 \times 9) = (14 \times 4) \times 9$ •	• Commutative Property of Multiplication
$1 \times 3 = 3 \times 1$ •	• Associative Property of Multiplication
$7 \times 3 = 3 \times 7$ •	• Identity Property of Multiplication

Name ______________________

Properties

Common Core **COMMON CORE STANDARD—5.OA.A.1**
Perform operations with multi-digit whole numbers and with decimals to hundredths.

Use properties to find the sum or product.

1. 6×89

$6 \times (90 - 1)$
$(6 \times 90) - (6 \times 1)$
$540 - 6$

534

2. $93 + (68 + 7)$

______

3. $5 \times 23 \times 2$

______

4. 8×51

______

5. $34 + 0 + 18 + 26$

______

6. 6×107

______

Complete the equation, and tell which property you used.

7. $(3 \times 10) \times 8 =$ ______ $\times (10 \times 8)$

______

8. $16 + 31 = 31 +$ ______

______

Problem Solving Real World

9. The Metro Theater has 20 rows of seats with 18 seats in each row. Tickets cost \$5. The theater's income in dollars if all seats are sold is $(20 \times 18) \times 5$. Use properties to find the total income.

______

10. The numbers of students in the four sixth-grade classes at Northside School are 26, 19, 34, and 21. Use properties to find the total number of students in the four classes.

______

11. WRITE *Math* Explain how you could mentally find 8×45 by using the Distributive Property.

______

Lesson Check (5.OA.A.1)

1. To find 19 + (11 + 37), Lennie added 19 and 11. Then he added 37 to the sum. What property did he use?

2. Marla did 65 sit-ups each day for one week. Use the Distributive Property to show an expression you can use to find the total number of sit-ups Marla did during the week.

Spiral Review (Reviews 4.OA.B.4, 4.NBT.B.5, 4.NBT.B.6, 5.NBT.A.1)

3. The average sunflower has 34 petals. What is the best estimate of the total number of petals on 57 sunflowers?

4. A golden eagle flies a distance of 290 miles in 5 days. If the eagle flies the same distance each day of its journey, how far does the eagle fly per day?

5. What is the value of the underlined digit in the following number?

   2,9<u>8</u>3,785

6. What best describes the number 5? Write *prime, composite, neither prime nor composite, or both prime and composite.*

FOR MORE PRACTICE GO TO THE **Personal Math Trainer**

ALGEBRA
Lesson 1.4

Name ______________________

Powers of 10 and Exponents

Essential Question How can you use an exponent to show powers of 10?

Number and Operations in Base Ten—5.NBT.A.2
MATHEMATICAL PRACTICES
MP2, MP7, MP8

Unlock the Problem

Expressions with repeated factors, such as 10 × 10 × 10, can be written by using a base with an exponent. The **base** is the number that is used as the repeated factor. The **exponent** is the number that tells how many times the base is used as a factor.

$$10 \times 10 \times 10 = 10^3 = 1{,}000$$

(3 factors; base; exponent)

Word form: the third power of ten

Exponent form: 10^3

Activity Use base-ten blocks.

Materials ■ base-ten blocks

What is 10 × 1,000 written with an exponent?

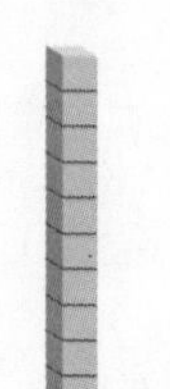

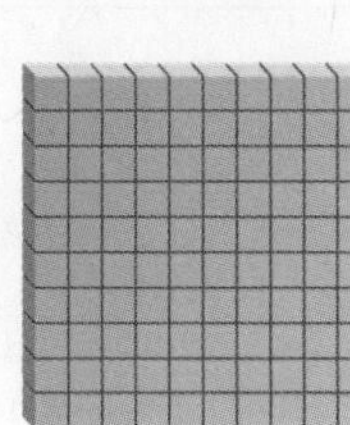
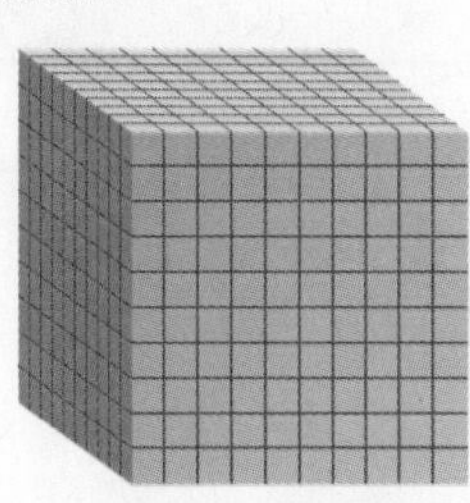

1 one	10 ones	100 ones	1,000 ones
1	1 × 10	1 × 10 × 10	1 × 10 × 10 × 10
10^0	10^1	10^2	10^3

- How many ones are in 1? ______
- How many ones are in 10? ______
- How many tens are in 100? ______
  Think: 10 groups of 10 or 10 × 10
- How many hundreds are in 1,000? ______
  Think: 10 groups of 100 or 10 × (10 × 10)
- How many thousands are in 10,000? ______

In the box at the right, draw a quick picture to show 10,000.

Use [T] for 1,000.

10,000 ones
1 × 10 × 10 × 10 × 10
$10^{\square}$

So, 10 × 1,000 is $10^{\square}$.

Example Multiply a whole number by a power of ten.

Hummingbirds beat their wings very fast. The smaller the hummingbird is, the faster its wings beat. The average hummingbird beats its wings about 3×10^3 times a minute. How many times a minute is that, written as a whole number?

Multiply 3 by powers of ten. Look for a pattern.

$3 \times 10^0 = 3 \times 1 =$ ____________

$3 \times 10^1 = 3 \times 10 =$ ____________

$3 \times 10^2 = 3 \times 10 \times 10 =$ ____________

$3 \times 10^3 = 3 \times 10 \times 10 \times 10 =$ ____________

So, the average hummingbird beats its wings about ____________ times a minute.

Math Talk MATHEMATICAL PRACTICES 8

Generalize Explain how using an exponent simplifies an expression.

- MATHEMATICAL PRACTICE 7 **Look for a Pattern** What pattern do you see?

____

____

Share and Show

Write in exponent form and word form.

1. 10×10

Exponent form: ____________

Word form: ____________

____

2. $10 \times 10 \times 10 \times 10$

Exponent form: ____________

Word form: ____________

____

Find the value.

3. 10^2

____

4. 4×10^2

____

5. 7×10^3

____

Name ______________________

On Your Own

Write in exponent form and word form.

6. $10 \times 10 \times 10$

exponent form: ______________

word form: ______________

____

7. $10 \times 10 \times 10 \times 10 \times 10$

exponent form: ______________

word form: ______________

____

Find the value.

8. 10^4

____

9. 2×10^3

____

10. 6×10^4

____

GO DEEPER **Complete the pattern.**

11. $12 \times 10^0 = 12 \times 1 =$ ______________

$12 \times 10^1 = 12 \times 10 =$ ______________

$12 \times 10^2 = 12 \times 100 =$ ______________

$12 \times 10^3 = 12 \times 1{,}000 =$ ______________

$12 \times 10^4 = 12 \times 10{,}000 =$ ______________

12. MATHEMATICAL PRACTICE 2 **Reason Abstractly** $10^3 = 10 \times 10^n$
What is the value of n?

Think: $10^3 = 10 \times$ ______ $\times$ ______,

or $10 \times$ ______________

The value of n is ______________.

13. WRITE *Math* Explain how to write 50,000 using exponents.

____

____

14. GO DEEPER One year, Mr. James travels 9×10^3 miles for his job. The next year he traveled 1×10^4 miles. How many more miles did he travel the second year than he did the first year. Explain.

____

____

Unlock the Problem

15. THINK SMARTER Lake Superior is the largest of the Great Lakes. It covers a surface area of about 30,000 square miles. How can you show the estimated area of Lake Superior as a whole number multiplied by a power of ten?

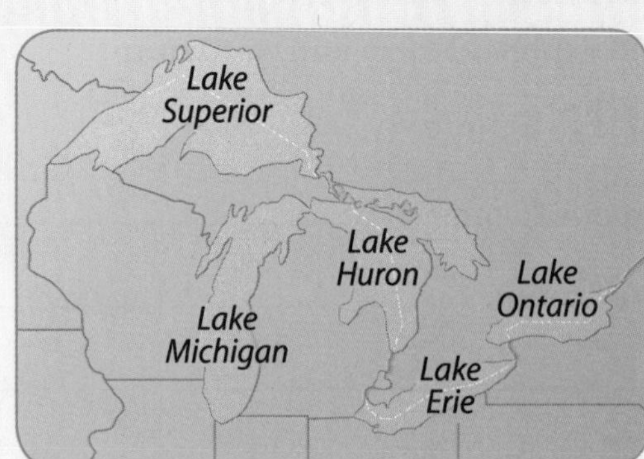

a. What are you asked to find?

____

b. How can you use a pattern to find the answer?

____

c. Write a pattern using the whole number 3 and powers of ten.

$3 \times 10^0 = 3 \times 1 =$ _______

$3 \times 10^1 = 3 \times 10 =$ _______

$3 \times 10^2 =$ _______ $=$ _______

$3 \times 10^3 =$ _______ $=$ _______

$3 \times 10^4 =$ _______ $=$ _______

d. Complete the sentence.
The estimated area of Lake Superior is _______.

16. The Earth's diameter through the equator is about 8,000 miles. What is the Earth's estimated diameter written as a whole number multiplied by a power of ten?

____

17. THINK SMARTER Yolanda says 10^5 is the same as 50 because 10×5 equals 50. What was Yolanda's mistake?

____

____

Name ______________________

Powers of 10 and Exponents

Common Core **COMMON CORE STANDARD—5.NBT.A.2**
Understand the place value system.

Write in exponent form and word form.

1. $10 \times 10 \times 10$

exponent form: 10^3

word form: the third power of ten

2. 10×10

exponent form: ______

word form: ______

3. $10 \times 10 \times 10 \times 10$

exponent form: ______

word form: ______

Find the value.

4. 10^3 ______

5. 4×10^2 ______

6. 7×10^3 ______

7. 8×10^0 ______

Problem Solving Real World

8. The moon is about 240,000 miles from Earth. What is this distance written as a whole number multiplied by a power of ten?

______

9. The sun is about 93×10^6 miles from Earth. What is this distance written as a whole number?

______

10. WRITE *Math* Consider 7×10^3. Write a pattern to find the value of the expression.

______

Lesson Check (5.NBT.A.2)

1. Write the expression that shows "3 times the sixth power of 10."

2. Gary mails 10^3 flyers to clients in one week. How many flyers does Gary mail?

Spiral Review (Reviews 4.NBT.B.5, 4.NBT.B.6)

3. Harley is loading 625 bags of cement onto small pallets. Each pallet holds 5 bags. How many pallets will Harley need?

4. Marylou buys a package of 500 jewels to decorate 4 different pairs of jeans. She uses the same number of jewels on each pair of jeans. How many jewels will she use for each pair of jeans?

5. Manny buys 4 boxes of straws for his restaurant. There are 500 straws in each box. How many straws does he buy?

6. Cammie goes to the gym to exercise 4 times per week. Altogether, how many times does she go to the gym in 10 weeks?

FOR MORE PRACTICE GO TO THE **Personal Math Trainer**

Name ______________________________

Multiplication Patterns

Essential Question How can you use a basic fact and a pattern to multiply by a 2-digit number?

Common Core Number and Operations in Base Ten—5.NBT.A.2
MATHEMATICAL PRACTICES MP2, MP3, MP8

Unlock the Problem — Real World

How close have you been to a bumblebee?

The actual length of a queen bumblebee is about 20 millimeters. The photograph shows part of a bee under a microscope, at 10 times its actual size. What would the length of the bee appear to be at a magnification of 300 times its actual size?

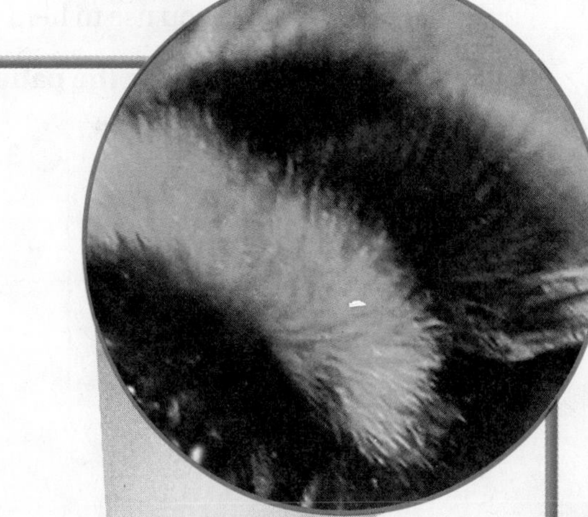

Use a basic fact and a pattern.

Multiply. 300×20

$3 \times 2 = 6$ ← basic fact

$30 \times 2 = (3 \times 2) \times 10^1 = 60$

$300 \times 2 = (3 \times 2) \times 10^2 =$ ______________

$300 \times 20 = (3 \times 2) \times (100 \times 10) = 6 \times 10^3 =$ ______________

So, the length of the bee would appear to be about ______________ millimeters.

Math Talk MATHEMATICAL PRACTICES 8

Generalize What pattern do you see in the number sentences and the exponents?

- What would the length of the bee shown in the photograph appear to be if the microscope shows it at 10 times its actual size?

  ____

Example Use mental math and a pattern.

Multiply. $50 \times 8{,}000$

$5 \times 8 = 40$ ← basic fact

$5 \times 80 = (5 \times 8) \times 10^1 = 400$

$5 \times 800 = (5 \times 8) \times 10^2 =$ ______________

$50 \times 800 = (5 \times 8) \times (10 \times 100) = 40 \times 10^3 =$ ______________

$50 \times 8{,}000 = (5 \times 8) \times (10 \times 1{,}000) = 40 \times 10^4 =$ ______________

Share and Show 

Use mental math and a pattern to find the product.

1. $30 \times 4{,}000 =$ ______

What basic fact can you use to help you find $30 \times 4{,}000$? ______

Use mental math to complete the pattern.

2. $1 \times 1 = 1$

$1 \times 10^1 =$ ______

$1 \times 10^2 =$ ______

$1 \times 10^3 =$ ______

3. $7 \times 8 = 56$

$(7 \times 8) \times 10^1 =$ ______

$(7 \times 8) \times 10^2 =$ ______

$(7 \times 8) \times 10^3 =$ ______

4. $6 \times 5 =$ ______

$(6 \times 5) \times$ ______ $= 300$

$(6 \times 5) \times$ ______ $= 3{,}000$

$(6 \times 5) \times$ ______ $= 30{,}000$

Math Talk MATHEMATICAL PRACTICES 3

Apply Tell how to find $50 \times 9{,}000$ by using a basic fact and pattern.

On Your Own

Use mental math to complete the pattern.

5. $9 \times 5 = 45$

$(9 \times 5) \times 10^1 =$ ______

$(9 \times 5) \times 10^2 =$ ______

$(9 \times 5) \times 10^3 =$ ______

6. $3 \times 7 = 21$

$(3 \times 7) \times 10^1 =$ ______

$(3 \times 7) \times 10^2 =$ ______

$(3 \times 7) \times 10^3 =$ ______

7. $5 \times 4 =$ ______

$(5 \times 4) \times$ ______ $= 200$

$(5 \times 4) \times$ ______ $= 2{,}000$

$(5 \times 4) \times$ ______ $= 20{,}000$

Use mental math and a pattern to find the product.

8. $(6 \times 6) \times 10^1 =$ ______

9. $(7 \times 4) \times 10^3 =$ ______

10. $(9 \times 8) \times 10^2 =$ ______

11. $(4 \times 3) \times 10^2 =$ ______

12. $(2 \times 5) \times 10^3 =$ ______

13. $(2 \times 8) \times 10^2 =$ ______

14. $(6 \times 5) \times 10^3 =$ ______

15. $(8 \times 8) \times 10^4 =$ ______

16. $(7 \times 8) \times 10^4 =$ ______

17. THINK SMARTER What does the product of any whole-number factor multiplied by 100 always have? Explain.

______

______

______

Name ______________________________

Use mental math to complete the table.

18. 1 roll = 50 dimes **Think:** 50 dimes per roll × 20 rolls = (5 × 2) × (10 × 10)

Rolls	20	30	40	50	60	70	80	90	100
Dimes	10×10^2								

19. 1 roll = 40 quarters **Think:** 40 quarters per roll × 20 rolls = (4 × 2) × (10 × 10)

Rolls	20	30	40	50	60	70	80	90	100
Quarters	8×10^2								

	×	6	70	800	9,000
20.	80			64×10^3	
21.	90				81×10^4

Problem Solving • Applications

Use the table for 22–24.

Arthropod Lengths	
Arthropod	Length (in millimeters)
Cluster Fly	9
Crab Spider	5
Fire Ant	4
Tree Hopper	6

22. **What if** you magnified the image of a cluster fly by 9×10^3? What would the length appear to be?

____

23. GO DEEPER If you magnified the images of a fire ant by 4×10^3 and a tree hopper by 3×10^3, which insect would appear longer? How much longer?

____

WRITE Math • Show Your Work

24. MATHEMATICAL PRACTICE 2 **Reason Quantitatively** John wants to magnify the image of a fire ant and a crab spider so they appear to be the same length. How many times their actual sizes would he need to magnify each image?

____

____

Connect to Health

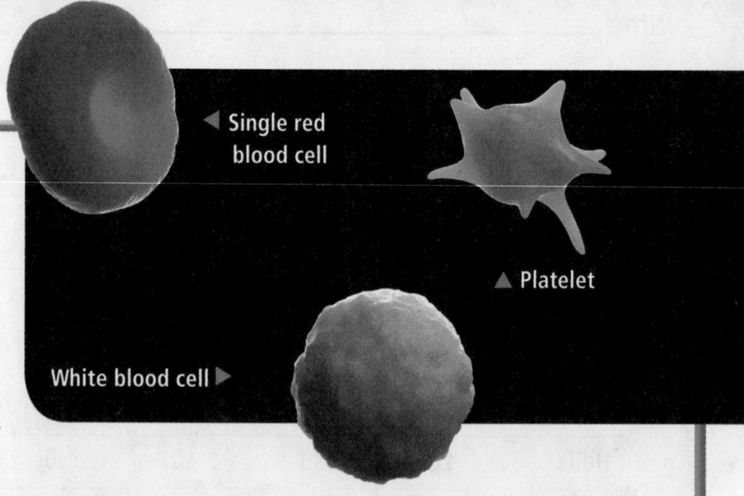

Blood Cells

Blood is necessary for all human life. It contains red blood cells and white blood cells that nourish and cleanse the body and platelets that stop bleeding. The average adult has about 5 liters of blood.

Use patterns and mental math to solve.

25. GO DEEPER A human body has about 30 times as many platelets as white blood cells. A small sample of blood has 8×10^3 white blood cells. About how many platelets are in the sample?

26. Basophils and monocytes are types of white blood cells. A blood sample has about 5 times as many monocytes as basophils. If there are 60 basophils in the sample, about how many monocytes are there?

27. Lymphocytes and eosinophils are types of white blood cells. A blood sample has about 10 times as many lymphocytes as eosinophils. If there are 2×10^2 eosinophils in the sample, about how many lymphocytes are there?

28. THINK SMARTER An average person has 6×10^2 times as many red blood cells as white blood cells. A small sample of blood has 7×10^3 white blood cells. About how many red blood cells are in the sample?

29. THINK SMARTER Kyle says 20×10^4 is the same as 20,000. He reasoned that since he saw 4 as the exponent he should write 4 zeros in his answer. Is Kyle correct?

Name ______________________________

Multiplication Patterns

Practice and Homework
Lesson 1.5

COMMON CORE STANDARD—5.NBT.A.2
Understand the place value system.

Use mental math to complete the pattern.

1. $8 \times 3 = 24$
   $(8 \times 3) \times 10^1 =$ 240
   $(8 \times 3) \times 10^2 =$ 2,400
   $(8 \times 3) \times 10^3 =$ 24,000

2. $5 \times 6 =$ ________
   $(5 \times 6) \times 10^1 =$ ________
   $(5 \times 6) \times 10^2 =$ ________
   $(5 \times 6) \times 10^3 =$ ________

3. $3 \times$ ________ $= 27$
   $(3 \times 9) \times 10^1 =$ ________
   $(3 \times 9) \times 10^2 =$ ________
   $(3 \times 9) \times 10^3 =$ ________

4. ______ $\times 4 = 28$
   $(7 \times 4) \times$ ________ $= 280$
   $(7 \times 4) \times$ ________ $= 2{,}800$
   $(7 \times 4) \times$ ________ $= 28{,}000$

5. $6 \times 8 =$ ________
   $(6 \times 8) \times 10^2 =$ ________
   $(6 \times 8) \times 10^3 =$ ________
   $(6 \times 8) \times 10^4 =$ ________

6. ________ $\times 4 = 16$
   $(4 \times 4) \times 10^2 =$ ________
   $(4 \times 4) \times 10^3 =$ ________
   $(4 \times 4) \times 10^4 =$ ________

Use mental math and a pattern to find the product.

7. $(2 \times 9) \times 10^2 =$ ________

8. $(8 \times 7) \times 10^2 =$ ________

9. $(3 \times 7) \times 10^3 =$ ________

10. $(5 \times 9) \times 10^4 =$ ________

11. $(4 \times 8) \times 10^4 =$ ________

12. $(8 \times 8) \times 10^3 =$ ________

Problem Solving

13. The Florida Everglades welcomes about 2×10^3 visitors per day. Based on this, about how many visitors come to the Everglades per week?

____

____

14. The average person loses about 8×10^1 strands of hair each day. About how many strands of hair would the average person lose in 9 days?

____

____

15. **WRITE** *Math* Do the products 40×500 and 40×600 have the same number of zeros? Explain.

____

____

Lesson Check (5.NBT.A.2)

1. How many zeros are in the product $(6 \times 5) \times 10^3$?

2. Addison studies a tarantula that is 30 millimeters long. Suppose she uses a microscope to magnify the spider by 4×10^2. How long will the spider appear to be?

Spiral Review (Reviews 4.OA.A.3, 4.NBT.B.5)

3. Hayden has 6 rolls of dimes. There are 50 dimes in each roll. How many dimes does he have altogether?

4. An adult ticket to the zoo costs $20 and a child's ticket costs $10. How much will it cost for Mr. and Mrs. Brown and their 4 children to get into the zoo?

5. At a museum, 100 posters are displayed in each of 4 rooms. Altogether, how many posters are displayed?

6. A store sells a gallon of milk for $3. A baker buys 30 gallons of milk for his bakery. How much will he have to pay?

FOR MORE PRACTICE GO TO THE Personal Math Trainer

Name ____________________

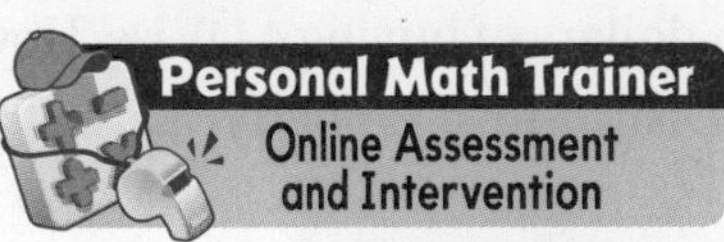

Vocabulary

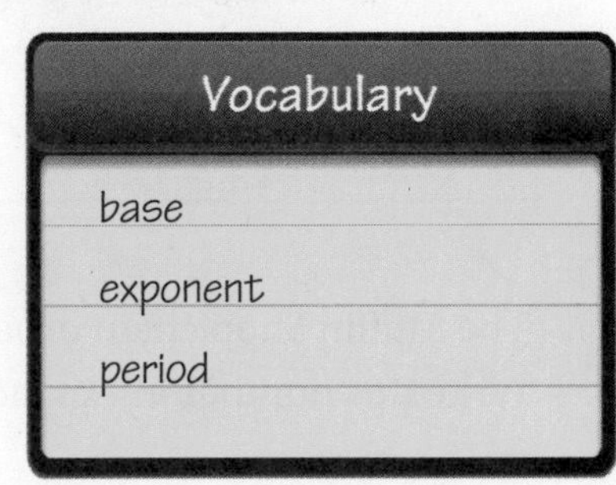

Choose the best term for the box.

1. A group of three digits separated by commas in a multidigit number is a ____________. (p. 11)

2. An ____________ is the number that tells how many times a base is used as a factor. (p. 23)

Concepts and Skills

Complete the sentence. (5.NBT.A.1)

3. 7 is $\frac{1}{10}$ of ________.

4. 800 is 10 times as much as ________.

Write the value of the underlined digit. (5.NBT.A.1)

5. $6{,}5\underline{8}1{,}678$ ____________

6. $125{,}\underline{6}34$ ____________

7. $3\underline{4}{,}634{,}803$ ____________

8. $2{,}\underline{7}64{,}835$ ____________

Complete the equation, and tell which property you used. (5.OA.A.1)

9. $8 \times (14 + 7) =$ ________ $+ (8 \times 7)$

____

10. $7 + (8 + 12) =$ ________ $+ 12$

____

Find the value. (5.NBT.A.2)

11. 10^3 ____________

12. 6×10^2 ____________

13. 4×10^4 ____________

Use mental math and a pattern to find the product. (5.NBT.A.2)

14. $70 \times 300 =$ ____________

15. $(3 \times 4) \times 10^3 =$ ____________

16. DVDs are on sale for $24 each. Felipe writes the expression 4×24 to find the cost in dollars of buying 4 DVDs. How can you rewrite Felipe's expression using the Distributive Property? (5.OA.A.1)

17. The Muffin Shop chain of bakeries sold 745,305 muffins last year. Write this number in expanded form. (5.NBT.A.1)

18. The soccer field at Mario's school has an area of 6,000 square meters. How can Mario show the area as a whole number multiplied by a power of ten? (5.NBT.A.2)

19. Ms. Alonzo ordered 4,000 markers for her store. Only $\frac{1}{10}$ of them arrived. How many markers did she receive? (5.NBT.A.1)

20. GO DEEPER Mark wrote the highest score he made on his new video game as the product of $70 \times 6{,}000$. Use the Associative and Commutative Properties to show how Mark can calculate this product mentally. (5.NBT.A.2)

Name ______________________

Multiply by 1-Digit Numbers

Essential Question How do you multiply by 1-digit numbers?

Common Core **Number and Operations in Base Ten—5.NBT.B.5**

MATHEMATICAL PRACTICES
MP1, MP2, MP3

Unlock the Problem

Each day an airline flies 9 commercial jets from New York to London, England. Each plane holds 293 passengers. If every seat is taken on all flights, how many passengers fly on this airline from New York to London in 1 day?

▲ **The Queen's Guard protects Britain's Royal Family and their residences.**

Use place value and regrouping.

STEP 1 Estimate: 293 × 9

Think: 300 × 9 = ____________

STEP 2 Multiply the ones.

$$\begin{array}{r} \scriptstyle 2 \\ 293 \\ \times \quad 9 \\ \hline 7 \end{array}$$

9 × 3 ones = ________ ones

Write the ones and the regrouped tens.

STEP 3 Multiply the tens.

$$\begin{array}{r} \scriptstyle 82 \\ 293 \\ \times \quad 9 \\ \hline 37 \end{array}$$

9 × 9 tens = ________ tens

Add the regrouped tens.

________ tens + 2 tens = ________ tens

Write the tens and the regrouped hundreds.

STEP 4 Multiply the hundreds.

$$\begin{array}{r} \scriptstyle 82 \\ 293 \\ \times \quad 9 \\ \hline 2{,}637 \end{array}$$

9 × 2 hundreds = ________ hundreds

Add the regrouped hundreds.

________ hundreds + 8 hundreds = ________ hundreds

Write the hundreds.

So, in 1 day, ______________ passengers fly from New York to London.

Math Talk MATHEMATICAL PRACTICES 1

Describe how to record the 27 ones when you multiply 3 by 9 in Step 2.

• MATHEMATICAL PRACTICE 1 **Evaluate Reasonableness** How can you tell if your answer is reasonable? ____________

____

Example

A commercial airline makes several flights each week from New York to Paris, France. If the airline serves 1,978 meals on its flights each day, how many meals are served for the entire week?

To multiply a greater number by a 1-digit number, repeat the process of multiplying and regrouping until every place value is multiplied.

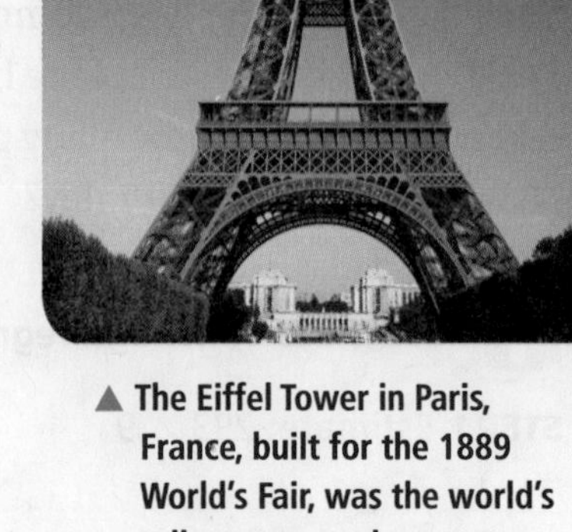

▲ The Eiffel Tower in Paris, France, built for the 1889 World's Fair, was the world's tallest man-made structure for 40 years.

STEP 1 Estimate. 1,978 × 7

Think: 2,000 × 7 = __________

STEP 2 Multiply the ones.

$$\begin{array}{r} {}^{5} \\ 1{,}978 \\ \times \quad 7 \\ \hline 6 \end{array}$$

7 × 8 ones = ______ ones

Write the ones and the regrouped tens.

STEP 3 Multiply the tens.

$$\begin{array}{r} {}^{55} \\ 1{,}978 \\ \times \quad 7 \\ \hline 46 \end{array}$$

7 × 7 tens = ______ tens

Add the regrouped tens.

______ tens + 5 tens = ______ tens

Write the tens and the regrouped hundreds.

STEP 4 Multiply the hundreds.

$$\begin{array}{r} {}^{6\,55} \\ 1{,}978 \\ \times \quad 7 \\ \hline 846 \end{array}$$

7 × 9 hundreds = ______ hundreds

Add the regrouped hundreds.

______ hundreds + 5 hundreds = ______ hundreds

Write the hundreds and the regrouped thousands.

STEP 5 Multiply the thousands.

$$\begin{array}{r} {}^{6\,55} \\ 1{,}978 \\ \times \quad 7 \\ \hline 13{,}846 \end{array}$$

7 × 1 thousand = ______ thousands

Add the regrouped thousands.

______ thousands + 6 thousands = ______ thousands

Write the thousands. Compare your answer to the estimate to see if it is reasonable.

So, in 1 week, __________ meals are served on flights from New York to Paris.

Name ______________________________

Share and Show

Complete to find the product.

1. 6 × 796 **Estimate:** 6 × ________ = ________

796 × 6	Multiply the ones and regroup.	3 796 × 6 6	Multiply the tens and add the regrouped tens. Regroup.	53 796 × 6 76	Multiply the hundreds and add the regrouped hundreds.

Estimate. Then find the product.

2. Estimate: ________

$$\begin{array}{r} 608 \\ \times \quad 8 \\ \hline \end{array}$$

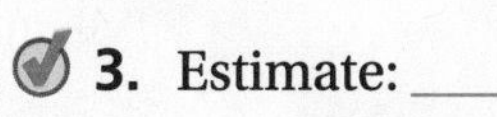

3. Estimate: ________

$$\begin{array}{r} 556 \\ \times \quad 4 \\ \hline \end{array}$$

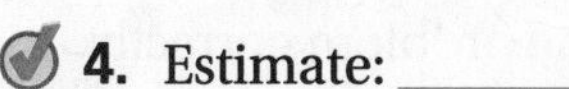

4. Estimate: ________

$$\begin{array}{r} 1,925 \\ \times \quad 7 \\ \hline \end{array}$$

On Your Own

MATHEMATICAL PRACTICE 2 Use Reasoning **Algebra** **Solve for the unknown numbers.**

5.
$$\begin{array}{r} 396 \\ \times \quad 6 \\ \hline 2,3\square6 \end{array}$$

6.
$$\begin{array}{r} 5,12\square \\ \times \quad 8 \\ \hline \square16 \end{array}$$

7.
$$\begin{array}{r} 8,5\square6 \\ \times \quad 7 \\ \hline 60,03\square \end{array}$$

Practice: Copy and Solve **Estimate. Then find the product.**

8. 116 × 3
9. 338 × 4
10. 6 × 219
11. 7 × 456

12. THINKSMARTER A commercial airline makes a flight each day from New York to Paris, France. The aircraft seats 524 passengers and serves 2 meals to each passenger per flight. If all the seats are filled each flight, how many meals are served in one week?

____

Problem Solving • Applications

13. THINK SMARTER **What's the Error?** The Plattsville Glee Club is sending 8 of its members to a singing contest in Cincinnati, Ohio. The cost will be $588 per person. How much will it cost for the entire group of 8 students to attend?

Both Brian and Jermaine solve the problem. Brian says the answer is $40,704. Jermaine's answer is $4,604.

Estimate the cost. A reasonable estimate is __________.

Although Jermaine's answer seems reasonable, neither Brian nor Jermaine solved the problem correctly. Find the errors in Brian's and Jermaine's work. Then, solve the problem correctly.

Brian

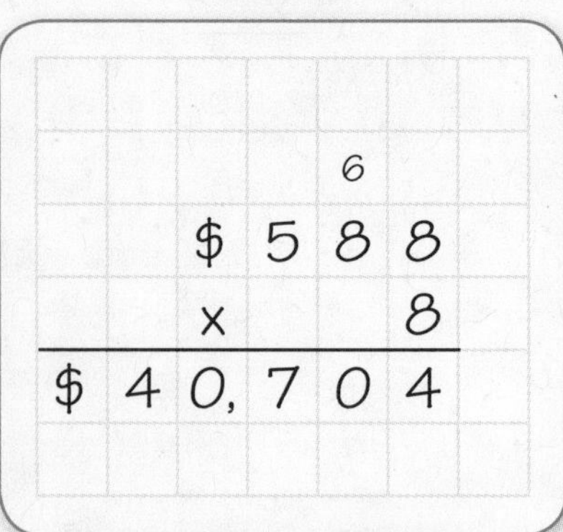

Jermaine

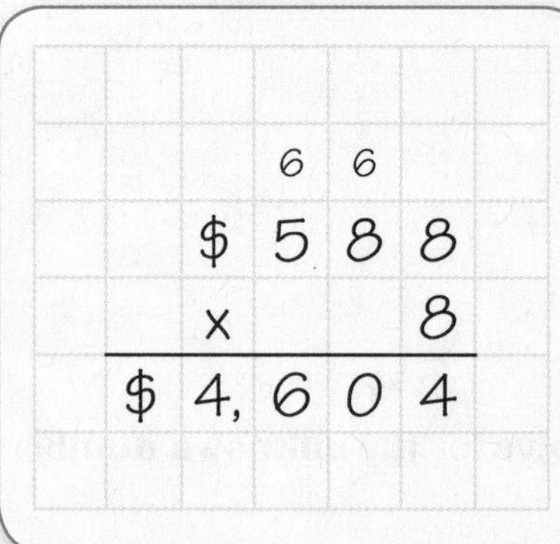

Correct Answer

- MATHEMATICAL PRACTICE 3 **Verify the Reasoning of Others** What error did Brian make? Explain.

___

___

- What error did Jermaine make? Explain.

___

___

14. GO DEEPER How could you predict that Jermaine's answer might be incorrect using your estimate? ___

___

___

Name ______________________________

Multiply by 1-Digit Numbers

COMMON CORE STANDARD—5.NBT.B.6
Perform operations with multi-digit whole numbers and with decimals to hundredths.

Estimate. Then find the product.

1. Estimate: 3,600

$$\begin{array}{r} {}^{1\,5} \\ 416 \\ \times \quad 9 \\ \hline 3{,}744 \end{array}$$

2. Estimate: ________

$$\begin{array}{r} 1{,}374 \\ \times \quad 6 \\ \hline \end{array}$$

3. Estimate: ________

$$\begin{array}{r} 726 \\ \times \quad 5 \\ \hline \end{array}$$

Estimate. Then find the product.

4. 4 × 979
5. 503 × 7
6. 5 × 4,257
7. 6,018 × 9
8. 758 × 6
9. 3 × 697
10. 2,141 × 8
11. 7 × 7,956

Problem Solving Real World

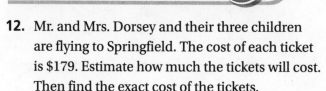

12. Mr. and Mrs. Dorsey and their three children are flying to Springfield. The cost of each ticket is $179. Estimate how much the tickets will cost. Then find the exact cost of the tickets.

____

____

____

13. Ms. Tao flies roundtrip twice yearly between Jacksonville and Los Angeles on business. The distance between the two cities is 2,150 miles. Estimate the distance she flies for both trips. Then find the exact distance.

____

____

____

14. **WRITE** *Math* Show how to solve the problem 378 × 6 using place value with regrouping. Explain how you knew when to regroup.

____

____

Lesson Check (5.NBT.B.5)

1. Mr. Nielson works 154 hours each month. He works 8 months each year. How many hours does Mr. Nielson work each year?

2. Sasha lives 1,493 miles from her grandmother. One year, Sasha's family made 4 round trips to visit her grandmother. How many miles did they travel in all?

Spiral Review (Reviews 4.NBT.A.2, 4.NBT.A.3, 4.NF.C.6, 5.NBT.A.1)

3. Yuna missed 5 points out of 100 points on her math test. What decimal number represents the part of her math test that she answered correctly?

4. Which symbol makes the statement true? Write >, <, or =.

   602,163 ◯ 620,163

5. The number below represents the number of fans that attended Chicago Cubs baseball games in 2008. What is this number written in standard form?

   $(3 \times 1{,}000{,}000) + (3 \times 100{,}000) + (2 \times 100)$

6. A fair was attended by 755,082 people altogether. What is this number rounded to the nearest ten thousand?

FOR MORE PRACTICE GO TO THE **Personal Math Trainer**

Name ________________________________

Multiply by Multi-Digit Numbers

Essential Question How do you multiply by multi-digit numbers?

Number and Operations in Base Ten—5.NBT.B.5

MATHEMATICAL PRACTICES
MP1, MP4, MP6

Unlock the Problem (Real World)

A tiger can eat as much as 40 pounds of food at a time but it may go for several days without eating anything. Suppose a Siberian tiger in the wild eats an average of 18 pounds of food per day. How much food will the tiger eat in 28 days if he eats that amount each day?

Use place value and regrouping.

STEP 1 **Estimate:** 28 × 18

Think: 30 × 20 = __________

STEP 2 Multiply by the ones.

$$\begin{array}{r} 28 \\ \times\ 18 \\ \hline \square \end{array}$$

28 × 8 ones = ______ ones

STEP 3 Multiply by the tens.

$$\begin{array}{r} 28 \\ \times\ 18 \\ \hline \square \\ \square \end{array}$$

28 × 1 ten = ______ tens, or ______ ones

STEP 4 Add the partial products.

$$\begin{array}{rl} 28 & \\ \times\ 18 & \\ \hline \square & \leftarrow 28 \times 8 \\ +\ \square & \leftarrow 28 \times 10 \\ \hline \square & \end{array}$$

So, on average, a Siberian tiger may eat __________ pounds of food in 28 days.

Remember

Use patterns of zeros to find the product of multiples of 10.

3 × 4 = 12

3 × 40 = 120   30 × 40 = 1,200

3 × 400 = 1,200   300 × 40 = 12,000

Example

A Siberian tiger was observed sleeping 1,287 minutes during the course of one day. If he slept for that long every day, how many minutes would he sleep in one year? Assume there are 365 days in one year.

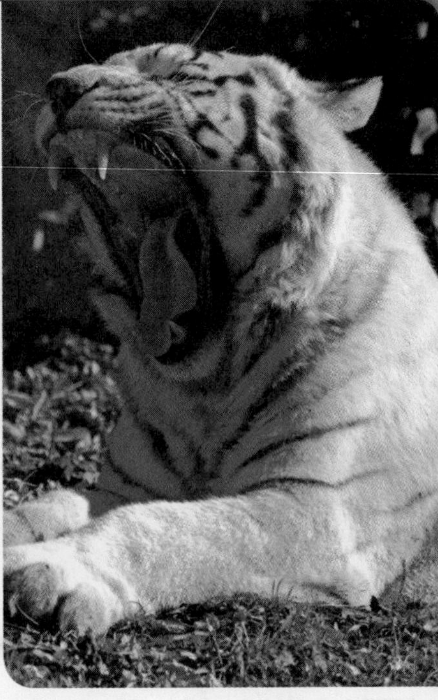

STEP 1 **Estimate:** 1,287 × 365

Think: 1,000 × 400 = ____________

STEP 2 Multiply by the ones.

$$\begin{array}{r} 1{,}287 \\ \times\ 365 \\ \hline \end{array}$$

1,287 × 5 ones = ____________ ones

STEP 3 Multiply by the tens.

$$\begin{array}{r} 1{,}287 \\ \times\ 365 \\ \hline \end{array}$$

1,287 × 6 tens = ____________ tens, or ____________ ones

STEP 4 Multiply by the hundreds.

$$\begin{array}{r} 1{,}287 \\ \times\ 365 \\ \hline \end{array}$$

1,287 × 3 hundreds = ____________ hundreds, or ____________ ones

STEP 5 Add the partial products.

$$\begin{array}{r} 1{,}287 \\ \times\ 365 \\ \hline \end{array}$$

← 1,287 × 5

← 1,287 × 60

\+ ← 1,287 × 300

So, the tiger would sleep ____________ minutes in one year.

MATHEMATICAL PRACTICES 6

Are there different numbers you could have used in Step 1 to find an estimate that is closer to the actual answer? Explain.

Name ______________________________

Share and Show

MATH BOARD

Complete to find the product.

1.

		6	4
×		4	3
+			

← 64 × ____

← 64 × ____

2.

		5	7	1
	×		3	8
+				

← 571 × ____

← 571 × ____

Estimate. Then find the product.

3. Estimate: ________

$$\begin{array}{r} 24 \\ \times\ 15 \\ \hline \end{array}$$

4. Estimate: ________

$$\begin{array}{r} 37 \\ \times\ 63 \\ \hline \end{array}$$

5. Estimate: ________

$$\begin{array}{r} 384 \\ \times\ 45 \\ \hline \end{array}$$

On Your Own

Estimate. Then find the product.

6. Estimate: ________

$$\begin{array}{r} 28 \\ \times\ 22 \\ \hline \end{array}$$

7. Estimate: ________

$$\begin{array}{r} 93 \\ \times\ 76 \\ \hline \end{array}$$

8. Estimate: ________

$$\begin{array}{r} 5{,}271 \\ \times\ 129 \\ \hline \end{array}$$

Practice: Copy and Solve **Estimate. Then find the product.**

9. 54 × 31 **10.** 42 × 26 **11.** 38 × 64 **12.** 63 × 16

13. 204 × 41 **14.** 534 × 25 **15.** 722 × 39 **16.** 957 × 243

17. GO DEEPER One case of books weighs 35 pounds. One case of magazines weighs 23 pounds. A book store wants to ship 72 cases of books and 94 cases of magazines to another store. What is the total weight of the shipment?

____

Problem Solving • Applications 

Use the table for 18–20.

18. How much sleep does a jaguar get in 1 year?

____

19. THINKSMARTER In 1 year, how many more hours of sleep does a giant armadillo get than a platypus?

Animal Sleep Amounts	
Animal	**Amount (usual hours per week)**
Jaguar	77
Giant Armadillo	127
Owl Monkey	119
Platypus	98
Three-Toed Sloth	101

____

20. MATHEMATICAL PRACTICE 1 **Make Sense of Problems** Owl monkeys sleep during the day, waking about 15 minutes after sundown to find food. At midnight, they rest for an hour or two, then continue to feed until sunrise. They live about 27 years. How many hours of sleep does an owl monkey that lives 27 years get in its lifetime?

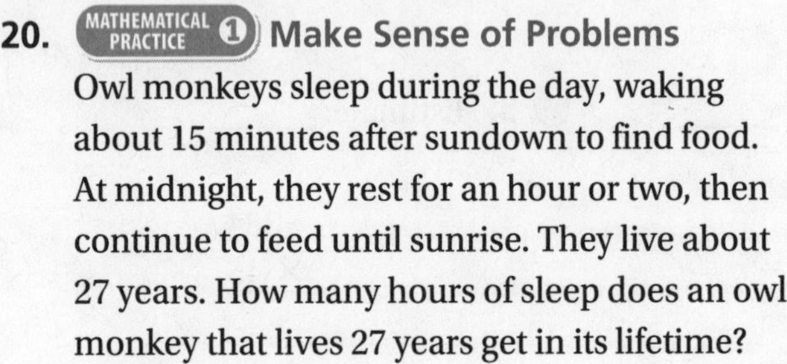

____

WRITE Math • Show Your Work

21. GO DEEPER Tickets to a museum cost \$17 each. For a field trip, the museum offers a \$4 discount on each ticket. How much will tickets for 32 students cost?

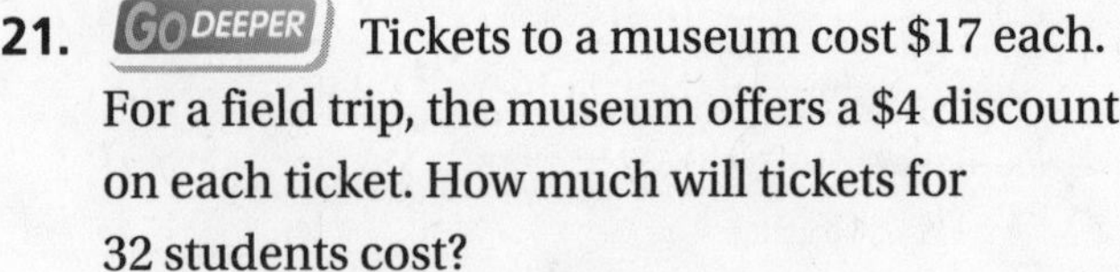

____

22. THINKSMARTER Rachel earns \$21 per day. For 22a–22d, select True or False for each statement.

22a. Rachel earns \$421 for 20 days of work.
○ True ○ False

22b. Rachel earns \$315 for 15 days of work.
○ True ○ False

22c. Rachel earns \$273 for 13 days of work.
○ True ○ False

22d. Rachel earns \$250 for 13 days of work.
○ True ○ False

Name ______________________

Multiply by Multi-Digit Numbers

COMMON CORE STANDARD—5.NBT.B.5
Perform operations with multi-digit whole numbers and with decimals to hundredths.

Estimate. Then find the product.

1. Estimate: 4,000

```
    82
 ×  49
   738
+ 3280
 4,018
```

2. Estimate: ______

```
   92
×  68
```

3. Estimate: ______

```
  1,537
×   242
```

4. 23 × 67

5. 309 × 29

6. 612 × 87

Problem Solving Real World

7. A company shipped 48 boxes of canned dog food. Each box contains 24 cans. How many cans of dog food did the company ship in all?

8. There were 135 cars in a rally. Each driver paid a \$25 fee to participate in the rally. How much money did the drivers pay in all?

9. WRITE Math Write a problem multiplying a 3-digit number by a 2-digit number. Show all the steps to solve it by using place value and regrouping and by using partial products.

Lesson Check (5.NBT.B.5)

1. A chessboard has 64 squares. At a chess tournament 84 chessboards were used. How many squares are there on 84 chessboards?

2. Last month, a manufacturing company shipped 452 boxes of ball bearings. Each box contains 48 ball bearings. How many ball bearings did the company ship last month?

Spiral Review (5.NBT.A.1, 5.NBT.A.2, 5.NBT.B.5, 5.NBT.B.6)

3. What is the standard form of the number three million, sixty thousand, five hundred twenty?

4. What number completes the following equation?

   $8 \times (40 + 7) = (8 \times \square) + (8 \times 7)$

5. The population of Clarksville is about 6,000 people. What is the population written as a whole number multiplied by a power of ten?

6. A sporting goods store ordered 144 cans of tennis balls. Each can contains 3 balls. How many tennis balls did the store order?

FOR MORE PRACTICE GO TO THE **Personal Math Trainer**

Name ______________________________

Relate Multiplication to Division

Essential Question How is multiplication used to solve a division problem?

Common Core **Number and Operations in Base Ten—5.NBT.B.6**

MATHEMATICAL PRACTICES
MP2, MP3, MP6, MP7

You can use the relationship between multiplication and division to solve a division problem. Using the same numbers, multiplication and division are opposite, or **inverse operations.**

3	×	8	=	24		24	÷	3	=	8
↑		↑		↑		↑		↑		↑
factor		factor		product		dividend		divisor		quotient

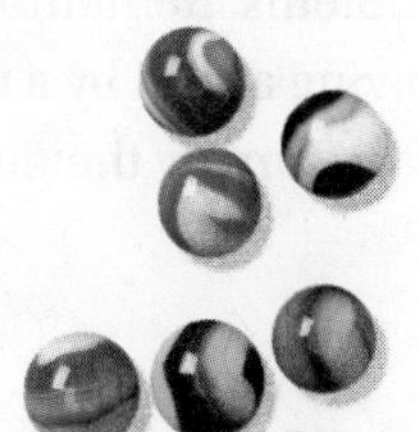

Unlock the Problem Real World

Joel and 5 friends collected 126 marbles. They shared the marbles equally. How many marbles will each person get?

- Underline the dividend.
- What is the divisor? ______

One Way Make an array.

- Outline a rectangular array on the grid to model 126 squares arranged in 6 rows of the same length. Shade each row a different color.

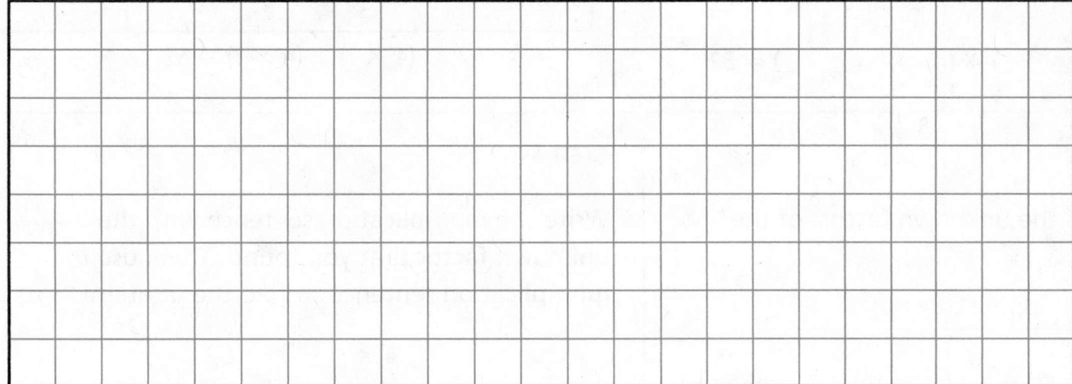

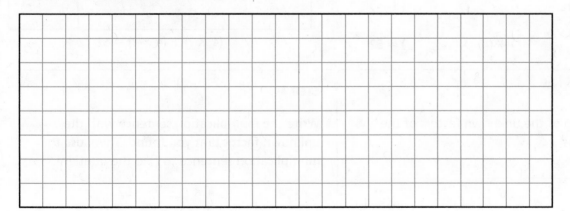

- How many squares are shaded in each row? ______
- Use the array to complete the multiplication sentence. Then, use the multiplication sentence to complete the division sentence.

6 × ______ = 126 126 ÷ 6 = ______

So, each of the 6 friends will get ______ marbles.

Another Way Use the Distributive Property.

Divide. 52 ÷ 4

You can use the Distributive Property and an area model to solve division problems. Remember that the Distributive Property states that multiplying a sum by a number is the same as multiplying each addend in the sum by the number and then adding the products.

STEP 1

Write a related multiplication sentence for the division problem.

Think: Use the divisor as a factor and the dividend as the product. The quotient will be the unknown factor.

52 ÷ 4 = ■

4 × ■ = 52

?

4 52

4 × ? = 52

STEP 2

Use the Distributive Property to break apart the large area into smaller areas for partial products that you know.

(40 + 12) = 52

(4 × ______) + (4 × ______) = 52

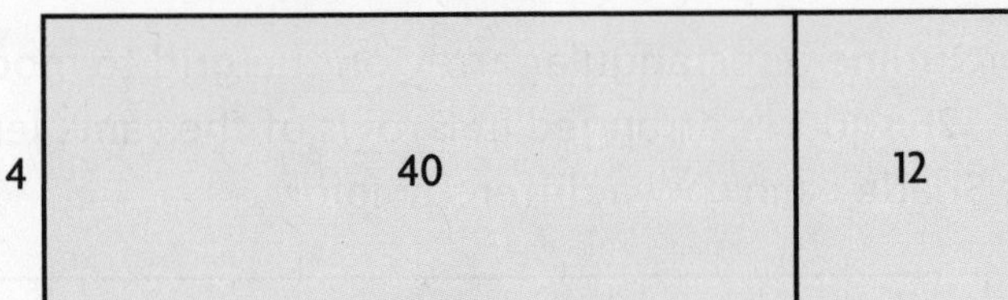

(4 × ?) + (4 × ?) = 52

STEP 3

Find the sum of the unknown factors of the smaller areas.

______ + ______ = ______

STEP 4

Write the multiplication sentence with the unknown factor that you found. Then, use the multiplication sentence to find the quotient.

4 × ______ = 52

52 ÷ 4 = ______

- MATHEMATICAL PRACTICE 6 **Explain** how you can use the Distributive Property to find the quotient of 96 ÷ 8.

____

____

____

Name ______________________________

Share and Show

1. Brad has 72 toy cars that he puts into 4 equal groups. How many cars does Brad have in each group? Use the array to show your answer.

$4 \times$ ______ $= 72$ $\quad 72 \div 4 =$ ______

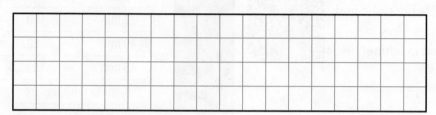

Use multiplication and the Distributive Property to find the quotient.

2. $108 \div 6 =$ ______

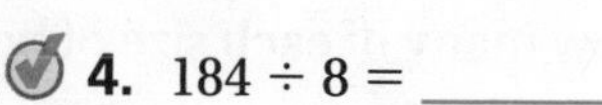

3. $84 \div 6 =$ ______

4. $184 \div 8 =$ ______

MATHEMATICAL PRACTICES 7

Look for Structure How does using multiplication help you solve a division problem?

On Your Own

Use multiplication and the Distributive Property to find the quotient.

5. $60 \div 4 =$ ______

6. $144 \div 6 =$ ______

7. $252 \div 9 =$ ______

Find each quotient. Then compare. Write <, >, or =.

8. $51 \div 3$ ◯ $68 \div 4$

______ ______

9. $252 \div 6$ ◯ $135 \div 3$

______ ______

10. $110 \div 5$ ◯ $133 \div 7$

______ ______

Problem Solving • Applications

Use the table to solve 11–12.

11. THINKSMARTER Mr. Henderson has 2 bouncy-ball vending machines. He buys one bag of the 27-millimeter balls and one bag of the 40-millimeter balls. He puts an equal number of each in the 2 machines. How many bouncy balls does he put in each machine?

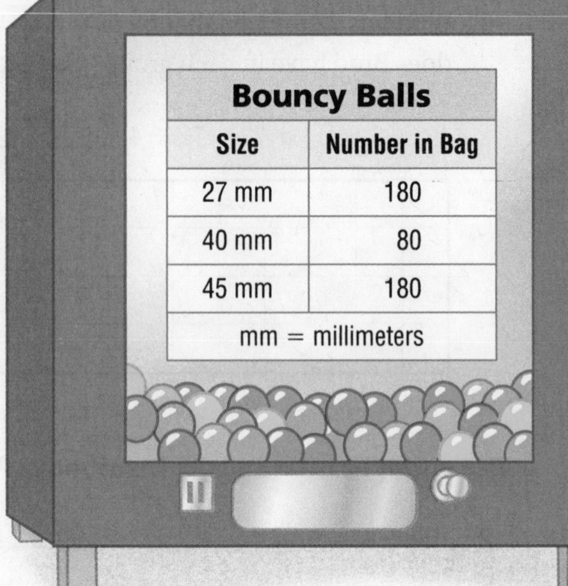

Bouncy Balls

Size	Number in Bag
27 mm	180
40 mm	80
45 mm	180

mm = millimeters

____

12. GO DEEPER Lindsey buys a bag of each size of bouncy ball. She wants to put the same number of each size of bouncy ball into 5 party-favor bags. How many of each size of bouncy ball will she put in a bag?

____

13. MATHEMATICAL PRACTICE 3 **Verify the Reasoning of Others** Sandra writes $(4 \times 30) + (4 \times 2)$ and says the quotient for $128 \div 4$ is 8. Is she correct? Explain.

____

____

____

____

WRITE Math • **Show Your Work**

Personal Math Trainer

14. THINKSMARTER+ Joe collected 45 seashells. Joe wants to share his seashells with 5 of his friends equally. How many seashells will each friend get? Use the array to show your answer.

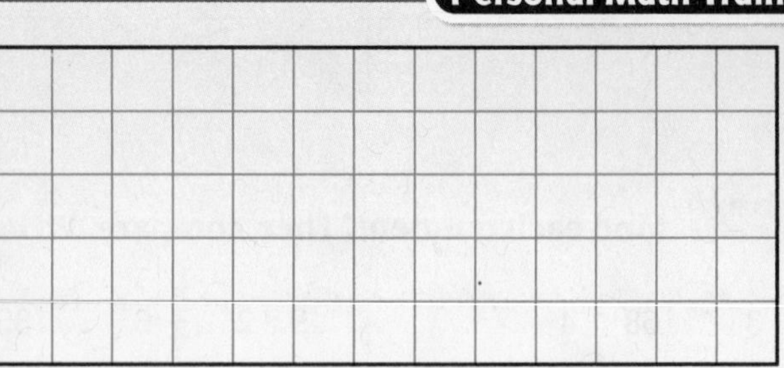

Use the multiplication sentence to complete the division sentence.

$5 \times$ ☐ $= 45$ $45 \div 5 =$ ☐

Name ____________________

Practice and Homework
Lesson 1.8

Relate Multiplication to Division

Common Core Standard—5.NBT.B.6
Perform operations with multi-digit whole numbers and with decimals to hundredths.

Use multiplication and the Distributive Property to find the quotient.

1. 70 ÷ 5 = 14

(5 × 10) + (5 × 4) = 70

5 × 14 = 70

2. 96 ÷ 6 = ______

3. 85 ÷ 5 = ______

4. 171 ÷ 9 = ______

5. 102 ÷ 6 = ______

6. 210 ÷ 5 = ______

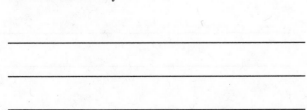

Problem Solving Real World

7. Ken is making gift bags for a party. He has 64 colored pens and wants to put the same number in each bag. How many bags will Ken make if he puts 4 pens in each bag?

8. Maritza is buying wheels for her skateboard shop. She ordered a total of 92 wheels. If wheels come in packages of 4, how many packages will she receive?

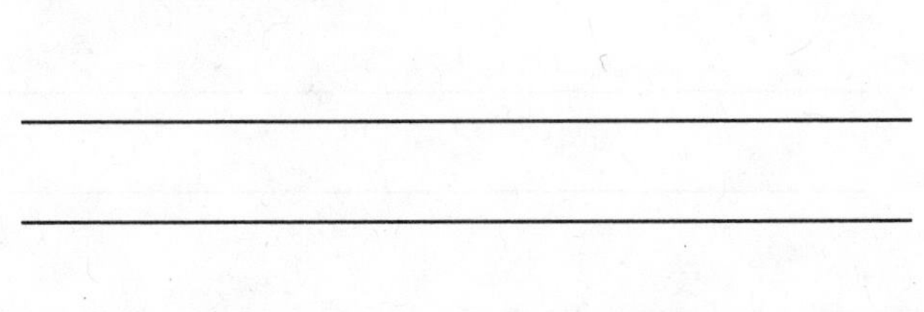

9. WRITE Math For the problem 135 ÷ 5, draw two different ways to break apart the array. Use the Distributive Property to write products for each different way.

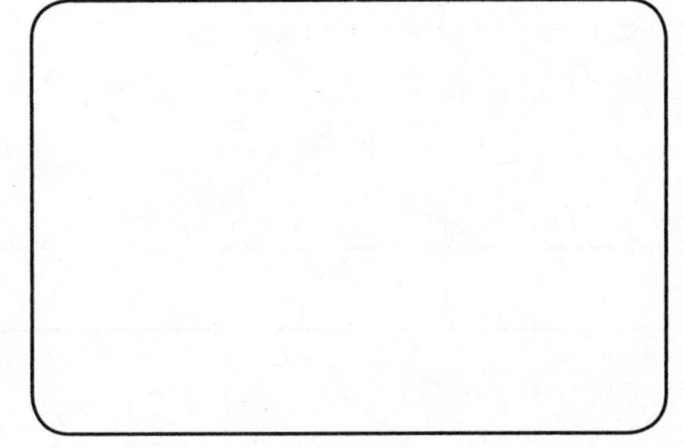

Lesson Check (5.NBT.B.6)

1. Write an expression using the Distributive Property that can be used to find the quotient of $36 \div 3$.

2. Write an expression using the Distributive Property that can be used to find the quotient of $126 \div 7$.

Spiral Review (4.OA.A.3, 5.NBT.A.1, 5.NBT.A.2)

3. Allison separates 23 stickers into 4 equal piles. How many stickers does she have left over?

4. A website had 2,135,789 hits. What is the value of the digit 3?

5. The area of Arizona is 114,006 square miles. What is the expanded form of this number?

6. What is the value of the fourth power of ten?

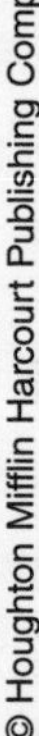

FOR MORE PRACTICE GO TO THE **Personal Math Trainer**

Name ________________________________

Problem Solving • Multiplication and Division

Essential Question How can you use the strategy *solve a simpler problem* to help you solve a division problem?

Number and Operations in Base Ten—5.NBT.B.6

MATHEMATICAL PRACTICES
MP1, MP2, MP3

Unlock the Problem

Real World

Mark works at an animal shelter. To feed 9 dogs, Mark empties eight 18-ounce cans of dog food into a large bowl. If he divides the food equally among the dogs, how many ounces of food will each dog get?

Use the graphic organizer below to help you solve the problem.

Read the Problem

What do I need to find?

I need to find ________________________________

____.

What information do I need to use?

I need to use the number of ______________, the number of ______________ in each can, and the number of dogs that need to be fed.

How will I use the information?

I can ______________ to find the total number of ounces. Then I can solve a simpler problem to ______________ that total by 9.

Solve the Problem

- First, multiply to find the total number of ounces of dog food.

  $8 \times 18 =$ ______

- To find the number of ounces each dog gets, I'll need to divide.

  $144 \div$ ______ $= \blacksquare$

- To find the quotient, I break 144 into two simpler numbers that are easier to divide.

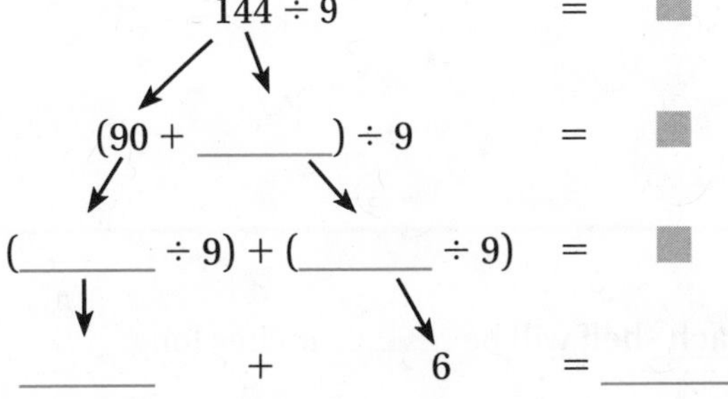

$144 \div 9 = \blacksquare$

$(90 +$ ______$) \div 9 = \blacksquare$

$($______ $\div 9) + ($______ $\div 9) = \blacksquare$

______ $+ 6 =$ ______

So, each dog gets ______ ounces of food.

Try Another Problem

Michelle is building shelves for her room. She has a plank 137 inches long that she wants to cut into 7 shelves of equal length. The plank has jagged ends, so she will start by cutting 2 inches off each end. How long will each shelf be?

137 inches

Read the Problem	Solve the Problem
What do I need to find?	
What information do I need to use?	
How will I use the information?	

So, each shelf will be _____ inches long.

MATHEMATICAL PRACTICES 1

Analyze Explain how the strategy you used helped you solve the problem.

Name ______________________________

Unlock the Problem

√ Underline what you need to find.

√ Circle the numbers you need to use.

Share and Show MATH BOARD

1. To make concrete mix, Monica pours 34 pounds of cement, 68 pounds of sand, 14 pounds of small pebbles, and 19 pounds of large pebbles into a large wheelbarrow. If she pours the mixture into 9 equal-size bags, how much will each bag weigh?

First, find the total weight of the mixture.

____

Then, divide the total by the number of bags. Break the total into two simpler numbers to make the division easier, if necessary.

Finally, find the quotient and solve the problem.

So, each bag will weigh ______ pounds.

2. **What if** Monica pours the mixture into 5 equal-size bags? How much will each bag weigh?

____

3. Taylor is building doghouses to sell. Each doghouse requires 3 full sheets of plywood which Taylor cuts into new shapes. The plywood is shipped in bundles of 14 full sheets. How many doghouses can Taylor make from 12 bundles of plywood?

____

4. Eileen is planting a garden. She has seeds for 60 tomato plants, 55 sweet corn plants, and 21 cucumber plants. She plants them in 8 rows, with the same number of plants in each row. How many seeds are planted in each row?

____

WRITE Math • Show Your Work

On Your Own

5. GO DEEPER Starting on day 1 with 1 jumping jack, Keila doubles the number of jumping jacks she does every day. How many jumping jacks will Keila do on day 10?

____

6. MATHEMATICAL PRACTICE 2 **Represent a Problem** Starting in the blue square, in how many different ways can you draw a line that passes through every square without picking up your pencil or crossing a line you've already drawn? Show the ways.

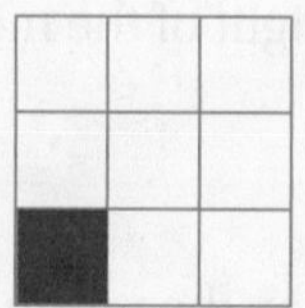

____

7. On April 11, Millie bought a lawn mower with a 50-day guarantee. If the guarantee begins on the date of purchase, what is the first day on which the mower will no longer be guaranteed?

____

8. THINK SMARTER The teacher of a jewelry-making class had a supply of 236 beads. Her students used 29 beads to make earrings and 63 beads to make bracelets. They will use the remaining beads to make necklaces with 6 beads on each necklace. How many necklaces will the students make?

____

9. THINK SMARTER Susan is making 8 casseroles. She uses 9 cans of beans. Each can is 16-ounces. If she divides the beans equally among 8 casseroles, how many ounces of beans will be in each casserole? Show your work.

____

____

____

Name ______________________

Problem Solving • Multiplication and Division

COMMON CORE STANDARD—5.NBT.B.6
Perform operations with multi-digit whole numbers and with decimals to hundredths.

Solve the problems below. Show your work.

1. Dani is making punch for a family picnic. She adds 16 fluid ounces of orange juice, 16 fluid ounces of lemon juice, and 8 fluid ounces of lime juice to 64 fluid ounces of water. How many 8-ounce glasses of punch can she fill?

$16 + 16 + 8 + 64 = 104$ fluid ounces

$104 \div 8 = (40 + 64) \div 8$

$= (40 \div 8) + (64 \div 8)$

$= 5 + 8$, or 13

13 glasses

2. Ryan has nine 14-ounce bags of popcorn to repackage and sell at the school fair. A small bag holds 3 ounces. How many small bags can he make?

____

3. Bianca is making scarves to sell. She has 33 pieces of blue fabric, 37 pieces of green fabric, and 41 pieces of red fabric. Suppose Bianca uses 3 pieces of fabric to make 1 scarf. How many scarves can she make?

____

4. Jasmine has 8 packs of candle wax to make scented candles. Each pack contains 14 ounces of wax. Jasmine uses 7 ounces of wax to make one candle. How many candles can she make?

____

5. **WRITE** *Math* Rewrite Problem 4 on page 57 with different numbers. Solve the new problem and show your work.

____

____

____

Lesson Check (5.NBT.B.6)

1. Joyce is helping her aunt create craft kits. Her aunt has 138 pipe cleaners, and each kit will include 6 pipe cleaners. What is the total number of craft kits they can make?

2. Stefan plants seeds for 30 carrot plants and 45 beet plants in 5 rows, with the same number of seeds in each row. How many seeds are planted in each row?

Spiral Review (Reviews 4.NBT.A.3, 5.NBT.B.5, 5.NBT.B.6)

3. Georgia wants to evenly divide 84 trading cards among 6 friends. How many cards will each friend get?

4. Maria has 144 marbles. Emanuel has 4 times the number of marbles Maria has. How many marbles does Emanuel have?

5. The Conservation Society bought and planted 45 cherry trees. Each tree cost $367. What was the total cost of planting the trees?

6. A sports arena covers 710,430 square feet of ground. A newspaper reported that the arena covers about 700,000 square feet of ground. To what place value was the number rounded?

FOR MORE PRACTICE GO TO THE Personal Math Trainer

Name ______________________

Numerical Expressions

Essential Question How can you use a numerical expression to describe a situation?

Operations and Algebraic Thinking—5.OA.A.1, 5.OA.A.2

MATHEMATICAL PRACTICES
MP3, MP4, MP6

Unlock the Problem

A **numerical expression** is a mathematical phrase that has numbers and operation signs but does not have an equal sign.

Tyler caught 15 small bass, and his dad caught 12 small bass in the Memorial Bass Tourney in Tidioute, PA. Write a numerical expression to represent how many fish they caught in all.

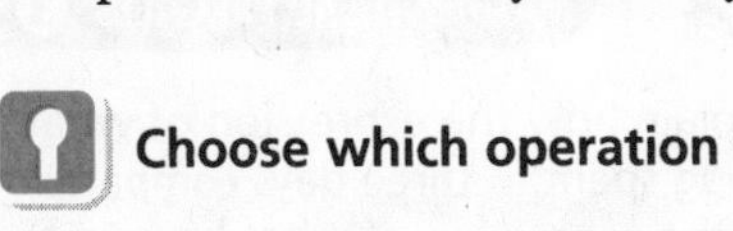

Choose which operation to use.

You need to join groups of different sizes, so use addition.

15 small bass	plus	12 small bass
↓	↓	↓
15	+	12

So, 15 + 12 represents how many fish they caught in all.

Example 1 Write an expression to match the words.

A Addition

Emma has 11 fish in her aquarium. She buys 4 more fish.

fish	plus	more fish
↓	↓	↓
11	+	4

B Subtraction

Lucia has 128 stamps. She uses 38 stamps on party invitations.

stamps	minus	stamps used
↓	↓	↓
128	−	______

C Multiplication

Karla buys 5 books. Each book costs $3.

books	multiplied by	cost per book
↓	↓	↓
______	×	______

D Division

Four players share 52 cards equally.

cards	divided by	players
↓	↓	↓
______	÷	______

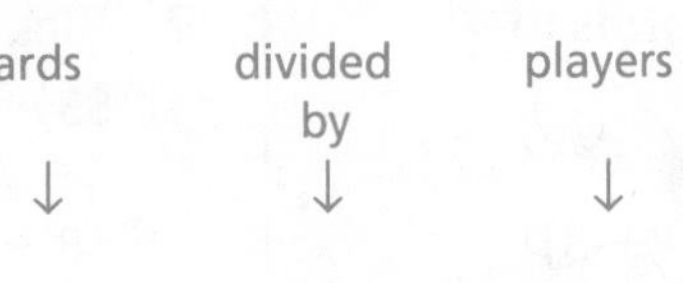

Math Talk MATHEMATICAL PRACTICES 4

What does the expression model in each example?

Expressions with Parentheses The meaning of the words in a problem will tell you where to place the parentheses in an expression.

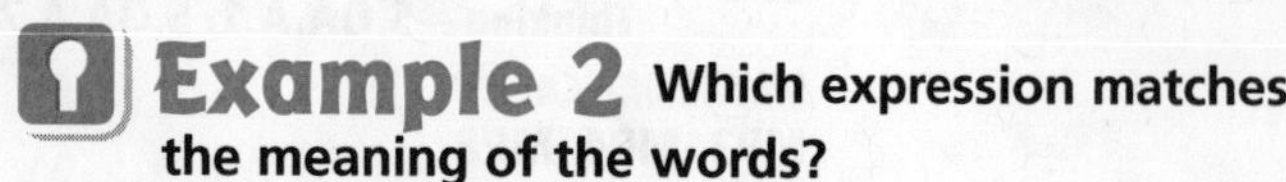

Example 2 Which expression matches the meaning of the words?

- Underline the events for each day.
- Circle the number of days these events happened.

Doug went fishing for 3 days. Each day he put $15 in his pocket. At the end of each day, he had $5 left. How much money did Doug spend by the end of the trip?

Think: Each day he took $15 and had $5 left. He did this for 3 days.

($15 − $5) ← **Think:** What expression can you write to show how much money Doug spends in one day?

3 × ($15 − $5) ← **Think:** What expression can you write to show how much money Doug spends in three days?

MATHEMATICAL PRACTICES 3

Explain how the expression of what Doug spent in three days compares to the expression of what he spent in one day?

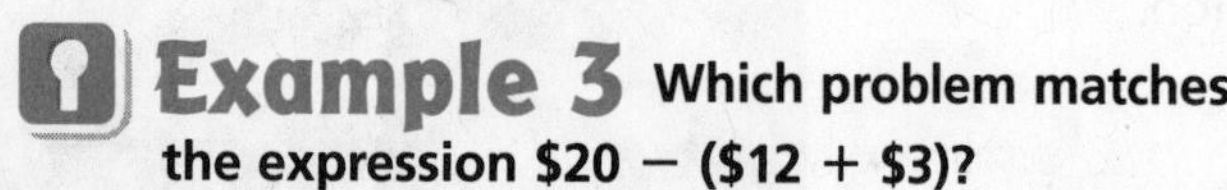

Example 3 Which problem matches the expression $20 − ($12 + $3)?

Kim has $20 to spend for her fishing trip. She spends $12 on a fishing pole. Then she finds $3. How much money does Kim have now?

List the events in order.

First: Kim has $20.

Next: ________________.

Then: ________________.

Do these words match the expression? __________

Kim has $20 to spend for her fishing trip. She spends $12 on a fishing pole and $3 on bait. How much money does Kim have now?

List the events in order.

First: Kim has $20.

Next: ________________.

Then: ________________.

Do these words match the expression? __________

Share and Show

Circle the expression that matches the words.

1. Teri had 18 worms. She gave 4 worms to Susie and 3 worms to Jamie.

   (18 − 4) + 3   18 − (4 + 3)

2. Rick had $8. He then worked 4 hours for $5 each hour.

   $8 + (4 × $5)   ($8 + 4) × $5

Name ______________________________

Write an expression to match the words.

3. Greg drives 26 miles on Monday and 90 miles on Tuesday.

____

4. Lynda has 27 fewer fish than Jack. Jack has 80 fish.

____

Write words to match the expression.

5. 34 − 17

____

____

6. $6 \times (12 - 4)$

____

____

MATHEMATICAL PRACTICES 6

Is $4 \times 8 = 32$ an expression? Explain why or why not.

On Your Own

Write an expression to match the words.

7. José shared 12 party favors equally among 6 friends.

____

8. Braden has 14 baseball cards. He finds 5 more baseball cards.

____

9. Isabelle bought 12 bottles of water at $2 each.

____

10. Monique had $20. She spent $5 on lunch and $10 at the bookstore.

____

Write words to match the expression.

11. 36 ÷ 9

____

____

12. $35 - (16 + 11)$

____

____

Draw a line to match the expression with the words.

13. Fred catches 25 fish. Then he releases 10 fish and catches 8 more. •

Nick has 25 pens. He gives 10 pens to one friend and 8 pens to another friend. •

Jan catches 15 fish and lets 6 fish go. •

Libby catches 15 fish and lets 6 fish go for three days in a row. •

• $3 \times (15 - 6)$

• $15 - 6$

• $25 - (10 + 8)$

• $(25 - 10) + 8$

Problem Solving • Applications

Use the rule and the table for 14–15.

Type of Fish	Length (in inches)
Lemon Tetra	2
Strawberry Tetra	3
Giant Danio	5
Tiger Barb	3
Swordtail	5

Aquarium Fish

▲ The rule for the number of fish in an aquarium is to allow 1 gallon of water for each inch of length.

14. MATHEMATICAL PRACTICE 4 **Write an Expression** to represent the total number of lemon tetras that could be in a 20-gallon aquarium.

____

15. THINK SMARTER There are tiger barbs in a 15-gallon aquarium and giant danios in a 30-gallon aquarium. Write a numerical expression to represent the greatest total number of fish that could be in both aquariums.

____

16. GO DEEPER Write a word problem for an expression that is three times as great as (15 + 7). Then write the expression.

____

____

____

____

____

17. THINK SMARTER Daniel bought 30 tokens when he arrived at the festival. He won 8 more tokens for getting the highest score at the basketball contest, but lost 6 tokens at the ring toss game. Write an expression to find the number of tokens Daniel has left.

____

WRITE ▸ Math • **Show Your Work**

Name ______________________

Numerical Expressions

Common Core **COMMON CORE STANDARD—5.OA.A.1, 5.OA.A.2** *Write and interpret numerical expressions.*

Write an expression to match the words.

1. Ethan collected 16 seashells. He lost 4 of them while walking home.

$16 - 4$

2. Yasmine bought 4 bracelets. Each bracelet cost $3.

____

3. Amani did 10 jumping jacks. Then she did 7 more.

____

4. Darryl has a board that is 8 feet long. He cuts it into pieces that are each 2 feet long.

____

Write words to match the expression.

5. $3 + (4 \times 12)$

____

6. $36 \div 4$

____

7. $24 - (6 + 3)$

____

Problem Solving Real World

8. Kylie has 14 polished stones. Her friend gives her 6 more stones. Write an expression to match the words.

____

9. Rashad had 25 stamps. He shared them equally among himself and 4 friends. Then Rashad found 2 more stamps in his pocket. Write an expression to match the words.

____

10. WRITE ▸ *Math* Write a numerical expression. Then write words to match the expression.

____

Lesson Check (5.OA.A.1)

1. Jenna bought 3 packs of bottled water, with 8 bottles in each pack. Then she gave 6 bottles away. Write an expression to match the words.

2. Stephen had 24 miniature cars. He gave 4 cars to his brother. Then he passed the rest of the cars out equally among 4 of his friends. Which operation would you use to represent the first part of this situation?

Spiral Review (5.NBT.A.2, 5.NBT.B.5, 5.NBT.B.6)

3. To find 36 + 29 + 14, Joshua rewrote the expression as 36 + 14 + 29. What property did Joshua use to rewrite the expression?

4. There are 6 baskets on the table. Each basket has 144 crayons in it. How many crayons are there?

5. Mr. Anderson wrote $(7 \times 9) \times 10^3$ on the board. What is the value of that expression?

6. Barbara mixes 54 ounces of granola and 36 ounces of raisins. She divides the mixture into 6-ounce servings. How many servings does she make?

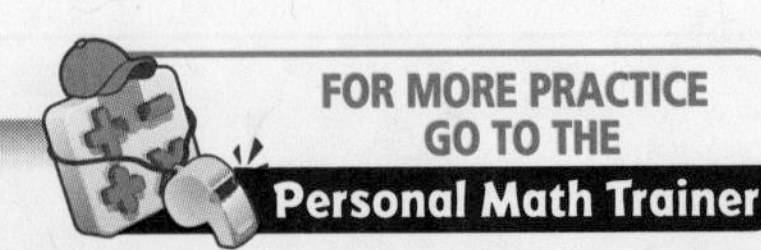

Name ____________________

Evaluate Numerical Expressions

Essential Question In what order must operations be evaluated to find the solution to a problem?

Operations and Algebraic Thinking—5.OA.A.1

MATHEMATICAL PRACTICES
MP2, MP3, MP4

CONNECT Remember that a numerical expression is a mathematical phrase that uses only numbers and operation symbols.

$(5 - 2) \times 7$ $72 \div 9 + 16$ $(24 - 15) + 32$

To **evaluate**, or find the value of, a numerical expression with more than one type of operation, you must follow rules called the **order of operations.** The order of operations tells you in what order you should evaluate an expression.

Order of Operations

1. Perform operations in parentheses.
2. Multiply and divide from left to right.
3. Add and subtract from left to right.

Unlock the Problem

A bread recipe calls for 4 cups of wheat flour and 2 cups of rye flour. To triple the recipe, how many cups of flour are needed in all?

Evaluate $3 \times 4 + 3 \times 2$ to find the total number of cups.

A Gabriela did not follow the order of operations correctly.

Gabriela	
$3 \times 4 + 3 \times 2$	First, I added.
$3 \times 7 \times 2$	Then, I multiplied.
42	

Explain why Gabriela's answer is not correct.

____

B Follow the order of operations by multiplying first and then adding.

Name________
$3 \times 4 + 3 \times 2$

So, ______ cups of flour are needed.

Evaluate Expressions with Parentheses To evaluate an expression with parentheses, follow the order of operations. Perform the operations in parentheses first. Multiply from left to right. Then add and subtract from left to right.

Example

Each batch of granola Lena makes uses 3 cups of oats, 1 cup of raisins, and 2 cups of nuts. Lena wants to make 5 batches of granola. How many cups of oats, raisins, and nuts will she need in all?

Write the expression. $5 \times (3 + 1 + 2)$

First, perform the operations in parentheses. $5 \times (\_\_\_\_)$

Then multiply. ______

So, Lena will use ______ cups of oats, raisins, and nuts in all.

- MATHEMATICAL PRACTICE 2 **Reason Quantitatively** What if Lena makes 4 batches? Will this change the numerical expression? Explain.

____

Try This! Rewrite the expression with parentheses to equal the given value.

A $6 + 12 \times 8 - 3$; value: 141

- Evaluate the expression without the parentheses. ________
- Try placing the parentheses in the expression so the value is 141.

Think: Will the placement of the parentheses increase or decrease the value of the expression?

- Use order of operations to check your work.

$6 + 12 \times 8 - 3$

B $5 + 28 \div 7 - 4$; value: 11

- Evaluate the expression without the parentheses. ________
- Try placing the parentheses in the expression so that the value is 11.

Think: Will the placement of the parentheses increase or decrease the value of the expression?

- Use order of operations to check your work.

$5 + 28 \div 7 - 4$

Name ____________________

Share and Show

Evaluate the numerical expression.

1. $10 + 36 \div 9$

   Think: I need to divide first.

   ______

2. $10 + (25 - 10) \div 5$

   ______

3. $9 - (3 \times 2) + 8$

   ______

MATHEMATICAL PRACTICES 3

Raina evaluated the expression $5 \times 2 + 2$ by adding first and then multiplying. Will her answer be correct? **Apply the order of operations.**

On Your Own

Evaluate the numerical expression.

4. $(4 + 49) - 4 \times 10$ ______

5. $5 + 17 - 100 \div 5$ ______

6. $36 - (8 + 5)$ ______

7. $125 - (68 + 7)$ ______

Rewrite the expression with parentheses to equal the given value.

8. $100 - 30 \div 5$
   value: 14

   ____

9. $12 + 17 - 3 \times 2$
   value: 23

   ____

10. $9 + 5 \div 5 + 2$
    value: 2

    ____

11. THINK SMARTER Each pitcher of power smoothie that Ginger makes has 2 scoops of pineapple, 3 scoops of strawberries, 1 scoop of spinach, and 1 scoop of kale. If Ginger makes 7 pitchers of power smoothies, how many scoops will she use in all? Write and evaluate a numerical expression containing parentheses.

    ____

    ____

12. MATHEMATICAL PRACTICE 2 **Reason Abstractly** The value of $100 - 30 \div 5$ with parentheses can have a value of 14 or 94. Explain.

    ____

    ____

    ____

Unlock the Problem Real World

13. GO DEEPER A movie theater has 4 groups of seats. The largest group of seats, in the middle, has 20 rows, with 20 seats in each row. There are 2 smaller groups of seats on the sides, each with 20 rows and 6 seats in each row. A group of seats in the back has 5 rows, with 30 seats in each row. How many seats are in the movie theater?

back | side | middle | side

a. What do you need to know? ______

______

b. What operation can you use to find the number of seats in the back group of seats? Write the expression. ______

c. What operation can you use to find the number of seats in both groups of side seats? Write the expression.

______

d. What operation can you use to find the number of seats in the middle group? Write the expression.

______

e. Write an expression to represent the total number of seats in the theater.

______

______

f. How many seats are in the theater? Show the steps you use to solve the problem.

______

______

14. THINK SMARTER Write and evaluate two equivalent numerical expressions that show the Distributive Property of Multiplication.

______

______

15. THINK SMARTER Rosalie evaluates the numerical expression $4 + 5 \times 2 - 1$.

Rosalie's first step should be to [add / subtract / multiply].

Name ____________________

Evaluate Numerical Expressions

Common Core **COMMON CORE STANDARD—5.OA.A.1**
Write and interpret numerical expressions.

Evaluate the numerical expression.

1. $24 \times 5 - 41$
   $120 - 41$
   79
2. $(32 - 20) \div 4$
   ____
3. $16 \div (2 + 6)$
   ____
4. $27 + 5 \times 6$
   ____

Rewrite the expression with parentheses to equal the given value.

5. $3 \times 4 - 1 + 2$
   value: 11
   ____
6. $2 \times 6 \div 2 + 1$
   value: 4
   ____
7. $5 + 3 \times 2 - 6$
   value: 10
   ____

Problem Solving Real World

8. Sandy has several pitchers to hold lemonade for the school bake sale. Two pitchers can hold 64 ounces each, and four pitchers can hold 48 ounces each. How many total ounces can Sandy's pitchers hold?

   ____

9. At the bake sale, Jonah sold 4 cakes for $8 each and 36 muffins for $2 each. What was the total amount, in dollars, that Jonah received from these sales?

   ____

10. **WRITE** *Math* Give two examples that show how using parentheses can change the order in which operations are performed in an expression.

   ____

   ____

Lesson Check (5.OA.A.1)

1. What is the value of the expression $4 \times (4 - 2) + 6$?

2. Lannie ordered 12 copies of the same book for his book club members. The books cost $19 each, and the order has a $15 shipping charge. What is the total cost of Lannie's order?

Spiral Review (5.NBT.A.1, 5.NBT.A.2, 5.NBT.B.5, 5.NBT.B.6)

3. A small company packs 12 jars of jelly into each of 110 boxes to bring to the farmers' market. How many jars of jelly does the company pack in all?

4. June has 42 sports books, 85 mystery books, and 69 nature books. She arranges her books equally on 7 shelves. How many books are on each shelf?

5. Last year, a widget factory produced one million, twelve thousand, sixty widgets. What is this number written in standard form?

6. A company has 3 divisions. Last year, each division earned a profit of $\$5 \times 10^5$. What was the total profit the company earned last year?

FOR MORE PRACTICE GO TO THE **Personal Math Trainer**

Name ______________________________

Grouping Symbols

Essential Question In what order must operations be evaluated to find a solution when there are parentheses within parentheses?

Operations and Algebraic Thinking—5.OA.A.1

MATHEMATICAL PRACTICES
MP2, MP4

Unlock the Problem Real World

Mary's weekly allowance is $8 and David's weekly allowance is $5. Every week they each spend $2 on lunch. Write a numerical expression to show how many weeks it will take them together to save enough money to buy a video game for $45.

- Underline Mary's weekly allowance and how much she spends.
- Circle David's weekly allowance and how much he spends.

Use parentheses and brackets to write an expression.

You can use parentheses and brackets to group operations that go together. Operations in parentheses and brackets are performed first.

STEP 1 Write an expression to represent how much Mary and David save each week.

- How much money does Mary save each week?

Think: Each week Mary gets $8 and spends $2.

(____________)

- How much money does David save each week?

Think: Each week David gets $5 and spends $2.

(____________)

- How much money do Mary and David save together each week? ______________________________

STEP 2 Write an expression to represent how many weeks it will take Mary and David to save enough money for the video game.

- How many weeks will it take Mary and David to save enough for a video game?

Think: I can use brackets to group operations a second time. $45 is divided by the total amount of money saved each week.

__________ ÷ [______________________________]

Math Talk MATHEMATICAL PRACTICES 4

Modeling Explain why brackets are placed around the part of the expression that represents the amount of money Mary and David save each week.

Evaluate Expressions with Grouping Symbols When evaluating an expression with different grouping symbols (parentheses, brackets, and braces), perform the operation in the innermost set of grouping symbols first, evaluating the expression from the inside out.

Juan gets $6 for his weekly allowance and spends $4 of it. His sister Tina gets $7 for her weekly allowance and spends $3 of it. Their mother's birthday is in 4 weeks. If they spend the same amount each week, how much money can they save together in that time to buy her a present?

- Write the expression using parentheses and brackets. 4 × [($6 – $4) + ($7 – $3)]
- Perform the operations in the parentheses first. 4 × [______ + ______]
- Next perform the operations in the brackets. 4 × ______
- Then multiply. ______

So, Juan and Tina will be able to save ___________ for their mother's birthday present.

- MATHEMATICAL PRACTICE 2 **Connect Symbols and Words** What if only Tina saves any money? Will this change the numerical expression? Explain.

____

Try This! **Follow the order of operations.**

A 4 × {[(5 – 2) × 3] + [(2 + 4) × 2]}

- Perform the operations in the parentheses. 4 × {[3 × 3] + [______ × ______]}
- Perform the operations in the brackets. 4 × {9 + ______}
- Perform the operations in the braces. 4 × ______
- Multiply. ______

B 32 ÷ {[(3 × 2) + 7] – [(6 – 4) + 7]}

- Perform the operations in the parentheses. 32 ÷ {[______ + ______] – [______ + ______]}
- Perform the operations in the brackets. 32 ÷ {______ – ______}
- Perform the operations in the braces. 32 ÷ ______
- Divide. ______

Name ___________________________

Evaluate the numerical expression.

1. 12 + [(15 − 5) + (9 − 3)]

   12 + [10 + ______]

   12 + ______

   ______

2. 5 × [(26 − 4) − (4 + 6)]

   ______

3. 36 ÷ [(18 − 10) − (8 − 6)]

   ______

On Your Own

Evaluate the numerical expression.

4. 4 + [(16 − 4) + (12 − 9)]

   ______

5. 24 − [(10 − 7) + (16 − 9)]

   ______

6. 3 × {[(12 − 8) × 2] + [(11 − 9) × 3]}

   ______

Problem Solving • Applications

7. MATHEMATICAL PRACTICE 4 **Use Symbols** Write the expression 2 × 8 + 20 − 12 ÷ 6 with parentheses and brackets two different ways so one value is less than 10 and the other value is greater than 50.

   ______

8. GO DEEPER Wilma works at a bird sanctuary and stores birdseed in plastic containers. She has 3 small containers that hold 8 pounds of birdseed each and 6 large containers that hold 12 pounds of birdseed each. Each container was full until she used 4 pounds of bird seed. She wants to put some of the remaining birdseed into 30 bird feeders that can hold 2 pounds each. How much birdseed does she have left over? Show the expression you used to find your answer.

   ______

Unlock the Problem Real World

9. THINK SMARTER Dan has a flower shop. Each day he displays 24 roses. He gives away 10 and sells the rest. Each day he displays 36 carnations. He gives away 12 and sells the rest. What expression can you use to find out how many roses and carnations Dan sells in a week?

a. What information are you given? ____________

____

____

b. What are you being asked to do? ____________

____

____

c. What expression shows how many roses Dan sells in one day? ____________

d. What expression shows how many carnations Dan sells in one day? ____________

e. Write an expression to represent the total number of roses and carnations Dan sells in one day. ____________

f. Write the expression that shows how many roses and carnations Dan sells in a week. ____________

Personal Math Trainer

10. THINK SMARTER + A gift shop had 500 coloring pencils. The shop sold 3 sets of 20 coloring pencils, 6 sets of 12 coloring pencils, and 10 sets of 18 coloring pencils. Write a numerical expression to show how many coloring pencils are left. Evaluate the numerical expression using order of operations. Show your work.

____

____

Name ______________________________

Grouping Symbols

COMMON CORE STANDARD—5.OA.A.1
Write and interpret numerical expressions.

Evaluate the numerical expression.

1. $5 \times [(11 - 3) - (13 - 9)]$

$5 \times [8 - (13 - 9)]$

$5 \times [8 - 4]$

5×4

20

2. $30 - [(9 \times 2) - (3 \times 4)]$

____

3. $[(25 - 11) + (15 - 9)] \div 5$

____

4. $8 \times \{[(7 + 4) \times 2] - [(11 - 7) \times 4]\}$

____

5. $\{[(8 - 3) \times 2] + [(5 \times 6) - 5]\} \div 5$

____

Problem Solving Real World

Use the information at the right for 6 and 7.

Joan has a cafe. Each day, she bakes 24 muffins. She gives away 3 and sells the rest. Each day, she also bakes 36 bagels. She gives away 4 and sells the rest.

6. Write an expression to represent the total number of muffins and bagels Joan sells in 5 days.

____

7. Evaluate the expression to find the total number of muffins and bagels Joan sells in 5 days.

____

8. WRITE *Math* Explain how to use grouping symbols to organize information appropriately.

____

____

Lesson Check (5.OA.A.1)

1. What is the value of the expression?

$30 + [(6 \div 3) + (3 + 4)]$

2. Find the value of the following expression.

$[(17 - 9) \times (3 \times 2)] \div 2$

Spiral Review (5.OA.A.2, 5.NBT.A.1, 5.NBT.B.5)

3. What is $\frac{1}{10}$ of 200?

4. The Park family is staying at a hotel near an amusement park for 3 nights. The hotel costs $129 per night. How much will their 3-night stay in the hotel cost?

5. Vidal bought 2 pizzas and cut each into 8 slices. He and his friends ate 10 slices. Write an expression to match the words.

6. What is the value of the underlined digit in 783,5<u>4</u>9,201?

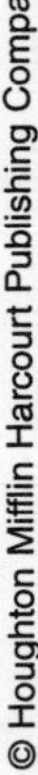

FOR MORE PRACTICE GO TO THE **Personal Math Trainer**

Name ___________________________

Chapter 1 Review/Test

Personal Math Trainer
Online Assessment and Intervention

1. Find the property that each equation shows.
Write the equation in the correct box.

$15 \times (7 \times 9) = (15 \times 7) \times 9$	$23 + 4 + 109 = 4 + 23 + 109$
$13 + (3 + 7) = (13 + 3) + 7$	$87 \times 3 = 3 \times 87$
$1 \times 9 = 9$	$0 + 16 = 16$

Identity Property of Addition	Commutative Property of Multiplication	Identity Property of Multiplication
Associative Property of Multiplication	Commutative Property of Addition	Associative Property of Addition

2. For 2a–2d, select True or False for each statement.

2a. 170 is $\frac{1}{10}$ of 17 ○ True ○ False

2b. 660 is 10 times as much as 600 ○ True ○ False

2c. 900 is $\frac{1}{10}$ of 9,000 ○ True ○ False

2d. 4,400 is 10 times as much as 440 ○ True ○ False

GO DIGITAL Assessment Options Chapter Test

3. Select other ways to write 700,562. Mark all that apply.

Ⓐ $(7 \times 100{,}000) + (5 \times 1{,}000) + (6 \times 10) + (2 \times 1)$

Ⓑ seven hundred thousand, five hundred sixty-two

Ⓒ $700{,}000 + 500 + 60 + 2$

Ⓓ 7 hundred thousands + 5 hundreds + 62 tens

4. Carrie has 140 coins. She has 10 times as many coins as she had last month. How many coins did Carrie have last month?

__________ coins

5. Valerie earns $24 per hour. Which expression can be used to show how much money she earns in 7 hours?

Ⓐ $(7 + 20) + (7 + 4)$

Ⓑ $(7 \times 20) + (7 \times 4)$

Ⓒ $(7 + 20) \times (7 + 4)$

Ⓓ $(7 \times 20) \times (7 \times 4)$

6. The table shows the equations Ms. Valez discussed in math class today.

Equations
$6 \times 10^0 = 6$
$6 \times 10^1 = 60$
$6 \times 10^2 = 600$
$6 \times 10^3 = 6{,}000$

Explain the pattern of zeros in the product when multiplying by powers of 10.

Name ______________________________

7. It is 3,452 miles round trip to Craig's aunt's house. If he travels to her house 3 times this year, how many miles did he travel in all?

____________ miles

8. Lindsey earns $33 per day at her part-time job. Complete the table to show the total amount Lindsey earns.

Lindsey's Earnings	
Number of Days	**Total Amount**
3	
8	
14	

Personal Math Trainer

9. THINK SMARTER+ Jackie followed these steps to evaluate the expression $15 - (37 + 8) \div 3$.

$37 + 8 = 45$

$45 - 15 = 30$

$30 \div 3 = 10$

Mark looks at Jackie's work and says she made a mistake. He says she should have divided by 3 before she subtracted.

Part A

Which student is correct? Explain how you know.

Part B

Evaluate the expression.

10. Carmine buys 8 plates for \$1 each. He also buys 4 bowls. Each bowl costs twice as much as each plate. The store is having a sale that gives Carmine \$3 off the bowls. Which numerical expression shows how much he spent?

Ⓐ $(8 \times 1) + [(4 \times 16) - 3]$

Ⓑ $(8 \times 1) + [4 \times (16 - 3)]$

Ⓒ $(8 \times 1) + [(4 \times 2) - 3]$

Ⓓ $(8 \times 4) + [(4 \times 2) - 3]$

11. Evaluate the numerical expression.

$2 + (65 + 7) \times 3 = \square$

12. An adult elephant eats about 300 pounds of food each day. Write an expression to represent the number of pounds of food a herd of 12 elephants eat in 5 days.

13. Jason is solving a homework problem.

Arianna buys 5 boxes of granola bars. Each box contains 12 granola bars. Arianna eats 4 bars.

Jason writes a numerical expression to represent the situation. His expression, $(12 - 4) \times 5$, has a mistake.

Part A

Explain Jason's mistake.

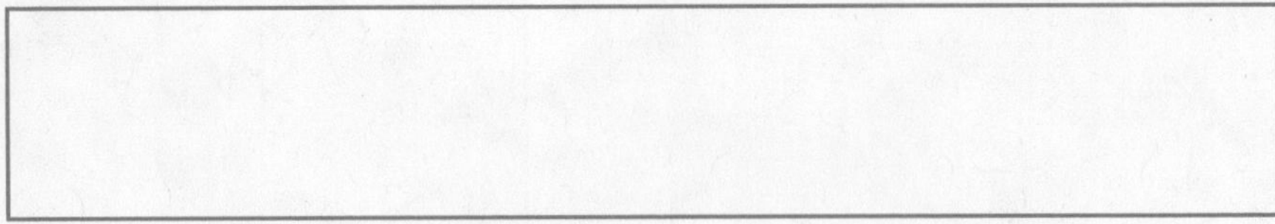

Part B

Write an expression to show how many granola bars are left, and then solve it.

Name ___________________________

14. Paula collected 75 stickers. She shares her stickers with 5 of her friends equally. How many stickers will each friend get?

Part A

Use the array to show your answer.

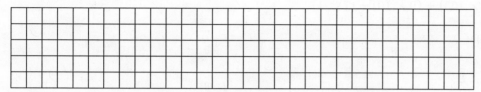

Part B

Use the multiplication sentence to complete the division sentence.

5 × ☐ = 75 75 ÷ 5 = ☐

15. GO DEEPER Mario is making dinner for 9 people. Mario buys 6 containers of soup. Each container is 18 ounces. If everyone gets the same amount of soup, how much soup will each person get? How can you solve a simpler problem to help you find the solution?

16. Jill wants to find the quotient. Use multiplication and the Distributive Property to help Jill find the quotient.

144 ÷ 8 = ☐

Multiplication ☐

Distributive Property ☐

17. If Jeannie eats 1,840 calories a day, how many calories will she have eaten after 182 days?

__________ calories

18. There are 8 teachers going to the science museum. If each teacher pays $15 to get inside, how much did the teachers pay?

$ ____________

19. Select other ways to write 50,897. Mark all that apply.

Ⓐ $(5 \times 10{,}000) + (8 \times 100) + (9 \times 10) + (7 \times 1)$

Ⓑ $50{,}000 + 800 + 90 + 7$

Ⓒ $5{,}000 + 800 + 90 + 7$

Ⓓ fifty thousand, eight hundred ninety-seven

20. For numbers 20a–20b, select True or False.

20a.	$55 - (12 + 2)$, value: 41	○ True	○ False
20b.	$25 + (14 - 4) \div 5$, value: 27	○ True	○ False

21. Tara bought 2 bottles of juice a day for 15 days. On the 16th day, Tara bought 7 bottles of juice.

Write an expression that matches the words.

22. Select other ways to express 10^2. Mark all that apply.

Ⓐ 20

Ⓑ 100

Ⓒ $10 + 2$

Ⓓ 10×2

Ⓔ $10 + 10$

Ⓕ 10×10

Chapter 2

Divide Whole Numbers

Show What You Know

Personal Math Trainer
Online Assessment and Intervention

Check your understanding of important skills.

Name ______________________________

▶ Meaning of Division **Use counters to solve.** (3.OA.A.2)

1. Divide 18 counters into 3 equal groups. How many counters are in each group?

   ______ counters

2. Divide 21 counters into 7 equal groups. How many counters are in each group?

   ______ counters

▶ Multiply 3-Digit and 4-Digit Numbers **Multiply.** (4.NBT.B.5)

3. $\begin{array}{r} 321 \\ \times \quad 4 \\ \hline \end{array}$

4. $\begin{array}{r} 518 \\ \times \quad 7 \\ \hline \end{array}$

5. $\begin{array}{r} 4{,}092 \\ \times \quad 6 \\ \hline \end{array}$

6. $\begin{array}{r} 8{,}264 \\ \times \quad 9 \\ \hline \end{array}$

▶ Estimate with 1-Digit Divisors **Estimate the quotient.** (4.NBT.B.6)

7. $2\overline{)312}$

8. $4\overline{)189}$

9. $6\overline{)603}$

10. $3\overline{)1{,}788}$

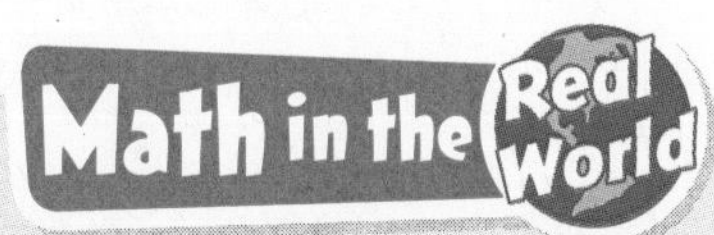

The height of the Gateway Arch shown on the Missouri quarter is 630 feet, or 7,560 inches. Find how many 4-inch stacks of quarters make up the height of the Gateway Arch. If there are 58 quarters in a 4-inch stack, how many quarters high is the arch?

Vocabulary Builder

▶ Visualize It

Complete the Flow Map using the words with a ✓.

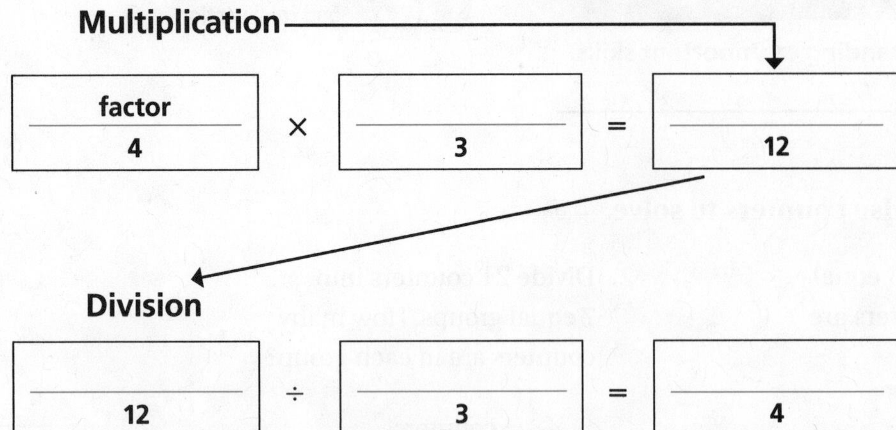

Review Words
compatible numbers
✓ dividend
✓ divisor
estimate
✓ factor
partial quotients
✓ product
✓ quotient
remainder

▶ Understand Vocabulary

Use the review words to complete each section.

1. You can ______________________ to find a number that is close to the exact amount.

2. Numbers that are easy to compute with mentally are called ______________________.

3. The ______________________ is the amount left over when a number cannot be divided evenly.

4. A method of dividing in which multiples of the divisor are subtracted from the dividend and then the quotients are added together is called ______________________.

5. The number that is to be divided in a division problem is the ______________________.

6. The ______________________ is the number, not including the remainder, that results from dividing.

GO DIGITAL
• Interactive Student Edition
• Multimedia *e*Glossary

Chapter 2 Vocabulary

compatible numbers

números compatibles

7

dividend

dividendo

18

divisor

divisor

19

factor

factor

27

partial quotient

cociente parcial

47

product

producto

54

quotient

cociente

57

remainder

residuo

59

The number that is to be divided in a division problem

Example: 36 ÷ 6 or 6)36

dividend

Numbers that are easy to compute with mentally

A number multiplied by another number to find a product

Example: 46 × 3 = 138

factors

The number that divides the dividend

Example: 15 ÷ 3 or 3)15

divisor

The answer to a multiplication problem

Example: 3 × 15 = 45

product

A method of dividing in which multiples of the divisor are subtracted from the dividend and then the quotients are added together

Example:

```
  5)125          ← partial quotients
   −50   10 × 5     10
    75
   −50   10 × 5     10
    25
   −25    5 × 5    + 5
     0              25
```


The amount left over when a number cannot be divided equally

Example:

```
   102 r2 ← remainder
  6)614
   −6
    01
   −0
    14
   −12
     2 ← remainder
```


The number that results from dividing

Example: 8 ÷ 4 = 2

quotient

Matchup

Word Box
- compatible numbers
- dividend
- divisor
- factor
- partial quotient
- product
- quotient
- remainder

For 2–3 players

Materials

- 1 set of word cards

How to Play

1. Put the cards face-down in rows. Take turns to play.
2. Choose two cards and turn them over.
   - If the cards show a word and its meaning, it's a match. Keep the pair and take another turn.
   - If the cards do not match, turn them over again.
3. The game is over when all cards have been matched. The players count their pairs. The player with the most pairs wins.

The Write Way

Reflect

Choose one idea. Write about it.

- Describe a situation in which you might use compatible numbers to estimate.
- Write a paragraph that uses at least **three** of these words.
  dividend divisor quotient remainder
- Megan has $340 to spend on party favors for 16 guests. Tell how Megan can use partial quotients to figure out how much she can spend on each guest.
- A hiker wants to travel the same number of miles each day to complete a 128-mile trail. Explain and illustrate two different options for completing the trail. Draw your picture on another sheet of paper.

Name ______________________________

Place the First Digit

Essential Question How can you tell where to place the first digit of a quotient without dividing?

Number and Operations in Base Ten—5.NBT.B.6

MATHEMATICAL PRACTICES
MP1, MP4, MP6

Unlock the Problem

Real World

Tania has 8 purple daisies. In all, she counts 128 petals on her flowers. If each flower has the same number of petals, how many petals are on one flower?

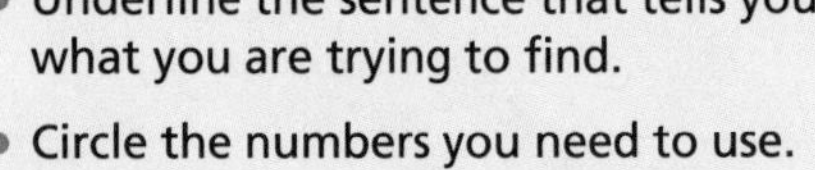

- Underline the sentence that tells you what you are trying to find.
- Circle the numbers you need to use.
- How will you use these numbers to solve the problem?

____

Divide. 128 ÷ 8

STEP 1 Use an estimate to place the first digit in the quotient.

Estimate. 160 ÷ _____ = _____

The first digit of the quotient will be in the ____________ place.

STEP 2 Divide the tens.

Divide. 12 tens ÷ 8
Multiply. 8 × 1 ten

Subtract. 12 tens − _______ tens

Check. _______ tens cannot be shared among 8 groups without regrouping.

STEP 3 Regroup any tens left as ones. Then, divide the ones.

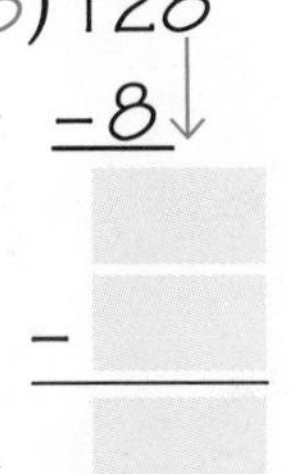

Divide. 48 ones ÷ 8
Multiply. 8 × 6 ones

Subtract. 48 ones − _______ ones

Check. _______ ones cannot be shared among 8 groups.

Since 16 is close to the estimate of _______, the answer is reasonable.

So, there are 16 petals on one flower.

Math Talk MATHEMATICAL PRACTICES 6

Explain how estimating the quotient helps you at both the beginning and the end of a division problem.

Example

Divide. Use place value to place the first digit. 4,236 ÷ 5

Remember

Remember to estimate the quotient first.

Estimate: 4,000 ÷ 5 = ______

STEP 1 Use place value to place the first digit.

5)4,236

Look at the thousands.

4 thousands cannot be shared among 5 groups without regrouping.

Look at the hundreds.

______ hundreds can be shared among 5 groups.

The first digit is in the ______ place.

STEP 2 Divide the hundreds.

```
   8
5)4,236
–
```

Divide. ______ hundreds ÷ ______

Multiply. ______ × ______ hundreds

Subtract. ______ hundreds – ______ hundreds

Check. ______ hundreds cannot be shared among 5 groups without regrouping.

STEP 3 Divide the tens.

```
   84
5)4,236
 −40↓
   23
  −20
    3
```

Divide. ______

Multiply. ______

Subtract. ______

Check. ______

______

STEP 4 Divide the ones.

```
   847
5)4,236
 −40
   23
  −20↓
    36
   −35
     1
```

Divide. ______

Multiply. ______

Subtract. ______

Check. ______

______

So, 4,236 ÷ 5 is ______ r______.

MATHEMATICAL PRACTICES 6

Explain how you know if your answer is reasonable.

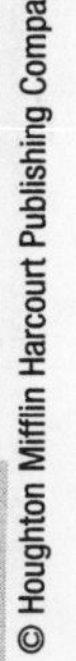

Name ______________________________

Share and Show MATH BOARD

Divide.

1. $4\overline{)457}$

✓ 2. $5\overline{)1{,}035}$

✓ 3. $8\overline{)1{,}766}$

MATHEMATICAL PRACTICES 6

Use Math Vocabulary As you divide, explain how you know when to place a zero in the quotient.

On Your Own

Divide.

4. $8\overline{)275}$

5. $3\overline{)468}$

6. $4\overline{)3{,}220}$

7. $6\overline{)618}$

8. GO DEEPER Ryan earned $376 by working for 4 days. If he earned the same amount each day, how much could he earn working 5 days?

____

Practice: Copy and Solve **Divide.**

9. $645 \div 8$

10. $942 \div 6$

11. $723 \div 7$

12. $3{,}478 \div 9$

13. $3{,}214 \div 5$

14. $492 \div 4$

15. $2{,}403 \div 9$

16. $2{,}205 \div 6$

17. GO DEEPER Will the first digit of the quotient of $2{,}589 \div 4$ be in the hundreds or the thousands place? **Explain** how you can decide without finding the quotient.

____

____

____

____

Unlock the Problem

18. MATHEMATICAL PRACTICE 4 **Interpret a Result** Rosa has a garden divided into sections. She has 125 daisy plants. If she plants an equal number of the daisy plants in each of 3 sections, how many daisy plants will be in each section? How many daisy plants will be left over?

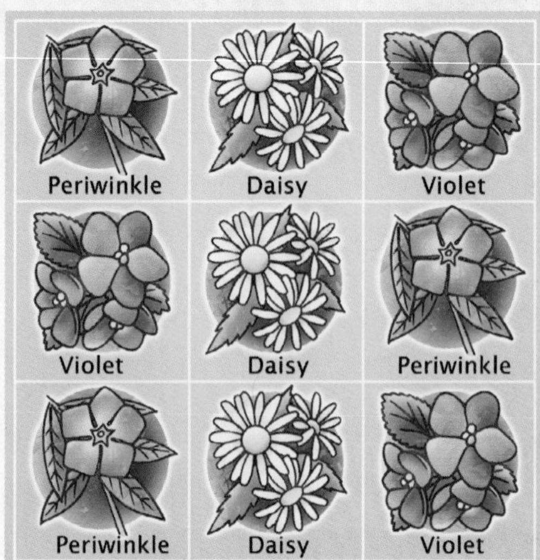

a. What information will you use to solve the problem?

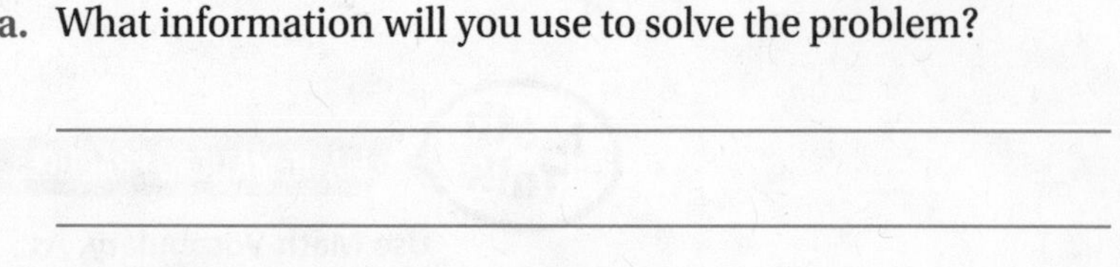

____

____

b. How will you use division to find the number of daisy plants left over?

____

____

____

c. Show the steps you use to solve the problem.
Estimate: 120 ÷ 3 = ______

d. Complete the sentences:

Rosa has ______ daisy plants. She puts an equal number in each of ______ sections.

Each section has ______ plants. Rosa has ______ daisy plants left over.

19. THINK SMARTER One case can hold 3 boxes. Each box can hold 3 binders. How many cases are needed to hold 126 binders?

____

20. THINK SMARTER For 20a–20b, choose Yes or No to indicate whether the first digit of the quotient is in the hundreds place.

20a. 1,523 ÷ 23 ○ Yes ○ No

20b. 2,315 ÷ 9 ○ Yes ○ No

Name ______________________

Place the First Digit

Common Core **COMMON CORE STANDARD—5.NBT.B.6**
Perform operations with multi-digit whole numbers and with decimals to hundredths.

Divide.

1. $4\overline{)388}$

$$\begin{array}{r} 97 \\ 4\overline{)388} \\ -36 \\ \hline 28 \\ -28 \\ \hline 0 \end{array}$$

97

2. $3\overline{)579}$

3. $8\overline{)712}$

4. $9\overline{)204}$

5. $2{,}117 \div 3$

6. $520 \div 8$

7. $1{,}812 \div 4$

8. $3{,}476 \div 6$

Problem Solving

9. The school theater department made \$2,142 on ticket sales for the three nights of their play. The department sold the same number of tickets each night and each ticket cost \$7. How many tickets did the theater department sell each night?

10. Andreus made \$625 mowing yards. He worked for 5 consecutive days and earned the same amount of money each day. How much money did Andreus earn per day?

11. WRITE *Math* Write a word problem that must be solved by using division. Include the equation and the solution, and explain how to place the first digit in the quotient.

Lesson Check (5.NBT.B.6)

1. Kenny is packing cans into bags at the food bank. He can pack 8 cans into each bag. How many bags will Kenny need for 1,056 cans?

2. Liz polishes rings for a jeweler. She can polish 9 rings per hour. How many hours will it take her to polish 315 rings?

Spiral Review (5.NBT.A.2, 5.NBT.B.5, 5.NBT.B.6)

3. Fiona uses 256 fluid ounces of juice to make 1 bowl of punch. How many fluid ounces of juice will she use to make 3 bowls of punch?

4. Len wants to write the number 100,000 using a base of 10 and an exponent. What number should he use as the exponent?

5. A family pass to the amusement park costs $54. Using the Distributive Property, write an expression that can be used to find the cost in dollars of 8 family passes.

6. Gary is catering a picnic. There will be 118 guests at the picnic, and he wants each guest to have a 12-ounce serving of salad. How much salad should he make?

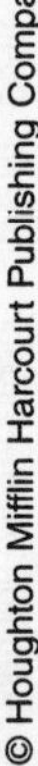

FOR MORE PRACTICE GO TO THE Personal Math Trainer

Name ______________________

Divide by 1-Digit Divisors

Essential Question How do you solve and check division problems?

Number and Operations in Base Ten—5.NBT.B.6

MATHEMATICAL PRACTICES
MP1, MP2, MP8

Unlock the Problem

Jenna's family is planning a trip to Oceanside, California. They will begin their trip in Scranton, Pennsylvania, and will travel 2,754 miles over 9 days. If the family travels an equal number of miles every day, how far will they travel each day?

- Underline the sentence that tells you what you are trying to find.
- Circle the numbers you need to use.

Divide. 2,754 ÷ 9

STEP 1

Use an estimate to place the first digit in the quotient.

Estimate. 2,700 ÷ 9 = ____________

The first digit of the quotient is in

the ____________ place.

STEP 2

Divide the hundreds.

STEP 3

Divide the tens.

STEP 4

Divide the ones.

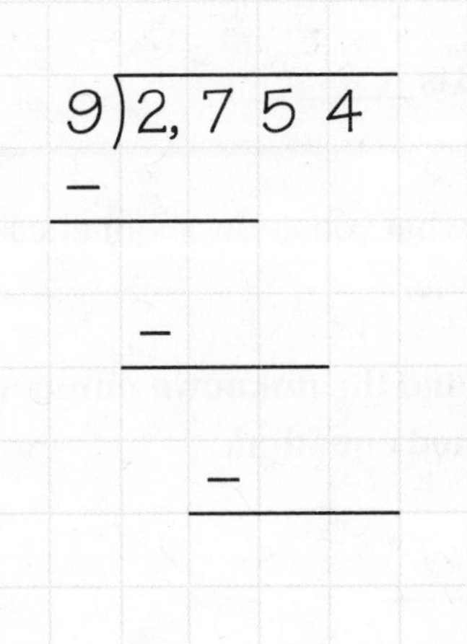

Since ____________ is close to the estimate of ____________, the answer is reasonable.

So, Jenna's family will travel ____________ miles each day.

Math Talk MATHEMATICAL PRACTICES 2

Reasoning Explain how you know the quotient is 306 and not 36.

CONNECT Division and multiplication are inverse operations. Inverse operations are opposite operations that undo each other. You can use multiplication to check your answer to a division problem.

Example Divide. Check your answer.

To check your answer to a division problem, multiply the quotient by the divisor. If there is a remainder, add it to the product. The result should equal the dividend.

```
   102 r2          102   ← quotient
6)614            ×   6   ← divisor
 −6               ____
  01
 −0              +   2   ← remainder
  14              ____   ← dividend
 −12
   2
```

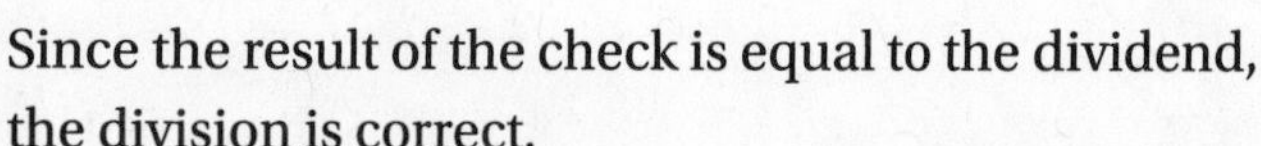

Since the result of the check is equal to the dividend, the division is correct.

So, 614 ÷ 6 is ________.

You can use what you know about checking division to find an unknown value.

Try This! **Find the unknown number by finding the value of *n* in the related equation.**

A

$7\overline{)}$ with quotient 63

$n = 7 \times 63$

dividend divisor quotient

Multiply the divisor and the quotient.

$n =$ ________

B

$6\overline{)752}$ with quotient 125 r ___

$752 = 6 \times 125 + n$

dividend divisor quotient remainder

Multiply the divisor and the quotient.

$752 = 750 + n$

Think: What number added to 750 equals 752?

$n =$ ________

Name ____________________

Share and Show MATH BOARD

Divide. Check your answer.

1. $8\overline{)624}$ Check.

2. $4\overline{)3,220}$ Check.

3. $4\overline{)1,027}$ Check.

MATHEMATICAL PRACTICES 8

Generalize Explain how multiplication can help you check a quotient.

On Your Own

Divide.

4. $6\overline{)938}$

5. $4\overline{)762}$

6. $3\overline{)5,654}$

7. $8\overline{)475}$

Practice: Copy and Solve Divide.

8. $4\overline{)671}$

9. $9\overline{)2,023}$

10. $3\overline{)4,685}$

11. $8\overline{)948}$

12. $1,326 \div 4$

13. $5,868 \div 6$

14. $566 \div 3$

15. $3,283 \div 9$

MATHEMATICAL PRACTICE 2 **Use Reasoning** **Algebra** **Find the value of n in each equation. Write what n represents in the related division problem.**

16. $n = 4 \times 58$

$n =$ ____________

17. $589 = 7 \times 84 + n$

$n =$ ____________

18. $n = 5 \times 67 + 3$

$n =$ ____________

Problem Solving • Applications

Use the table to solve 19–21.

Large Gold Nuggets Found		
Name	**Weight**	**Location**
Welcome Stranger	2,284 troy ounces	Australia
Welcome	2,217 troy ounces	Australia
Willard	788 troy ounces	California

19. If the Welcome gold nugget were turned into 3 equal-sized gold bricks, how many troy ounces would each brick weigh?

____

20. **Pose a Problem** Look back at Problem 19. Write a similar problem by changing the nugget and the number of bricks. Then solve the problem.

____

____

____

WRITE Math • Show Your Work

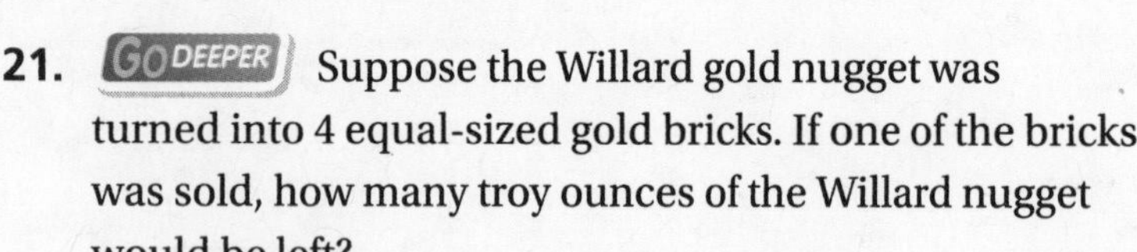

21. GO DEEPER Suppose the Willard gold nugget was turned into 4 equal-sized gold bricks. If one of the bricks was sold, how many troy ounces of the Willard nugget would be left?

____

22. THINK SMARTER There are 246 students going on a field trip to pan for gold. If they are going in vans that hold 9 students each, how many vans are needed? How many students will ride in the van that isn't full?

____

23. THINK SMARTER Lily's teacher wrote the division problem on the board. Using the vocabulary box, label the parts of the division problem. Then, using the vocabulary, explain how Lily can check whether her teacher's quotient is correct.

____

____

quotient | divisor | dividend

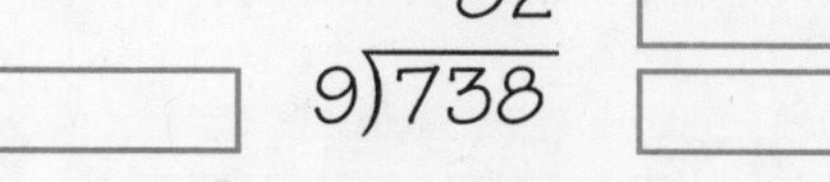

Name ______________________

Divide by 1-Digit Divisors

COMMON CORE STANDARD—5.NBT.B.6
Perform operations with multi-digit whole numbers and with decimals to hundredths.

Divide.

1. $4\overline{)724}$

2. $5\overline{)312}$

3. $278 \div 2$

4. $336 \div 7$

181
4)724
−4
32
−32
04
− 4
0

181

Find the value of *n* in each equation. Write what *n* represents in the related division problem.

5. $n = 3 \times 45$

6. $643 = 4 \times 160 + n$

7. $n = 6 \times 35 + 4$

Problem Solving Real World

8. Randy has 128 ounces of dog food. He feeds his dog 8 ounces of food each day. How many days will the dog food last?

9. Angelina bought a 64-ounce can of lemonade mix. She uses 4 ounces of mix for each pitcher of lemonade. How many pitchers of lemonade can Angelina make from the can of mix?

10. WRITE ▸ *Math* Use a map to plan a trip in the United States. Find the number of miles between your current location and your destination, and divide the mileage by the number of days or hours that you wish to travel.

Lesson Check (5.NBT.B.6)

1. A color printer will print 8 pages per minute. How many minutes will it take to print a report that has 136 pages?

2. A postcard collector has 1,230 postcards. If she displays them on pages that hold 6 cards each, how many pages does she need?

Spiral Review (5.NBT.A.1, 5.NBT.B.5, 5.NBT.B.6)

3. Francis is buying a stereo system for $196. She wants to pay for it in four equal monthly installments. What is the amount she will pay each month?

4. A bakery bakes 184 loaves of bread in 4 hours. How many loaves does the bakery bake in 1 hour?

5. Marvin collects trading cards. He stores them in boxes that hold 235 cards each. If Marvin has 4 boxes full of cards, how many cards does he have in his collection?

6. What is the value of the digit 7 in 870,541?

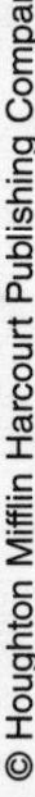

FOR MORE PRACTICE GO TO THE **Personal Math Trainer**

Name ______________________________

Division with 2-Digit Divisors

Essential Question How can you use base-ten blocks to model and understand division of whole numbers?

Common Core **Number and Operations in Base Ten—5.NBT.B.6**

MATHEMATICAL PRACTICES
MP1, MP3, MP4, MP6

Investigate

Materials ■ base-ten blocks

There are 156 students in the Carville Middle School chorus. The music director wants the students to stand with 12 students in each row for the next concert. How many rows will there be?

A. Use base-ten blocks to model the dividend, 156.

B. Place 2 tens below the hundred to form a rectangle. How many groups of 12 does the rectangle show? How much of the dividend is not shown in this rectangle?

____

C. Combine the remaining tens and ones into as many groups of 12 as possible. How many groups of 12 are there?

____

D. Place these groups of 12 on the right side of the rectangle to make a larger rectangle.

E. The final rectangle shows ______ groups of 12.

So, there will be ______ rows of 12 students.

Draw Conclusions

1. MATHEMATICAL PRACTICE 6 **Explain** why you still need to make groups of 12 after Step B.

____

____

2. MATHEMATICAL PRACTICE 6 Describe how you can use base-ten blocks to **model** the quotient $176 \div 16$.

____

____

____

Make Connections

The two sets of groups of 12 that you found in the Investigate are partial quotients. First you found 10 groups of 12 and then you found 3 more groups of 12. Sometimes you may need to regroup before you can show a partial quotient.

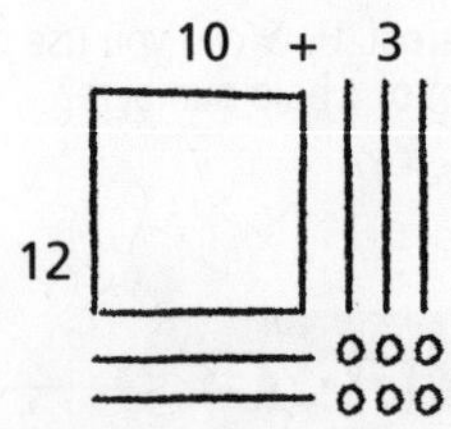

You can use a quick picture to record the partial products.

Divide. 180 ÷ 15

MODEL Use base-ten blocks.

STEP 1 Model the dividend, 180, as 1 hundred 8 tens.

Model the first partial quotient by making a rectangle with the hundred and 5 tens. In the Record section, cross out the hundred and tens you use.

The rectangle shows ________ groups of 15.

STEP 2 Additional groups of 15 cannot be made without regrouping.

Regroup 1 ten as 10 ones. In the Record section, cross out the regrouped ten.

There are now ________ tens and ________ ones.

STEP 3 Decide how many additional groups of 15 can be made with the remaining tens and ones. The number of groups is the second partial quotient.

Make your rectangle larger by including these groups of 15. In the Record section, cross out the tens and ones you use.

There are now ________ groups of 15.

RECORD Use quick pictures.

Draw the first partial quotient.

Draw the first and second partial quotients.

So, 180 ÷ 15 is ________.

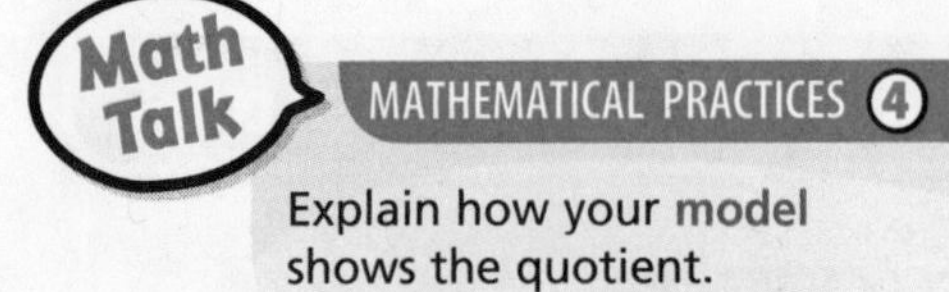

Explain how your model shows the quotient.

Share and Show

Use the quick picture to divide.

1. 143 ÷ 13

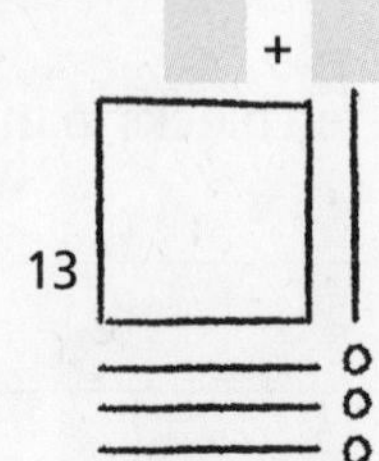

Name ___________________________

Divide. Use base-ten blocks.

2. 168 ÷ 12

3. 154 ÷ 14

4. 187 ÷ 11

Divide. Draw a quick picture.

5. 165 ÷ 11

6. 216 ÷ 18

7. 182 ÷ 13

8. 228 ÷ 12

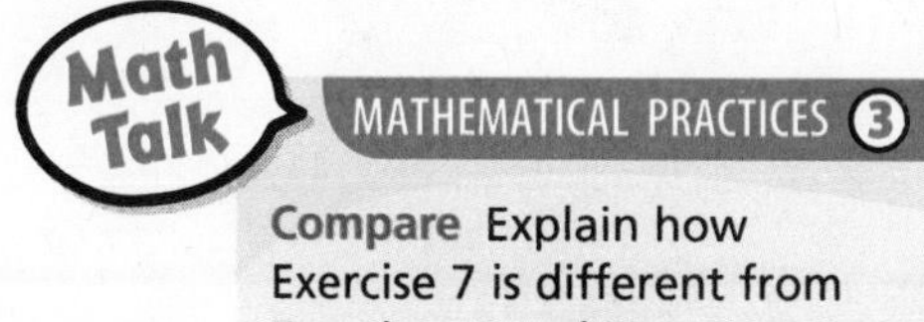

Math Talk
MATHEMATICAL PRACTICES 3
Compare Explain how Exercise 7 is different from Exercises 6 and 8.

9. GO DEEPER On Monday, the Mars rover traveled 330 cm. On Tuesday, it traveled 180 cm. If the rover stopped every 15 cm to recharge, how many more times did it need to recharge on Monday than on Tuesday?

____

Connect to Social Studies

Pony Express

The Pony Express used men riding horses to deliver mail between St. Joseph, Missouri, and Sacramento, California, from April, 1860 to October, 1861. The trail between the cities was approximately 2,000 miles long. The first trip from St. Joseph to Sacramento took 9 days 23 hours. The first trip from Sacramento to St. Joseph took 11 days 12 hours.

Solve.

10. THINK SMARTER Two Pony Express riders each rode part of a 176-mile trip. Each rider rode the same number of miles. They changed horses every 11 miles. How many horses did each rider use?

11. GO DEEPER Suppose a Pony Express rider was paid $192 for 12 weeks of work. If he was paid the same amount each week, how much was he paid for 3 weeks of work?

12. MATHEMATICAL PRACTICE 1 **Analyze** Suppose three riders rode a total of 240 miles. If they used a total of 16 horses, and rode each horse the same number of miles, how many miles did they ride before replacing each horse?

13. THINK SMARTER Suppose it took 19 riders a total of 11 days 21 hours to ride from St. Joseph to Sacramento. If they all rode the same number of hours, how many hours did each rider ride?

14. THINK SMARTER+ Scientists collect 144 rock samples. The samples will be divided among 12 teams of scientists for analysis. Draw a quick picture to show how the samples can be divided among the 12 teams.

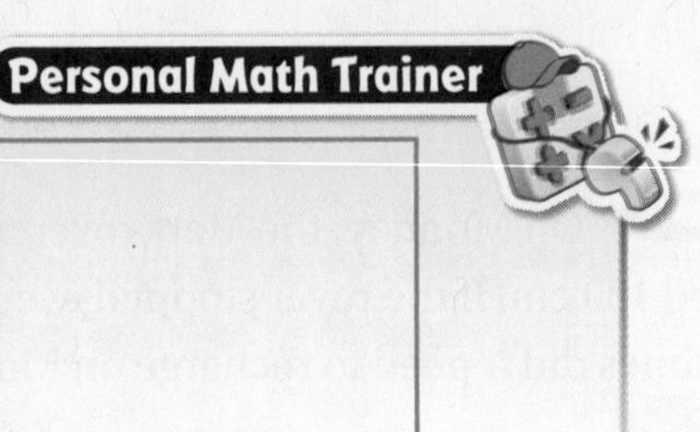

Name ______________________

Division with 2-Digit Divisors

COMMON CORE STANDARD—5.NBT.B.6
Perform operations with multi-digit whole numbers and with decimals to hundredths.

Use the quick picture to divide.

1. 132 ÷ 12 = 11

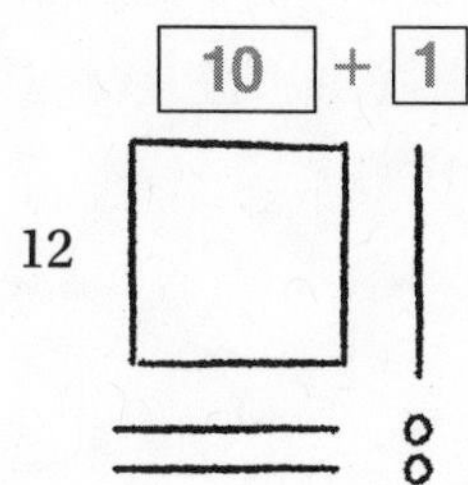

2. 168 ÷ 14 = ______

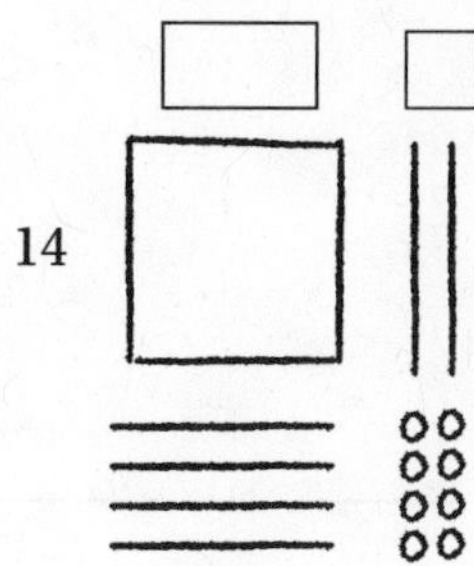

Divide. Draw a quick picture.

3. 192 ÷ 16 = ______

4. 169 ÷ 13 = ______

Problem Solving Real World

5. There are 182 seats in a theater. The seats are evenly divided into 13 rows. How many seats are in each row?

____

6. There are 156 students at summer camp. The camp has 13 cabins. An equal number of students sleep in each cabin. How many students sleep in each cabin?

____

7. WRITE Math Write a division problem that has a 3-digit dividend and a divisor between 10 and 20. Show how to solve it by drawing a quick picture.

____

____

Lesson Check (5.NBT.B.6)

1. There are 198 students in the soccer league. There are 11 players on each soccer team. How many soccer teams are there?

2. Jason earned $187 for 17 hours of work. How much did Jason earn per hour?

Spiral Review (5.OA.A.2, 5.NBT.A.1, 5.NBT.B.5, 5.NBT.B.6)

3. What is the number written in standard form: six million, seven hundred thousand, twenty?

4. What is the following sentence written as an expression? "Add the product of 3 and 6 to 4."

5. To transport 228 people to an island, the island ferry makes 6 different trips. On each trip, the ferry carries the same number of people. How many people does the ferry transport on each trip?

6. Isabella sells 36 tickets to the school talent show. Each ticket costs $14. How much money does Isabella collect for the tickets she sells?

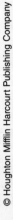

FOR MORE PRACTICE GO TO THE Personal Math Trainer

Name ________________________

Partial Quotients

Essential Question How can you use partial quotients to divide by 2-digit divisors?

Common Core **Number and Operations in Base Ten—5.NBT.B.6**
MATHEMATICAL PRACTICES
MP1, MP3, MP8

Unlock the Problem

People in the United States eat about 23 pounds of pizza per person every year. If you ate that much pizza each year, how many years would it take you to eat 775 pounds of pizza?

- Rewrite in one sentence the problem you are asked to solve.

____

____

Divide by using partial quotients.

775 ÷ 23

STEP 1

Subtract multiples of the divisor from the dividend until the remaining number is less than the multiple. The easiest partial quotients to use are multiples of 10.

STEP 2

Subtract smaller multiples of the divisor until the remaining number is less than the divisor. Then add the partial quotients to find the quotient.

COMPLETE THE DIVISION PROBLEM.

$$\begin{array}{r} 23\overline{)775} \\ - \\ \hline 545 \end{array}$$

10 × 23 | 10

775 ÷ 23 is ______ r ______.

So, it would take you more than 33 years to eat 775 pounds of pizza.

Remember

Depending on the question, a remainder may or may not be used in answering the question. Sometimes the quotient is adjusted based on the remainder.

Example

Myles is helping his father with the supply order for his pizza shop. For next week, the shop will need 1,450 ounces of mozzarella cheese. Each package of cheese weighs 32 ounces. Complete Myles's work to find how many packages of mozzarella cheese he needs to order.

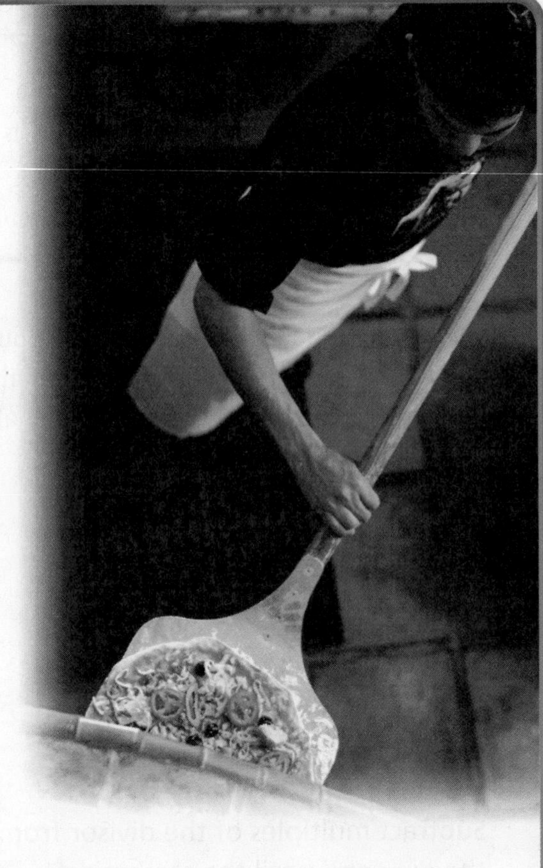

```
32)1,450
  − 320      ______ × 32  |  [  ]
   1,130
  − 320      ______ × 32  |  [  ]
     810
  − 320      ______ × 32  |  [  ]
     490
  − 320      ______ × 32  |  [  ]
     170
  − 160      ______ × 32  | + [  ]
      10
```

MATHEMATICAL PRACTICES 8

Generalize What does the remainder represent? Explain how a remainder will affect your answer.

1,450 ÷ 32 is ______ r ______.

So, he needs to order ______ packages of mozzarella cheese.

Try This! Use different partial quotients to solve the problem above.

32)1,450

Math Idea

Using different multiples of the divisor to find partial quotients provides many ways to solve a division problem. Some ways are quicker, but all result in the same answer.

Name ______________________________

Share and Show

Divide. Use partial quotients.

1. $18\overline{)648}$

2. $62\overline{)3,186}$

3. $858 \div 57$

Math Talk

MATHEMATICAL PRACTICES 8

Generalize Explain what the greatest possible whole-number remainder is if you divide any number by 23.

On Your Own

Divide. Use partial quotients.

4. $73\overline{)584}$

5. $51\overline{)1,831}$

6. $82\overline{)2,964}$

7. $892 \div 26$

8. $1,056 \div 48$

9. $2,950 \div 67$

Practice: Copy and Solve **Divide. Use partial quotients.**

10. $653 \div 42$

11. $946 \div 78$

12. $412 \div 18$

13. $871 \div 87$

14. $1,544 \div 34$

15. $2,548 \div 52$

16. $2,740 \div 83$

17. $4,135 \div 66$

18. GO DEEPER The 5th grade is having a picnic this Friday. There will be 182 students and 274 adults. Each table seats 12 people. How many tables are needed?

____

Problem Solving • Applications

Use the table to solve 19–22.

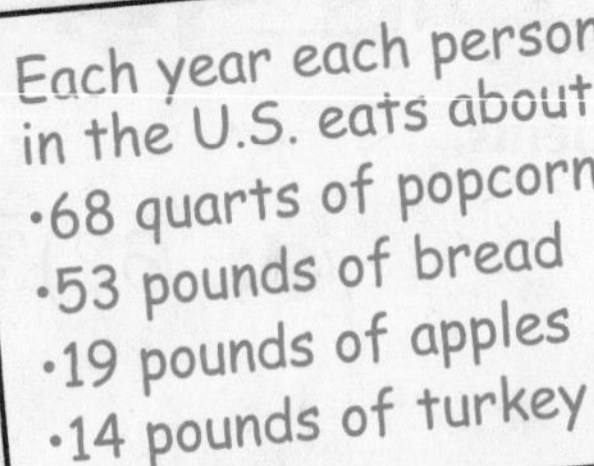

Each year each person
in the U.S. eats about...
•68 quarts of popcorn
•53 pounds of bread
•19 pounds of apples
•14 pounds of turkey

19. How many years would it take for a person in the United States to eat 855 pounds of apples?

20. How many years would it take for a person in the United States to eat 1,120 pounds of turkey?

21. GO DEEPER If 6 people in the United States each eat the average amount of popcorn for 5 years, how many quarts of popcorn will they eat?

22. MATHEMATICAL PRACTICE 1 **Make Sense of Problems** In the United States, a person eats more than 40,000 pounds of bread in a lifetime if he or she lives to be 80 years old. Does this statement make sense, or is it nonsense? Explain.

23. THINK SMARTER In a study, 9 people ate a total of 1,566 pounds of potatoes in 2 years. If each person ate the same amount each year, how many pounds of potatoes did each person eat in 1 year?

24. THINK SMARTER Nyree divided 495 by 24 using partial quotients. Find the quotient and remainder. Explain your answer using numbers and words.

$24\overline{)495}$

Name ______________________________

Partial Quotients

Common Core **COMMON CORE STANDARD—5.NBT.B.6**
Perform operations with multi-digit whole numbers and with decimals to hundredths.

Divide. Use partial quotients.

1. $18\overline{)236}$

$$\begin{array}{rll} 18\overline{)236} & & \\ -180 & \leftarrow 10 \times 18 & 10 \\ \hline 56 & & \\ -36 & \leftarrow 2 \times 18 & 2 \\ \hline 20 & & \\ -18 & \leftarrow 1 \times 18 & +1 \\ \hline 2 & & 13 \end{array}$$

236 ÷ 18 is 13 r2.

2. $36\overline{)540}$

3. $27\overline{)624}$

4. 514 ÷ 28

5. 322 ÷ 14

6. 715 ÷ 25

Problem Solving Real World

7. A factory processes 1,560 ounces of olive oil per hour. The oil is packaged into 24-ounce bottles. How many bottles does the factory fill in one hour?

____

8. A pond at a hotel holds 4,290 gallons of water. The groundskeeper drains the pond at a rate of 78 gallons of water per hour. How long will it take to drain the pond?

____

9. WRITE *Math* Explain how using partial quotients to divide is similar to using the Distributive Property to multiply.

____

____

____

Lesson Check (5.NBT.B.6)

1. Yvette has 336 eggs to put into cartons. She puts one dozen eggs into each carton. How many cartons does she fill?

2. Ned mows a 450 square-foot garden in 15 minutes. How many square feet of the garden does he mow in one minute?

Spiral Review (5.NBT.A.1, 5.NBT.B.5, 5.NBT.B.6)

3. Raul has 56 bouncy balls. He puts the balls into 4 green gift bags. If he puts the same number of balls into each bag, how many balls does he put into each green bag?

4. Marcia uses 5 ounces of chicken stock to make one batch of soup. She has a total of 400 ounces of chicken stock. How many batches of soup can Marcia make?

5. Michelle buys 13 bags of gravel for her fish aquarium. If each bag weighs 12 pounds, how many pounds of gravel did she buy?

6. What is the number 4,305,012 written in expanded notation?

FOR MORE PRACTICE GO TO THE Personal Math Trainer

Name ___________________________

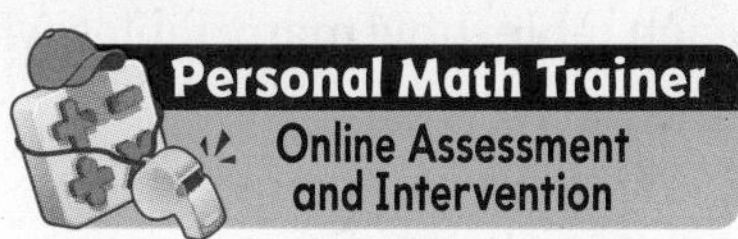

Concepts and Skills

1. Explain how estimating the quotient helps you place the first digit in the quotient of a division problem. (5.NBT.B.6)

____

____

2. Explain how to use multiplication to check the answer to a division problem. (5.NBT.B.6)

____

____

____

Divide. (5.NBT.B.6)

3. $633 \div 3$	4. $487 \div 8$	5. $1,641 \div 4$	6. $2,765 \div 9$

Divide. Use partial quotients. (5.NBT.B.6)

7. $156 \div 13$	8. $318 \div 53$	9. $1,562 \div 34$	10. $4,024 \div 68$

11. Emma is planning a party for 128 guests. If 8 guests can be seated at each table, how many tables will be needed for seating at the party? (5.NBT.B.6)

12. Tickets for the basketball game cost $14 each. If the sale of the tickets brought in $2,212, how many tickets were sold? (5.NBT.B.6)

13. Margo used 864 beads to make necklaces for the art club. She made 24 necklaces with the beads. If each necklace has the same number of beads, how many beads did Margo use for each necklace? (5.NBT.B.6)

14. Angie needs to buy 156 candles for a party. Each package has 8 candles. How many packages should Angie buy? (5.NBT.B.6)

15. GO DEEPER Max delivers 8,520 pieces of mail in one year. If he delivers the same number of pieces of mail each month, about how many pieces of mail does he deliver in 2 months? Explain your steps. (5.NBT.B.6)

Name ______________________

Estimate with 2-Digit Divisors

Essential Question How can you use compatible numbers to estimate quotients?

Common Core **Number and Operations in Base Ten—5.NBT.B.6**
MATHEMATICAL PRACTICES
MP1, MP2, MP3

CONNECT You can estimate quotients using compatible numbers that are found by using basic facts and patterns.

$35 \div 5 = 7$ ← basic fact
$350 \div 50 = 7$
$3{,}500 \div 50 = 70$
$35{,}000 \div 50 = 700$

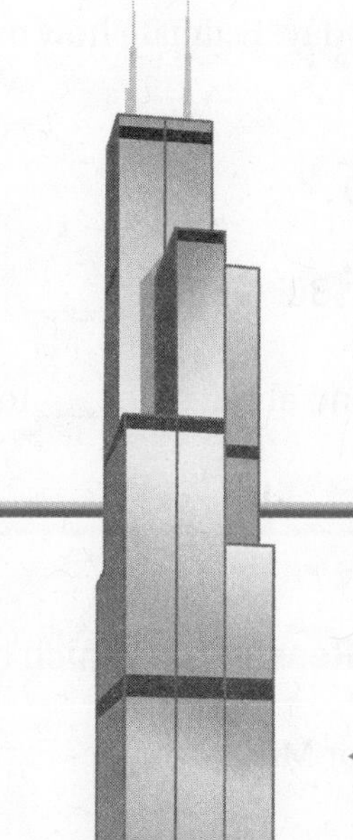

◀ Willis Tower, formerly known as the Sears Tower, is the tallest building in the United States.

Unlock the Problem Real World

The observation deck of the Willis Tower in Chicago, Illinois, is 1,353 feet above the ground. Elevators lift visitors to that level in 60 seconds. About how many feet do the elevators travel per second?

Estimate. $1{,}353 \div 60$

STEP 1

Use two sets of compatible numbers to find two different estimates.

$1{,}353 \div 60$	$1{,}353 \div 60$
↓	↓
$1{,}200 \div 60$	$1{,}800 \div 60$

STEP 2

Use patterns and basic facts to help estimate.

$12 \div 6 =$ _____	$18 \div 6 =$ _____
$120 \div 60 =$ _____	_____ ÷ _____ = _____
$1{,}200 \div 60 =$ _____	_____ ÷ _____ = _____

The elevators travel about _____ to _____ feet per second.

The more reasonable estimate is ______________ because

______________ is closer to 1,353 than ______________ is.

So, the observation deck elevators in the Willis Tower travel about _____ feet per second.

Example Estimate money.

Miriam saved $650 to spend during her 18-day trip to Chicago. She doesn't want to run out of money before the trip is over, so she plans to spend about the same amount each day. Estimate how much she can spend each day.

Estimate. 18)$650

$600 ÷ ______ = $30 or ____________ ÷ 20 = $40

So, Miriam can spend about ______ to ______ each day.

MATHEMATICAL PRACTICES 1

Analyze Would it be more reasonable to have an estimate or an exact answer for this example? Explain your reasoning.

- MATHEMATICAL PRACTICE 2 **Use Reasoning** Which estimate do you think is the better one for Miriam to use? Explain your reasoning. ____________

Try This! Use compatible numbers.

Find two estimates.	Estimate the quotient.
52)415	38)$2,764

Share and Show

Use compatible numbers to find two estimates.

1. 22)154

140 ÷ 20 = ______

160 ÷ 20 = ______

2. 68)503

3. 81)7,052

4. 33)291

5. 58)2,365

6. 19)5,312

Name ________________________________

On Your Own

Use compatible numbers to find two estimates.

7. $42\overline{)396}$

8. $59\overline{)413}$

9. $28\overline{)232}$

Use compatible numbers to estimate the quotient.

10. $19\overline{)228}$

11. $25\overline{)\$595}$

12. $86\overline{)7{,}130}$

13. GO DEEPER At an orchard, 486 green apples are to be organized into 12 green baskets and 633 red apples are to be organized into 31 red baskets. Use estimation to decide which color basket has more apples. About how many apples are in each basket of that color?

____

14. A store owner bought a large box of 5,135 paper clips. He wants to repackage the paper clips into 18 smaller boxes. Each box should contain about the same number of paper clips. About how many paper clips should the store owner put into each box?

____

15. Explain how you can use compatible numbers to estimate the quotient of $925 \div 29$.

____

____

____

____

Problem Solving • Applications 

Use the picture to solve 16–17.

16. THINKSMARTER Use estimation to decide which building has the tallest floors. About how many meters is each floor?

____

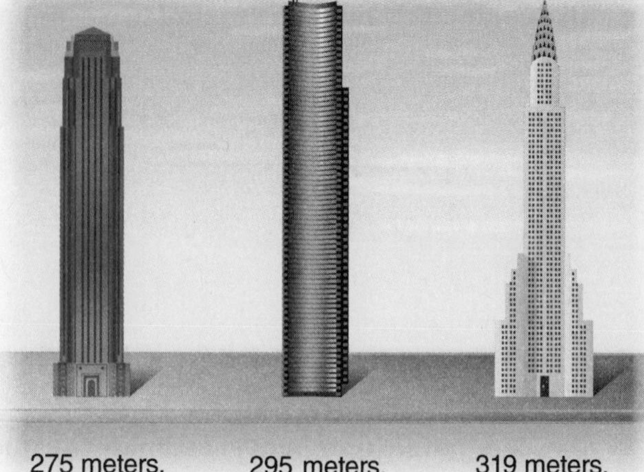

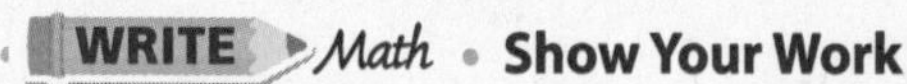

275 meters, 64 floors, Williams Tower, Texas	295 meters, 76 floors, Columbia Center, Washington	319 meters, 77 floors, Chrysler Building, New York

17. MATHEMATICAL PRACTICE 3 **Make Arguments** About how many meters tall is each floor of the Chrysler Building? Use what you know about estimating quotients to justify your answer.

____

____

18. WRITE Math Explain how you know whether the quotient of 298 ÷ 31 is closer to 9 or to 10.

____

____

____

WRITE Math • **Show Your Work**

19. GO DEEPER Eli needs to save $235. To earn money, he plans to mow lawns and charge $21 for each. Write two estimates Eli could use to determine the number of lawns he needs to mow. Decide which estimate you think is the better one for Eli to use. Explain your reasoning.

____

____

____

20. THINKSMARTER Anik built a tower of cubes. It was 594 millimeters tall. The height of each cube was 17 millimeters. About how many cubes did Anik use? Explain your answer.

____

____

Name ______________________________

Estimate with 2-Digit Divisors

Common Core **COMMON CORE STANDARD—5.NBT.B.6**
Perform operations with multi-digit whole numbers and with decimals to hundredths.

Use compatible numbers to find two estimates.

1. $18\overline{)1{,}322}$

1,200 ÷ 20 = 60

1,400 ÷ 20 = 70

2. $12\overline{)478}$

3. 336 ÷ 12

4. 2,242 ÷ 33

Use compatible numbers to estimate the quotient.

5. $82\overline{)5{,}514}$

6. $61\overline{)5{,}320}$

7. $28\overline{)776}$

8. $23\overline{)1{,}624}$

Problem Solving (Real World)

9. A cubic yard of topsoil weighs 4,128 pounds. About how many 50-pound bags of topsoil can you fill with one cubic yard of topsoil?

____

10. An electronics store places an order for 2,665 USB flash drives. One shipping box holds 36 flash drives. About how many boxes will it take to hold all the flash drives?

____

11. WRITE *Math* Create a division problem with a 2-digit divisor. Using more than 1 set of compatible numbers, observe what happens when you estimate using a different divisor, a different dividend, and when both are different. Using a calculator, compare the estimates to the answer and describe the differences.

____

____

____

____

____

____

____

Lesson Check (5.NBT.B.6)

1. Marcy has 567 earmuffs in stock. If she can put 18 earmuffs on each shelf, about how many shelves does she need for all the earmuffs?

2. Howard pays $327 for one dozen collector's edition baseball cards. About how much does he pay for each baseball card?

Spiral Review (5.NBT.A.1, 5.NBT.B.5, 5.NBT.B.6)

3. Andrew can frame 9 pictures each day. He has an order for 108 pictures. How many days will it take him to complete the order?

4. Madeleine can type 3 pages in one hour. How many hours will it take her to type a 123-page report?

5. Suppose you round 43,257,529 to 43,300,000. To what place value did you round the number?

6. Grace's catering company received an order for 118 apple pies. Grace uses 8 apples to make one apple pie. How many apples does she need to make all 118 pies?

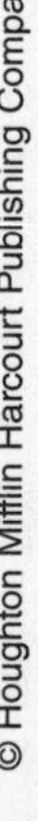

FOR MORE PRACTICE GO TO THE Personal Math Trainer

Name ______________________________

Divide by 2-Digit Divisors

Essential Question How can you divide by 2-digit divisors?

Number and Operations in Base Ten—5.NBT.B.6

MATHEMATICAL PRACTICES
MP1, MP2, MP8

Unlock the Problem

Mr. Yates owns a smoothie shop. To mix a batch of his famous orange smoothies, he uses 18 ounces of freshly squeezed orange juice. Each day he squeezes 560 ounces of fresh orange juice. How many batches of orange smoothies can Mr. Yates make in a day?

- Underline the sentence that tells you what you are trying to find.
- Circle the numbers you need to use.

Divide. 560 ÷ 18 **Estimate.** ______________

STEP 1 Use the estimate to place the first digit in the quotient.

18)560

The first digit of the quotient will be in the ______________ place.

STEP 2 Divide the tens.

```
    3
18)560
  -54
    2
```

Divide. 56 tens ÷ 18

Multiply. ______________

Subtract. ______________

Check. 2 tens cannot be shared among 18 groups without regrouping.

STEP 3 Divide the ones.

```
   31 r2
18)560
  -54↓
    20
   -18
     2
```

Divide. ______________

Multiply. ______________

Subtract. ______________

Check. ______________

____

Since 31 is close to the estimate of 30, the answer is reasonable. So, Mr. Yates can make 31 batches of orange smoothies each day.

MATHEMATICAL PRACTICES 1

Describe what the remainder 2 represents.

Example

Every Wednesday, Mr. Yates orders fruit. He has set aside $1,250 to purchase Valencia oranges. Each box of Valencia oranges costs $41. How many boxes of Valencia oranges can Mr. Yates purchase?

You can use multiplication to check your answer.

Divide. 1,250 ÷ 41

DIVIDE

Estimate. ____________

```
     30 r20
41)1,250
  −
  ____

  −
  ____

```

CHECK YOUR WORK

```
     30            
   × 41            
   ____            
     30          +  
 + 1,200         _______
 _______          1,250 ✓
```

So, Mr. Yates can buy ______ boxes of Valencia oranges.

Try This! **Divide. Check your answer.**

A $63\overline{)756}$

B $22\overline{)4,692}$

Name ___________________________

Share and Show 

Divide. Check your answer.

1. $28\overline{)620}$

2. $64\overline{)842}$

3. $53\overline{)2,340}$

✓4. 723 ÷ 31

5. 1,359 ÷ 45

✓6. 7,925 ÷ 72

Math Talk MATHEMATICAL PRACTICES 8

Generalize Explain why you can use multiplication to check division.

On Your Own

Divide. Check your answer.

7. $16\overline{)346}$

8. $34\overline{)421}$

9. $77\overline{)851}$

10. $21\overline{)1,098}$

11. $32\overline{)6,466}$

12. $45\overline{)9,500}$

13. GO DEEPER A city has 7,204 recycle bins. The city gives half of the recycle bins to its citizens. The rest of the recycle bins are divided into 23 equal groups for city parks. How many recycle bins are left over?

____

Practice: Copy and Solve **Divide. Check your answer.**

14. 775 ÷ 35

15. 820 ÷ 41

16. 805 ÷ 24

17. 1,166 ÷ 53

18. 1,989 ÷ 15

19. 3,927 ÷ 35

Problem Solving • Applications

Use the list at the right to solve 20–22.

Smoothie Main Ingredients
Orange Tango Smoothie
18 ounces orange juice
12 ounces mango juice
Royal Purple Smoothie
22 ounces grape juice
8 ounces apple juice
Crazy Cranberry Smoothie
20 ounces cranberry juice
10 ounces passion fruit juice

20. GO DEEPER A smoothie shop receives a delivery of 968 ounces of grape juice and 720 ounces of orange juice. How many more Royal Purple smoothies than Orange Tango smoothies can be made with the shipment of juices?

____

21. THINK SMARTER The shop has 1,260 ounces of cranberry juice and 650 ounces of passion fruit juice. If the juices are used to make Crazy Cranberry smoothies, which juice will run out first? How much of the other juice will be left over?

____

____

22. MATHEMATICAL PRACTICE 2 **Use Reasoning** In the refrigerator, there are 680 ounces of orange juice and 410 ounces of mango juice. How many Orange Tango smoothies can be made? Explain your reasoning.

____

____

____

____

____

____

23. THINK SMARTER + For 23a–23b, select True or False for each statement.

23a. 1,585 ÷ 16 is 99 r1. ○ True ○ False

23b. 1,473 ÷ 21 is 70 r7. ○ True ○ False

Name ______________________________

Divide by 2-Digit Divisors

COMMON CORE STANDARD—5.NBT.B.6
Perform operations with multi-digit whole numbers and with decimals to hundredths.

Divide. Check your answer.

1. 385 ÷ 12

$$\begin{array}{r} 32 \text{ r1} \\ 12\overline{)385} \\ -36 \\ \hline 25 \\ -24 \\ \hline 1 \end{array}$$

2. 837 ÷ 36

3. 1,650 ÷ 55

4. 5,634 ÷ 18

5. $28\overline{)6{,}440}$

6. $52\overline{)5{,}256}$

7. $85\overline{)1{,}955}$

8. $46\overline{)5{,}624}$

Problem Solving

9. The factory workers make 756 machine parts in 36 hours. Suppose the workers make the same number of machine parts each hour. How many machine parts do they make each hour?

____

10. One bag holds 12 bolts. Several bags filled with bolts are packed into a box and shipped to the factory. The box contains a total of 2,760 bolts. How many bags of bolts are in the box?

____

11. **WRITE** *Math* Choose a problem that you solved in the lesson, and solve the same problem using the partial quotients method. Compare the methods to solve the problems. Name the method you like better, and explain why.

____

____

____

____

Lesson Check (5.NBT.B.6)

1. A bakery packages 868 muffins into 31 boxes. The same number of muffins are put into each box. How many muffins are in each box?

2. Maggie orders 19 identical gift boxes. The Ship-Shape Packaging Company packs and ships the boxes for $1,292. How much does it cost to pack and ship each box?

Spiral Review (5.NBT.A.1, 5.NBT.B.6)

3. What is the standard form of the number four million, two hundred sixteen thousand, ninety?

4. Kelly and 23 friends go roller skating. They pay a total of $186. About how much does it cost for one person to skate?

5. In two days, Gretchen drinks seven 16-ounce bottles of water. She drinks the water in 4 equal servings. How many ounces of water does Gretchen drink in each serving?

6. What is the value of the underlined digit in 5,<u>4</u>36,788?

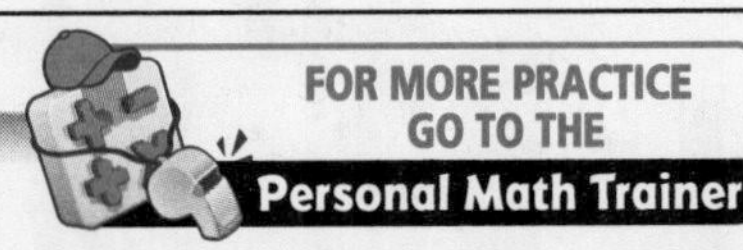

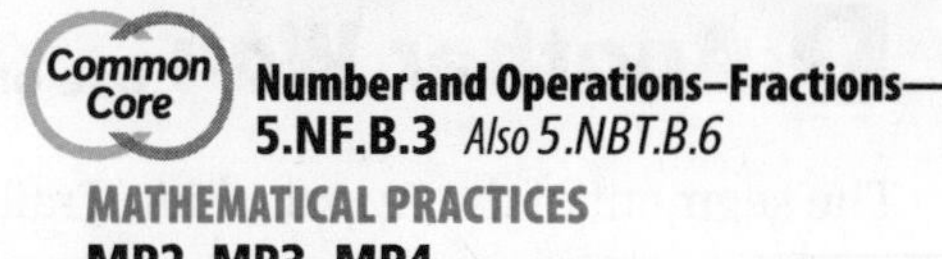

Name ______________________________

Interpret the Remainder

Essential Question When solving a division problem, when do you write the remainder as a fraction?

Number and Operations–Fractions—5.NF.B.3 *Also 5.NBT.B.6*

MATHEMATICAL PRACTICES
MP2, MP3, MP4

Unlock the Problem Real World

Scott and his family want to hike a trail that is 1,365 miles long. They will hike equal parts of the trail on 12 different hiking trips. How many miles will Scott's family hike on each trip?

- Circle the dividend you will use to solve the division problem.
- Underline the divisor you will use to solve the division problem.

When you solve a division problem with a remainder, the way you interpret the remainder depends on the situation and the question. Sometimes you need to use both the quotient and the remainder. You can do that by writing the remainder as a fraction.

One Way Write the remainder as a fraction.

First, divide to find the quotient and remainder.

Then, decide how to use the quotient and remainder to answer the question.

- The ____________ represents the number of trips Scott and his family plan to take.
- The ____________ represents the whole-number part of the number of miles Scott and his family will hike on each trip.
- The ____________ represents the number of miles left over.
- The remainder represents 9 miles, which can also be divided into 12 parts and written as a fraction.

$\frac{\text{remainder}}{\text{divisor}} \rightarrow$ ____________

- Write the quotient with the remainder written as a fraction in simplest form.

____

$12\overline{)1,365}$

So, Scott and his family will hike ____________ miles on each trip.

The segment of the Appalachian Trail that runs through Pennsylvania is 232 miles long. Scott and his family want to hike 9 miles each day on the trail. How many days will they hike exactly 9 miles?

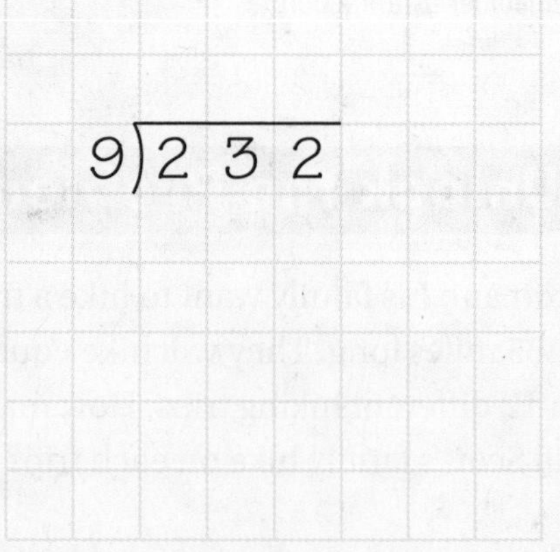

- Divide to find the quotient and the remainder.
- Since the remainder shows that there are not enough miles left for another 9-mile day, it is not used in the answer.

So, they will hike exactly 9 miles on each of ______ days.

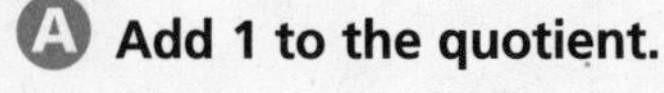

A Add 1 to the quotient.

What is the total number of days that Scott will need to hike 232 miles?

- To hike the 7 remaining miles, he will need 1 more day.

So, Scott will need ______ days to hike 232 miles.

B Use the remainder as the answer.

If Scott hikes 9 miles each day except the last day, how many miles will he hike on the last day?

- The remainder is 7.

So, Scott will hike ______ miles on the last day.

Try This!

A sporting goods store is going to ship 1,252 sleeping bags. Each shipping carton can hold 8 sleeping bags. How many cartons are needed to ship all of the sleeping bags?

$$\begin{array}{r} 1\square\square \\ 8\overline{)1,252} \\ -8 \\ \hline 45 \\ -\square \\ \hline \square 2 \\ -\square \\ \hline \square \end{array}$$

Since there are ______ sleeping bags left over,

______ cartons will be needed for all of the sleeping bags.

MATHEMATICAL PRACTICES 4

Modeling Explain why you would not write the remainder as a fraction when you find the number of cartons needed in the Try This.

Name ______________________

Share and Show MATH BOARD

Interpret the remainder to solve.

1. Erika and Bradley want to hike the Big Cypress Trail. They will hike a total of 75 miles. If Erika and Bradley plan to hike for 12 days, how many miles will they hike each day?

$12\overline{)75}$ r

a. Divide to find the quotient and remainder.

b. Decide how to use the quotient and remainder to answer the question.

____

2. **What if** Erika and Bradley want to hike 14 miles each day? How many days will they hike exactly 14 miles?

____

3. Dylan's hiking club is planning to stay overnight at a camping lodge. Each large room can hold 15 hikers. There are 154 hikers. How many rooms will they need?

____

On Your Own

Interpret the remainder to solve.

4. GO DEEPER The students in a class of 24 share 48 apple slices and 36 orange slices equally among them. How many pieces of fruit did each student get?

____

5. Fiona has 212 stickers to put in her sticker book. Each page holds 18 stickers. How many pages does Fiona need for all of her stickers?

____

6. A total of 123 fifth-grade students are going to Fort Verde State Historic Park. Each bus holds 38 students. All of the buses are full except one. How many students will be in the bus that is not full?

____

7. MATHEMATICAL PRACTICE 3 **Verify the Reasoning of Others** Sheila is going to divide a 36-inch piece of ribbon into 5 equal pieces. She says each piece will be 7 inches long. What is Sheila's error?

____

____

____

Unlock the Problem

8. Maureen has 243 ounces of trail mix. She puts an equal number of ounces in each of 15 bags. How many ounces of trail mix does Maureen have left over?

a. What do you need to find? ______________________

b. How will you use division to find how many ounces of trail mix are left over?

____

____

c. Show the steps you use to solve the problem.

d. Complete the sentences.

Maureen has ________ ounces of trail mix.

She puts an equal number of ounces in each of ________ bags.

Each bag has ________ ounces.

Maureen has ________ ounces of trail mix left over.

9. THINK SMARTER James has 884 feet of rope. There are 12 teams of hikers. If James gives an equal amount of rope to each team, how much rope will each team receive?

____

10. THINK SMARTER Rory works at a produce packing plant. She packed 2,172 strawberries last week and put them in containers with 8 strawberries in each one. How many containers of strawberries did Rory fill with 8 strawberries? Explain how you used the quotient and the remainder to answer the question.

____

____

____

Name ______________________

Interpret the Remainder

COMMON CORE STANDARD—5.NF.B.3
Apply and extend previous understandings of multiplication and division to multiply and divide fractions.

Interpret the remainder to solve.

1. Warren spent 140 hours making 16 wooden toy trucks for a craft fair. If he spent the same amount of time making each truck, how many hours did he spend making each truck?

$$\begin{array}{r} 8 \\ 16\overline{)140} \\ -128 \\ \hline 12 \end{array}$$

$8\frac{3}{4}$ hours

2. Marcia has 412 flowers for centerpieces. She uses 8 flowers for each centerpiece. How many centerpieces can she make?

____

3. A campground has cabins that can each hold 28 campers. There are 148 campers visiting the campground. How many cabins are full if 28 campers are in each cabin?

____

4. Jenny has 220 ounces of cleaning solution that she wants to divide equally among 12 large containers. How much cleaning solution should she put in each container?

____

5. **WRITE** ▸ *Math* Suppose you have 192 marbles in groups of 15 marbles each. Find the number of groups of marbles that you have. Write the quotient with the remainder written as a fraction. Explain what the fraction part of your answer means.

____

____

____

____

Lesson Check (5.NF.B.3)

1. Henry and 28 classmates go to the roller skating rink. Each van can hold 11 students. If all of the vans are full except one, how many students are in the van that is not full?

2. Candy buys 20 ounces of mixed nuts. She puts an equal number of ounces in each of 3 bags. How many ounces of mixed nuts will be in each bag? Write the answer as a whole number and a fraction.

Spiral Review (5.NBT.B.5, 5.NBT.B.6)

3. Jayson earns $196 each week bagging groceries at the store. He saves half his earnings each week. How much money does Jayson save per week?

4. Desiree swims laps for 25 minutes each day. How many minutes does she spend swimming laps in 14 days?

5. Steve is participating in a bike-a-thon for charity. He will bike 144 miles per day for 5 days. How many miles will Steve bike in the five days?

6. Kasi is building a patio. He has 136 bricks. He wants the patio to have 8 rows, each with the same number of bricks. How many bricks will Kasi put in each row?

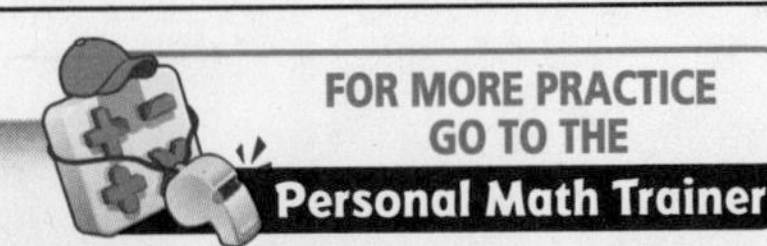

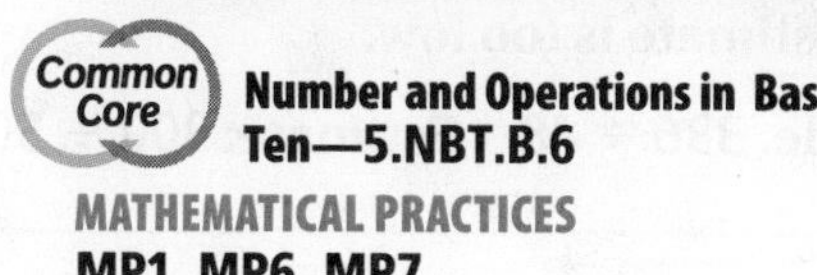

Name ______________________________

Adjust Quotients

Essential Question How can you adjust the quotient if your estimate is too high or too low?

Common Core **Number and Operations in Base Ten—5.NBT.B.6**
MATHEMATICAL PRACTICES
MP1, MP6, MP7

CONNECT When you estimate to decide where to place the first digit, you can also try using the first digit of your estimate to find the first digit of your quotient. Sometimes an estimate is too low or too high.

Divide. 3,382 ÷ 48

Estimate. 3,000 ÷ 50 = 60

Try 6 tens.

If an estimate is too low, the difference will be greater than the divisor.

```
     6
48)3,382
  -2 88
     50
```

Since the estimate is too low, adjust by increasing the number in the quotient.

Divide. 453 ÷ 65

Estimate. 490 ÷ 70 = 7

Try 7 ones.

If an estimate is too high, the product with the first digit will be too large and cannot be subtracted.

```
     7
65)453
  -455
```

Since the estimate is too high, adjust by decreasing the number in the quotient.

Unlock the Problem Real World

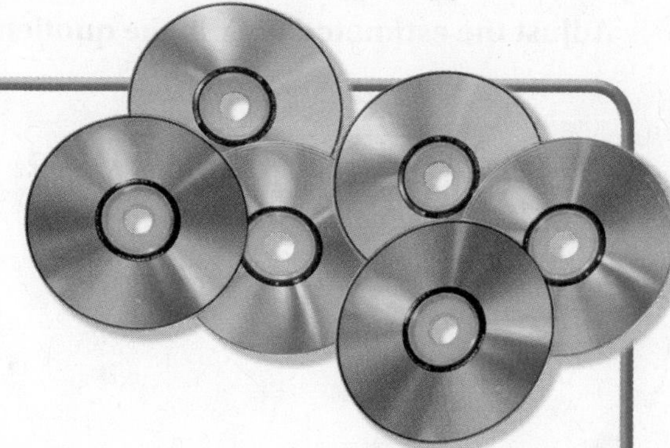

A new music group makes 6,127 copies of its first CD. The group sells 75 copies of the CD at each of its shows. How many shows does it take the group to sell all of the CDs?

Divide. 6,127 ÷ 75 **Estimate.** 6,300 ÷ 70 = 90

STEP 1 Use the estimate, 90. Try 9 tens.

- Is the estimate too high, too low, or correct?

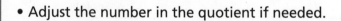

____

- Adjust the number in the quotient if needed.

STEP 2 Estimate the next digit in the quotient.
Divide the ones.
Estimate: 140 ÷ 70 = 2. Try 2 ones.

- Is the estimate too high, too low, or correct?

____

- Adjust the number in the quotient if needed.

```
75)6,127
```

So, it takes the group ______ shows to sell all of the CDs.

Try This! **When the difference is equal to or greater than the divisor, the estimate is too low.**

Divide. 336 ÷ 48 **Estimate.** 300 ÷ 50 = 6

Use the estimate.

Try 6 ones.

$$48\overline{)336}\ \text{quotient } 6$$

Since ____________, the estimate is ________.

336 ÷ 48 = ______

Adjust the estimated digit in the quotient if needed. Then divide.

Try ____________.

MATHEMATICAL PRACTICES 6

Explain why using the closest estimate could be useful in solving a division problem.

Share and Show

Adjust the estimated digit in the quotient, if needed. Then divide.

1. $41\overline{)1,546}$ (estimated quotient digit: 4)
2. $16\overline{)416}$ (estimated quotient digit: 2)
3. $34\overline{)2,831}$ (estimated quotient digit: 9)

Divide.

4. $19\overline{)915}$
5. $28\overline{)1,825}$
6. $45\overline{)3,518}$

MATHEMATICAL PRACTICES 1

Evaluate Explain how you know whether an estimated quotient is too low or too high.

Name ___________________________

On Your Own

Divide.

7. $15\overline{)975}$

8. $37\overline{)264}$

9. $34\overline{)6,837}$

Practice: Copy and Solve **Divide.**

10. 452 ÷ 31

11. 592 ÷ 74

12. 785 ÷ 14

13. 601 ÷ 66

14. 1,067 ÷ 97

15. 2,693 ÷ 56

16. 1,488 ÷ 78

17. 2,230 ÷ 42

18. 4,295 ÷ 66

MATHEMATICAL PRACTICE 7 **Identify Relationships** **Algebra** **Write the unknown number for each ■.**

19. ■ ÷ 33 = 11

■ = __________

20. 1,092 ÷ 52 = ■

■ = __________

21. 429 ÷ ■ = 33

■ = __________

22. MATHEMATICAL PRACTICE 6 **Explain a Method** A deli served 1,288 sandwiches in 4 weeks. If it served the same number of sandwiches each day, how many sandwiches did it serve in 1 day? Explain how you found your answer.

____

____

____

23. THINKSMARTER Kainoa collects trading cards. He has 1,025 baseball cards, 713 basketball cards, and 836 football cards. He wants to put all of them in albums. Each page in the albums holds 18 cards. How many pages will he need to hold all of his cards?

____

Unlock the Problem Real World

24. GO DEEPER A banquet hall serves 2,394 pounds of turkey during a 3-week period. If the same amount is served each day, how many pounds of turkey does the banquet hall serve each day?

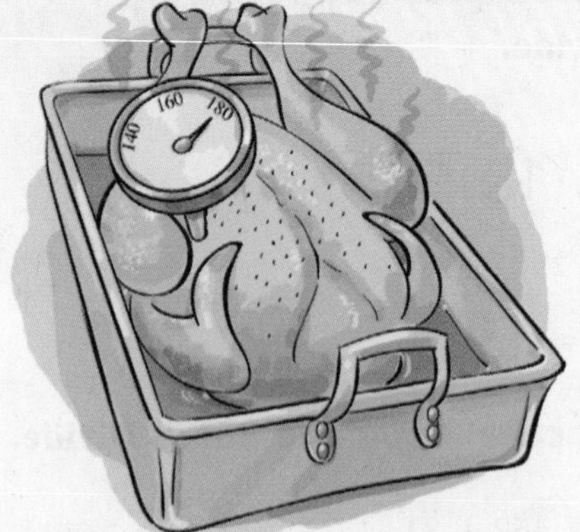

a. What do you need to find? ______________________

____

b. What information are you given? ______________________

____

c. What other information will you use?

____

____

____

d. Find how many days there are in 3 weeks.

There are ______ days in 3 weeks.

e. Divide to solve the problem.

f. Complete the sentence.
The banquet hall serves ____________ of turkey each day.

25. Marcos mixes 624 ounces of lemonade. He wants to fill the 52 cups he has with equal amounts of lemonade. How much lemonade should he put in each cup?

____

26. THINK SMARTER Oliver estimates the first digit in the quotient.

$$75\overline{)6{,}234}\quad \text{quotient: } 9$$

Oliver's estimate is

correct.
too high.
too low

Name ______________________

Adjust Quotients

Adjust the estimated digit in the quotient, if needed. Then divide.

COMMON CORE STANDARD—5.NBT.B.6
Perform operations with multi-digit whole numbers and with decimals to hundredths.

1. 16)976 — estimated quotient 5

```
      5
 16)976
   -80
    17

      61
 16 )976
    -96
     16
    -16
      0
```

2. 24)689 — estimated quotient 3

3. 65)2,210 — estimated quotient 3

4. 38)7,035 — estimated quotient 2

Divide.

5. 2,961 ÷ 47

6. 2,072 ÷ 86

7. 44)2,910

8. 82)4,018

Problem Solving

9. A copier prints 89 copies in one minute. How long does it take the copier to print 1,958 copies?

____

10. Erica is saving her money to buy a dining room set that costs $580. If she saves $29 each month, how many months will she need to save to have enough money to buy the set?

____

11. WRITE Math Explain the different ways that you can use multiplication to estimate and solve division problems.

____

____

____

____

____

____

Lesson Check (5.NBT.B.6)

1. Gail ordered 5,675 pounds of flour for the bakery. The flour comes in 25-pound bags. How many bags of flour will the bakery receive?

2. Simone is in a bike-a-thon for a fundraiser. She receives $15 in pledges for every mile she bikes. If she wants to raise $510, how many miles does she need to bike?

Spiral Review (5.OA.A.2, 5.NBT.A.1, 5.NBT.B.6)

3. Lina makes beaded bracelets. She uses 9 beads to make each bracelet. How many bracelets can she make with 156 beads?

4. A total of 1,056 students from different schools enter the county science fair. Each school enters exactly 32 students. How many schools participate in the science fair?

5. What is $\frac{1}{10}$ of 6,000?

6. Christy buys 48 barrettes. She shares the barrettes equally between herself and her 3 sisters. Write an expression to represent the number of barrettes each girl gets.

FOR MORE PRACTICE GO TO THE Personal Math Trainer

Name ______________________________

Problem Solving • Division

Essential Question How can the strategy *draw a diagram* help you solve a division problem?

Common Core **Number and Operations in Base Ten—5.NBT.B.6**
MATHEMATICAL PRACTICES
MP1, MP3, MP4

Unlock the Problem (Real World)

Sean and his family chartered a fishing boat for the day. Sean caught a blue marlin and an amberjack. The weight of the blue marlin was 12 times as great as the weight of the amberjack. The combined weight of both fish was 273 pounds. How much did each fish weigh?

Read the Problem

What do I need to find?	What information do I need to use?	How will I use the information?
I need to find ______________ ______________.	I need to know that Sean caught a total of ______ pounds of fish and the weight of the blue marlin was ______ times as great as the weight of the amberjack.	I can use the strategy ______________ and then divide. I can draw and use a bar model to write the division problem that helps me find the weight of each fish.

Solve the Problem

I will draw one box to show the weight of the amberjack. Then I will draw a bar of 12 boxes of the same size to show the weight of the blue marlin. I can divide the total weight of the two fish by the total number of boxes.

amberjack [___]

blue marlin [___ | ___ | ___ | ___ | ___ | ___ | ___ | ___ | ___ | ___ | ___ | ___]

273 pounds

$$\begin{array}{r} 2 \\ 13\overline{)273} \\ -26 \\ \hline \square \\ -\square \\ \hline \square \end{array}$$

Write the quotient in each box. Multiply it by 12 to find the weight of the blue marlin.

So, the amberjack weighed __________ pounds and the blue marlin weighed __________ pounds.

Try Another Problem

Jason, Murray, and Dana went fishing. Dana caught a red snapper. Jason caught a tuna with a weight 3 times as great as the weight of the red snapper. Murray caught a sailfish with a weight 12 times as great as the weight of the red snapper. If the combined weight of the three fish was 208 pounds, how much did the tuna weigh?

Read the Problem

What do I need to find?	What information do I need to use?	How will I use the information?

Solve the Problem

So, the tuna weighed _______ pounds.

- How can you check if your answer is correct? ____________________

____

MATHEMATICAL PRACTICES 1

Analyze Explain how you could use another strategy to solve this problem.

Name ______________________

Share and Show MATH BOARD

1. Paula caught a tarpon with a weight that was 10 times as great as the weight of a permit fish she caught. The total weight of the two fish was 132 pounds. How much did each fish weigh?

First, draw one box to represent the weight of the permit fish and ten boxes to represent the weight of the tarpon.

Next, divide the total weight of the two fish by the total number of boxes you drew. Place the quotient in each box.

Last, find the weight of each fish.

The permit fish weighed _______ pounds.

The tarpon weighed _______ pounds.

2. What if the weight of the tarpon was 11 times the weight of the permit fish, and the total weight of the two fish was 132 pounds? How much would each fish weigh?

permit fish: _______ pounds

tarpon: _______ pounds

3. Jon caught four fish that weighed a total of 252 pounds. The kingfish weighed twice as much as the amberjack and the white marlin weighed twice as much as the kingfish. The weight of the tarpon was 5 times the weight of the amberjack. How much did each fish weigh?

amberjack: _______ pounds

kingfish: _______ pounds

marlin: _______ pounds

tarpon: _______ pounds

WRITE Math • **Show Your Work**

On Your Own

Use the table to solve 4–5.

Kevin's Supply List for a Saltwater Aquarium	
40-gal tank	\$170
Aquarium light	\$30
Filtration system	\$65
Thermometer	\$2
15-lb bag of gravel	\$13
Large rocks	\$3 per lb
Clown fish	\$20 each
Damselfish	\$7 each

4. THINK SMARTER Kevin bought 3 bags of gravel to cover the bottom of his fish tank. He has 8 pounds of gravel left over. How much gravel did Kevin use to cover the bottom of the tank?

5. MATHEMATICAL PRACTICE 3 **Apply** Look back at Problem 4. Write a similar problem by changing the number of bags of gravel and the amount of gravel left.

6. THINK SMARTER The crew on a fishing boat caught four fish that weighed a total of 1,092 pounds. The tarpon weighed twice as much as the amberjack and the white marlin weighed twice as much as the tarpon. The weight of the tuna was 5 times the weight of the amberjack. How much did each fish weigh?

7. GO DEEPER A fish market bought two swordfish at a rate of \$13 per pound. The cost of the larger fish was 3 times as great as the cost of the smaller fish. The total cost of the two fish was \$3,952. How much did each fish weigh?

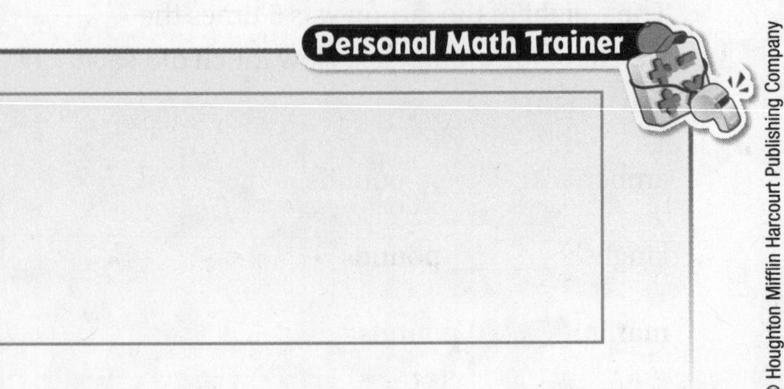

8. THINK SMARTER+ Eric and Stephanie took their younger sister Melissa to pick apples. Eric picked 4 times as many apples as Melissa. Stephanie picked 6 times as many apples as Melissa. Eric and Stephanie picked 150 apples together. Draw a diagram to find the number of apples Melissa picked.

Name ______________________

Problem Solving • Division

COMMON CORE STANDARD—5.NBT.B.6
Perform operations with multi-digit whole numbers and with decimals to hundredths.

Show your work. Solve each problem.

1. Duane has 12 times as many baseball cards as Tony. Between them, they have 208 baseball cards. How many baseball cards does each boy have?

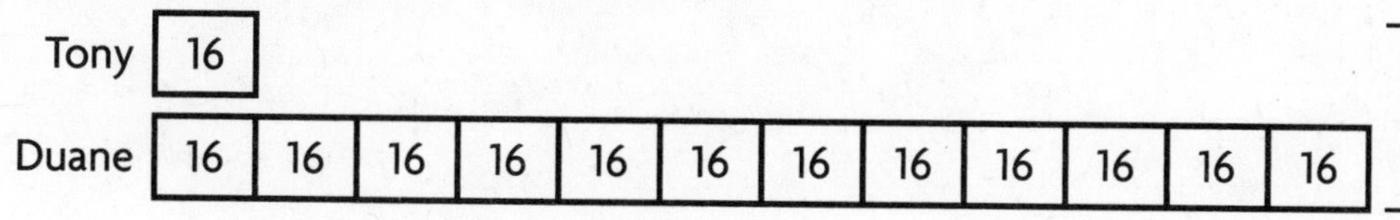

$208 \div 13 = 16$

Tony: 16 cards; Duane: 192 cards

2. Hallie has 10 times as many pages to read for her homework assignment as Janet. Altogether, they have to read 264 pages. How many pages does each girl have to read?

____

3. Kelly has 4 times as many songs on her music player as Lou. Tiffany has 6 times as many songs on her music player as Lou. Altogether, they have 682 songs on their music players. How many songs does Kelly have?

____

4. **WRITE** *Math* Create a word problem that uses division. Draw a bar model to help you write an equation to solve the problem.

____

____

Lesson Check (5.NBT.B.6)

1. Chelsea has 11 times as many art brushes as Monique. If they have 60 art brushes altogether, how many brushes does Chelsea have?

2. Jo has a gerbil and a German shepherd. The shepherd eats 14 times as much food as the gerbil. Altogether, they eat 225 ounces of dry food per week. How many ounces of food does the German shepherd eat per week?

Spiral Review (5.NBT.B.5, 5.NBT.B.6, 5.NF.B.3)

3. Jeanine is twice as old as her brother Marc. If the sum of their ages is 24, how old is Jeanine?

4. Larry is shipping nails that weigh a total of 53 pounds. He divides the nails equally among 4 shipping boxes. How many pounds of nails does he put in each box?

5. Annie plants 6 rows of small flower bulbs in a garden. She plants 132 bulbs in each row. How many bulbs does Annie plant?

6. Next year, four elementary schools will each send 126 students to Bedford Middle School. What is the total number of students the elementary schools will send to the middle school?

FOR MORE PRACTICE GO TO THE Personal Math Trainer

Name ______________________________

Chapter 2 Review/Test

Personal Math Trainer
Online Assessment and Intervention

1. Choose the word that makes the sentence true.
The first digit in the quotient of 1,875 ÷ 9

will be in the [ones / tens / hundreds / thousands] place.

2. For 2a–2d, select True or False to indicate whether the quotient is correct.

2a. 225 ÷ 9 = 25 ○ True ○ False

2b. 154 ÷ 7 = 22 ○ True ○ False

2c. 312 ÷ 9 = 39 ○ True ○ False

2d. 412 ÷ 2 = 260 ○ True ○ False

3. Chen is checking a division problem by doing the following:

```
  152
×   4
─────
 
+   2
─────
 
```

What problem is Chen checking?

GO DIGITAL Assessment Options Chapter Test

4. Isaiah wrote this problem in his notebook. Using the vocabulary boxes, label the parts of the division problem. Then, using the vocabulary, explain how Isaiah can check whether his quotient is correct.

____

____

____

5. Tammy says the quotient of 793 ÷ 6 is 132 r1. Use multiplication to show if Tammy's answer is correct.

6. Jeffery wants to save the same amount of money each week to buy a new bike. He needs \$252. If he wants the bike in 14 weeks, how much money should Jeffery save each week?

\$ ____________

7. Dana is making a seating chart for an awards banquet. There are 184 people coming to the banquet. If 8 people can be seated at each table, how many tables will be needed for the awards banquet?

____________ tables

Name ____________________

8. Darrel divided 575 by 14 by using partial quotients. What is the quotient? Explain your answer using numbers and words.

____

____

____

9. For 9a–9c, choose Yes or No to indicate whether the statement is correct.

9a. 5,210 ÷ 17 is 306 r8. ○ Yes ○ No

9b. 8,808 ÷ 42 is 209 r30. ○ Yes ○ No

9c. 1,248 ÷ 24 is 51. ○ Yes ○ No

10. Divide. Draw a quick picture.

156 ÷ 12 = ☐

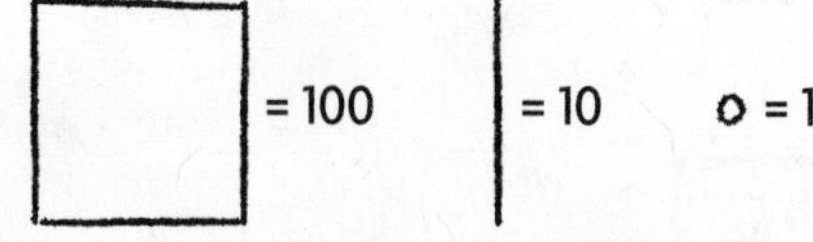

11. Divide. Show your work.

$17\overline{)5,210}$

12. Choose the compatible numbers that will give the best estimate for 429 ÷ 36.

○ 300		○ 60
○ 350	and	○ 50
○ 440		○ 40

13. GO DEEPER Samuel needs 233 feet of wood to build a fence. The wood comes in lengths of 11 feet.

Part A

How many total pieces of wood will Samuel need? Explain your answer.

Part B

Theresa needs twice as many feet of wood as Samuel. How many pieces of wood does Theresa need? Explain your answer.

Name ______________________________

Personal Math Trainer

14. THINK SMARTER+ Russ and Vickie are trying to solve this problem: There are 146 students taking buses to the museum. If each bus holds 24 students, how many buses will they need?

Russ says the students need 6 buses. Vickie says they need 7 buses. Who is correct? Explain your reasoning.

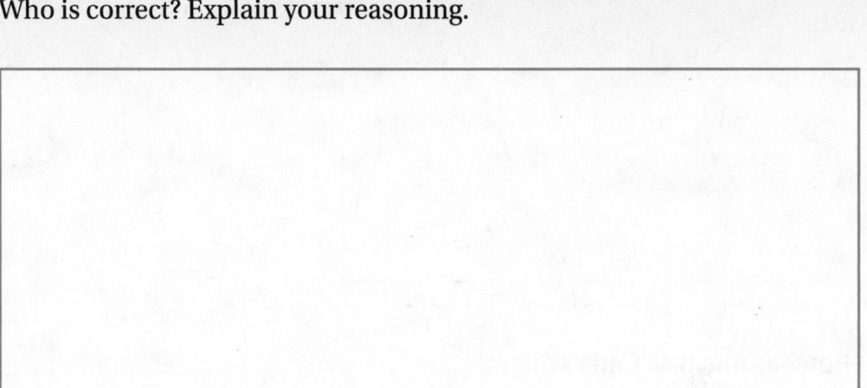

15. Write the letter for each quick picture under the division problem it represents.

A

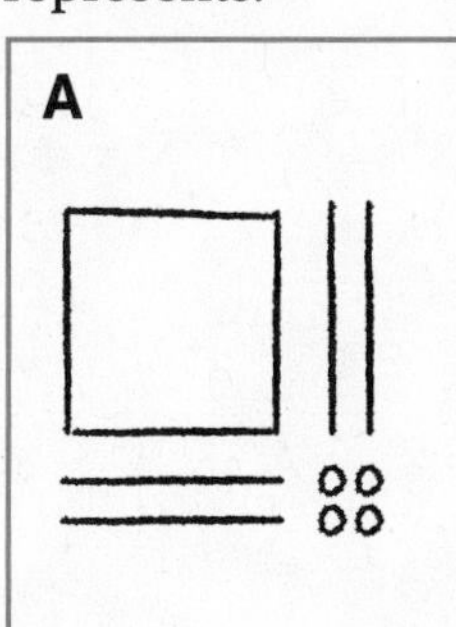

B

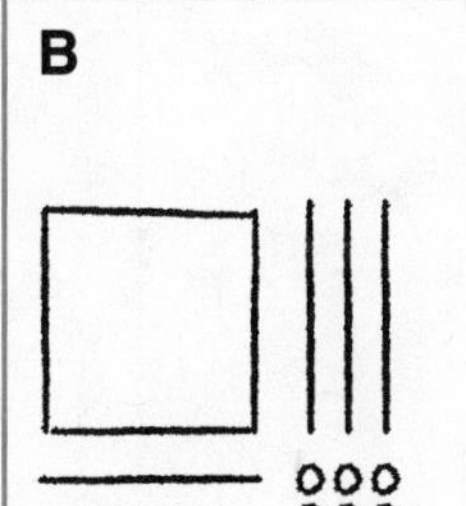

C

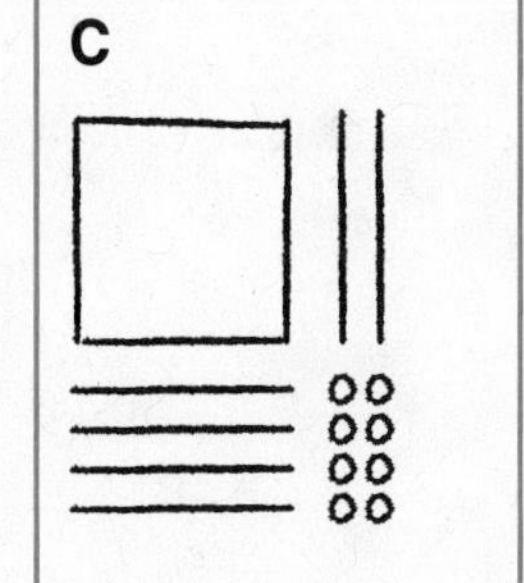

$156 \div 12 = 13$	$168 \div 12 = 14$	$144 \div 12 = 12$

16. Steve is buying apples for the fifth grade. Each bag holds 12 apples. If there are 75 students total, how many bags of apples will Steve need to buy if he wants to give one apple to each student?

__________ bags

17. Rasheed needs to save $231. To earn money, he plans to wash cars and charge $12 per car. Write two estimates Rasheed could use to determine how many cars he needs to wash.

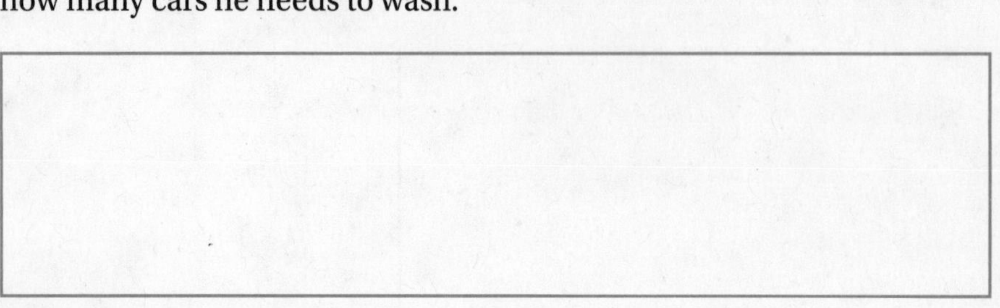

18. Paula has a dog that weighs 3 times as much as Carla's dog. The total weight of the dogs is 48 pounds. How much does Paula's dog weigh?

Draw a diagram to find the weight of Paula's dog.

19. Dylan estimates the first digit in the quotient.

$$\begin{array}{r} 6 \\ 46\overline{)3{,}662} \end{array}$$

Dylan's estimate is [too high. / too low].

Chapter 3

Add and Subtract Decimals

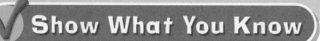

Show What You Know

Check your understanding of important skills.

Name ______________________

2-Digit Addition and Subtraction **Find the sum or difference.** (3.NBT.A.2)

1.

	Hundreds	Tens	Ones
		5	8
+		7	6

2.

	Hundreds	Tens	Ones
		8	2
−		4	7

Decimals Greater Than One **Write the word form and the expanded form for each.** (5.NBT.A.3a)

3. 3.4 ______________________ ______________________

4. 2.51 ______________________ ______________________

Relate Fractions and Decimals **Write as a decimal or a fraction.** (4.NF.C.6)

5. 0.8 ______

6. $\frac{5}{100}$ ______

7. 0.46 ______

8. $\frac{6}{10}$ ______

9. 0.90 ______

10. $\frac{35}{100}$ ______

Jason has 4 tiles. Each tile has a number printed on it. The numbers are 2, 3, 6, and 8. A decimal number is formed using the tiles and the clues. Find the number.

Clues

- The digit in the tens place is the greatest number.
- The digit in the tenths place is less than the digit in the hundredths place.
- The digit in the ones place is greater than the digit in the hundredths place.

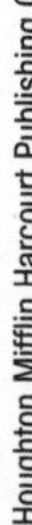

Vocabulary Builder

▶ Visualize It

Use the ✓ words to complete the tree map.

Estimation

Review Words

✓ benchmark
✓ hundredth
✓ place value
✓ round
✓ tenth

Preview Words

sequence
term
✓ thousandth

▶ Understand Vocabulary

Read the description. Which word do you think is described?

1. One of one hundred equal parts ________________
2. The value of each digit in a number based on the location of the digit ________________
3. To replace a number with one that is simpler and is approximately the same size as the original number ________________
4. An ordered set of numbers ________________
5. One of ten equal parts ________________
6. A familiar number used as a point of reference ________________
7. One of one thousand equal parts ________________
8. Each of the numbers in a sequence ________________

• Interactive Student Edition
• Multimedia eGlossary

Chapter 3 Vocabulary

benchmark punto de referencia 2	**hundredth** centésimo 30
place value valor posicional 50	**round** redondear 60
sequence sucesión 63	**tenth** décimo 65
term término 66	**thousandth** milésimo 67

One of 100 equal parts

Example: $0.56 = \frac{56}{100}$ = fifty-six hundredths

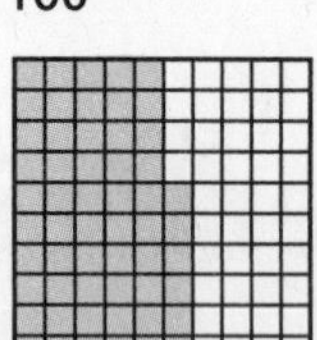

To replace a number with one that is simpler and is approximately the same size as the original number

Example: 114.6 rounded to the nearest ten is 110 and to the nearest one is 115.

One of ten equal parts

Example: $0.7 = \frac{7}{10}$ = seven tenths

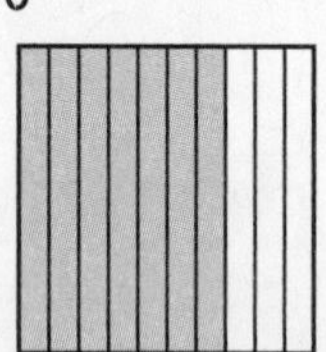

One of 1,000 equal parts

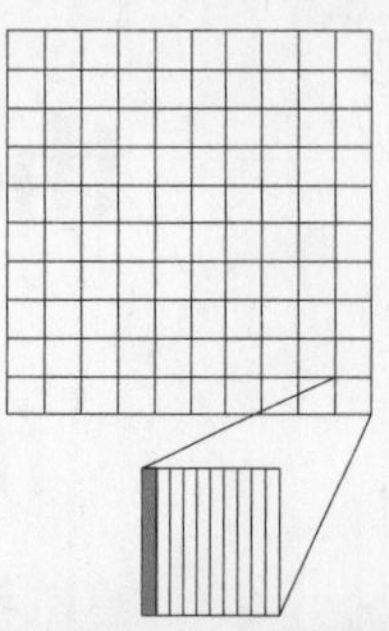

A familiar number used as a point of reference

The value of each digit in a number based on the location of the digit

Example:

MILLIONS			THOUSANDS			ONES		
Hundreds	Tens	Ones	Hundreds	Tens	Ones	Hundreds	Tens	Ones
		1,	3	9	2,	0	0	0
		1 × 1,000,000	3 × 100,000	9 × 10,000	2 × 1,000	0 × 100	0 × 10	0 × 1
		1,000,000	300,000	90,000	2,000	0	0	0

An ordered list of numbers

Example:

2, 3.25, 4.50, 5.75

sequence

A number in a sequence

Example:

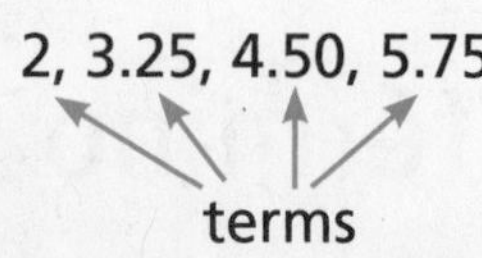

Pick It

Word Box
- benchmark
- hundredth
- place value
- round
- sequence
- tenth
- term
- thousandths

For 3 players

Materials
- 4 sets of word cards

How to Play
1. Each player is dealt 5 cards. The remaining cards are a draw pile.
2. To take a turn, ask any player if he or she has a word that matches one of your word cards.
3. If the player has the word, he or she gives the card to you, and you must define the word.
   - If you are correct, keep the card and put the matching pair in front of you. Take another turn.
   - If you are wrong, return the card. Your turn is over.
4. If the player does not have the word, he or she answers, "Pick it." Then you take a card from the draw pile.
5. If the card you draw matches one of your word cards, follow the directions for Step 3 above. If it does not, your turn is over.
6. The game is over when one player has no cards left. The player with the most pairs wins.

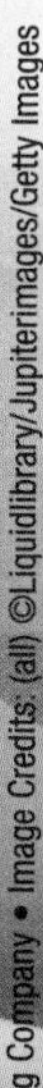

The Write Way

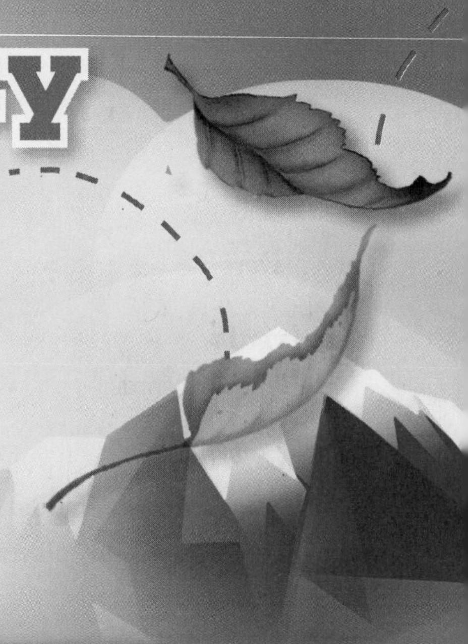

Reflect

Choose one idea. Write about it.

- Compare and contrast a hundredth and a thousandth. Tell how they are alike and how they are different.
- Explain how to use benchmarks to estimate: 0.28 + 0.71
- A phone company charges a base fee of $10 per month. Then, each minute used costs 10 cents more. Use a sequence to tell how much 20, 30, and 40 minutes would cost.
- Write a note to a friend about something you learned in Chapter 3.

Name ______________________

Thousandths

Essential Question How can you describe the relationship between two decimal place-value positions?

Common Core **Number and Operations in Base Ten—5.NBT.A.1**
Also 5.NBT.A.3a
MATHEMATICAL PRACTICES
MP4, MP5, MP7

Investigate

Materials ■ color pencils ■ straightedge

Thousandths are smaller parts than hundredths. If one hundredth is divided into ten equal parts, each part is one **thousandth**.

Use the model at the right to show tenths, hundredths, and thousandths.

A. Divide the larger square into 10 equal columns or rectangles. Shade one rectangle. What part of the whole is the shaded rectangle? Write that part as a decimal and a fraction.

____

B. Divide each rectangle into 10 equal squares. Use a second color to shade in one of the squares. What part of the whole is the shaded square? Write that part as a decimal and a fraction.

____

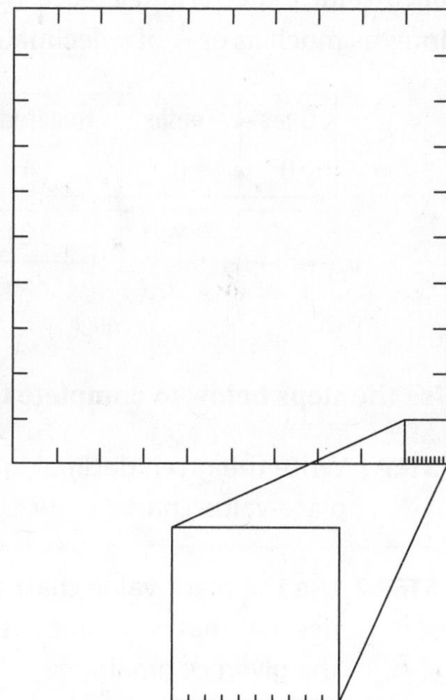

C. Divide the enlarged hundredths square into 10 equal columns or rectangles. If each hundredths square is divided into ten equal rectangles, how many parts will the model have?

____

Use a third color to shade one rectangle of the enlarged hundredths square. What part of the whole is the shaded rectangle? Write that part as a decimal and a fraction.

____

Math Talk MATHEMATICAL PRACTICES 4

There are 10 times as many hundredths as there are tenths. Explain how the model shows this.

Draw Conclusions

1. Explain what each shaded part of your model in the Investigate section shows. What fraction can you write that relates each shaded part to the next greater shaded part? ______

______

2. MATHEMATICAL PRACTICE 5 **Use a Concrete Model** Identify and describe a part of your model that shows one thousandth. Explain how you know.

______

______

______

Make Connections

The relationship of a digit in different place-value positions is the same with decimals as it is with whole numbers. You can use your understanding of place-value patterns and a place-value chart to write decimals that are 10 times as much as or $\frac{1}{10}$ of a decimal.

Ones	• Tenths	Hundredths	Thousandths
0 •	0	4	
	?	0.04	?

10 times as much · $\frac{1}{10}$ of

______ is 10 times as much as 0.04.

______ is $\frac{1}{10}$ of 0.04.

Use the steps below to complete the table.

STEP 1 Write the given decimal in a place-value chart.

STEP 2 Use the place-value chart to write a decimal that is 10 times as much as the given decimal.

STEP 3 Use the place-value chart to write a decimal that is $\frac{1}{10}$ of the given decimal.

Decimal	10 times as much as	$\frac{1}{10}$ of
0.03		
0.1		
0.07		

Math Talk — MATHEMATICAL PRACTICES 7

Look for Structure Explain the pattern you see when you move one decimal place value to the right and one decimal place value to the left.

Name ______________________

Share and Show MATH BOARD

Write the decimal shown by the shaded parts of each model.

1. 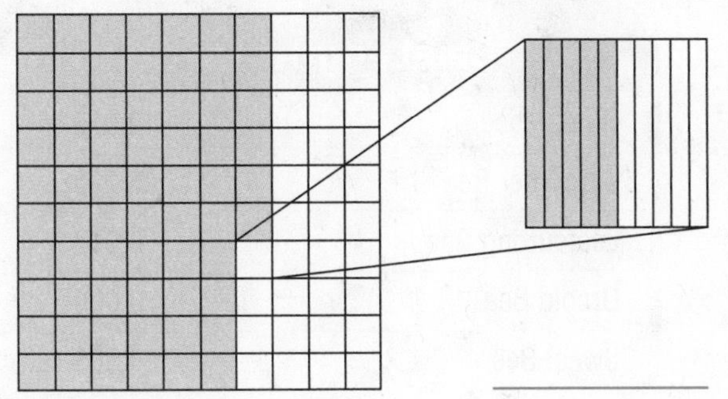
______

2. 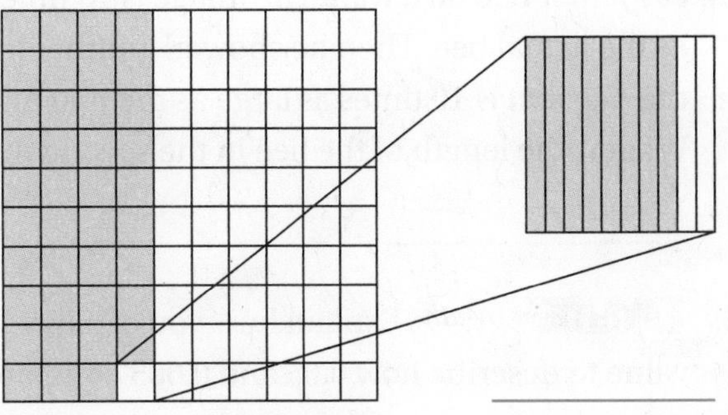
______

3. 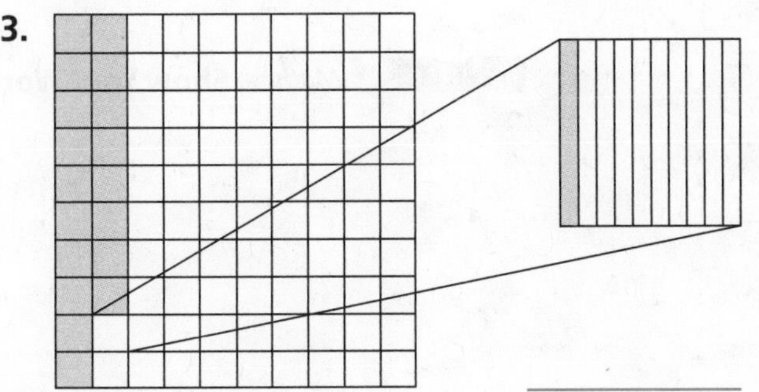
______

4. 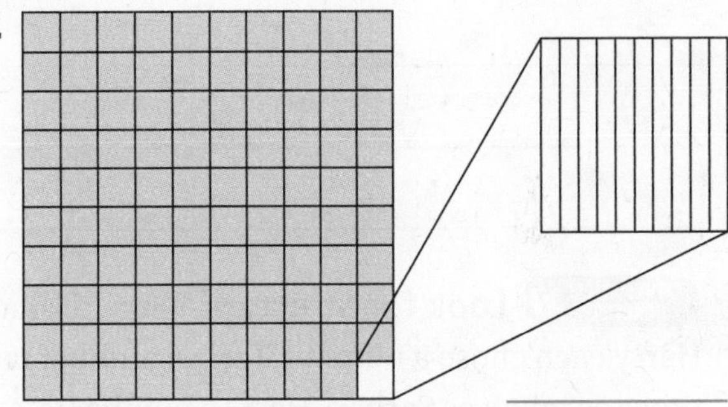
______

Complete the sentence.

5. 0.6 is 10 times as much as ______.

6. 0.007 is $\frac{1}{10}$ of ______.

7. 0.008 is $\frac{1}{10}$ of ______.

8. 0.5 is 10 times as much as ______.

Use place-value patterns to complete the table.

	Decimal	10 times as much as	$\frac{1}{10}$ of
9.	0.2		
10.	0.07		
11.	0.05		
12.	0.4		

	Decimal	10 times as much as	$\frac{1}{10}$ of
13.	0.06		
14.	0.9		
15.	0.3		
16.	0.08		

Problem Solving • Applications

Use the table for 17 and 20.

Bee Lengths (in meters)	
Bumblebee	0.019
Carpenter Bee	0.025
Leafcutting Bee	0.014
Orchid Bee	0.028
Sweat Bee	0.006

17. GO DEEPER A science teacher showed an image of a carpenter bee on a wall. The image is 10 times as large as the actual bee. Then he showed another image of the bee that is 10 times as large as the first image. What is the length of the bee in the second image?

18. WRITE Math Explain how you can use place value to describe how 0.05 and 0.005 compare.

19. MATHEMATICAL PRACTICE 7 **Look for Structure** Terry, Sasha, and Harry each chose a number. Terry's number is ten times as much as Sasha's. Harry's number is $\frac{1}{10}$ of Sasha's. Sasha's number is 0.4. What number did each person choose?

20. THINK SMARTER An atlas beetle is about 0.14 of a meter long. How does the length of the atlas beetle compare to the length of a leafcutting bee?

WRITE Math • **Show Your Work**

21. THINK SMARTER Choose the numbers that make the statement true.

0.65 is 10 times as much as [0.065 / 0.65 / 6.5 / 65.0] and $\frac{1}{10}$ of [0.065 / 0.65 / 6.5 / 65.0].

Name ______________________

Thousandths

COMMON CORE STANDARD—5.NBT.A.1
Understand the place value system.

Write the decimal shown by the shaded parts of each model.

1.

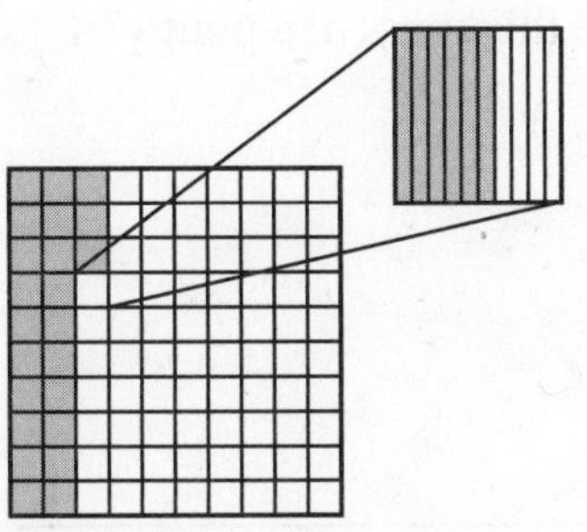

0.236

Think: 2 tenths, 3 hundredths, and 6 thousandths are shaded

2.

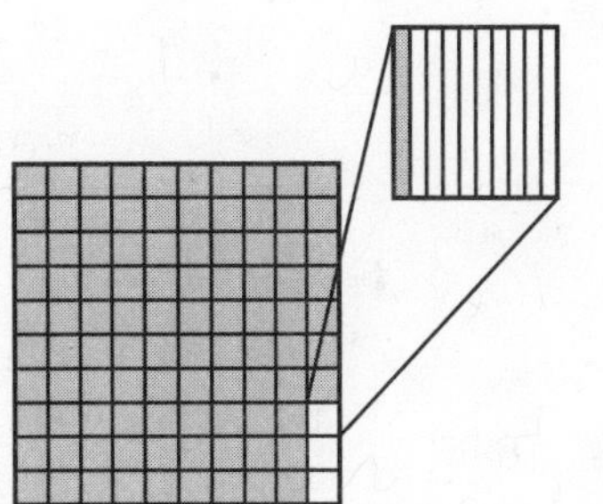

____

Complete the sentence.

3. 0.4 is 10 times as much as __________.

4. 0.003 is $\frac{1}{10}$ of __________.

Use place-value patterns to complete the table.

Decimal	10 times as much as	$\frac{1}{10}$ of
5. 0.1		
6. 0.09		

Decimal	10 times as much as	$\frac{1}{10}$ of
7. 0.08		
8. 0.2		

Problem Solving Real World

9. The diameter of a dime is seven hundred five thousandths of an inch. Complete the table by recording the diameter of a dime.

U.S. Coins	
Coin	**Diameter (in inches)**
Penny	0.750
Nickel	0.835
Dime	
Quarter	0.955
Half dollar	1.205

10. What is the value of the 5 in the diameter of a half dollar?

____

11. Which coins have a diameter with a 5 in the hundredths place?

____

12. WRITE Math Write four decimals with the digit 4 in a different place in each—ones, tenths, hundredths, and thousandths. Then write a statement that compares the value of the digit 4 in the different decimals.

____

Lesson Check (5.NBT.A.1)

1. Write a decimal that is $\frac{1}{10}$ of 3.0.

2. A penny is 0.061 inch thick. What is the value of the 6 in the thickness of a penny?

Spiral Review (5.OA.A.1, 5.OA.A.2, 5.NBT.A.1)

3. What is the number seven hundred thirty-one million, nine hundred thirty-four thousand, thirty written in standard form?

4. A city has a population of 743,182 people. What is the value of the digit 3?

5. Write an expression to match the words "three times the sum of 8 and 4".

6. A family of 2 adults and 3 children goes to a play. Admission costs $8 per adult and $5 per child. What expression would show the total admission cost for the family?

FOR MORE PRACTICE GO TO THE **Personal Math Trainer**

Name ______________________

Place Value of Decimals

Essential Question How do you read, write, and represent decimals through thousandths?

Number and Operations in Base Ten—5.NBT.A.3a
Also 5.NBT.A.1

MATHEMATICAL PRACTICES
MP2, MP7

Unlock the Problem

The Brooklyn Battery Tunnel in New York City is 1.726 miles long. It is the longest underwater tunnel for vehicles in the United States. To understand this distance, you need to understand the place value of each digit in 1.726.

You can use a place-value chart to understand decimals. Whole numbers are to the left of the decimal point. Decimals are to the right of the decimal point. The thousandths place is to the right of the hundredths place.

▲ The Brooklyn Battery Tunnel passes under the East River.

Tens	Ones	• Tenths	Hundredths	Thousandths
	1	• 7	2	6
	1×1	$7 \times \frac{1}{10}$	$2 \times \frac{1}{100}$	$6 \times \frac{1}{1,000}$
	1.0	0.7	0.02	0.006

} Value

The place value of the digit 6 in 1.726 is thousandths. The value of 6 in 1.726 is $6 \times \frac{1}{1,000}$, or 0.006.

Standard Form: 1.726

Word Form: one and seven hundred twenty-six thousandths

Expanded Form: $1 \times 1 + 7 \times \left(\frac{1}{10}\right) + 2 \times \left(\frac{1}{100}\right) + 6 \times \left(\frac{1}{1,000}\right)$

MATHEMATICAL PRACTICES 7

Look for Structure Explain how the place value of the last digit in a decimal can help you read a decimal.

Try This! **Use place value to read and write decimals.**

A **Standard Form:** 2.35

Word Form: two and ______________________

Expanded Form: $2 \times 1 +$ ______________________

B **Standard Form:** __________

Word Form: three and six hundred fourteen thousandths

Expanded Form: __________ $+ 6 \times \left(\frac{1}{10}\right) +$ __________ $+$ __________

 **Example** **Use a place-value chart.**

A common garden spider spins a web with its silk that is about 0.003 millimeter thick. A commonly used sewing thread is about 0.3 millimeter thick. How does the thickness of the spider silk and the thread compare?

STEP 1 Write the numbers in a place-value chart.

Ones •	Tenths	Hundredths	Thousandths
•			
•			

STEP 2

Count the number of decimal place-value positions to the digit 3 in 0.3 and 0.003.

0.3 has ______ fewer decimal places than 0.003

2 fewer decimal places: $10 \times 10 =$ ________

0.3 is ________ times as much as 0.003

0.003 is ________ of 0.3

So, the thread is ________ times as thick as the garden spider's silk. The thickness of the garden spider's silk is

________ that of the thread.

You can use place-value patterns to rename a decimal.

Try This! **Use place-value patterns.**

Rename 0.3 using other place values.

0.300	3 tenths	$3 \times \frac{1}{10}$
0.300	______ hundredths	______ $\times \frac{1}{100}$
0.300	________	________

Name ______________________

Share and Show

MATH BOARD

1. Complete the place-value chart to find the value of each digit.

Ones •	Tenths	Hundredths	Thousandths
3 •	5	2	4
3×1		$2 \times \frac{1}{100}$	
	0.5		

} Value

Write the value of the underlined digit.

2. 0.5$\underline{4}$3

3. 6.$\underline{2}$34

4. 3.95$\underline{4}$

Write the number in two other forms.

5. 0.253

6. 7.632

On Your Own

Write the value of the underlined digit.

7. 0.4$\underline{9}$6

8. 2.$\underline{7}$26

9. 1.06$\underline{6}$

10. 6.$\underline{3}$99

11. 0.00$\underline{2}$

12. 14.37$\underline{1}$

Write the number in two other forms.

13. 0.489

14. 5.916

Problem Solving • Applications 

Use the table for 15–16.

Average Annual Rainfall (in meters)	
California	0.564
New Mexico	0.372
New York	1.041
Wisconsin	0.820
Maine	1.074

15. What is the value of the digit 7 in New Mexico's average annual rainfall?

16. GO DEEPER Which of the states has an average annual rainfall with the least number in the thousandths place? What is another way to write the total annual rainfall in this state?

WRITE Math
Show Your Work

17. MATHEMATICAL PRACTICE 2 **Reason Quantitatively** Damian wrote the number four and twenty-three thousandths as 4.23. Describe and correct his error.

18. THINK SMARTER Dan used a meter stick to measure some seedlings in his garden. One day, a corn stalk was 0.85 m tall. A tomato plant was 0.850 m. A carrot top was 0.085 m. Which plant was shortest?

19. WRITE Math Explain how you know that the digit 6 does not have the same value in the numbers 3.675 and 3.756.

20. THINK SMARTER What is the value of the underlined digit? Mark all that apply.

0.5<u>8</u>9

- ○ 0.8
- ○ 0.08
- ○ eight tenths
- ○ eight hundredths
- ○ $8 \times (\frac{1}{10})$

Name ______________________

Place Value of Decimals

Common Core **COMMON CORE STANDARD—5.NBT.A.3a**
Understand the place value system.

Write the value of the underlined digit.

1. 0.2<u>8</u>7 **2.** 5.<u>3</u>49 **3.** 2.70<u>4</u>

8 hundredths, or 0.08

4. 9.<u>1</u>54 **5.** 4.00<u>6</u> **6.** 7.2<u>5</u>8

Write the number in two other forms.

7. 0.326

8. 8.517

9. 0.924

10. 1.075

Problem Solving Real World

11. In a gymnastics competition, Paige's score was 37.025. What is Paige's score written in word form?

12. Jake's batting average for the softball season is 0.368. What is Jake's batting average written in expanded form?

13. WRITE ▸ *Math* Write five decimals that have at least 3 digits to the right of the decimal point. Write the expanded form and the word form for each number.

Lesson Check (5.NBT.A.3a)

1. When Mindy went to China, she exchanged $1 for 6.589 Yuan. What digit is in the hundredths place of 6.589?

2. The diameter of the head of a screw is 0.306 inch. What is this number written in word form?

Spiral Review (5.OA.A.1, 5.OA.A.2, 5.NBT.B.5, 5.NF.B.3)

3. Each car on a commuter train can seat 114 passengers. If the train has 7 cars, how many passengers can the train seat?

4. What is the value of the expression $(9 + 15) \div 3 + 2$?

5. Danica has 15 stickers. She gives 3 to one friend and gets 4 from another friend. What expression would match the words?

6. There are 138 people seated at the tables in a banquet hall. Each table can seat 12 people. All the tables are full except one. How many full tables are there?

FOR MORE PRACTICE GO TO THE **Personal Math Trainer**

Name ______________________________

Compare and Order Decimals

Essential Question How can you use place value to compare and order decimals?

Number and Operations in Base Ten—5.NBT.A.3b

MATHEMATICAL PRACTICES
MP2, MP6

Unlock the Problem

The table lists some of the mountains in the United States that are over two miles high. How does the height of Cloud Peak in Wyoming compare to the height of Boundary Peak in Nevada?

▲ The Tetons are located in Grand Teton National Park.

Mountain Heights

Mountain and State	Height (in miles)
Boundary Peak, Nevada	2.488
Cloud Peak, Wyoming	2.495
Grand Teton Peak, Wyoming	2.607
Wheeler Peak, New Mexico	2.493

One Way Use place value.

Line up the decimal points. Start at the left. Compare the digits in each place-value position until the digits are different.

STEP 1 Compare the ones.

2.495
↓
2.488

2 = 2

STEP 2 Compare the tenths.

2.495
↓
2.488

4 ◯ 4

STEP 3 Compare the hundredths.

2.495
↓
2.488

9 ◯ 8

Since 9 ◯ 8, then 2.495 ◯ 2.488, and 2.488 ◯ 2.495.

So, the height of Cloud Peak is ____________ the height of Boundary Peak.

Another Way Use a place-value chart to compare.

Compare the height of Cloud Peak to Wheeler Peak.

Ones	•	Tenths	Hundredths	Thousandths
2	•	4	9	5
2	•	4	9	3

2 = 2   4 = ______   9 = ______   5 > ______

Since 5 ◯ 3, then 2.495 ◯ 2.493, and 2.493 ◯ 2.495.

So, the height of Cloud Peak is ____________ the height of Wheeler Peak.

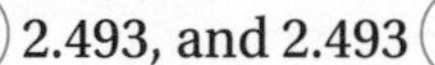

MATHEMATICAL PRACTICES 2

Reasoning Explain why it is important to line up the decimal points when comparing decimals.

Order Decimals You can use place value to order decimal numbers.

Example

Mount Whitney in California is 2.745 miles high, Mount Rainier in Washington is 2.729 miles high, and Mount Harvard in Colorado is 2.731 miles high. Order the heights of these mountains from least to greatest. Which mountain has the least height? Which mountain has the greatest height?

STEP 1

Line up the decimal points. There are the same number of ones. Circle the tenths and compare.

2.745 **Whitney**

2.729 **Rainier**

2.731 **Harvard**

There are the same number of tenths.

STEP 2

Underline the hundredths and compare. Order from least to greatest.

2.745 **Whitney**

2.729 **Rainier**

2.731 **Harvard**

Since ◯ < ◯ < ◯, the heights in order from least to greatest are ________, ________, ________.

So, ____________ has the least height and ____________ has the greatest height.

Math Talk MATHEMATICAL PRACTICES 2

Reasoning Explain why you do not compare the digits in the thousandths place to order the heights of the 3 mountains.

Try This! **Use a place-value chart.**

What is the order of 1.383, 1.321, 1.456, and 1.32 from greatest to least?

- Write each number in the place-value chart. Compare the digits, beginning with the greatest place value.
- Compare the ones. The ones are the same.
- Compare the tenths. 4 > 3.

Ones	• Tenths	Hundredths	Thousandths
1 •	3	8	3
1 •			
1 •			
1 •			

The greatest number is ________.
Circle the greatest number in the place-value chart.

- Compare the remaining hundredths. 8 > 2.

The next greatest number is ________.
Draw a rectangle around the number.

- Compare the remaining thousandths. 1 > 0.

So, the order of the numbers from greatest to least is: ________________.

Name ______________________________

Share and Show

1. Use the place-value chart to compare the two numbers. What is the greatest place-value position where the digits differ?

Ones	•	Tenths	Hundredths	Thousandths
3	•	4	7	2
3	•	4	4	5

____

Compare. Write <, >, or =.

2. 4.563 ◯ 4.536

3. 5.640 ◯ 5.64

4. 8.673 ◯ 8.637

Name the greatest place-value position where the digits differ. Name the greater number.

5. 3.579; 3.564

6. 9.572; 9.637

7. 4.159; 4.152

Order from least to greatest.

8. 4.08; 4.3; 4.803; 4.038

9. 1.703; 1.037; 1.37; 1.073

On Your Own

Compare. Write <, >, or =.

10. 8.72 ◯ 8.720

11. 5.4 ◯ 5.243

12. 1.036 ◯ 1.306

13. 2.573 ◯ 2.753

14. 9.300 ◯ 9.3

15. 6.76 ◯ 6.759

Order from greatest to least.

16. 2.007; 2.714; 2.09; 2.97

17. 0.275; 0.2; 0.572; 0.725

18. 5.249; 5.43; 5.340; 5.209

19. 0.678; 1.678; 0.587; 0.687

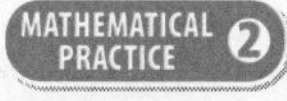

Use Reasoning **Algebra** **Find the unknown digit to make each statement true.**

20. 3.59 > 3.5 ☐ 1 > 3.572

21. 6.837 > 6.83 ☐ > 6.835

22. 2.45 < 2. ☐ 6 < 2.461

Problem Solving • Applications

Use the table for 23–26.

Mountains Over Three Miles High

Mountain and Location	Height (in miles)
Mount Blackburn, Alaska	3.104
Mount Bona, Alaska	3.134
Mount Steele, Yukon	3.152

23. In comparing the height of the mountains, which is the greatest place value where the digits differ?

____

24. MATHEMATICAL PRACTICE 6 **Use Math Vocabulary** How does the height of Mount Steele compare to the height of Mount Blackburn? Compare the heights using words.

____

____

25. GO DEEPER Explain how to order the heights of the mountains from greatest to least.

____

____

____

26. THINK SMARTER What if the height of Mount Blackburn were 0.05 mile greater? Would it then be the mountain with the greatest height? Explain.

____

____

____

27. THINK SMARTER Orlando kept a record of the total rainfall each month for 5 months.

Month	Rainfall (in.)
March	3.75
April	4.42
May	4.09
June	3.09
July	4.04

Order the months from the least amount of rainfall to the greatest amount of rainfall.

Least   Greatest

Name ______________________

Compare and Order Decimals

Practice and Homework
Lesson 3.3

Common Core COMMON CORE STANDARD—5.NBT.A.3b
Understand the place value system.

Compare. Write <, >, or =.

1. 4.735 (<) 4.74
2. 2.549 ( ) 2.549
3. 3.207 ( ) 3.027
4. 8.25 ( ) 8.250
5. 5.871 ( ) 5.781
6. 9.36 ( ) 9.359

Order from greatest to least.

7. 3.008; 3.825; 3.09; 3.18

   ____

8. 0.386; 0.3; 0.683; 0.836

   ____

Algebra **Find the unknown digit to make each statement true.**

9. 2.48 > 2.4 ___ 1 > 2.463

   ____

10. 5.723 < 5.72 ___ < 5.725

    ____

11. 7.64 < 7. ___ 5 < 7.68

    ____

Problem Solving

12. The completion times for three runners in a 100-yard dash are 9.75 seconds, 9.7 seconds, and 9.675 seconds. Which is the least time?

    ____

13. In a discus competition, an athlete threw the discus 63.37 meters, 62.95 meters, and 63.7 meters. Order the distances from least to greatest.

    ____

14. **WRITE** *Math* Write a word problem that can be solved by ordering three decimals to thousandths. Include a solution.

    ____

    ____

Lesson Check (5.NBT.A.3b)

Jay, Alana, Evan, and Stacey work together to complete a science experiment. The table at the right shows the amount of liquid left in each of their beakers at the end of the experiment.

Student	Amount of liquid (liters)
Jay	0.8
Alana	1.05
Evan	1.2
Stacey	0.75

1. Whose beaker has the greatest amount of liquid left in it?

2. Whose beaker has the least amount of liquid left in it?

Spiral Review (5.OA.A.1, 5.OA.A.2, 5.NBT.A.3a, 5.NF.B.3)

3. Janet walked 3.75 miles yesterday. What is the word form of 3.75?

4. A dance school allows a maximum of 15 students per class. If 112 students sign up for dance class, how many classes does the school need to offer to accommodate all the students?

5. What is the value of the expression $[(29 + 18) + (17 - 8)] \div 8$?

6. Cathy cut 2 apples into 6 slices each. She ate 9 slices. What expression matches the words?

FOR MORE PRACTICE GO TO THE **Personal Math Trainer**

Name ______________________________

Round Decimals

Essential Question How can you use place value to round decimals to a given place?

Common Core **Number and Operations in Base Ten—5.NBT.A.4**
MATHEMATICAL PRACTICES
MP3, MP6, MP8

Unlock the Problem (Real World)

The Gold Frog of South America is one of the smallest frogs in the world. It is 0.386 of an inch long. What is this length rounded to the nearest hundredth of an inch?

- Underline the length of the Gold Frog.
- Is the frog's length about the same as the length or the width of a large paper clip?

____

One Way Use a place-value chart.

- Write the number in a place-value chart and circle the digit in the place to which you want to round.
- In the place-value chart, underline the digit to the right of the place to which you are rounding.
- If the digit to the right is less than 5, the digit in the place to which you are rounding stays the same. If the digit to the right is 5 or greater, the digit in the rounding place increases by 1.
- Drop the digits after the place to which you are rounding.

Ones	• Tenths	Hundredths	Thousandths
0	• 3	8	6

Think: Does the digit in the rounding place stay the same or increase by 1?

So, to the nearest hundredth of an inch, a Gold Frog is about ______ of an inch long.

Another Way Use place value.

The Little Grass Frog is the smallest frog in North America. It is 0.437 of an inch long.

A **What is the length of the frog to the nearest hundredth of an inch?**

0.437 $7 > 5$
↓
0.44

So, to the nearest hundredth of an inch, the frog is about ____________ of an inch long.

B **What is the length of the frog to the nearest tenth of an inch?**

0.437 $3 < 5$
↓
0.4

So, to the nearest tenth of an inch, the frog is about ____________ of an inch long.

Example

The Goliath Frog is the largest frog in the world. It is found in the country of Cameroon in West Africa. The Goliath Frog can grow to be 11.815 inches long. How long is the Goliath Frog to the nearest inch?

STEP 1 Write 11.815 in the place-value chart.

Tens	Ones •	Tenths	Hundredths	Thousandths
	•			

STEP 2 Find the place to which you want to round. Circle the digit.

MATHEMATICAL PRACTICES 3

Apply How would your answer change if the frog were 11.286 inches long?

STEP 3 Underline the digit to the right of the place to which you are rounding. Then round.

Think: Does the digit in the rounding place stay the same or increase by 1?

So, to the nearest inch, the Goliath Frog is about ______ inches long.

- MATHEMATICAL PRACTICE 8 **Generalize** Explain why any number less than 12.5 and greater than or equal to 11.5 would round to 12 when rounded to the nearest whole number.

Try This! **Round.** 14.603

A **To the nearest hundredth:**

Tens	Ones •	Tenths	Hundredths	Thousandths
	•			

Circle and underline the digits as you did above to help you round to the nearest hundredth.

So, 14.603 rounded to the nearest hundredth is ____________.

B **To the nearest whole number:**

Tens	Ones •	Tenths	Hundredths	Thousandths
	•			

Circle and underline the digits as you did above to help you round to the nearest whole number.

So, 14.603 rounded to the nearest whole number is ____________.

Name ______________________________

Share and Show 

Write the place value of the underlined digit. Round each number to the place of the underlined digit.

1. 0.67̲3

2. 4.2̲82

3. 12̲.917

Name the place value to which each number was rounded.

4. 0.982 to 0.98

5. 3.695 to 4

6. 7.486 to 7.5

On Your Own

Write the place value of the underlined digit. Round each number to the place of the underlined digit.

7. 0.5̲92

8. 6̲.518

9. 0.80̲9

10. 3.3̲34

11. 12.0̲74

12. 4.49̲4

Name the place value to which each number was rounded.

13. 0.328 to 0.33

14. 2.607 to 2.61

15. 12.583 to 13

Round 16.748 to the place named.

16. tenths ________

17. hundredths ________

18. ones ________

19. WRITE *Math* Explain what happens when you round 4.999 to the nearest tenth.

Problem Solving • Applications

Use the table for 20–22.

Insect Speeds (meters per second)	
Insect	**Speed**
Dragonfly	6.974
Horsefly	3.934
Bumblebee	2.861
Honeybee	2.548
Housefly	1.967

20. GO DEEPER The speeds of two insects when rounded to the nearest whole number are the same. Which two insects are they?

____

21. What is the speed of the housefly rounded to the nearest hundredth?

____

22. THINK SMARTER **What's the Error?** Mark said that the speed of a dragonfly rounded to the nearest tenth was 6.9 meters per second. Is he correct? If not, what is his error?

____

____

____

WRITE ▸ Math
Show Your Work

23. MATHEMATICAL PRACTICE 6 A rounded number for the speed of an insect is 5.67 meters per second. What are the fastest and slowest speeds to the thousandths that could round to 5.67 meters per second? **Explain.**

____

____

____

____

24. THINK SMARTER The price of a certain box of cereal at the grocery store is \$0.258 per ounce. For 24a–24c, select True or False for each statement.

24a. Rounded to the nearest whole number, the price is \$1 per ounce. ○ True ○ False

24b. Rounded to the nearest tenth, the price is \$0.3 per ounce. ○ True ○ False

24c. Rounded to the nearest hundredth, the price is \$0.26 per ounce. ○ True ○ False

Name ______________________________

Round Decimals

Common Core **COMMON CORE STANDARD—5.NBT.A.4**
Understand the place value system.

Write the place value of the underlined digit. Round each number to the place of the underlined digit.

1. $0.\underline{7}82$ ______ ______

2. $\underline{4}.735$ ______ ______

3. $2.\underline{3}48$ ______ ______

4. $0.5\underline{0}6$ ______ ______

5. $15.\underline{1}86$ ______ ______

6. $8.4\underline{6}5$ ______ ______

Name the place value to which each number was rounded.

7. 0.546 to 0.55 ______

8. 4.805 to 4.8 ______

9. 6.493 to 6 ______

Round 18.194 to the place named.

10. tenths ______

11. hundredths ______

12. ones ______

Problem Solving Real World

13. The population density of Montana is 6.699 people per square mile. What is the population density per square mile of Montana rounded to the nearest whole number?

______

14. Alex is mailing an envelope that weighs 0.346 pound. What is the weight of the envelope rounded to the nearest hundredth?

______

15. WRITE Math Describe how to round 3.987 to the nearest tenth.

______
______
______

Lesson Check (5.NBT.A.4)

1. Ms. Ari buys and sells diamonds. She has a diamond that weighs 1.825 carats. What is the weight of Ms. Ari's diamond rounded to the nearest hundredth?

2. A machinist uses a special tool to measure the diameter of a small pipe. The measurement tool reads 0.276 inch. What is this measure rounded to the nearest tenth?

Spiral Review (5.NBT.A.1, 5.NBT.A.2, 5.NBT.A.3b, 5.NBT.B.6)

3. Four ice skaters participate in an ice skating competition. The table shows their scores. Who has the highest score?

Name	Points
Natasha	75.03
Taylor	75.39
Rowena	74.98
Suki	75.3

4. Write a decimal that is $\frac{1}{10}$ of 0.9.

5. The population of Foxville is about 12×10^3 people. Which is another way to write this number?

6. Joseph needs to find the quotient of $3,216 \div 8$. In what place is the first digit in the quotient?

Name ______________________________

Decimal Addition

Essential Question How can you use base-ten blocks to model decimal addition?

Number and Operations in Base Ten—5.NBT.B.7

MATHEMATICAL PRACTICES
MP5, MP6, MP8

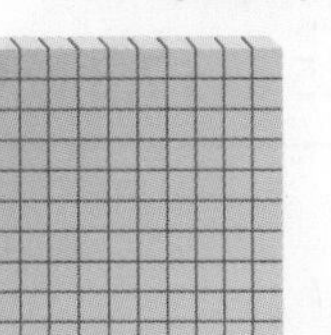

1 one | 0.1 one tenth | 0.01 one hundredth

CONNECT You can use base-ten blocks to help you find sums of decimals.

Investigate

Hands On

Materials ■ base-ten blocks

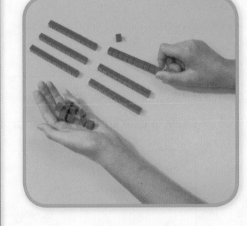

A. Use base-ten blocks to model the sum of 0.34 and 0.27.

B. Add the hundredths first by combining them.

- Do you need to regroup the hundredths? Explain.

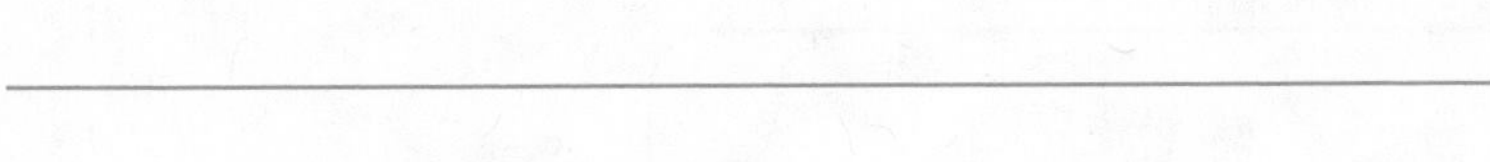

C. Add the tenths by combining them.

- Do you need to regroup the tenths? Explain.

D. Record the sum. $0.34 + 0.27 =$ ________

Draw Conclusions

1. **What if** you combine the tenths first and then the hundredths? Explain how you would regroup.

2. MATHEMATICAL PRACTICE 6 If you add two decimals that are each greater than 0.5, will the sum be less than or greater than 1.0? **Explain.**

Make Connections

You can use a quick picture to add decimals greater than 1.

STEP 1

Model the sum of 2.5 and 2.8 with a quick picture.

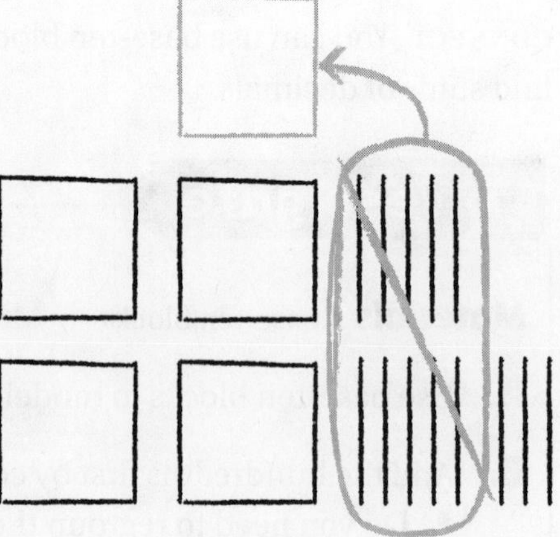

STEP 2

Add the tenths.

- Are there more than 9 tenths? ______
  If there are more than 9 tenths, regroup.

Add the ones.

STEP 3

Draw a quick picture of your answer. Then record.

2.5 + 2.8 = ______

Share and Show

Complete the quick picture to find the sum.

1. 1.37 + 1.85 = ______

MATHEMATICAL PRACTICES 8

Generalize Explain how you know where to write the decimal point in the sum.

Name ______________________

Add. Draw a quick picture.

2. $0.9 + 0.7 =$ ________

3. $0.65 + 0.73 =$ ________

4. $1.3 + 0.7 =$ ________

5. $2.72 + 0.51 =$ ________

Problem Solving • Applications

Personal Math Trainer

6. THINK SMARTER + Carissa bought 2.35 pounds of chicken and 2.7 pounds of turkey for lunches this week. She used a quick picture to find the amount of lunch meat. Does Carissa's work make sense? Explain.

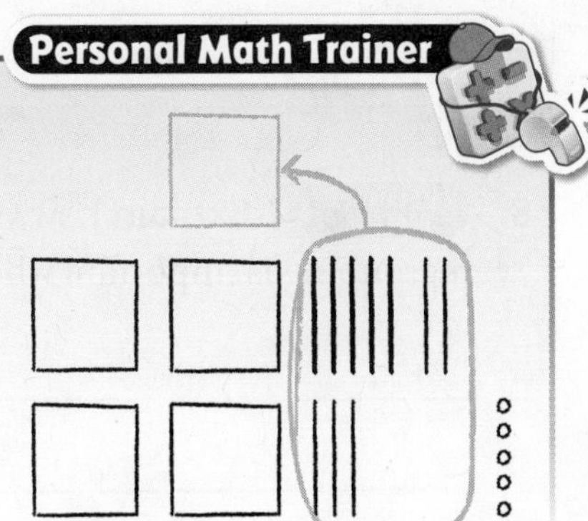

____

____

____

Math Talk MATHEMATICAL PRACTICES 6

Explain how you solved Exercise 4.

THINKSMARTER Sense or Nonsense?

7. Robyn and Jim used quick pictures to model 1.85 + 2.73.

Robyn's Work

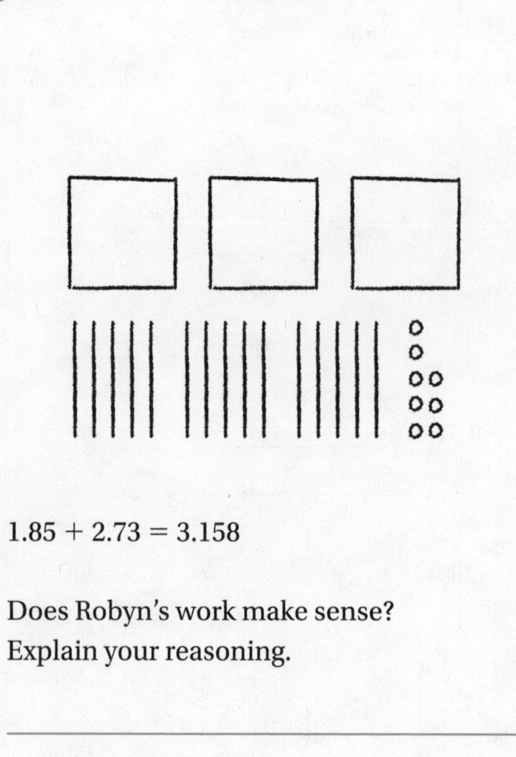

1.85 + 2.73 = 3.158

Does Robyn's work make sense? Explain your reasoning.

Jim's Work

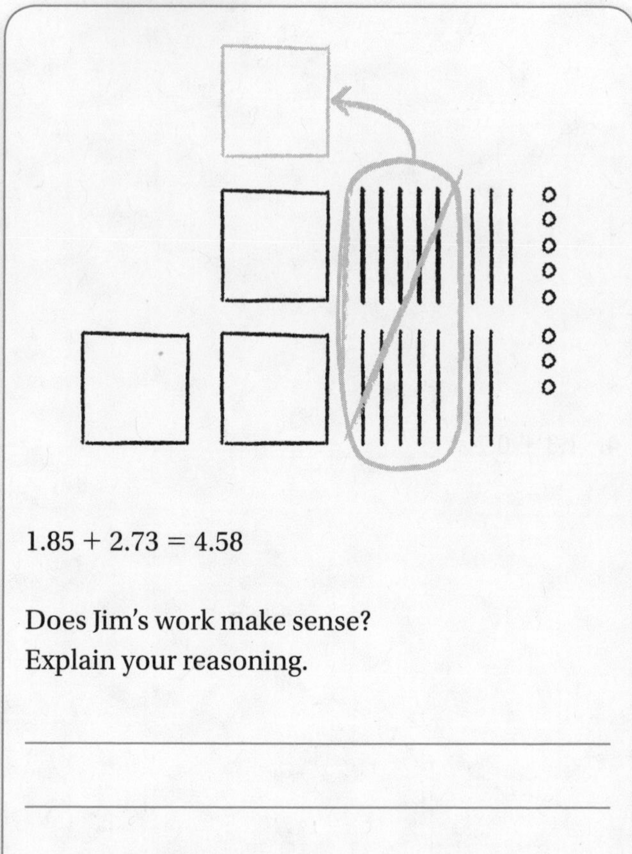

1.85 + 2.73 = 4.58

Does Jim's work make sense? Explain your reasoning.

8. MATHEMATICAL PRACTICE 6 **Explain** how you would help Robyn understand that regrouping is important when adding decimals.

9. GO DEEPER Write a decimal addition problem that requires regrouping the hundredths. Explain how you know you will need to regroup.

Name ______________________

Decimal Addition

Common Core **COMMON CORE STANDARD—5.NBT.B.7**
Perform operations with multi-digit whole numbers and with decimals to hundredths.

Add. Draw a quick picture.

1. 0.5 + 0.6 = 1.1 **2.** 0.15 + 0.36 = ________ **3.** 0.8 + 0.7 = ________

4. 0.35 + 0.64 = ________ **5.** 0.54 + 0.12 = ________ **6.** 0.51 + 0.28 = ________

Problem Solving Real World

7. Draco bought 0.6 pound of bananas and 0.9 pound of grapes at the farmers' market. What is the total weight of the fruit?

____

8. Nancy biked 2.65 miles in the morning and 3.19 miles in the afternoon. What total distance did she bike?

____

9. WRITE ▸ *Math* Explain why drawing a quick picture is helpful when adding decimals.

____

____

____

Lesson Check (5.NBT.B.7)

1. What is the sum of 2.5 and 1.9?

2. Keisha walked 0.65 hour in the morning and 0.31 hour in the evening. How many hours did she walk altogether?

Spiral Review (5.OA.A.1, 5.NBT.B.5, 5.NBT.B.6)

3. Jodi walks 35 minutes a day. If she walks for 240 days, how many minutes altogether does Jodi walk?

4. The Speeders soccer team charged $12 to wash each car at a fundraiser car wash. The team collected a total of $672 by the end of the day. How many cars did the team wash?

5. David records the number of visitors to the snake exhibit each day for 6 days. His data are shown in the table. If admission is $7 per person, how much money did the snake exhibit make over the 6 days?

Visitors to the Snake Exhibit					
30	25	44	12	25	32

6. What is the value of the expression?

$$6 + 18 \div 3 \times 4$$

FOR MORE PRACTICE GO TO THE Personal Math Trainer

Name ______________________________

Lesson 3.6

Decimal Subtraction

Essential Question How can you use base-ten blocks to model decimal subtraction?

Number and Operations in Base Ten—5.NBT.B.7

MATHEMATICAL PRACTICES
MP2, MP5, MP8

CONNECT You can use base-ten blocks to help you find the difference between two decimals.

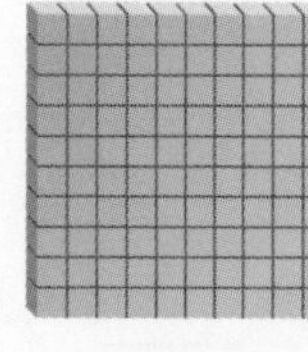

1 one | 0.1 one tenth | 0.01 one hundredth

Investigate

Materials ■ base-ten blocks

A. Use base-ten blocks to find 0.84 − 0.56.
Model 0.84.

B. Subtract 0.56. Start by removing 6 hundredths.

- Do you need to regroup to subtract? **Explain.**

____

____

C. Subtract the tenths. Remove 5 tenths.

D. Record the difference. 0.84 − 0.56 = ____________

Draw Conclusions

1. **What if** you remove the tenths first and then the hundredths? Explain how you would regroup.

____

____

2. MATHEMATICAL PRACTICE 8 **Generalize** If two decimals are both less than 1.0, what do you know about the difference between them? Explain.

____

____

Make Connections

You can use quick pictures to subtract decimals that need to be regrouped.

STEP 1

- Use a quick picture to model 2.82 − 1.47.
- Subtract the hundredths.
- Are there enough hundredths to remove? ________
  If there are not enough hundredths, regroup.

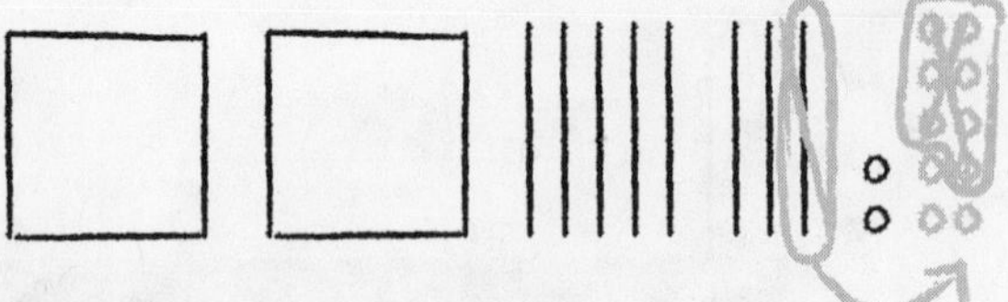

STEP 2

- Subtract the tenths.
- Are there enough tenths to remove? ________
  If there are not enough tenths, regroup.
- Subtract the ones.

STEP 3

Draw a quick picture of your answer. Then record the answer.

$2.82 - 1.47 =$ ____________

MATHEMATICAL PRACTICES 2

Reasoning Explain why you have to regroup in Step 1.

Name ___________________________

Share and Show

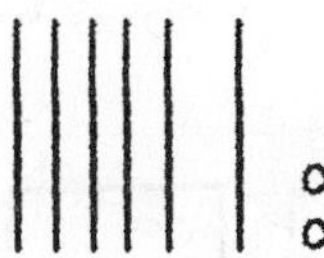

Complete the quick picture to find the difference.

1. 0.62 − 0.18 = ____________

Subtract. Draw a quick picture.

2. 3.41 − 1.74 = ____________

3. 0.84 − 0.57 = ____________

4. 4.05 − 1.61 = ____________

5. 1.37 − 0.52 = ____________

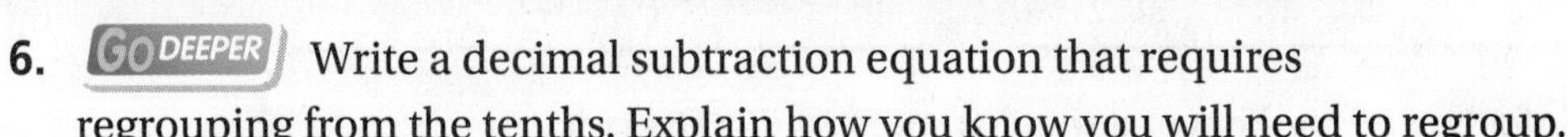

Problem Solving • Applications

6. GO DEEPER Write a decimal subtraction equation that requires regrouping from the tenths. Explain how you know you will need to regroup.

____

____

____

MATHEMATICAL PRACTICES 5

Use Tools Explain how you can use a quick picture to find 0.81 − 0.46.

THINK SMARTER Pose a Problem

7. Antonio left his MathBoard on his desk during lunch. The quick picture below shows the problem he was working on when he left.

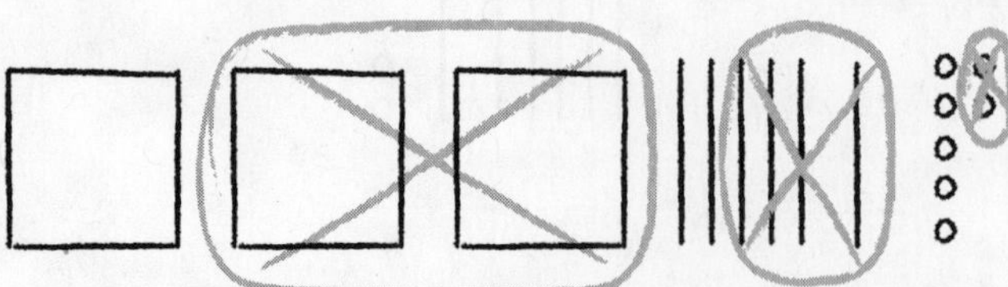

Write a word problem that can be solved using the quick picture above.

Pose a problem.

Solve your problem.

- MATHEMATICAL PRACTICE 2 **Use Reasoning** Describe how you can change the problem by changing the quick picture.

8. THINK SMARTER The price of a box of markers at a retail store is \$4.65. The price of a box of markers at the school bookstore is \$3.90. How much more do the markers cost at the retail store? Explain how you can use a quick picture to solve the problem.

Name ________________________

Decimal Subtraction

Practice and Homework Lesson 3.6

COMMON CORE STANDARD—5.NBT.B.7
Perform operations with multi-digit whole numbers and with decimals to hundredths.

Subtract. Draw a quick picture.

1. 0.7 − 0.2 = 0.5

2. 0.45 − 0.24 = ________

3. 0.92 − 0.51 = ________

4. 4.1 − 2.7 = ________

5. 3.12 − 2.52 = ________

6. 3.6 − 1.8 = ________

Problem Solving Real World

7. Yelina made a training plan to run 5.6 miles per day. So far, she has run 3.1 miles today. How much farther does she have to run to meet her goal for today?

____

8. Tim cut a 2.3-foot length of pipe from a pipe that was 4.1 feet long. How long is the remaining piece of pipe?

____

9. WRITE ▸ *Math* Describe a problem involving decimals that you would use a quick picture to solve. Then solve the problem.

____

____

____

Lesson Check (5.NBT.B.7)

1. Janice wants to jog 3.25 miles on the treadmill. She has jogged 1.63 miles. How much farther does she have to jog to meet her goal?

2. A new teen magazine has a readership goal of 3.5 million. Its current readership is 2.8 million. How much does its readership need to increase to meet this goal?

Spiral Review (5.OA.A.1, 5.NBT.A.1, 5.NBT.A.2, 5.NBT.B.6)

3. What is the value of the underlined digit in 91,<u>7</u>64,350?

4. How many zeros are in the product $(6 \times 5) \times 10^3$?

5. To evaluate the following expression, what step should you do first?

$$7 \times (4 + 16) \div 4 - 2$$

6. In the past two weeks, Sue earned $513 at her part-time job. She worked a total of 54 hours. About how much did Sue earn per hour?

FOR MORE PRACTICE GO TO THE **Personal Math Trainer**

Name ________________________

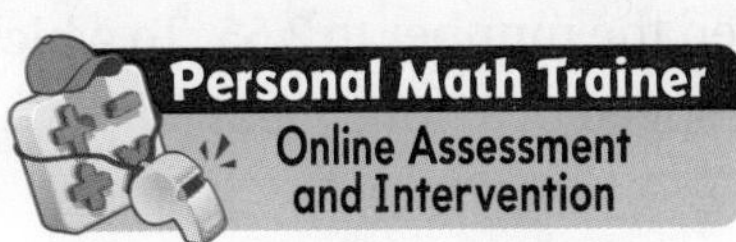

Concepts and Skills

1. **Explain** how you can use base-ten blocks to find 1.54 + 2.37. (5.NBT.B.7)

____

____

____

Complete the sentence. (5.NBT.A.1)

2. 0.04 is $\frac{1}{10}$ of __________.

3. 0.06 is 10 times as much as __________.

Write the value of the underlined digit. (5.NBT.A.3a)

4. 6.5<u>4</u>

5. 0.<u>8</u>37

6. 8.70<u>2</u>

7. <u>9</u>.173

Compare. Write <, >, or =. (5.NBT.A.3b)

8. 6.52 ◯ 6.520

9. 3.589 ◯ 3.598

10. 8.483 ◯ 8.463

Write the place value of the underlined digit. Round each number to the place of the underlined digit. (5.NBT.A.4)

11. 0.<u>7</u>24

12. <u>2</u>.576

13. 4.7<u>6</u>9

Draw a quick picture to find the sum or difference. (5.NBT.B.7)

14. 2.46 + 0.78 = __________

15. 3.27 − 1.84 = __________

16. Marco read that a honeybee can fly up to 2.548 meters per second. He rounded the number to 2.55. To which place value did Marco round the speed of a honeybee? (5.NBT.A.4)

____

17. What is the relationship between 0.04 and 0.004? (5.NBT.A.1)

____

18. Jodi drew a quick picture to model the answer for 3.14 − 1.75. Draw what her picture might look like. (5.NBT.B.7)

19. The average annual rainfall in California is 0.564 of a meter per year. What is the value of the digit 4 in that number? (5.NBT.A.3a)

____

20. Jan ran 1.256 miles on Monday, 1.265 miles on Wednesday, and 1.268 miles on Friday. What were her distances from greatest to least? (5.NBT.A.3b)

____

Name ______________________

Estimate Decimal Sums and Differences

Essential Question How can you estimate decimal sums and differences?

Number and Operations in Base Ten—5.NBT.B.7

MATHEMATICAL PRACTICES
MP2, MP5, MP6

Unlock the Problem

A singer is recording a CD. The lengths of the three songs are 3.4 minutes, 2.78 minutes, and 4.19 minutes. About how much recording time will be on the CD?

Use rounding to estimate.

Remember

To round a number, determine the place to which you want to round.

- If the digit to the right is less than 5, the digit in the rounding place stays the same.
- If the digit to the right is 5 or greater, the digit in the rounding place increases by 1.

Round to the nearest whole number. Then add.

$$\begin{array}{r} 3.4 \\ 2.78 \\ +\,4.19 \\ \hline \end{array} \qquad \begin{array}{r} 3 \\ \square \\ +\,\square \\ \hline \square \end{array}$$

So, there will be about ______ minutes of recording time on the CD.

Try This! Use rounding to estimate.

A Round to the nearest whole dollar. Then subtract.

$$\begin{array}{r} \$27.95 \\ -\,\$11.72 \\ \hline \end{array}$$

To the nearest dollar, \$27.95 – \$11.72 is about __________.

B Round to the nearest ten dollars. Then subtract.

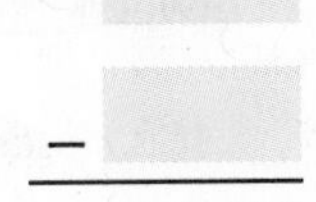

$$\begin{array}{r} \$27.95 \\ -\,\$11.72 \\ \hline \end{array}$$

To the nearest ten dollars, \$27.95 – \$11.72 is about __________.

- MATHEMATICAL PRACTICE 5 **Use Appropriate Tools** Do you want an overestimate or an underestimate when you estimate the total cost of items you want to buy? Explain.

____

____

____

Use Benchmarks Benchmarks are familiar numbers used as points of reference. You can use the benchmarks 0, 0.25, 0.50, 0.75, and 1 to estimate decimal sums and differences.

Example 1 Use benchmarks to estimate. 0.18 + 0.43

Locate and graph a point on the number line for each decimal. Identify which benchmark each decimal is closer to.

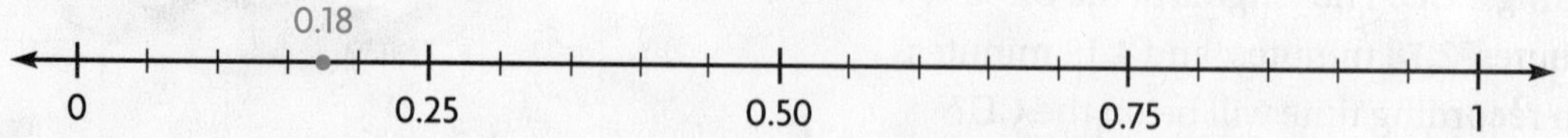

Think: 0.18 is between 0 and 0.25.

It is closer to ______.

Think: 0.43 is between ______ and ______. It is closer to ______.

0.18 + 0.43

↓ ↓

______ + ______ = ______

So, 0.18 + 0.43 is about ______.

Example 2 Use benchmarks to estimate. 0.76 − 0.22

Locate and graph a point on the number line for each decimal. Identify which benchmark each decimal is closer to.

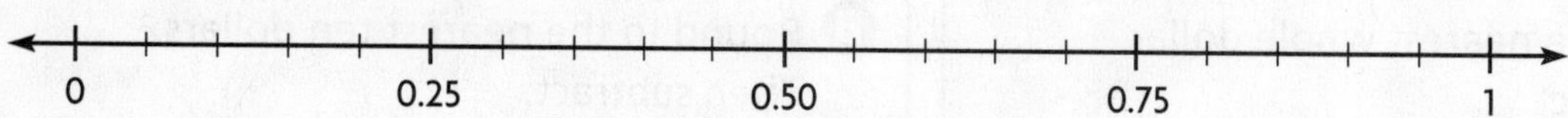

Think: 0.76 is between ______ and ______. It is closer to ______.

Think: 0.22 is between 0 and 0.25. It is closer to ______.

0.76 − 0.22

↓ ↓

______ − ______ = ______

So, 0.76 − 0.22 is about ______.

MATHEMATICAL PRACTICES 5

Use Tools Can you get different answers when using rounding or benchmarks to estimate a decimal difference? Use Example 2 to explain.

Name ______________________________

Share and Show

Use rounding to estimate.

1.
$$\begin{array}{r} 2.34 \\ 1.9 \\ +\ 5.23 \\ \hline \end{array}$$

2.
$$\begin{array}{r} 9.65 \\ -\ 3.12 \\ \hline \end{array}$$

✓ 3.
$$\begin{array}{r} \$19.75 \\ +\ \$\ 3.98 \\ \hline \end{array}$$

Use benchmarks to estimate.

4.
$$\begin{array}{r} 0.34 \\ 0.1 \\ +\ 0.25 \\ \hline \end{array}$$

✓ 5.
$$\begin{array}{r} 10.39 \\ -\ 4.28 \\ \hline \end{array}$$

MATHEMATICAL PRACTICES 6

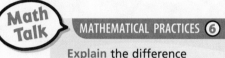

Explain the difference between an estimate and an exact answer.

On Your Own

Use rounding to estimate.

6.
$$\begin{array}{r} 0.93 \\ +\ 0.18 \\ \hline \end{array}$$

7.
$$\begin{array}{r} 7.41 \\ -\ 3.88 \\ \hline \end{array}$$

8.
$$\begin{array}{r} 14.68 \\ -\ 9.93 \\ \hline \end{array}$$

Use benchmarks to estimate.

9.
$$\begin{array}{r} 12.41 \\ -\ 6.47 \\ \hline \end{array}$$

10.
$$\begin{array}{r} 8.12 \\ +\ 5.52 \\ \hline \end{array}$$

11.
$$\begin{array}{r} 9.75 \\ -\ 3.47 \\ \hline \end{array}$$

Practice: Copy and Solve **Use rounding or benchmarks to estimate.**

12. 12.83 + 16.24

13. \$26.92 − \$11.13

14. 9.41 + 3.82

MATHEMATICAL PRACTICE 2 **Use Reasoning** **Estimate to compare. Write < or >.**

15. 2.74 + 4.22 ◯ 3.13 + 1.87

______ estimate ______ estimate

16. 6.25 − 2.39 ◯ 9.79 − 3.84

______ estimate ______ estimate

Problem Solving • Applications

Use the table to solve 17–18. Show your work.

17. For the week of April 4, 1964, the Beatles had the top four songs. About how long would it take to listen to these four songs?

Top Songs

Number	Song Title	Song Length (in minutes)
1	"Can't Buy Me Love"	2.30
2	"She Loves You"	2.50
3	"I Want to Hold Your Hand"	2.75
4	"Please Please Me"	2.00

18. **What's the Error?** Isabelle says she can listen to the first three songs in the table in 6 minutes.

19. THINK SMARTER Tracy ran a lap around the school track in 74.2 seconds. Malcolm ran a lap in 65.92 seconds. Estimate the difference in the times in which the students completed the lap.

Connect to Science

Nutrition

Your body needs protein to build and repair cells. You should get a new supply of protein each day. The average 10-year-old needs 35 grams of protein daily. You can find protein in foods like meat, vegetables, and dairy products.

Grams of Protein per Serving

Type of Food	Protein (in grams)
1 scrambled egg	6.75
1 cup shredded wheat cereal	5.56
1 oat bran muffin	3.99
1 cup low-fat milk	8.22

Use estimation to solve.

20. GO DEEPER Gina had a scrambled egg and a cup of low-fat milk for breakfast. She had an oat bran muffin for a morning snack. About how many more grams of protein did Gina have for breakfast than for a snack?

21. THINK SMARTER Pablo had a cup of shredded wheat cereal, a cup of low-fat milk, and one other item for breakfast. He had about 21 grams of protein. What was the third item Pablo had for breakfast?

Name ______________________

Estimate Decimal Sums and Differences

COMMON CORE STANDARD—5.NBT.B.7
Perform operations with multi-digit whole numbers and with decimals to hundredths.

Use rounding to estimate.

1. $\begin{array}{r} 5.38 \\ +6.14 \\ \hline \end{array}$

   $\begin{array}{r} 5 \\ +6 \\ \hline 11 \end{array}$

   ____

2. $\begin{array}{r} 2.57 \\ +0.14 \\ \hline \end{array}$

   ____

3. $\begin{array}{r} 10.39 \\ -4.28 \\ \hline \end{array}$

   ____

4. $\begin{array}{r} 7.92 \\ +5.37 \\ \hline \end{array}$

   ____

Use benchmarks to estimate.

5. $\begin{array}{r} 2.81 \\ +3.72 \\ \hline \end{array}$

   ____

6. $\begin{array}{r} 12.54 \\ +7.98 \\ \hline \end{array}$

   ____

7. $\begin{array}{r} 6.34 \\ +3.95 \\ \hline \end{array}$

   ____

8. $\begin{array}{r} 16.18 \\ -5.94 \\ \hline \end{array}$

   ____

Problem Solving

9. Elian bought 1.87 pounds of chicken and 2.46 pounds of turkey at the deli. About how many pounds of meat did he buy?

   ____

10. Jenna bought a gallon of milk at the store for $3.58. About how much change did she receive from a $20 bill?

   ____

11. **WRITE** *Math* Explain why estimation is an important skill to know when adding and subtracting decimals.

____

____

____

Lesson Check (5.NBT.B.7)

1. Regina has two electronic files. One has a size of 3.15 MB and the other has a size of 4.89 MB. What is the best estimate of the total size of the two electronic files?

2. Madison is training for a marathon. Her goal is to run 26.2 miles a day. She currently can run 18.5 miles in a day. About how many more miles does she need to run in a day to meet her goal?

Spiral Review (5.NBT.A.1, 5.NBT.A.3b, 5.NBT.A.4, 5.NBT.B.6)

3. A machine prints 8 banners in 120 seconds. How many seconds does it take to print one banner?

4. To what place value is the number rounded?

   5.319 to 5.3

5. The average distance from Mars to the Sun is about one hundred forty-one million, six hundred twenty thousand miles. How is this distance written in standard form?

6. Logan ate 1.438 pounds of grapes. His brother Ralph ate 1.44 pounds of grapes. Which brother ate more grapes?

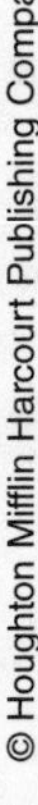

FOR MORE PRACTICE GO TO THE **Personal Math Trainer**

Name ________________________

Add Decimals

Essential Question How can place value help you add decimals?

Common Core **Number and Operations in Base Ten—5.NBT.B.7**

MATHEMATICAL PRACTICES
MP1, MP2, MP8

Unlock the Problem Real World

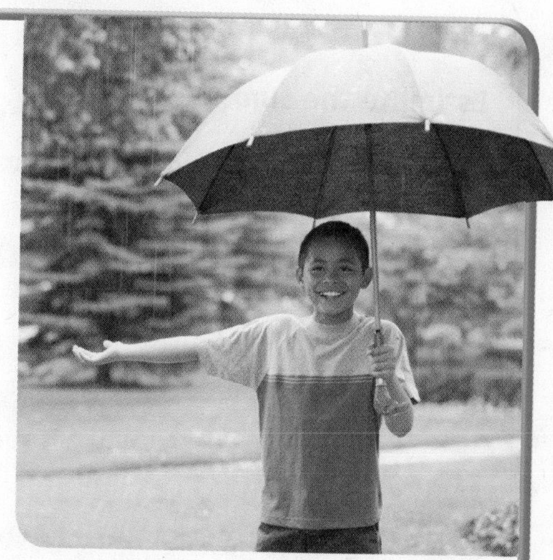

Henry recorded the amount of rain that fell during 2 hours. In the first hour, Henry measured 2.35 centimeters of rain. In the second hour, he measured 1.82 centimeters of rain.

Henry estimated that about 4 centimeters of rain fell in 2 hours. What is the total amount of rain that fell? How can you use this estimate to decide if your answer is reasonable?

Add. 2.35 + 1.82

- Add the hundredths first.

  5 hundredths + 2 hundredths = _______ hundredths.

- Then add the tenths and ones. Regroup as needed.

  3 tenths + 8 tenths = _______ tenths. Regroup.

  2 ones + 1 one + 1 regrouped one = _______ ones.

- Record the sum for each place value.

Draw a quick picture to check your work.

Math Talk MATHEMATICAL PRACTICES 8

Generalize Explain how you know when you need to regroup in a decimal addition problem.

So, _______ centimeters of rain fell.

Since _______ is close to the estimate, 4, the answer is reasonable.

Equivalent Decimals When adding decimals, you can use equivalent decimals to help keep the numbers aligned in each place. Write zeros to the right of the last digit as needed, so that the addends have the same number of decimal places.

Try This! **Estimate. Then find the sum.**

STEP 1

Estimate the sum.

20.4 + 13.76

↓ ↓

Estimate: 20 + 14 = ______

20.40 + 13.76 = ______

STEP 2

Find the sum.

Add the hundredths first.
Then, add the tenths, ones, and tens.
Regroup as needed.

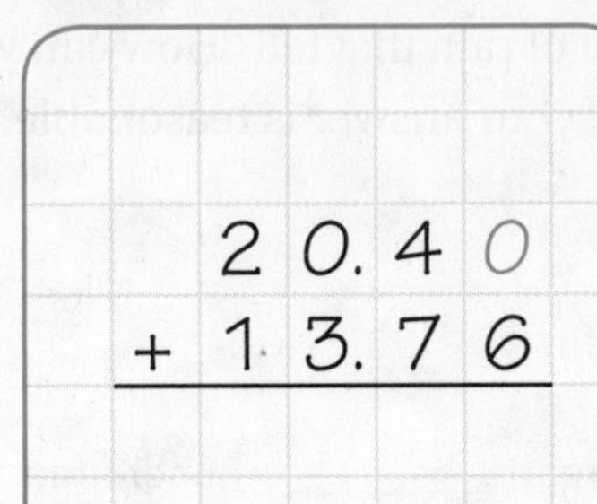

Think: 20.4 = 20.40

- **Evaluate Reasonableness** Is your answer reasonable? Explain.

______

Share and Show

MATH BOARD

Estimate. Then find the sum.

1. Estimate: ______

$$\begin{array}{r} 2.5 \\ +4.6 \\ \hline \end{array}$$

2. Estimate: ______

$$\begin{array}{r} 8.75 \\ +6.43 \\ \hline \end{array}$$

3. Estimate: ______

$$\begin{array}{r} 2.03 \\ +7.89 \\ \hline \end{array}$$

4. Estimate: ______

6.34 + 3.8 = ______

5. Estimate: ______

5.63 + 2.6 = ______

Math Talk

MATHEMATICAL PRACTICES 2

Reasoning Explain why it is important to remember to line up the place values in each number when adding or subtracting decimals.

Name ______________________________

On Your Own

Connect Symbols and Words **Find the sum.**

6. seven and twenty-five hundredths added to nine and four tenths

7. twelve and eight hundredths added to four and thirty-five hundredths

8. nineteen and seven tenths added to four and ninety-two hundredths

9. one and eighty-two hundredths added to fifteen and eight tenths

Practice: Copy and Solve **Find the sum.**

10. 7.99 + 8.34

11. 15.76 + 8.2

12. 9.6 + 5.49

13. 33.5 + 16.4

14. 9.84 + 21.52

15. 3.89 + 4.6

16. 42.19 + 8.8

17. 16.74 + 5.34

18. 27.58 + 83.9

19. THINKSMARTER Tania measured the growth of her plant each week. The first week, the plant's height measured 2.65 decimeters. During the second week, Tania's plant grew 0.7 decimeter. How tall was Tania's plant at the end of the second week? Describe the steps you took to solve the problem.

20. GO DEEPER Maggie had $35.13. Then her mom gave her $7.50 for watching her younger brother. She was paid $10.35 for her old roller skates. How much money does Maggie have now?

Unlock the Problem 

21. A city receives an average rainfall of 16.99 centimeters in August. One year, during the month of August, it rained 8.33 centimeters by August 15th. Then it rained another 4.65 centimeters through the end of the month. What was the total rainfall in centimeters for the month?

a. What do you need to find?

____

b. What information are you given?

____

____

c. How will you use addition to find the total number of centimeters of rain that fell?

____

d. Show how you solved the problem.

e. Complete the sentence. It rained ________ centimeters for the month.

Personal Math Trainer

22. THINKSMARTER+ Horatio caught a fish that weighed 1.25 pounds. Later he caught another fish that weighed 1.92 pounds. What was the combined weight of both fish? Use the digits on the tiles to solve the problem. Digits may be used more than once or not at all.

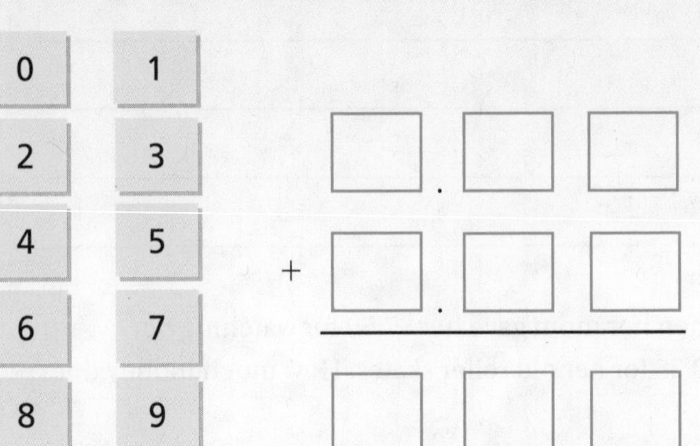

Name ______________________

Add Decimals

Common Core **COMMON CORE STANDARD—5.NBT.B.7**
Perform operations with multi-digit whole numbers and with decimals to hundredths.

Estimate. Then find the sum.

1. Estimate: ______

$$\begin{array}{r} 2.85 \\ +7.29 \\ \hline \end{array}$$

$$\begin{array}{r} {}^{1\,1} \\ 2.85 \\ +7.29 \\ \hline 10.14 \end{array}$$

2. Estimate: ______

$$\begin{array}{r} 4.23 \\ +6.51 \\ \hline \end{array}$$

______

3. Estimate: ______

$$\begin{array}{r} 6.8 \\ +4.2 \\ \hline \end{array}$$

______

4. Estimate: ______

$$\begin{array}{r} 2.7 \\ +5.37 \\ \hline \end{array}$$

______

Find the sum.

5. 6.8 + 4.4 ______

6. 6.87 + 5.18 ______

7. 3.14 + 2.9 ______

8. 16.18 + 5.94 ______

Problem Solving Real World

9. Marcela's dog gained 4.1 kilograms in two months. Two months ago, the dog's mass was 5.6 kilograms. What is the dog's current mass?

____

10. During last week's storm, 2.15 inches of rain fell on Monday and 1.68 inches of rain fell on Tuesday. What was the total amount of rainfall on both days?

____

11. WRITE *Math* Describe an addition problem that you may need to regroup hundredths to solve.

____

____

Lesson Check (5.NBT.B.7)

1. Lindsay has two packages she wants to mail. One package weighs 6.3 ounces, and the other package weighs 4.9 ounces. How much do the packages weigh together?

2. Anton rode his mountain bike three days in a row. He biked 12.1 miles on the first day, 13.4 miles on the second day, and 17.9 miles on the third day. How many total miles did Anton bike during the three days?

Spiral Review (5.NBT.A.1, 5.NBT.A.2, 5.NBT.B.6)

3. In the number 2,145,857, how does the digit 5 in the thousands place compare to the digit 5 in the tens place?

4. What is the value of 10^5?

5. Carmen works at a pet store. To feed 8 cats, she empties four 6-ounce cans of cat food into a large bowl. Carmen divides the food equally among the cats. How many ounces of food will each cat get?

6. There are 112 students in the Hammond Middle School marching band. The band director wants the students to march with 14 students in each row for the upcoming parade. How many rows will there be?

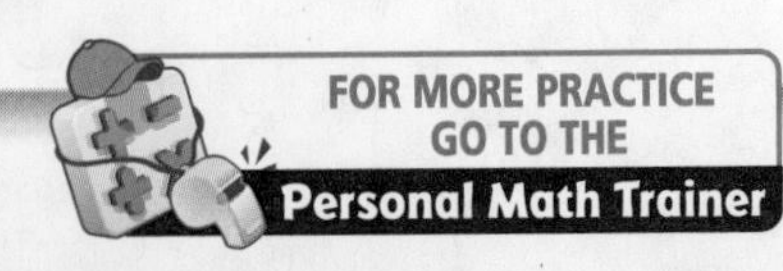

Name ______________________________

Subtract Decimals

Essential Question How can place value help you subtract decimals?

Number and Operations in Base Ten—5.NBT.B.7

MATHEMATICAL PRACTICES
MP1, MP2, MP5

Unlock the Problem (Real World)

Hannah has 3.36 kilograms of apples and 2.28 kilograms of oranges. Hannah estimates she has about 1 more kilogram of apples than oranges. How many more kilograms of apples than oranges does Hannah have? How can you use this estimate to decide if your answer is reasonable?

- What operation will you use to solve the problem?

  ____

- Circle Hannah's estimate to check that your answer is reasonable.

Subtract. 3.36 − 2.28

- Subtract the hundredths first. If there are not enough hundredths, regroup 1 tenth as 10 hundredths.

  ______ hundredths − 8 hundredths = 8 hundredths

- Then subtract the tenths and ones. Regroup as needed.

  ______ tenths − 2 tenths = 0 tenths

  ______ ones − 2 ones = 1 one

- Record the difference for each place value.

$$\begin{array}{r} 3.36 \\ -\ 2.28 \\ \hline \end{array}$$

Draw a quick picture to check your work.

So, Hannah has __________ more kilograms of apples than oranges.

Since __________ is close to 1, the answer is reasonable.

Math Talk MATHEMATICAL PRACTICES 2

Reasoning Explain how you know when to regroup in a decimal subtraction problem.

Try This! **Use addition to check.**

Since subtraction and addition are inverse operations, you can check subtraction by adding.

STEP 1

Find the difference.

Subtract the hundredths first.

Then, subtract the tenths, ones, and tens. Regroup as needed.

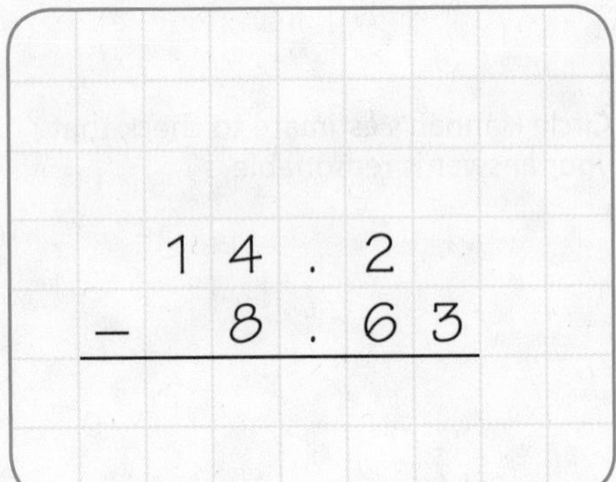

STEP 2

Check your answer.

Add the difference to the number you subtracted. If the sum matches the number you subtracted from, your answer is correct.

	← difference
+ 8.63	← number subtracted
	← number subtracted from

- MATHEMATICAL PRACTICE 1 **Evaluate** Is your answer correct? Explain.

Share and Show MATH BOARD

Estimate. Then find the difference.

1. Estimate: ______

5.83
−2.18

2. Estimate: ______

4.45
−1.86

3. Estimate: ______

4.03
−2.25

Find the difference. Check your answer.

4.

0.70
− 0.43

5.

13.2
− 8.04

6.

15.8
− 9.67

Name ___________________________

On Your Own

MATHEMATICAL PRACTICE 2 **Connect Symbols and Words** **Find the difference.**

7. three and seventy-two hundredths subtracted from five and eighty-one hundredths

____

8. one and six hundredths subtracted from eight and thirty-two hundredths

____

MATHEMATICAL PRACTICE 2 **Use Reasoning** **Algebra** **Write the unknown number for n.**

9. $5.28 - 3.4 = n$

$n =$ _______________

10. $n - 6.47 = 4.32$

$n =$ _______________

11. $11.57 - n = 7.51$

$n =$ _______________

Practice: Copy and Solve **Find the difference.**

12. $8.42 - 5.14$

13. $16.46 - 13.87$

14. $34.27 - 17.51$

15. $15.83 - 11.45$

16. $12.74 - 10.54$

17. $48.21 - 13.65$

WRITE Math • Show Your Work

18. GO DEEPER Beth finished a race in 3.35 minutes. Ana finished the race in 0.8 minute less than Beth. Fran finished the race in 1.02 minutes less than Ana. What was Fran's time to finish the race in minutes?

____

19. Fatima planted sunflower seeds in a flower patch. The tallest sunflower grew 2.65 meters tall. The height of the shortest sunflower was 0.34 meter less than the tallest sunflower. What was the height, in meters, of the shortest sunflower?

____

Unlock the Problem

20. THINKSMARTER In peanut butter, how many more grams of protein are there than grams of carbohydrates? Use the label at the right.

PEANUT BUTTER
Nutrition Facts
Serving Size 2 Tbsp (32.0 g)

Amount Per Serving	
Calories	190
Calories from Fat	190
	% Daily Value*
Total Fat 16g	25%
Saturated Fat 3g	18%
Polyunsaturated Fat 4.4g	
Monounsaturated Fat 7.8g	
Cholesterol 0mg	0%
Sodium 5mg	0%
Total Carbohydrates 6.2g	2%
Dietary Fiber 1.9g	8%
Sugars 2.5g	8%
Protein 8.1g	

*Based on a 2,000 calorie diet

a. What do you need to know? ____________

____

____

b. How will you use subtraction to find how many more grams of protein there are than grams of carbohydrates?

____

____

c. Show how you solved the problem.

d. Complete each sentence.

The peanut butter has ______ grams of protein.

The peanut butter has ______ grams of carbohydrates.

There are ______ more grams of protein than grams of carbohydrates in the peanut butter.

21. Kyle is building a block tower. Right now the tower stands 0.89 meter tall. How much higher does the tower need to be to reach a height of 1.74 meters?

____

22. THINKSMARTER Dialyn scored 2.5 points higher than Gina at a gymnastics event. Select the values that could represent each student's gymnastics score. Mark all that apply.

Ⓐ Dialyn: 18.4 points, Gina: 16.9 points

Ⓑ Dialyn: 15.4 points, Gina: 13.35 points

Ⓒ Dialyn: 16.2 points, Gina: 13.7 points

Ⓓ Dialyn: 19.25 points, Gina: 16.75 points

Name ______________________

Subtract Decimals

Common Core **COMMON CORE STANDARD—5.NBT.B.7**
Perform operations with multi-digit whole numbers and with decimals to hundredths.

Estimate. Then find the difference.

1. Estimate: 3

   6.5
   −3.9

   5 15
   6.5
   −3.9
   2.6

2. Estimate: ______

   4.23
   −2.51

3. Estimate: ______

   8.6
   −5.1

4. Estimate: ______

   2.71
   −1.34

Find the difference. Check your answer.

5. 16.3
   − 4.4

6. 12.56
   − 5.18

7. 11.63 − 6.7

8. 5.24 − 2.14

Problem Solving Real World

9. The height of a tree sapling was 3.15 inches last year. This year, the height is 5.38 inches. How much did the height of the tree sapling increase?

10. The temperature decreased from 71.5°F to 56.8°F overnight. How much did the temperature drop?

11. WRITE Math Write a decimal subtraction problem that requires regrouping to solve. Then solve the problem.

Lesson Check (5.NBT.B.7)

1. During training, Janice kayaked 4.68 miles on Monday and 5.61 miles on Tuesday. How much farther did she kayak on Tuesday?

2. Devon had a length of rope that was 4.78 meters long. He cut a 1.45-meter length from it. How much rope does he have left?

Spiral Review (5.OA.A.1, 5.NBT.A.3b, 5.NBT.B.6, 5.NBT.B.7)

3. A dairy farm has 9 pastures and 630 cows. The same number of cows are placed in each pasture. How many cows are in each pasture?

4. Moya records 6.75 minutes of an interview on one tape and 3.75 minutes of the interview on another tape. How long was the total interview?

5. Joanna, Dana, and Tracy shared some trail mix. Joanna ate 0.125 pound of trail mix, Dana ate 0.1 pound, and Tracy ate 0.12 pound of trail mix. List the friends in order from least to greatest amount of trail mix eaten.

6. The local park has 4 bike racks. Each bike rack can hold 15 bikes. There are 16 bikes in the bike racks. What expression shows the total number of empty spaces in the bike racks?

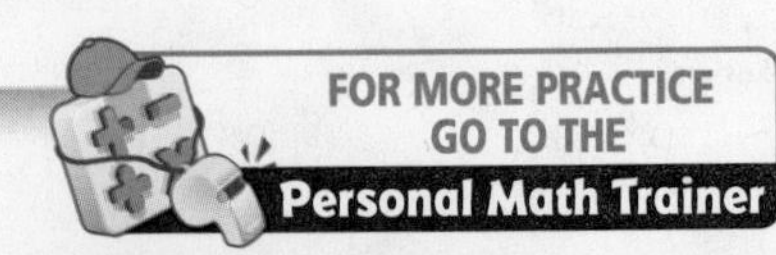

Name ___

Patterns with Decimals

Essential Question How can you use addition or subtraction to describe a pattern or create a sequence with decimals?

Number and Operations in Base Ten—5.NBT.B.7

MATHEMATICAL PRACTICES
MP7, MP8

Unlock the Problem

A state park rents canoes for guests to use at the lake. It costs $5.00 to rent a canoe for 1 hour, $6.75 for 2 hours, $8.50 for 3 hours, and $10.25 for 4 hours. If this pattern continues, how much should it cost Jason to rent a canoe for 7 hours?

A **sequence** is an ordered list of numbers. A **term** is each number in a sequence. You can find the pattern in a sequence by comparing one term with the next term.

STEP 1

Write the terms you know in a sequence. Then look for a pattern by finding the difference from one term in the sequence to the next.

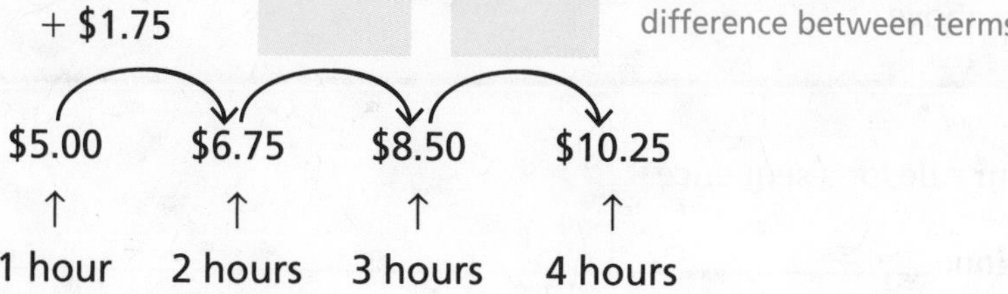

STEP 2

Write a rule that describes the pattern in the sequence.

Rule: ___

STEP 3

Extend the sequence to solve the problem.

$5.00, $6.75, $8.50, $10.25, ___, ___, ___

So, it should cost ___ to rent a canoe for 7 hours.

- MATHEMATICAL PRACTICE 7 **Look for a Pattern** What observation can you make about the pattern in the sequence that will help you write a rule?

___

___

Example Write a rule for the pattern in the sequence.

Then find the unknown terms in the sequence.

29.6, 28.3, 27, 25.7, ______, ______, ______, 20.5, 19.2

STEP 1 Look at the first few terms in the sequence.

Think: Is the sequence increasing or decreasing from one term to the next?

____

STEP 2 Write a rule that describes the pattern in the sequence.

What operation can be used to describe a sequence that increases?

____

What operation can be used to describe a sequence that decreases?

____

Rule: ______________________________

STEP 3 Use your rule to find the unknown terms.
Then complete the sequence above.

- Explain how you know whether your rule for a sequence would involve addition or subtraction. ______________________________

____

____

Try This!

A **Write a rule for the sequence. Then find the unknown term.**

65.9, 65.3, ______, 64.1, 63.5, 62.9

Rule: ______________________________

B **Write the first four terms of the sequence.**

Rule: start at 0.35, add 0.15

______, ______, ______, ______

Name ______________________________

Share and Show

Write a rule for the sequence.

1. 0.5, 1.8, 3.1, 4.4, ...

Think: Is the sequence increasing or decreasing?

Rule: ______________________________

2. 23.2, 22.1, 21, 19.9, ...

Rule: ______________________________

Write a rule for the sequence. Then find the unknown term.

3. 0.3, 1.5, ______ , 3.9, 5.1

Rule: ______________________________

4. 19.5, 18.8, 18.1, 17.4, ______

Rule: ______________________________

MATHEMATICAL PRACTICES 8

Compare Besides addition, what other operation can suggest an increase from one term to the next?

On Your Own

Write the first four terms of the sequence.

5. **Rule:** start at 10.64, subtract 1.45

______, ______, ______, ______

6. **Rule:** start at 0.87, add 2.15

______, ______, ______, ______

7. **Rule:** start at 19.3, add 1.8

______, ______, ______, ______

8. **Rule:** start at 29.7, subtract 0.4

______, ______, ______, ______

9. GO DEEPER Marta put $4.87 in her coin bank. Each day she added 1 quarter, 1 nickel, and 3 pennies. How much money was in her coin bank after 6 days? Describe the pattern you used to solve.

____

10. MATHEMATICAL PRACTICE 7 **Identify Relationships** Look at the list below. Do the numbers show a pattern? Explain how you know.

11.23, 10.75, 10.3, 9.82, 9.37, 8.89

____

____

Problem Solving • Applications

THINK SMARTER Pose a Problem

11. Bren has a deck of cards. As shown below, each card is labeled with a rule describing a pattern in a sequence. Select a card and decide on a starting number. Use the rule to write the first five terms in your sequence.

Add 1.6	Add 0.33	Add 6.5	Add 0.25	Add 1.15

Sequence: _____, _____, _____, _____, _____

Write a problem that relates to your sequence and requires the sequence be extended to solve.

Pose a Problem

Solve your problem.

12. THINK SMARTER Colleen and Tom are playing a number pattern game. Tom wrote the following sequence.

33.5, 34.6, 35.7, _______, 37.9

What is the unknown term in the sequence? ___________

Name ______________________________

Patterns with Decimals

COMMON CORE STANDARD—5.NBT.B.7
Perform operations with multi-digit whole numbers and with decimals to hundredths.

Write a rule for the sequence. Then find the unknown term.

1. 2.6, 3.92, 5.24, 6.56, 7.88

Think: 2.6 + ? = 3.92; 3.92 + ? = 5.24

2.6 + 1.32 = 3.92
3.92 + 1.32 = 5.24

Rule: add 1.32

2. 25.7, 24.1, ________, 20.9, 19.3

Rule: ______________________

Write the first four terms of the sequence.

3. Rule: start at 17.3, add 0.9

________, ________, ________, ________

4. Rule: start at 28.6, subtract 3.1

________, ________, ________, ________

Problem Solving (Real World)

5. The Ride-It Store rents bicycles. The cost is \$8.50 for 1 hour, \$13.65 for 2 hours, \$18.80 for 3 hours, and \$23.95 for 4 hours. If the pattern continues, how much will it cost Nate to rent a bike for 6 hours?

____

6. Lynne walks dogs every day to earn money. The fees she charges per month are 1 dog, \$40; 2 dogs, \$37.25 each; 3 dogs, \$34.50 each; 4 dogs, \$31.75 each. A pet store wants her to walk 8 dogs. If the pattern continues, how much will Lynne charge to walk each of the 8 dogs?

____

7. WRITE ▶ *Math* Give an example of a rule describing the pattern for a sequence. Then write the terms of the sequence for your rule.

____

____

Lesson Check (5.NBT.B.7)

1. A store has a sale on books. The price is $17.55 for one book, $16.70 each for 2 books, $15.85 each for 3 books, and $15 each for 4 books. If this pattern continues, how much per book will it cost to buy 7 books?

2. A bowling alley offers special weekly bowling rates. The weekly rates are 5 games for $15, 6 games for $17.55, 7 games for $20.10, and 8 games for $22.65. If this pattern continues, how much will it cost to bowl 10 games in a week?

Spiral Review (5.NBT.B.5, 5.NBT.B.6, 5.NBT.B.7)

3. Find the product.

$$\begin{array}{r} 284 \\ \times\ 36 \\ \hline \end{array}$$

4. At a sale, a shoe store sold 8 pairs of shoes for a total of $256. Each pair cost the same amount. What was the price of each pair of shoes?

5. Marcie jogged 0.8 mile on Wednesday and 0.9 mile on Thursday. How far did she jog on the two days?

6. Bob has 5.5 cups of flour. He uses 3.75 cups of flour. How much flour does Bob have left?

FOR MORE PRACTICE GO TO THE **Personal Math Trainer**

Name ______________________________

Problem Solving • Add and Subtract Money

Essential Question How can the strategy *make a table* help you organize and keep track of your bank account balance?

Common Core **Number and Operations in Base Ten—5.NBT.B.7**
MATHEMATICAL PRACTICES
MP1

At the end of May, Mrs. Freeman had a bank account balance of $442.37. Since then, she has written a check for $63.92 and made a deposit of $350.00. Mrs. Freeman says she has $729.45 in her bank account. Make a table to determine if Mrs. Freeman is correct.

Read the Problem

What do I need to find?

I need to find ______________________________

____

What information do I need to use?

I need to use the ______________________________

____

____

How will I use the information?

I need to make a table and use the information to ______

____

____

____

Solve the Problem

Mrs. Freeman's Checkbook			
May balance			$442.37
Check	$63.92		−$63.92
Deposit		$350.00	

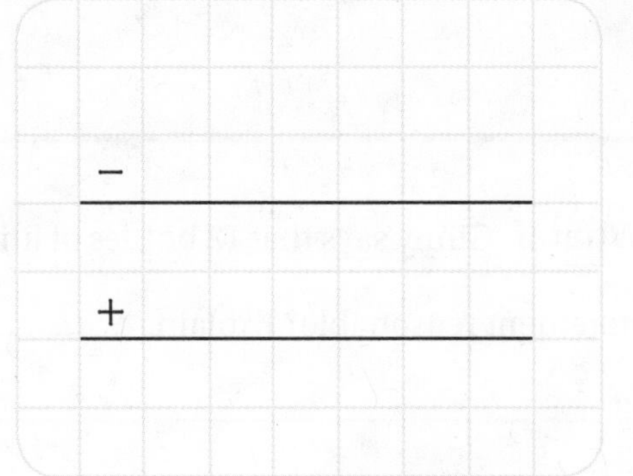

Mrs. Freeman's correct balance is __________.

1. MATHEMATICAL PRACTICE 1 **Evaluate Reasonableness** How can you tell if your answer is reasonable? ______________________________

____

Try Another Problem

Nick is buying juice for himself and 5 friends. Each bottle of juice costs $1.25. How much do 6 bottles of juice cost? Make a table to find the cost of 6 bottles of juice.

Use the graphic below to solve the problem.

Read the Problem	Solve the Problem
What do I need to find?	
What information do I need to use?	
How will I use the information?	So, the total cost of 6 bottles of juice is ______________.

2. **What if** Ginny says that 12 bottles of juice cost $25.00? Is Ginny's statement reasonable? Explain. ______________________________

3. If Nick had $10, how many bottles of juice could he buy? ________________

MATHEMATICAL PRACTICES 1

Describe how you could use another strategy to solve this problem.

Name ______________________________

Share and Show

1. Sara wants to buy a bottle of apple juice from a vending machine. She needs exactly $2.30. She has the following bills and coins:

Make and complete a table to find all the ways Sara could pay for the juice.

First, draw a table with a column for each type of bill or coin.

Next, fill in your table with each row showing a different way Sara can make exactly $2.30.

2. **What if** Sara decides to buy a bottle of water that costs $1.85? What are all the different ways she can make exactly $1.85 with the bills and coins she has? Which coin must Sara use?

3. At the end of August, Mr. Diaz had a balance of $441.62. Since then, he has written two checks for $157.34 and $19.74 and made a deposit of $575.00. Mr. Diaz says his balance is $739.54. Find Mr. Diaz's correct balance.

On Your Own

Use the following information to solve 4–6.

At Open Skate Night, admission is $3.75 with a membership card and $5.00 without a membership card. Skate rentals are $3.00.

4. GO DEEPER Aidan paid the admission for himself and two friends at Open Skate Night. Aidan had a membership card, but his friends did not. Aidan paid with a $20 bill. How much change should Aidan receive?

____

5. THINK SMARTER The Moores paid $6 more for skate rentals than the Cotters did. Together, the two families paid $30 for skate rentals. How many pairs of skates did the Moores rent?

____

WRITE Math
Show Your Work

6. MATHEMATICAL PRACTICE 1 **Analyze** Jennie and 5 of her friends are going to Open Skate Night. Jennie does not have a membership card. Only some of her friends have membership cards. What is the total amount that Jennie and her friends might pay for admission?

____

____

____

7. THINK SMARTER Marisol bought 5 movie tickets for a show. Each ticket cost $6.25. Complete the table to show the price of 2, 3, 4, and 5 tickets.

Number of Tickets	Price
1	$6.25
2	
3	
4	
5	

Name ______________________

Problem Solving • Add and Subtract Money

COMMON CORE STANDARD—5.NBT.B.7
Perform operations with multi-digit whole numbers and with decimals to hundredths.

Solve. Use the table to solve 1–2.

1. Dorian and Jack decided to go bowling. They each need to rent shoes and 1 lane, and Jack is a member. If Jack pays for both of them with $20, what change should he receive?

Bowl-a-Rama		
	Regular Cost	Member's Cost
Lane Rental (up to 4 people)	$9.75	$7.50
Shoe Rental	$3.95	$2.95

Calculate the cost: $7.50 + $3.95 + $2.95 = $14.40

Calculate the change: $20 − $14.40 = $5.60

2. Natalie and her friends decided to rent 4 lanes at regular cost for a party. Ten people need to rent shoes, and 4 people are members. What is the total cost for the party?

____

Use the following information to solve 3–5.

At the concession stand, medium sodas cost $1.25 and hot dogs cost $2.50.

3. Natalie's group brought in pizzas, but is buying the drinks at the concession stand. How many medium sodas can Natalie's group buy with $20? Make a table to show your answer.

____

4. Jack bought 2 medium sodas and 2 hot dogs. He paid with $20. What was his change?

____

5. How much would it cost to buy 3 medium sodas and 2 hot dogs?

____

6. WRITE Math Write a money problem that shows money being added to and subtracted from a bank account. Then solve the problem.

____

____

Lesson Check (5.NBT.B.7)

1. Prakrit bought a pack of paper for $5.69 and printer toner for $9.76. He paid with a $20 bill. What was his change?

2. Elysse paid for her sandwich and drink with a $10 bill and received $0.63 in change. The sandwich was $7.75. Sales tax was $0.47. What was the cost of her drink?

Spiral Review (5.NBT.A.1, 5.NBT.B.6, 5.NBT.B.7)

3. Tracie has saved $425 to spend during her 14-day vacation. About how much money can she spend each day?

4. What decimal is $\frac{1}{10}$ of 0.08?

5. Tyrone bought 2.25 pounds of Swiss cheese and 4.2 pounds of turkey at the deli. About how much was the weight of the two items?

6. Shelly ate 4.2 ounces of trail mix. Marshall ate 4.25 ounces of trail mix. How much more trail mix did Marshall eat?

FOR MORE PRACTICE GO TO THE **Personal Math Trainer**

Name ______________________________

Choose a Method

Essential Question Which method could you choose to find decimal sums and differences?

Common Core **Number and Operations in Base Ten—5.NBT.B.7**
MATHEMATICAL PRACTICES
MP1, MP2, MP5

Unlock the Problem

At a track meet, Steven entered the long jump. His jumps were 2.25 meters, 1.81 meters, and 3.75 meters. What was the total distance Steven jumped?

- Underline the sentence that tells you what you are trying to find.
- Circle the numbers you need to use.
- What operation will you use?

____

To find decimal sums, you can use properties and mental math or you can use paper and pencil.

One Way Use properties and mental math.

Add. 2.25 + 1.81 + 3.75

$2.25 + 1.81 + 3.75$

$= 2.25 + 3.75 + 1.81$ Commutative Property

$= (\_\_\_\_\_ + \_\_\_\_\_) + 1.81$ Associative Property

$= \_\_\_\_\_ + 1.81$

$= \_\_\_\_\_$

Another Way Use place-value.

Add. 2.25 + 1.81 + 3.75

$$\begin{array}{r} 2.25 \\ 1.81 \\ +\underline{3.75} \end{array}$$

So, the total distance Steven jumped was __________ meters.

MATHEMATICAL PRACTICES 5

Use Tools Explain why you might choose to use the properties to solve this problem.

Try This!

In 1924, William DeHart Hubbard won a gold medal with a long jump of 7.44 meters. In 2000, Roman Schurenko won the bronze medal with a jump of 8.31 meters. How much longer was Schurenko's jump than Hubbard's?

A **Use place-value.**

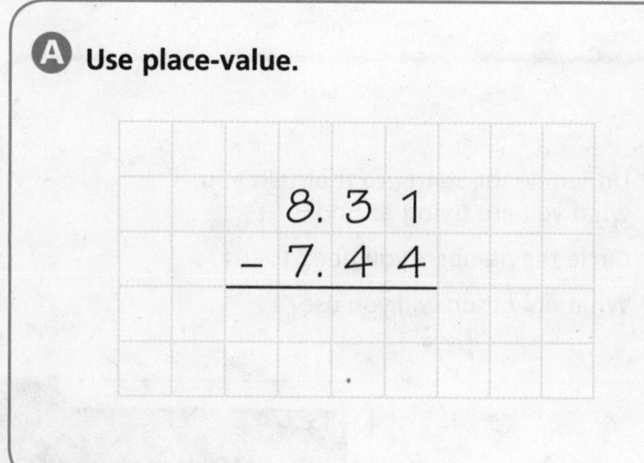

B **Use a calculator.**

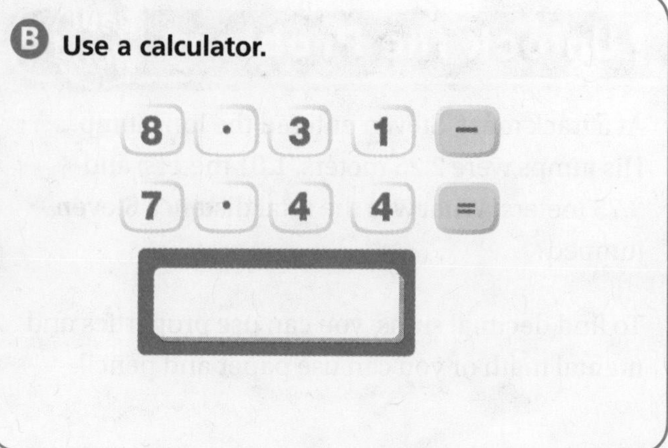

So, Schurenko's jump was __________ meter longer than Hubbard's.

- MATHEMATICAL PRACTICE 5 **Use Tools** Explain why you cannot use the Commutative Property or the Associative Property to find the difference between two decimals.

____

____

Share and Show MATH BOARD

Find the sum or difference.

1. $4.19 + 0.58$

2. $9.99 - 4.1$

3. $5.7 + 2.25 + 1.3$

4. $28.6 - 9.84$

5. $\$15.79 + \$32.81$

6. $38.44 - 25.86$

Name ____________________

On Your Own

Find the sum or difference.

7. $\begin{array}{r} \$18.39 \\ +\$\ \ 7.56 \\ \hline \end{array}$

8. $8.22 - 4.39$

9. $93.6 - 79.84$

10. $\begin{array}{r} 1.82 \\ 2.28 \\ +2.18 \\ \hline \end{array}$

Practice: Copy and Solve **Find the sum or difference.**

11. $6.3 + 2.98 + 7.7$

12. $27.96 - 16.2$

13. $12.63 + 15.04$

14. $9.24 - 2.68$

15. $\$18 - \$3.55$

16. $9.73 - 2.52$

17. $\$54.78 + \$43.62$

18. $7.25 + 0.25 + 1.5$

MATHEMATICAL PRACTICE 2 Use Reasoning **Algebra** **Find the missing number.**

19. $n - 9.02 = 3.85$

$n =$ ____________

20. $n + 31.53 = 62.4$

$n =$ ____________

21. $9.2 + n + 8.4 = 20.8$

$n =$ ____________

Problem Solving • Applications

22. GO DEEPER Jake needs 7.58 meters of wood to complete a school project. He buys a 2.25-meter plank of wood and a 3.12-meter plank of wood. How many more meters of wood does Jake need to buy?

____

23. THINK SMARTER Lori needs a length of twine 8.5 meters long to mark a row in her garden. Andrew needs a length of twine 7.25 meters long for his row. They have one length of twine that measures 16.27 meters. After they each take the lengths they need, how much twine will be left?

____

Use the table to solve 24–26.

2008 Men's Olympic Long Jump Results	
Medal	**Distance (in meters)**
Gold	8.34
Silver	8.24
Bronze	8.20

24. How much farther did the gold-medal winner jump than the silver medal winner?

____

25. MATHEMATICAL PRACTICE 1 The fourth-place competitor's jump measured 8.19 meters. If his jump had been 0.10 meter greater, what medal would he have received? **Describe** how you solved the problem.

____

____

____

26. In the 2004 Olympics, the gold medalist for the men's long jump had a jump of 8.59 meters. How much farther did the 2004 gold medalist jump compared to the 2008 gold medalist?

____

27. THINK SMARTER Alexander and Holly are solving the following word problem.

At the supermarket Carla buys 2.25 pounds of hamburger. She also buys 3.85 pounds of chicken. How many pounds of hamburger and chicken did Carla buy?

Alexander set up his problem as 2.25 + 3.85.
Holly set up her problem as 3.85 + 2.25.
Who is correct? Explain your answer and solve the problem.

____

____

____

Name ____________________

Practice and Homework
Lesson 3.12

Choose a Method

Common Core **COMMON CORE STANDARD—5.NBT.B.7**
Perform operations with multi-digit whole numbers and with decimals to hundredths.

Find the sum or difference.

1. $\begin{array}{r} 7.24 \\ +3.18 \\ \hline \end{array}$

$\begin{array}{r} \overset{1}{7}.24 \\ +3.18 \\ \hline 10.42 \end{array}$

2. $\begin{array}{r} 5.2 \\ 6.47 \\ +12.16 \\ \hline \end{array}$

3. $\begin{array}{r} 6.37 \\ -4.98 \\ \hline \end{array}$

4. $\begin{array}{r} 0.64 \\ 9.68 \\ +1.47 \\ \hline \end{array}$

5. $\begin{array}{r} 14.87 \\ +3.65 \\ \hline \end{array}$

6. $\begin{array}{r} 60.12 \\ -14.05 \\ \hline \end{array}$

7. $\begin{array}{r} 2.72 \\ +9.48 \\ \hline \end{array}$

8. $\begin{array}{r} 16.85 \\ +83.4 \\ \hline \end{array}$

9. \$13.60 − \$8.74 ____________

10. 13.65 + 6.90 + 4.35 ____________

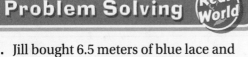

Problem Solving Real World

11. Jill bought 6.5 meters of blue lace and 4.12 meters of green lace. What was the total length of lace she bought?

____

12. Zack bought a coat for \$69.78. He paid with a \$100 bill and received \$26.73 in change. How much was the sales tax?

____

13. WRITE Math Write and solve a story problem for each method you can use to find decimal sums and differences.

____

____

____

Lesson Check (5.NBT.B.7)

1. Jin buys 4 balls of yarn for a total of $23.78. She pays with two $20 bills. What is her change?

____

2. Allan is measuring his dining room table to make a tablecloth. The table is 0.45 meter longer than it is wide. If it is 1.06 meters wide, how long is it?

____

Spiral Review (5.NBT.B.6, 5.NBT.B.7)

3. Write an expression using the Distributive Property that can be used to find the quotient $56 \div 4$.

____

4. Jane, Andre, and Maria pick apples. Andre picks three times as many pounds as Maria. Jane picks two times as many pounds as Andre. The total weight of the apples is 840 pounds. How many pounds of apples does Andre pick?

____

5. What is the sum $6.43 + 0.89$?

____

6. Hannah bought a total of 5.12 pounds of fruit at the market. She bought 2.5 pounds of pears, and she also bought some bananas. How many pounds of bananas did she buy?

____

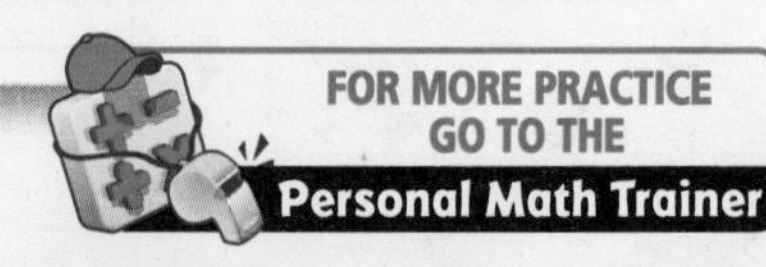

Name ______________________________

Chapter 3 Review/Test

Personal Math Trainer
Online Assessment and Intervention

1. Chaz kept a record of how many gallons of gas he purchased each day last week.

Day	Gas (in gallons)
Monday	4.5
Tuesday	3.9
Wednesday	4.258
Thursday	3.75
Friday	4.256

Order the days from least amount of gas Chaz purchased to greatest amount of gas Chaz purchased.

Least — Greatest

2. For 2a–2c, select True or False for each statement.

2a. 16.437 rounded to the nearest whole number is 16. ○ True ○ False

2b. 16.437 rounded to the nearest tenth is 16.4. ○ True ○ False

2c. 16.437 rounded to the nearest hundredth is 16.43. ○ True ○ False

Personal Math Trainer

3. THINK SMARTER+ Students are selling muffins at a school bake sale. One muffin costs $0.25, 2 muffins cost $0.37, 3 muffins cost $0.49, and 4 muffins cost $0.61. If this pattern continues, how much will 7 muffins cost? Explain how you found your answer.

GO DIGITAL Assessment Options Chapter Test

4. What is the value of the underlined digit? Mark all that apply.

0.<u>6</u>79

- ○ 0.6
- ○ six hundredths
- ○ 0.06
- ○ $6 \times \frac{1}{10}$
- ○ six tenths

5. Rowanda jogged 2.14 kilometers farther than Terrance. Select the values that could represent how far each student jogged. Mark all that apply.

- ○ Rowanda: 6.5 km, Terrance: 4.36 km
- ○ Rowanda: 4.8 km, Terrance: 2.76 km
- ○ Rowanda: 3.51 km, Terrance: 5.65 km
- ○ Rowanda: 7.24 km, Terrance: 5.1 km

6. Shade the model to show the decimal 0.542.

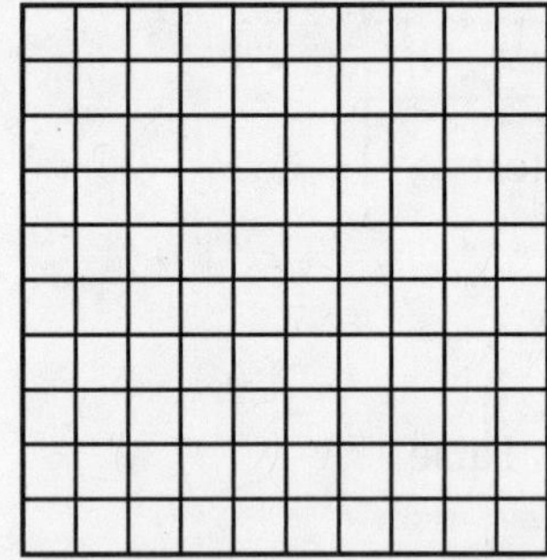

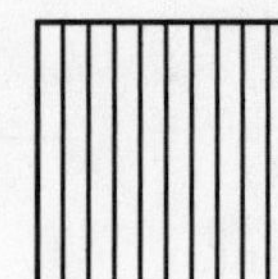

7. Benjamin rode his bicycle 3.6 miles on Saturday and 4.85 miles on Sunday. How many miles did he ride Saturday and Sunday combined? Use the digits on the tiles to solve the problem. Digits may be used more than once or not at all.

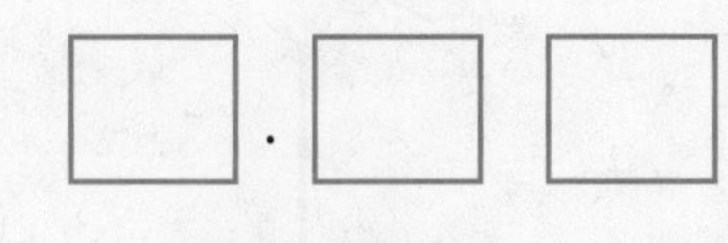

+ 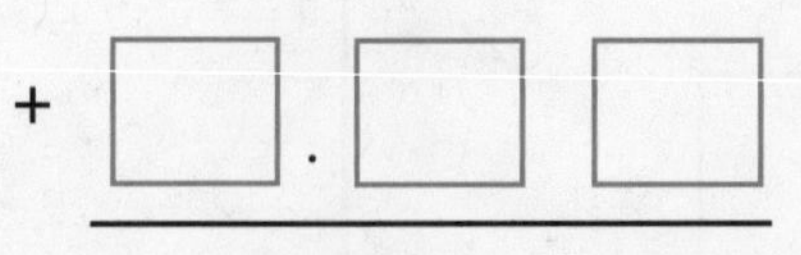

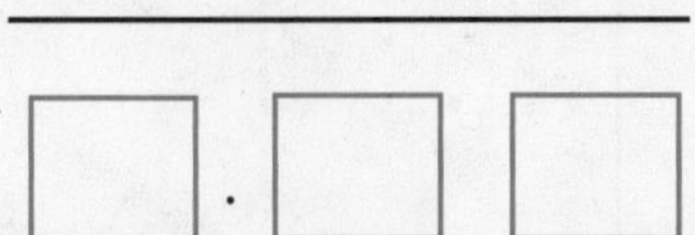

0	1
2	3
4	5
6	7
8	9

Name ___________________________

8. The school is 3.65 miles from Tonya's house and 1.28 miles from Jamal's house. How much farther from school is Tonya's house than Jamal's house? Explain how you can use a quick picture to solve the problem.

9. A vet measured the mass of two birds. The mass of the robin was 76.64 grams. The mass of the blue jay was 81.54 grams. Estimate the difference in the masses of the birds.

__________ grams

10. Rick bought 5 yogurt bars at a snack shop. Each yogurt bar cost $1.75. Complete the table to show the price of 2, 3, 4, and 5 yogurt bars.

Number of Yogurt Bars	Price
1	$1.75
2	
3	
4	
5	

11. Clayton Road is 2.25 miles long. Wood Pike Road is 1.8 miles long. Kisha used a quick picture to find the combined length of Clayton Road and Wood Pike Road. Does Kisha's work make sense? Explain why or why not.

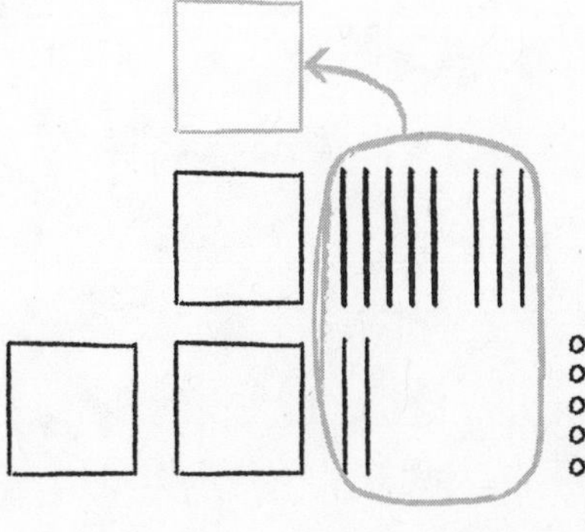

12. Bob and Ling are playing a number pattern game. Bob wrote the following sequence.

28.9, 26.8, 24.7, ____________, 20.5

What is the unknown term in the sequence?

[ ]

13. Rafael bought 2.15 pounds of potato salad and 4.2 pounds of macaroni salad to bring to a picnic. For 13a–13c, select Yes or No to indicate whether each statement is true.

13a. Rounded to the nearest whole number, Rafael bought 2 pounds of potato salad. ○ Yes ○ No

13b. Rounded to the nearest whole number, Rafael bought 4 pounds of macaroni salad. ○ Yes ○ No

13c. Rounded to the nearest tenth, Rafael bought 2.1 pounds of potato salad. ○ Yes ○ No

14. The four highest scores on the floor exercise at a gymnastics meet were 9.675, 9.25, 9.325, and 9.5 points. Choose the numbers that make the statement true.

The lowest of these four scores was [9.675 / 9.25 / 9.325 / 9.5] points. The highest of these four scores was [9.675 / 9.25 / 9.325 / 9.5] points.

Name ______________________

15. Michelle records the value of one euro in U.S. dollars each day for her social studies project. The table shows the data she has recorded so far.

Day	Value of 1 Euro (in U.S. dollars)
Monday	1.448
Tuesday	1.443
Wednesday	1.452
Thursday	1.458

On which two days was the value of 1 euro the same when rounded to the nearest hundredth of a dollar?

16. Miguel has $20. He spends $7.25 on a movie ticket, $3.95 for snacks, and $1.75 for bus fare each way. How much money does Miguel have left?

$ ________

17. GO DEEPER Yolanda's sunflower plant was 64.34 centimeters tall in July. During August, the plant grew 18.2 centimeters.

Part A

Estimate the height of Yolanda's plant at the end of August by rounding each value to the nearest whole number. Will your estimate be less than or greater than the actual height? Explain your reasoning.

Part B

What was the exact height of the plant at the end of August? Was the estimate less than or greater than the exact value?

18. Oscar ran the 100-yard dash in 12.41 seconds. Jesiah ran the 100-yard dash in 11.85 seconds. How many seconds faster was Jesiah's time than Oscar's time?

_______ second(s)

19. Choose the value that makes the statement true.

In the number 1.025, the value of the digit 2 is 2 [ones / tenths / hundredths / thousandths], and the value of the digit 5 is 5 [ones / tenths / hundredths / thousandths].

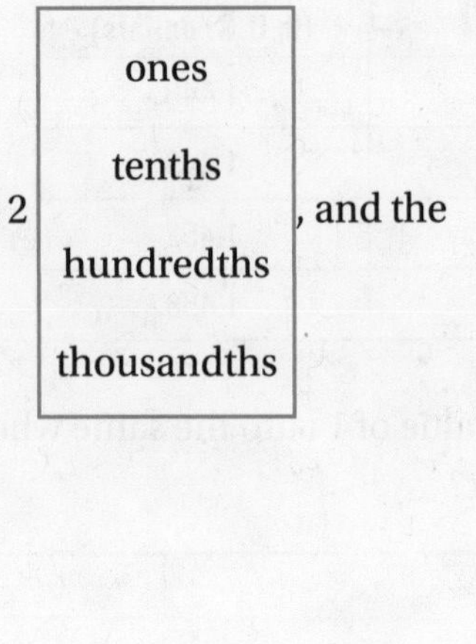

20. Troy and Lazetta are solving the following word problem.

Rosalie's cat weights 9.8 pounds. Her dog weighs 25.4 pounds. What is the weight of both animals combined.

Troy sets up his problem as 9.8 + 25.4. Lazetta sets up her problem as 25.4 + 9.8. Who is correct? Explain your answer and solve the problem.

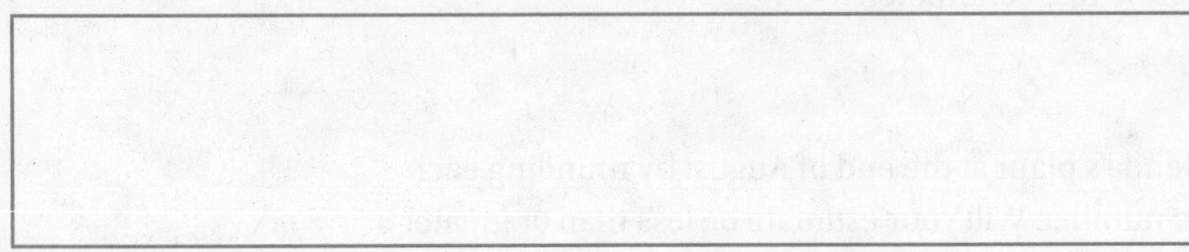

21. 0.84 is 10 times as much as [0.084 / 0.84 / 8.4 / 84] and $\frac{1}{10}$ of [0.084 / 0.84 / 8.4 / 84].

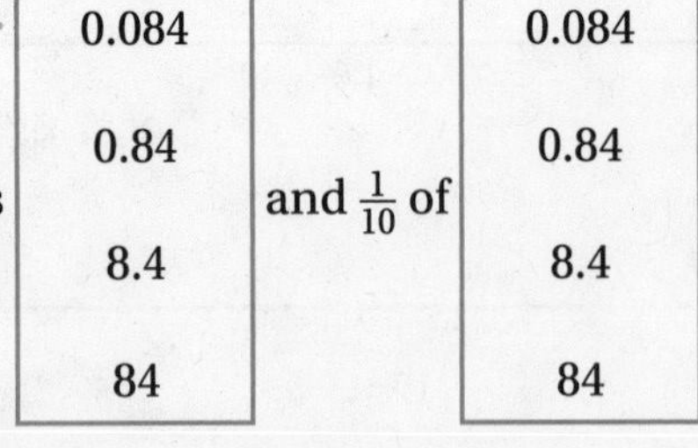

Multiply Decimals

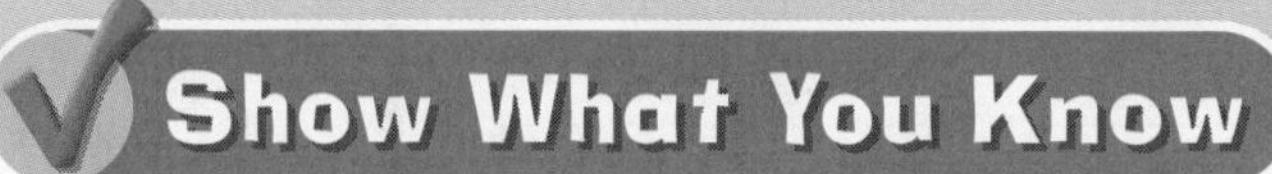

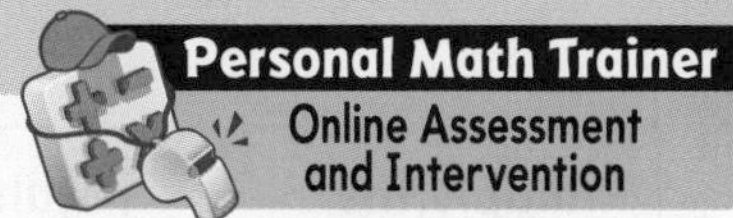

Check your understanding of important skills.

Name ______________________________

▶ Meaning of Multiplication **Complete.** (3.OA.A.1)

1. 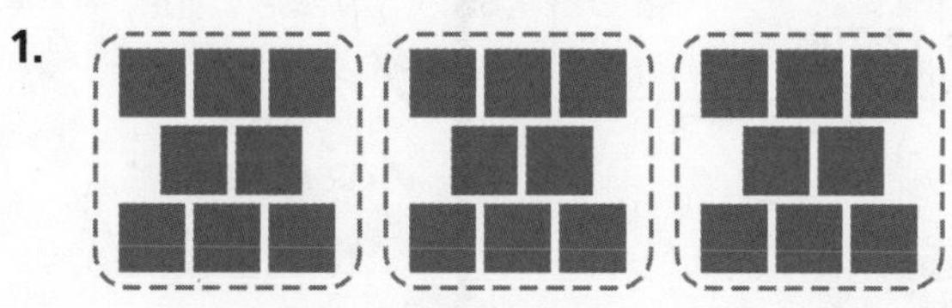

______ groups of ______ = ______

2.

______ groups of ______ = ______

▶ Decimals Greater Than One **Write the word form and the expanded form for each.** (5.NBT.A.3a)

3. 1.7

____

____

4. 5.62

____

____

▶ Multiply by 3-Digit Numbers **Multiply.** (4.NBT.B.5)

5. $\begin{array}{r} 321 \\ \times \quad 4 \\ \hline \end{array}$

6. $\begin{array}{r} 387 \\ \times \quad 5 \\ \hline \end{array}$

7. $\begin{array}{r} 126 \\ \times \ 13 \\ \hline \end{array}$

8. $\begin{array}{r} 457 \\ \times \ 35 \\ \hline \end{array}$

Staghorn Coral is a type of branching coral. It can add as much as 0.67 foot to its branches each year. Find how much a staghorn coral can grow in 5 years.

Vocabulary Builder

▶ Visualize It

Complete the flow map using the words with a ✓.

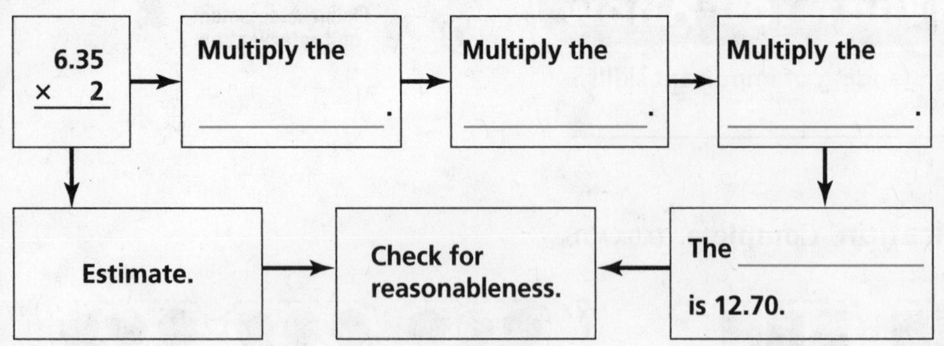

Review Words

- decimal
- expanded form
- ✓ hundredths
- multiplication
- ✓ ones
- pattern
- place value
- ✓ product
- ✓ tenths
- thousandths

▶ Understand Vocabulary

Read the description. What term do you think it describes?

1. It is the process used to find the total number of items in a given number of groups. ______________

2. It is a way to write a number that shows the value of each digit. ______________

3. It is one of one hundred equal parts. ______________

4. This is the result when you multiply two numbers. ______________

5. It is the value of a digit in a number based on the location of the digit. ______________

GO DIGITAL
- Interactive Student Edition
- Multimedia eGlossary

Chapter 4 Vocabulary

decimal decimal 11	**expanded form** forma desarrollada 25
hundredth centésimo 30	**pattern** patrón 48
place value valor posicional 50	**product** producto 54
tenth décimo 65	**thousandth** milésimo 67

A way to write numbers by showing the value of each digit

Example:
$832 = (8 \times 100) + (3 \times 10) + (2 \times 1)$
$3.25 = (3 \times 1) + \left(2 \times \frac{1}{10}\right) + \left(5 \times \frac{1}{100}\right)$

© Houghton Mifflin Harcourt Publishing Company

A number with one or more digits to the right of the decimal point.

Example: 0.5, 0.06, and 12.679 are decimals.

© Houghton Mifflin Harcourt Publishing Company

An ordered set of numbers or objects; the order helps you predict what will come next

Examples: 2, 4, 6, 8, 10

© Houghton Mifflin Harcourt Publishing Company

One of 100 equal parts

Example: $0.56 = \frac{56}{100}$ = fifty-six hundredths

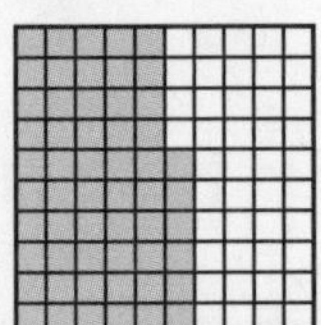

© Houghton Mifflin Harcourt Publishing Company

The answer to a multiplication problem

Example: $3 \times 15 = 45$

© Houghton Mifflin Harcourt Publishing Company

The value of each digit in a number based on the location of the digit

Example:

MILLIONS			THOUSANDS			ONES		
Hundreds	Tens	Ones	Hundreds	Tens	Ones	Hundreds	Tens	Ones
		1,	3	9	2,	0	0	0
		1 × 1,000,000	3 × 100,000	9 × 10,000	2 × 1,000	0 × 100	0 × 10	0 × 1
		1,000,000	300,000	90,000	2,000	0	0	0

© Houghton Mifflin Harcourt Publishing Company

One of 1,000 equal parts

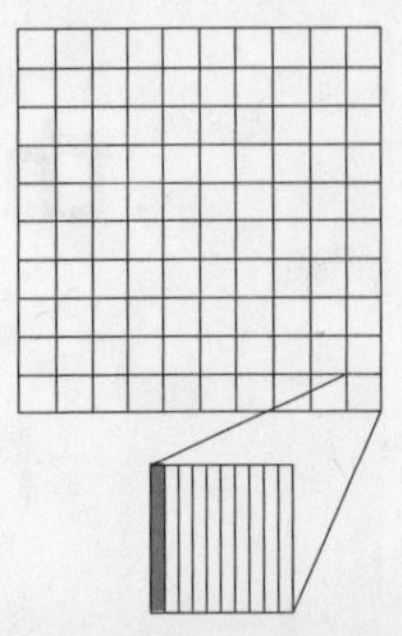

© Houghton Mifflin Harcourt Publishing Company

One of ten equal parts

Example: $0.7 = \frac{7}{10}$ = seven tenths

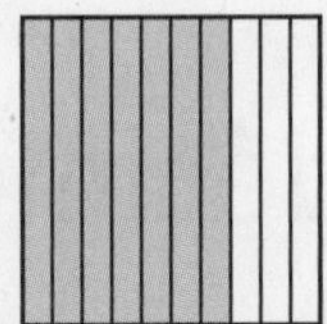

Bingo

Word Box
decimal
expanded form
hundredth
pattern
place value
product
tenth
thousandths

For 3–6 players

Materials

- 1 set of word cards
- 1 Bingo board for each player
- game markers

How to Play

1. The caller chooses a card and reads the definition. Then the caller puts the card in a second pile.
2. Players put a marker on the word that matches the definition each time they find it on their Bingo boards.
3. Repeat Steps 1 and 2 until a player marks 5 boxes in a line going down, across, or on a slant and calls "Bingo."
4. To check the answers, the player who said "Bingo" reads the words aloud while the caller checks the definitions.

The Write Way

Reflect

Choose one idea. Write about it.

- Kevin needs 1,000 pieces of ribbon for balloons at a school event. Each piece of ribbon has to be 2.25 feet long. Tell how Kevin can use a pattern to find how many yards of ribbon he needs.
- Compare the place value of the digit 8 in the following numbers.
  2.8 1.68 9.438
- Tell how using expanded form can help you solve a multiplication problem.
- Explain the steps of how to multiply two decimals. Include an example in your explanation.

Name ______________________________

Multiplication Patterns with Decimals

Essential Question How can patterns help you place the decimal point in a product?

Number and Operations in Base Ten—5.NBT.A.2 *Also 5.NBT.B.7*

MATHEMATICAL PRACTICES
MP2, MP3, MP6

Unlock the Problem (Real World)

Cindy is combining equal-sized rectangles from different fabric patterns to make a postage-stamp quilt. Each rectangle has an area of 0.75 of a square inch. If she uses 1,000 rectangles to make the quilt, what will be the area of the quilt?

 **Use the pattern to find the product.**

1 × 0.75 = 0.75

10 × 0.75 = 7.5

100 × 0.75 = 75.

1,000 × 0.75 = 750.

The quilt will have an area of __________ square inches.

1. As you multiply by increasing powers of 10, how does the position of the decimal point change in the product? ______________________________

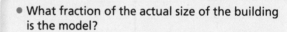

____

Place value patterns can be used to find the product of a number and the decimals 0.1 and 0.01.

 Example 1

Jorge is making a scale model of the Willis Tower in Chicago for a theater set. The height of the tower is 1,353 feet. If the model is $\frac{1}{100}$ of the actual size of the building, how tall is the model?

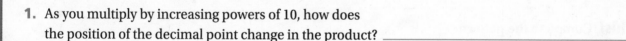

- What fraction of the actual size of the building is the model?

____

- Write the fraction as a decimal.

____

1 × 1,353 = 1,353

0.1 × 1,353 = 135.3

0.01 × 1,353 = ☐ ← $\frac{1}{100}$ of 1,353

Jorge's model of the Willis Tower is __________ feet tall.

2. As you multiply by decreasing powers of 10, how does the position of the decimal point change in the product?

____

____

Example 2

Three friends are selling items at an arts and crafts fair. Josey makes \$45.75 selling jewelry. Mark makes 100 times as much as Josey makes by selling his custom furniture. Carlos makes a tenth of the money Mark makes by selling paintings. How much money does each friend make?

Josey: \$45.75

Mark: ______ × \$45.75

Think: 1 × \$45.75 = ______

10 × \$45.75 = ______

100 × \$45.75 = ______

Carlos: ______ × ______

Think: 1 × ______ = ______

______ × ______ = ______

So, Josey makes \$45.75, Mark makes ______,

and Carlos makes ______.

Try This! **Complete the pattern.**

A $10^0 \times 4.78 =$ ______

$10^1 \times 4.78 =$ ______

$10^2 \times 4.78 =$ ______

$10^3 \times 4.78 =$ ______

B $38 \times 1 =$ ______

$38 \times 0.1 =$ ______

$38 \times 0.01 =$ ______

Share and Show

Complete the pattern.

1. $10^0 \times 17.04 = 17.04$

$10^1 \times 17.04 = 170.4$

$10^2 \times 17.04 = 1{,}704$

$10^3 \times 17.04 =$ ______

Think: The decimal point moves one place to the ______ for each increasing power of 10.

Name ____________________

Complete the pattern.

2. $1 \times 3.19 =$ ______

$10 \times 3.19 =$ ______

$100 \times 3.19 =$ ______

$1,000 \times 3.19 =$ ______

3. $45.6 \times 10^0 =$ ______

$45.6 \times 10^1 =$ ______

$45.6 \times 10^2 =$ ______

$45.6 \times 10^3 =$ ______

4. $1 \times 6,391 =$ ______

$0.1 \times 6,391 =$ ______

$0.01 \times 6,391 =$ ______

Math Talk MATHEMATICAL PRACTICES 6

Explain how you know that when you multiply the product of 10 × 34.1 by 0.1, the result will be 34.1.

On Your Own

MATHEMATICAL PRACTICE 2 **Use Reasoning** **Algebra** **Find the value of *n*.**

5. $n \times \$3.25 = \$325.00$

$n =$ ____________

6. $0.1 \times n = 89.5$

$n =$ ____________

7. $10^3 \times n = 630$

$n =$ ____________

8. GO DEEPER A glacier in Alaska moves about 29.9 meters a day. About how much farther will it move in 1,000 days than it will move in 100 days?

____

9. THINK SMARTER For 9a–9e, choose Yes or No to indicate whether the product is correct.

9a. $0.81 \times 10 = 0.081$ ○ Yes ○ No

9b. $0.33 \times 100 = 33$ ○ Yes ○ No

9c. $0.05 \times 100 = 5$ ○ Yes ○ No

9d. $0.70 \times 1,000 = 70$ ○ Yes ○ No

9e. $0.38 \times 10 = 0.038$ ○ Yes ○ No

Problem Solving • Applications

THINKSMARTER **What's the Error?**

10. Kirsten is making lanyards for a convention. She needs to make 1,000 lanyards and knows that 1 lanyard uses 1.75 feet of cord. How much cord will Kirsten need?

Kirsten's work is shown below.

$1 \times 1.75 = 1.75$

$10 \times 1.75 = 10.75$

$100 \times 1.75 = 100.75$

$1{,}000 \times 1.75 = 1{,}000.75$

Find and describe Kirsten's error.

Solve the problem using the correct pattern.

So, Kirsten needs __________ feet of cord to make 1,000 lanyards.

- MATHEMATICAL PRACTICE 3 **Compare Strategies** Describe how Kirsten could solve the problem without writing out the pattern.

Name ______________________

Multiplication Patterns with Decimals

COMMON CORE STANDARD—5.NBT.A.2
Understand the place value system.

Complete the pattern.

1. $2.07 \times 1 =$ 2.07

$2.07 \times 10 =$ 20.7

$2.07 \times 100 =$ 207

$2.07 \times 1{,}000 =$ 2,070

2. $1 \times 30 =$ ________

$0.1 \times 30 =$ ________

$0.01 \times 30 =$ ________

3. $10^0 \times 0.23 =$ ________

$10^1 \times 0.23 =$ ________

$10^2 \times 0.23 =$ ________

$10^3 \times 0.23 =$ ________

4. $390 \times 1 =$ ________

$390 \times 0.1 =$ ________

$390 \times 0.01 =$ ________

5. $1 \times 5 =$ ________

$0.1 \times 5 =$ ________

$0.01 \times 5 =$ ________

6. $1 \times 9{,}670 =$ ________

$0.1 \times 9{,}670 =$ ________

$0.01 \times 9{,}670 =$ ________

7. $874 \times 1 =$ ________

$874 \times 10 =$ ________

$874 \times 100 =$ ________

$874 \times 1{,}000 =$ ________

8. $10^0 \times 10 =$ ________

$10^1 \times 10 =$ ________

$10^2 \times 10 =$ ________

$10^3 \times 10 =$ ________

9. $10^0 \times 49.32 =$ ________

$10^1 \times 49.32 =$ ________

$10^2 \times 49.32 =$ ________

$10^3 \times 49.32 =$ ________

Problem Solving Real World

10. Nathan plants equal-sized squares of sod in his front yard. Each square has an area of 6 square feet. Nathan plants a total of 1,000 squares in his yard. What is the total area of the squares of sod?

____

11. Three friends are selling items at a bake sale. May makes $23.25 selling bread. Inez sells gift baskets and makes 100 times as much as May. Jo sells pies and makes one tenth of the money Inez makes. How much money does each friend make?

____

12. WRITE *Math* Explain how to use a pattern to find the product of a power of 10 and a decimal.

____

____

Lesson Check (5.NBT.A.2)

1. The length of the Titanic was 882 feet. Porter's history class is building a model of the Titanic. The model is $\frac{1}{100}$ of the actual length of the ship. How long is the model?

2. Ted is asked to multiply $10^2 \times 18.72$. How many places and in which direction should he move the decimal point to get the correct product?

Spiral Review (5.NBT.A.3b, 5.NBT.A.4, 5.NBT.B.6, 5.NBT.B.7)

3. The table shows the height in meters of some of the world's tallest buildings. What are the heights in order from least to greatest?

Building	Height (meters)
Zifeng Tower	457.2
International Finance Center	415.138
Burj Khalifa	828.142
Petronas Towers	452.018

4. Madison had \$187.56 in her checking account. She deposited \$49.73 and then used her debit card to spend \$18.64. What is Madison's new account balance?

5. What is 3.47 rounded to the nearest tenth?

6. The city gardener ordered 1,680 tulip bulbs for Riverside Park. The bulbs were shipped in 35 boxes with an equal number of bulbs in each box. How many tulip bulbs were in each box?

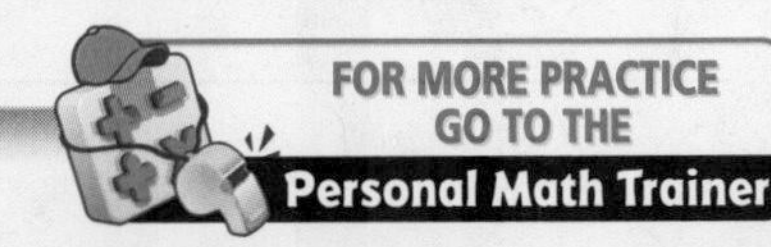

Name ______________________________

Multiply Decimals and Whole Numbers

Essential Question How can you use a model to multiply a whole number and a decimal?

Common Core **Number and Operations in Base Ten—5.NBT.B.7**
MATHEMATICAL PRACTICES
MP2, MP4, MP6

Investigate

Hands On

Materials ■ decimal models ■ color pencils

Giant tortoises move very slowly. They can travel a distance of about 0.17 mile in 1 hour. How far could a giant tortoise move if it travels at this same speed for 4 hours?

A. Complete the statement to describe the problem.

I need to find how many total miles are in ______ groups of ____________.

- Write an expression to represent the problem. ____________

B. Use the decimal model to find the answer.

- What does each small square in the decimal model represent?

____

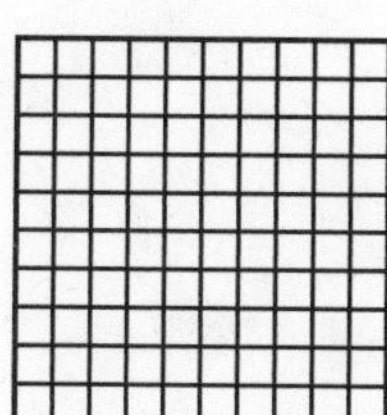

C. Shade a group of ______ squares to represent the distance a giant tortoise can move in 1 hour.

D. Use a different color to shade each additional group of ______ squares until you have ______ groups of ______ squares.

E. Record the total number of squares shaded. ______ squares

So, the giant tortoise can move ____________ mile in 4 hours.

MATHEMATICAL PRACTICES 4

Use Models Describe how the model helps you determine if your answer is reasonable.

Draw Conclusions

1. Explain why you used only one decimal model to show the product.

____

____

2. Explain how the product of 4 groups of 0.17 is similar to the product of 4 groups of 17. How is it different?

____

____

3. MATHEMATICAL PRACTICE 6 **Compare** the product of 0.17 and 4 with each of the factors. Which number has the greatest value? Explain how this is different than multiplying two whole numbers.

____

____

Make Connections

You can draw a quick picture to solve decimal multiplication problems.

Find the product. 3×0.46

STEP 1 Draw 3 groups of 4 tenths and 6 hundredths. Remember that a square is equal to 1.

STEP 2 Combine the hundredths and rename.

There are ______ hundredths. I will rename

______ hundredths as __________.

Cross out the hundredths you renamed.

STEP 3 Combine the tenths and rename.

There are ______ tenths. I will rename

______ tenths as __________.

Cross out the tenths you renamed.

STEP 4 Record the value shown by your completed quick picture.

So, $3 \times 0.46 =$ __________.

MATHEMATICAL PRACTICES 6

Compare Explain how renaming decimals is like renaming whole numbers.

Name ____________________

Share and Show 

Use the decimal model to find the product.

1. $5 \times 0.06 =$ ________

2. $2 \times 0.38 =$ ________

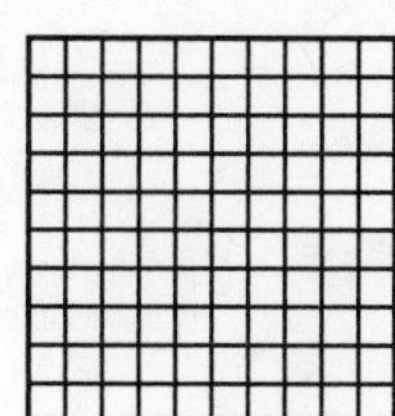

3. $4 \times 0.24 =$ ________

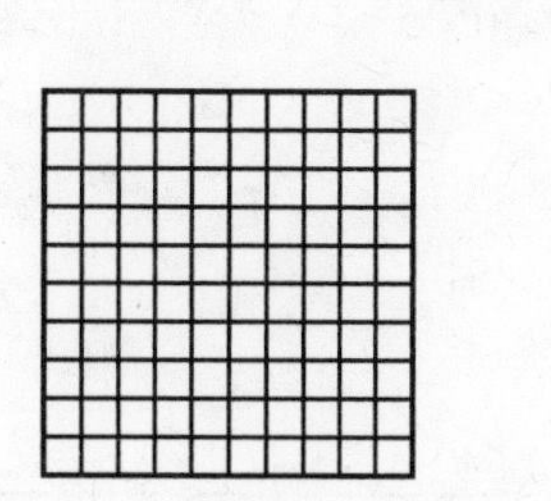

Find the product. Draw a quick picture.

4. $3 \times 0.62 =$ ________

5. $4 \times 0.32 =$ ________

6. WRITE ▶ *Math* Describe how you solved Exercise 5 using place value and renaming. ____________________

7. GO DEEPER Carrie has 0.73 liter of juice in her pitcher. Sanji's pitcher has 2 times as much juice as Carrie's pitcher. Lee's pitcher has 4 times as much juice as Carrie's pitcher. Sanji and Lee pour all their juice into a large bowl. How much juice is in the bowl?

____

Problem Solving • Applications

Use the table for 8–10.

Animal	Average Amount (liters per day)
Canada Goose	0.24
Cat	0.15
Mink	0.10
Opossum	0.30
Bald Eagle	0.16

Water Consumption

8. MATHEMATICAL PRACTICE 2 **Reason Quantitatively** Each day a bobcat drinks about 3 times as much water as a Canada goose drinks. How much water can a bobcat drink in one day?

____

9. THINK SMARTER River otters drink about 5 times as much water as a bald eagle drinks in a day. How much water can a river otter drink in 3 days?

____

10. GO DEEPER An animal shelter provides a bowl with 1.25 liters of water for 3 cats. About how much water will be left after the cats drink their average daily amount of water?

____

11. THINK SMARTER Yossi is shading the model to show 0.14×3.

Describe what Yossi should shade to show the product. Then shade in the correct amount of boxes that will show the product of 0.14×3.

______ groups of ______ small squares or ______ small squares

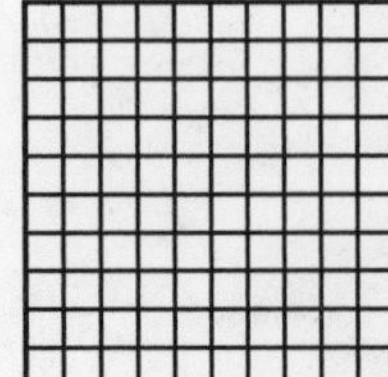

Name ______________________

Multiply Decimals and Whole Numbers

Use the decimal model to find the product.

COMMON CORE STANDARD—5.NBT.B.7
Perform operations with multi-digit whole numbers and with decimals to hundredths.

1. $4 \times 0.07 =$ 0.28

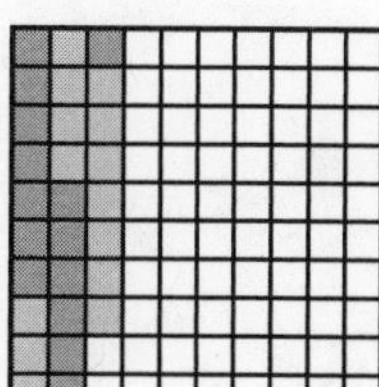

2. $3 \times 0.27 =$ ______

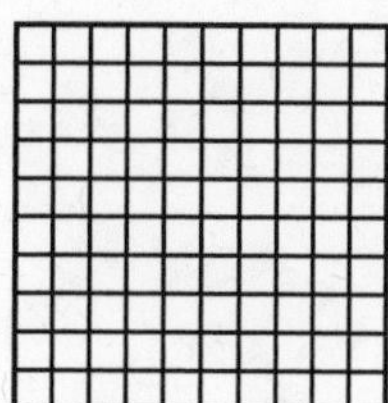

3. $2 \times 0.45 =$ ______

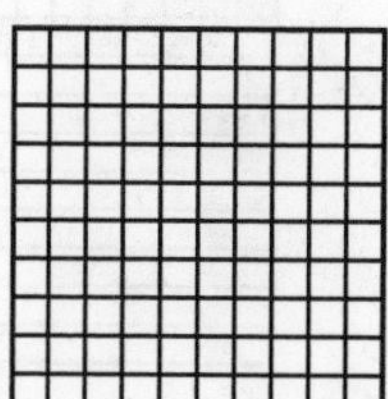

Find the product. Draw a quick picture.

4. $2 \times 0.8 =$ ______

5. $2 \times 0.67 =$ ______

6. $5 \times 0.71 =$ ______

7. $4 \times 0.23 =$ ______

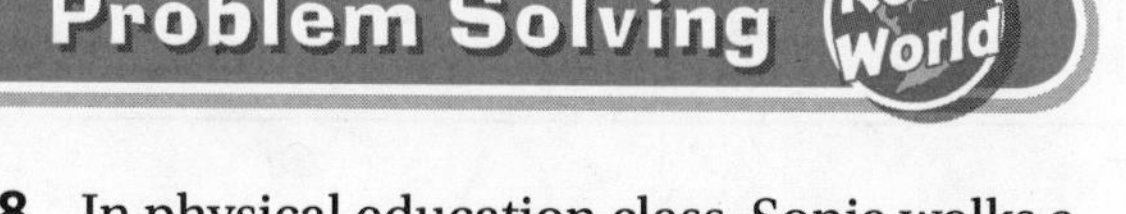

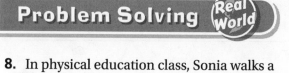

8. In physical education class, Sonia walks a distance of 0.12 mile in 1 minute. At that rate, how far can she walk in 9 minutes?

______

9. A certain tree can grow 0.45 meter in one year. At that rate, how much can the tree grow in 3 years?

______

10. WRITE *Math* Explain how multiplying a whole number and a decimal is similar to and different from multiplying whole numbers.

______

______

Lesson Check (5.NBT.B.7)

1. What multiplication sentence does the model represent?

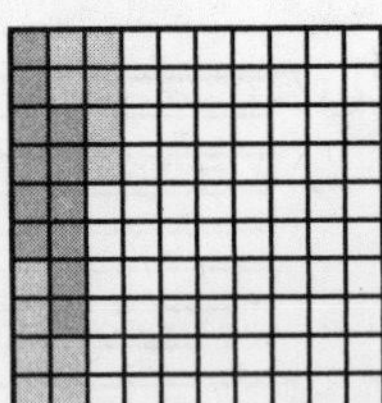

2. A certain type of lunch meat contains 0.5 gram of unsaturated fat per serving. How much unsaturated fat is in 3 servings of the lunch meat?

Spiral Review (5.OA.A.1, 5.NBT.A.2, 5.NBT.A.3b, 5.NF.B.3)

3. To find the value of the following expression, what operation should you do first?

   $20 - (7 + 4) \times 5$

4. Ella and three friends run in a relay race that is 14 miles long. Each person runs equal parts of the race. How many miles does each person run?

5. What symbol makes the statement true? Write >, <, or =.

   17.518 ◯ 17.581

6. Each number in the following sequence has the same relationship to the number immediately before it. How can you find the next number in the sequence?

   3, 30, 300, 3,000, . . .

FOR MORE PRACTICE GO TO THE **Personal Math Trainer**

Name ____________________

Multiplication with Decimals and Whole Numbers

Essential Question How can you use properties and place value to multiply a decimal and a whole number?

Common Core **Number and Operations in Base Ten—5.NBT.B.7** *Also 5.NBT.A.2*
MATHEMATICAL PRACTICES
MP2, MP3, MP6

Unlock the Problem (Real World)

In 2010, the United States Mint released a newly designed Lincoln penny. A Lincoln penny has a mass of 2.5 grams. If there are 5 Lincoln pennies on a tray, what is the total mass of the pennies?

- How much mass does one penny have?
  ____
- How many pennies are on the tray?
  ____
- Use grouping language to describe what you are asked to find.
  ____

Multiply. 5×2.5

Estimate the product. Round to the nearest whole number.

$5 \times$ _____ $=$ _____

One Way

Use the Distributive Property.

$5 \times 2.5 = 5 \times ($ _____ $+ 0.5)$

$= ($ _____ $\times 2) + (5 \times$ _____ $)$

$=$ _____ $+$ _____

$=$ _____

Math Talk MATHEMATICAL PRACTICES 2

Use Reason How does the estimate help you determine if the answer is reasonable?

Another Way **Show partial products.**

STEP 1 Multiply the tenths by 5.

```
  2.5
×   5
-----
 ____   ← 5 × 5 tenths = 25 tenths, or
             2 ones and 5 tenths
```

STEP 2 Multiply the ones by 5.

```
  2.5
×   5
-----
  2.5
 ____   ← 5 × 2 ones = 10 ones, or 1 ten
```

STEP 3 Add the partial products.

```
  2.5
×   5
-----
  2.5
+ 10
-----
 ____
```

So, 5 Lincoln pennies have a mass of __________ grams.

Example Use place value patterns.

Having a thickness of 1.35 millimeters, the dime is the thinnest coin produced by the United States Mint. If you stacked 8 dimes, what would be the total thickness of the stack?

Multiply. 8 × 1.35

STEP 1	STEP 2	STEP 3
Write the decimal factor as a whole number.	Multiply as with whole numbers.	Place the decimal point.
Think: 1.35 × 100 = 135		**Think:** 0.01 of 135 is 1.35. Find 0.01 of 1,080 and record the product.

$$\begin{array}{r} 1.35 \\ \times\ \ 8 \\ \hline ? \end{array} \xrightarrow{\times 100} \begin{array}{r} 135 \\ \times\ \ 8 \\ \hline 1{,}080 \end{array} \xrightarrow{\times 0.01} \begin{array}{r} 1.35 \\ \times\ \ 8 \\ \hline \square \end{array}$$

A stack of 15 dimes would have a thickness of ______ millimeters.

1. MATHEMATICAL PRACTICE 6 **Explain** how you know the product of 8 × 1.35 is greater than 8.

______

______

2. **What if** you multiplied 0.35 by 8? Would the product be less than or greater than 8? Explain.

______

______

Share and Show

Place the decimal point in the product.

1. $\begin{array}{r} 6.81 \\ \times\ \ 7 \\ \hline 4767 \end{array}$ **Think:** The place value of the decimal factor is hundredths.

2. $\begin{array}{r} 3.7 \\ \times\ 2 \\ \hline 74 \end{array}$

3. $\begin{array}{r} 19.34 \\ \times\ \ \ 5 \\ \hline 9670 \end{array}$

Name ______________________________

Find the product.

4. $\begin{array}{r} 6.32 \\ \times \quad 3 \\ \hline \end{array}$

5. $\begin{array}{r} 4.5 \\ \times \ 8 \\ \hline \end{array}$

6. $\begin{array}{r} 40.7 \\ \times \quad 5 \\ \hline \end{array}$

MATHEMATICAL PRACTICES 6

Explain a Method How can you determine if your answer to Exercise 6 is reasonable?

On Your Own

Find the product.

7. $\begin{array}{r} 4.93 \\ \times \quad 7 \\ \hline \end{array}$

8. $\begin{array}{r} 8.2 \\ \times \ 6 \\ \hline \end{array}$

9. $\begin{array}{r} 7.55 \\ \times \quad 8 \\ \hline \end{array}$

Practice: Copy and Solve **Find the product.**

10. 8×7.2

11. 3×1.45

12. 9×8.6

13. 6×0.79

14. 4×9.3

15. 7×0.81

16. 6×2.08

17. 5×23.66

18. GO DEEPER The cost to park a car in a parking lot is \$3.45 per hour. Maleek parked his car for 4 hours on Monday, 3 hours on Tuesday, and 2 hours on Wednesday. How much did he spend on parking in all?

____

Problem Solving • Applications 

Use the table for 19–20.

Coin	Mass (in grams)
Nickel	5.00
Dime	2.27
Quarter	5.67
Half Dollar	11.34
Dollar	8.1

19. GO DEEPER Sari has a bag containing 6 half-dollar and 3 dollar coins. What is the total mass of the coins in Sari's bag?

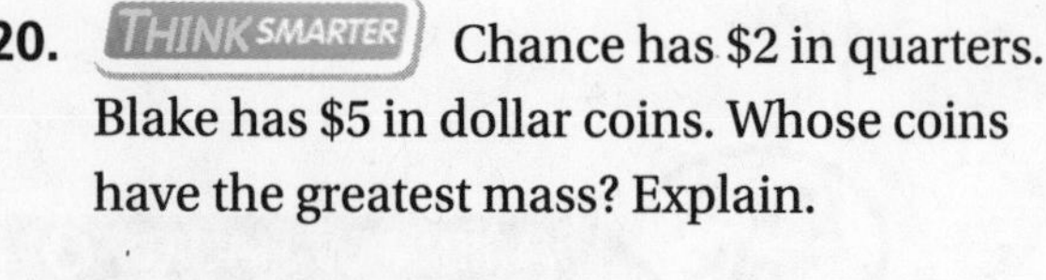

20. THINK SMARTER Chance has $2 in quarters. Blake has $5 in dollar coins. Whose coins have the greatest mass? Explain.

WRITE Math • Show Your Work

21. MATHEMATICAL PRACTICE 3 **Make Arguments** Julie multiplies 6.27 by 7 and claims the product is 438.9. Explain without multiplying how you know Julie's answer is not correct. Find the correct answer.

Personal Math Trainer

22. THINK SMARTER+ Rachel and Abby are trying to solve a science homework question. They need to find how much a rock that weighs 6 pounds on Earth would weigh on the moon. They know they can multiply weight on Earth by about 0.16 to find weight on the moon. Select the partial products Rachel and Abby would need to add to find the product of 6 and 0.16. Mark all that apply.

Ⓐ 0.22 Ⓑ 0.6 Ⓒ 3.65 Ⓓ 3.6 Ⓔ 0.36

Name ______________________________

Multiplication with Decimals and Whole Numbers

COMMON CORE STANDARDS—5.NBT.A.2, 5.NBT.B.7 *Perform operations with multi-digit whole numbers and with decimals to hundredths.*

Find the product.

1. $\begin{array}{r} 5.2 \\ \times \quad 4 \\ \hline 20.8 \end{array}$ **Think:** The place value of the decimal factor is tenths.

2. $\begin{array}{r} 9.8 \\ \times \quad 6 \\ \hline \end{array}$

3. $\begin{array}{r} 13.02 \\ \times \quad 5 \\ \hline \end{array}$

4. $\begin{array}{r} 8.42 \\ \times \quad 9 \\ \hline \end{array}$

5. $\begin{array}{r} 14.05 \\ \times \quad 7 \\ \hline \end{array}$

6. $\begin{array}{r} 23.82 \\ \times \quad 5 \\ \hline \end{array}$

7. 4×9.3

8. 3×7.9

9. 5×42.89

10. 8×2.6

11. 6×0.92

12. 9×1.04

13. 7×2.18

14. 3×19.54

Problem Solving Real World

15. A half-dollar coin issued by the United States Mint measures 30.61 millimeters across. Mikk has 9 half dollars. He lines them up edge to edge in a row. What is the total length of the row of half dollars?

____

16. One pound of grapes costs $3.49. Linda buys exactly 3 pounds of grapes. How much will the grapes cost?

____

17. WRITE *Math* Compare and contrast the methods you can use to multiply a whole number and a decimal.

____

____

Lesson Check (5.NBT.A.2, 5.NBT.B.7)

1. Pete wants to make turkey sandwiches for two friends and himself. He wants each sandwich to contain 3.5 ounces of turkey. How many ounces of turkey does he need?

2. Gasoline costs $3.37 per gallon. Mary's father puts 9 gallons of gasoline in the tank of his car. How much will the gasoline cost?

Spiral Review (5.OA.A.1, 5.OA.A.2, 5.NBT.B.6, 5.NBT.B.7)

3. A group of 5 boys and 8 girls goes to the fair. Admission costs $9 per person. What expression can show the total amount the group will pay?

4. Sue and 4 friends buy a box of 362 baseball cards at a yard sale. If they share the cards equally, how many cards will each person receive?

5. Sarah rides her bicycle 2.7 miles to school. She takes a different route home, which is 2.5 miles. How many miles does Sarah ride to and from school each day?

6. Tim has a box of 15 markers. He gives 3 markers each to 4 friends. What expression can show the number of markers Tim has left?

FOR MORE PRACTICE GO TO THE **Personal Math Trainer**

Name ______________________

Multiply Using Expanded Form

Essential Question How can you use expanded form and place value to multiply a decimal and a whole number?

Number and Operations in Base Ten—5.NBT.B.7 *Also 5.NBT.A.2*

MATHEMATICAL PRACTICES
MP1, MP3, MP6

Unlock the Problem

The length of a day is the amount of time it takes a planet to make a complete rotation on its axis. On Jupiter, there are 9.8 Earth hours in a day. How many Earth hours are there in 46 days on Jupiter?

You can use a model and partial products to solve the problem.

▲ A day on Jupiter is called a Jovian day.

One Way Use a model.

Multiply. 46 × 9.8

THINK	MODEL	RECORD
STEP 1 Rewrite the factors in expanded form, and label the model. 46 = ______ + ______ 9.8 = ______ + ______	Area model: columns labeled 9 and 0.8; rows labeled 40 and 6	9.8 × 46 ____ ← 40 × 9 ____ ← 40 × 0.8 ____ ← 6 × 9 + ____ ← 6 × 0.8 ____
STEP 2 Multiply to find the area of each section. The area of each section represents a partial product.		
STEP 3 Add the partial products.		

So, there are ____________ Earth hours in 46 days on Jupiter.

1. **What if** you wanted to find the number of Earth hours in 125 days on Jupiter? How would your model change?

____

____

Another Way Use place value patterns.

A day on the planet Mercury lasts about 58.6 Earth days. How many Earth days are there in 14 days on Mercury?

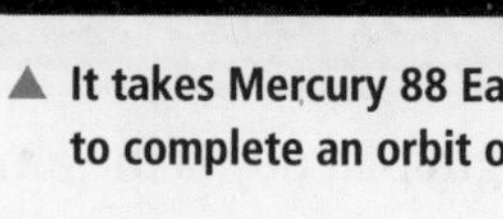

▲ It takes Mercury 88 Earth days to complete an orbit of the Sun.

Multiply. 14×58.6

STEP 1

Write the decimal factor as a whole number.

____

STEP 2

Multiply as with whole numbers.

____

STEP 3

Place the decimal point.

The decimal product is ____________ of the whole number product.

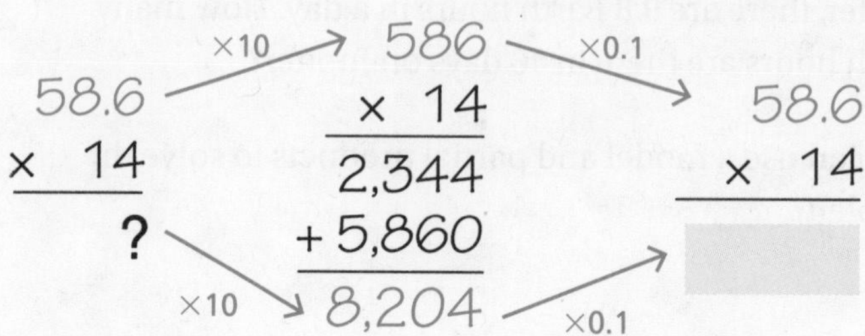

So, there are ____________ Earth days in 14 days on Mercury.

2. MATHEMATICAL PRACTICE 3 **Compare Strategies** What if you rewrite the problem as $(10 + 4) \times 58.6$ and used the Distributive Property to solve? Explain how this is similar to your model using place value.

____

____

Try This! Find the product.

A Use a model.

$52 \times 0.35 =$ ____________

B Use place value patterns.

$16 \times 9.18 =$ ____________

Name ___________________________

Draw a model to find the product.

1. $19 \times 0.75 =$ __________

	0.7	0.05
10		
9		

2. $27 \times 8.3 =$ __________

Find the product.

3. $18 \times 8.7 =$ __________

4. $23 \times 56.1 =$ __________

5. $47 \times 5.92 =$ __________

MATHEMATICAL PRACTICES 6

Describe how you could use an estimate to determine if your answer to Exercise 3 is reasonable.

On Your Own

Find the product.

6. $71 \times 8.3 =$ __________

7. $28 \times 0.19 =$ __________

8. THINKSMARTER A jacket costs $40 at the store. Max pays only 0.7 of the price because his father works at the store. Evan has a coupon for $10 off. Explain who will pay less for the jacket.

9. GO DEEPER An orchard sells apples in 3.5-pound bags. The orchard sells 45 bags of apples each day. How many pounds of apples does the orchard sell in 1 week?

Unlock the Problem  Real World

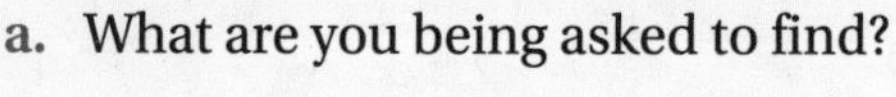

10. MATHEMATICAL PRACTICE 1 **Make Sense of Problems** While researching facts on the planet Earth, Kate learned that a true Earth day is about 23.93 hours long. How many hours are in 2 weeks on Earth?

a. What are you being asked to find?

____

____

b. What information do you need to know to solve the problem? ______________________________

____

____

c. Write an expression to represent the problem to be solved. ______________________________

d. Show the steps you used to solve the problem.

e. Complete the sentences.

On Earth, there are about __________ hours in a day, ______ days in 1 week, and ______ days in 2 weeks.

Since ______ × __________ = __________, there are about __________ hours in 2 weeks on Earth.

11. THINKSMARTER Use the numbers in the boxes to complete the number sentences. A number may be used more than once.

7.68	76.8	768

$48 \times 16 =$ __________

$48 \times 1.6 =$ __________ $4.8 \times 16 =$ __________

$0.48 \times 16 =$ __________ $48 \times 0.16 =$ __________

Name ______________________________

Multiply Using Expanded Form

Practice and Homework
Lesson 4.4

Common Core **COMMON CORE STANDARDS— 5.NBT.A.2, 5.NBT.B.7** *Perform operations with multi-digit whole numbers and with decimals to hundredths.*

Draw a model to find the product.

1. 37 × 9.5 = 351.5

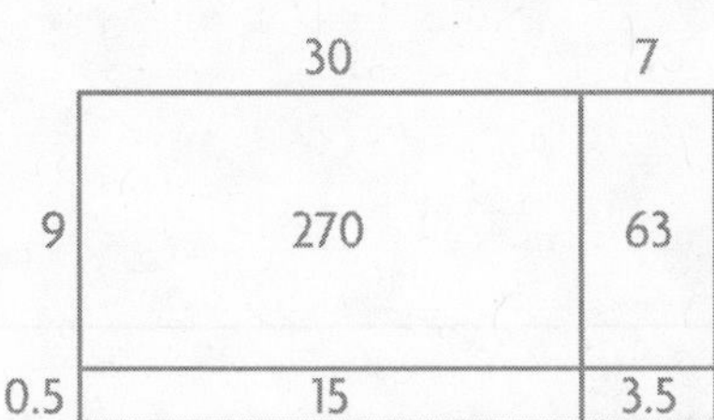

2. 84 × 0.24 = __________

Find the product.

3. 13 × 0.53 = __________

4. 27 × 89.5 = __________

5. 32 × 12.71 = __________

6. 17 × 0.52 = __________

7. 23 × 59.8 = __________

8. 61 × 15.98 = __________

Problem Solving

9. An object that weighs one pound on the moon will weigh about 6.02 pounds on Earth. Suppose a moon rock weighs 11 pounds on the moon. How much will the same rock weigh on Earth?

____

10. Tessa is on the track team. For practice and exercise, she runs 2.25 miles each day. At the end of 14 days, how many total miles will Tessa have run?

____

11. WRITE *Math* Compare the method of using expanded form and the method of using place value to multiply a decimal and a whole number.

____

____

Lesson Check (5.NBT.A.2, 5.NBT.B.7)

1. A baker is going to make 24 blueberry pies. She wants to make sure each pie contains 3.5 cups of blueberries. How many cups of blueberries will she need?

2. Aaron buys postcards while he is on vacation. It costs $0.28 to send one postcard. Aaron wants to send 12 postcards. How much will it cost Aaron to send all the postcards?

Spiral Review (5.NBT.A.1, 5.NBT.A.2, 5.NBT.B.6, 5.NBT.B.7)

3. What is the value of the digit 4 in the number 524,897,123?

4. How many zeros will be in the product $(6 \times 5) \times 10^3$?

5. Roast beef costs $8.49 per pound. What is the cost of 2 pounds of roast beef?

6. North Ridge Middle School collected 5,022 cans of food for a food drive. Each of the 18 homerooms collected the same number of cans. About how many cans did each homeroom collect?

FOR MORE PRACTICE GO TO THE Personal Math Trainer

Name ____________________

Problem Solving • Multiply Money

Essential Question How can the strategy *draw a diagram* help you solve a decimal multiplication problem?

Number and Operations in Base Ten—5.NBT.B.7

MATHEMATICAL PRACTICES
MP1, MP4

Unlock the Problem

A group of friends go to a local fair. Jayson spends \$3.75. Myra spends 3 times as much as Jayson. Teresa spends \$5.25 more than Myra. How much does Teresa spend?

Use the graphic organizer below to help you solve the problem.

Read the Problem

What do I need to find?

I need to find ____________________

____

____________________.

What information do I need to use?

I need to use the amount spent by __________ to find the amount spent by __________ and __________ at the fair.

How will I use the information?

I can draw a diagram to show ____________________

____

____________________.

Solve the Problem

The amount of money Myra and Teresa spend depends on the amount Jayson spends. Draw a diagram to compare the amounts without calculating. Then, use the diagram to find the amount each person spends.

Jayson	\$3.75			
Myra	____	____	____	
Teresa	____	____	____	\$5.25

Jayson: \$3.75

Myra: 3 × __________ = __________

Teresa: __________ + \$5.25 = __________

So, Teresa spent __________ at the fair.

Try Another Problem

Julie's savings account has a balance of $57.85 in January. By March, her balance is 4 times as much as her January balance. Between March and November, Julie deposits a total of $78.45. If she does not withdraw any money from her account, what should Julie's balance be in November?

Read the Problem	Solve the Problem
What do I need to find?	
What information do I need to use?	
How will I use the information?	So, Julie's savings account balance will be _______________ in November.

- **MATHEMATICAL PRACTICE 1** **Evaluate Reasonableness** How does the diagram help you determine if your answer is reasonable? _______________

____

Math Talk MATHEMATICAL PRACTICES 4

Use Diagrams Describe a different diagram you could use to solve the problem.

Name ________________

Share and Show

MATH BOARD

1. Manuel collects $45.18 for a fundraiser. Gerome collects $18.07 more than Manuel. Cindy collects 2 times as much as Gerome. How much money does Cindy collect for the fundraiser?

First, draw a diagram to show the amount Manuel collects.

Then, draw a diagram to show the amount Gerome collects.

Next, draw a diagram to show the amount Cindy collects.

Finally, find the amount each person collects.

Cindy collects ____________ for the fundraiser.

2. **What if** Gerome collects $9.23 more than Manuel? If Cindy still collects 2 times as much as Gerome, how much money would Cindy collect?

____

3. Jenn buys a pair of jeans for $24.99. Her friend Karen spends $3.50 more for the same pair of jeans. Vicki paid the same price as Karen for the jeans but bought 2 pairs. How much did Vicki spend?

____

4. GO DEEPER The fifth-grade students in Miguel's school formed 3 teams to raise money for the Penny Harvest fundraiser. Team A raised $65.45. Team B raised 3 times as much as Team A. Team C raised $20.15 more than Team B. How much money did Team C raise?

____

WRITE Math • Show Your Work

On Your Own

Use the sign for 5–7.

Surfer Joe's Surf Shop
T-shirt $12.75
Board Shorts $25.99
Sandals $8.95
Towel $5.65
Sunglasses $15.50

5. Nathan receives a coupon in the mail for $10 off of a purchase of $100 or more. If he buys 3 pairs of board shorts, 2 towels, and a pair of sunglasses, will he spend enough to use the coupon? How much will his purchase cost?

____

6. MATHEMATICAL PRACTICE 1 **Make Sense of Problems** Ana spends $33.90 on 3 different items. If she did not buy board shorts, which three items did Ana buy?

____

7. GO DEEPER Austin shops at Surfer Joe's Surf Shop before going to the beach. He buys 2 T-shirts, a pair of board shorts, and a towel. If he gives the cashier $60, how much change will Austin get back?

____

8. THINK SMARTER It costs $5.15 to rent a kayak for 1 hour at a local state park. The price per hour stays the same for up to 5 hours of rental. After 5 hours, the cost decreases to $3.75 per hour. How much would it cost to rent a kayak for 6 hours?

____

9. THINK SMARTER At a video game store it costs $10.45 to buy one movie. It costs 3 times as much to buy one video game. Choose the answer to complete the sentence.

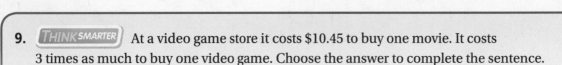

It would cost Jon [$20.90 / $31.35 / $41.80] to buy one movie and one video game.

Name ______________________

Problem Solving • Multiply Money

Common Core **COMMON CORE STANDARD—5.NBT.B.7**
Perform operations with multi-digit whole numbers and with decimals to hundredths.

Solve each problem.

1. Three friends go to the local farmers' market. Ashlee spends $8.25. Natalie spends 4 times as much as Ashlee. Patrick spends $9.50 more than Natalie. How much does Patrick spend?

Ashlee	$8.25				
Natalie	$8.25	$8.25	$8.25	$8.25	
Patrick	$8.25	$8.25	$8.25	$8.25	$9.50

4 × $8.25 = $33.00

$33.00 + $9.50 = $42.50

$42.50

2. Kimmy's savings account has a balance of $76.23 in June. By September, her balance is 5 times as much as her June balance. Between September and December, Kimmy deposits a total of $87.83 into her account. If she does not withdraw any money from her account, what should Kimmy's balance be in December?

____

3. Amy raises $58.75 to participate in a walk-a-thon. Jeremy raises $23.25 more than Amy. Oscar raises 3 times as much as Jeremy. How much money does Oscar raise?

____

4. **WRITE** *Math* Create a word problem that uses multiplication of money. Draw a bar model to help you write equations to solve the problem.

____

____

____

Lesson Check (5.NBT.B.7)

1. A family of two adults and four children is going to an amusement park. Admission is \$21.75 for adults and \$15.25 for children. What is the total cost of the family's admission?

2. Ms. Rosenbaum buys 5 crates of apples at the market. Each crate costs \$12.50. She also buys one crate of pears for \$18.75. What is the total cost of the apples and pears?

Spiral Review (5.OA.A.2, 5.NBT.A.2, 5.NBT.A.4, 5.NF.B.3)

3. How do you write $10 \times 10 \times 10 \times 10$ using exponents?

4. What number represents 125.638 rounded to the nearest hundredth?

5. The sixth-graders at Meadowbrook Middle School are going on a field trip. The 325 students and adults will ride in school buses. Each bus holds 48 people. How many school buses are needed?

6. A restaurant can seat 100 people. It has booths that seat 4 people and tables that seat 6 people. So far, 5 of the booths are full. What expression matches the situation?

FOR MORE PRACTICE GO TO THE **Personal Math Trainer**

Name ______________________________

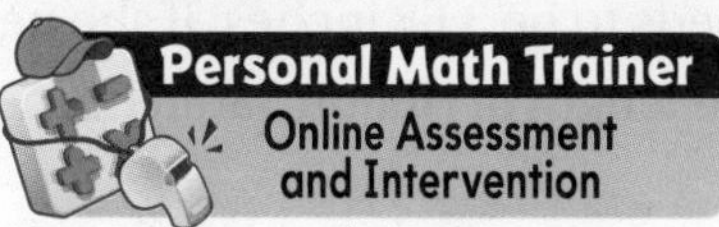

Concepts and Skills

1. **Explain** how you can use a quick picture to find 3×2.7. (5.NBT.B.7) ______________________________

____

____

Complete the pattern. (5.NBT.A.2)

2. $1 \times 3.6 =$ ________

$10 \times 3.6 =$ ________

$100 \times 3.6 =$ ________

$1{,}000 \times 3.6 =$ ________

3. $10^0 \times 17.55 =$ ________

$10^1 \times 17.55 =$ ________

$10^2 \times 17.55 =$ ________

$10^3 \times 17.55 =$ ________

4. $1 \times 29 =$ ________

$0.1 \times 29 =$ ________

$0.01 \times 29 =$ ________

Find the product. (5.NBT.B.7)

5. $\begin{array}{r} 3.14 \\ \times \quad 8 \\ \hline \end{array}$

6. 17×0.67

7. 29×7.3

Draw a diagram to solve. (5.NBT.B.7)

8. Julie spends $5.62 at the store. Micah spends 5 times as much as Julie. Jeremy spends $6.72 more than Micah. How much money does each person spend?

Julie: $5.62

Micah: ________

Jeremy: ________

9. Sarah is cutting ribbons for a pep rally. The length of each ribbon needs to be 3.68 inches. If she needs 1,000 ribbons, what is the length of ribbon Sarah needs? (5.NBT.A.2)

____

10. Adam is carrying books to the classroom for his teacher. Each books weighs 3.85 pounds. If he carries 4 books, how many pounds is Adam carrying? (5.NBT.B.7)

____

11. A car travels 54.9 miles in an hour. If the car continues at the same speed for 12 hours, how many miles will it travel? (5.NBT.B.7)

____

12. GO DEEPER Charlie saves $21.45 each month for 6 months. In the seventh month, he only saves $10.60. How much money will Charlie have saved after 7 months? (5.NBT.B.7)

____

Name ______________________

Decimal Multiplication

Essential Question How can you use a model to multiply decimals?

Common Core **Number and Operations in Base Ten—5.NBT.B.7**

MATHEMATICAL PRACTICES
MP2, MP3, MP8

Investigate

Materials ■ color pencils

The distance from Charlene's house to her school is 0.8 mile. Charlene rides her bike 0.7 of the distance and walks the rest of the way. How far does Charlene ride her bike to school?

You can use a decimal square to multiply decimals.

Multiply. 0.7 × 0.8

A. Draw a square with 10 equal columns.

- What decimal value does each column represent? ______

B. Using a color pencil, shade columns on the grid to represent the distance to Charlene's school.

- The distance to the school is 0.8 mile.

  How many columns did you shade? ______________

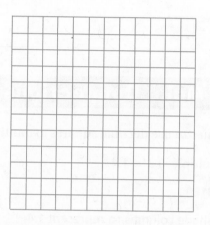

C. Divide the square into 10 equal rows.

- What decimal value does each row represent? ______

D. Using a different color, shade rows that overlap the shaded columns to represent the distance to school that Charlene rides her bike.

- What part of the distance to school does Charlene ride her bike? __________

- How many rows of the shaded columns did you shade?

  ____

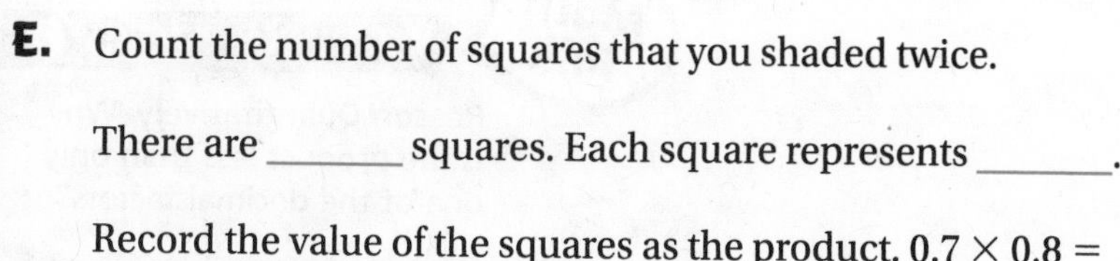

E. Count the number of squares that you shaded twice.

There are ______ squares. Each square represents ______.

Record the value of the squares as the product. 0.7 × 0.8 = __________

So, Charlene rides her bike for __________ mile.

Draw Conclusions

1. **Explain** how dividing the decimal square into 10 equal columns and rows shows that tenths multiplied by tenths is equal to hundredths.

____

____

____

2. MATHEMATICAL PRACTICE 8 **Draw Conclusions** Why is the part of the model representing the product less than either factor?

____

____

____

Make Connections

You can use decimal squares to multiply decimals greater than 1.

Multiply. 0.3×1.4

STEP 1

Shade columns to represent 1.4.

How many tenths are in 1.4?

____

STEP 2

Shade rows that overlap the shaded columns to represent 0.3.

How many rows of the shaded columns did you shade? _______________

STEP 3

Count the number of squares that you shaded twice. Record the product at the right.

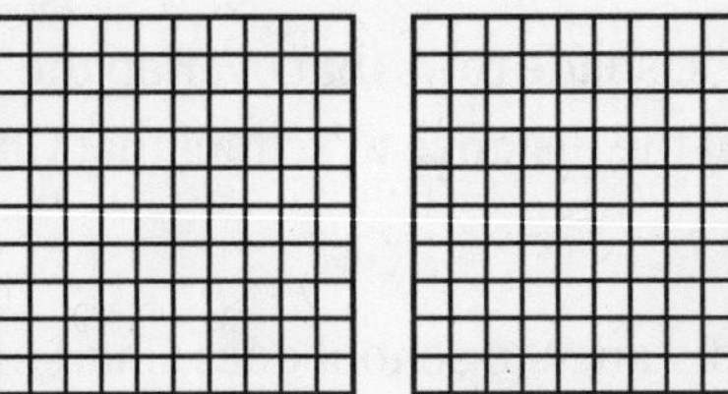

$0.3 \times 1.4 =$ _______________

MATHEMATICAL PRACTICES 2

Reason Quantitatively Why is the product less than only one of the decimal factors?

Name ___________________________

Share and Show MATH BOARD

Multiply. Use the decimal model.

1. 0.8 × 0.4 = ___________

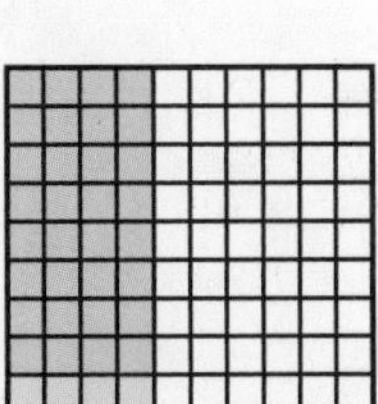

2. 0.1 × 0.7 = ___________

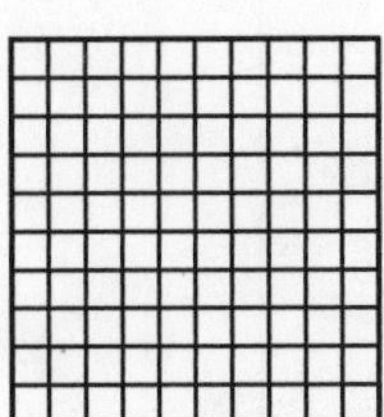

3. 0.4 × 1.6 = ___________

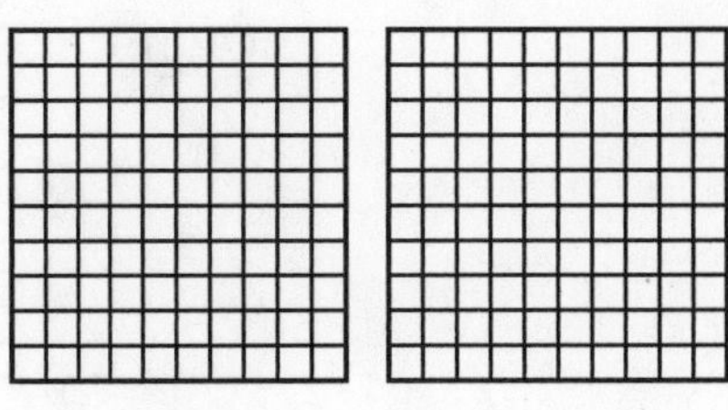

4. 0.3 × 0.4 = ___________

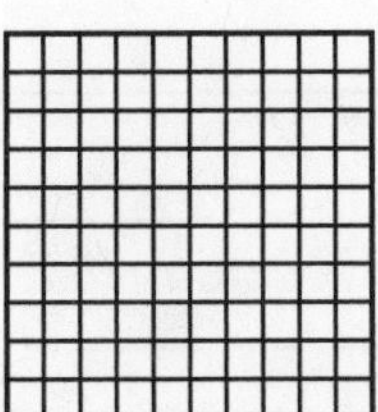

5. 0.9 × 0.6 = ___________

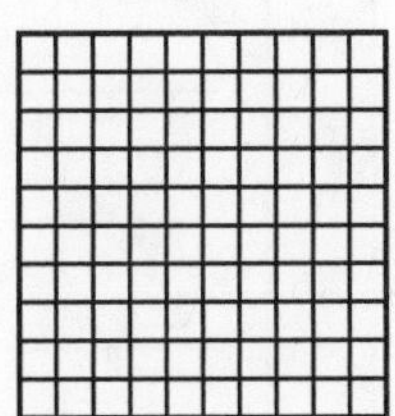

6. 0.5 × 1.2 = ___________

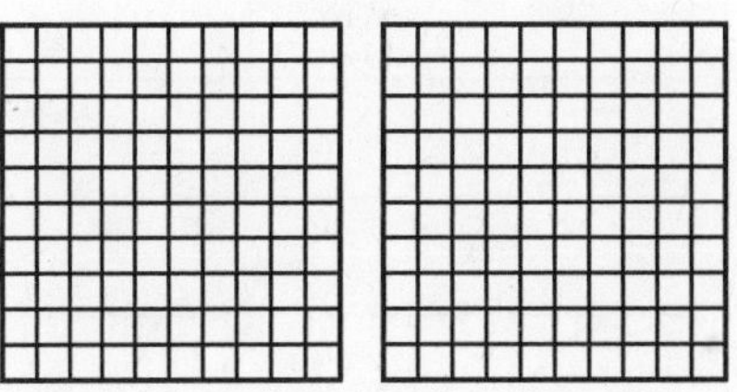

Problem Solving • Applications

7. GO DEEPER Rachel buys 1.5 pounds of grapes. She eats 0.3 of that amount on Tuesday and 0.2 of that amount on Wednesday. How many pounds of grapes are left?

____

WRITE Math • Show Your Work

8. THINK SMARTER A large bottle contains 1.2 liters of olive oil. A medium-sized bottle has 0.6 times the amount of olive oil as the large bottle. How much more olive oil does the large bottle contain than the medium-sized bottle?

____

9. MATHEMATICAL PRACTICE 3 **Compare Representations** Randy and Stacy used models to find 0.3 of 0.5. Both Randy's and Stacy's models are shown below. Whose model makes sense? Whose model is nonsense? Explain your reasoning below each model. Then record the correct answer.

Randy's Model

Stacy's Model

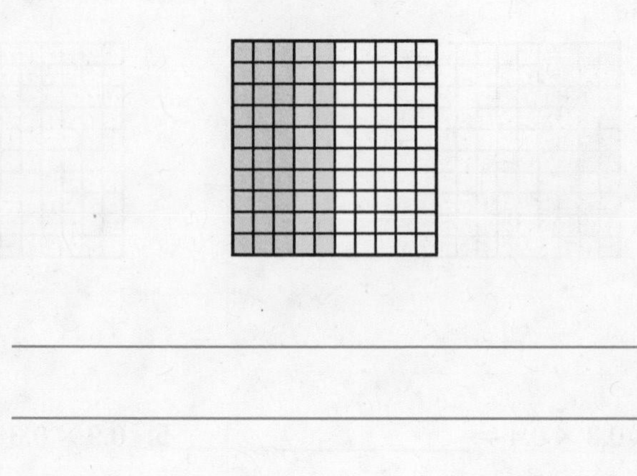

$0.3 \times 0.5 =$ ________

- For the answer that is nonsense, describe the error the student made.

10. THINK SMARTER Shade the model to show 0.2×0.6. Then find the product.

$0.2 \times 0.6 =$ ________

Name ______________________________

Decimal Multiplication

Common Core **COMMON CORE STANDARD—5.NBT.B.7**
Perform operations with multi-digit whole numbers and with decimals to hundredths.

Multiply. Use the decimal model.

1. 0.3 × 0.6 = 0.18

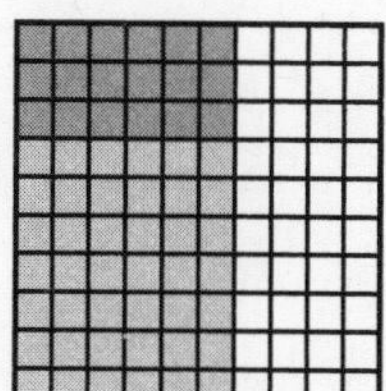

2. 0.2 × 0.8 = ____________

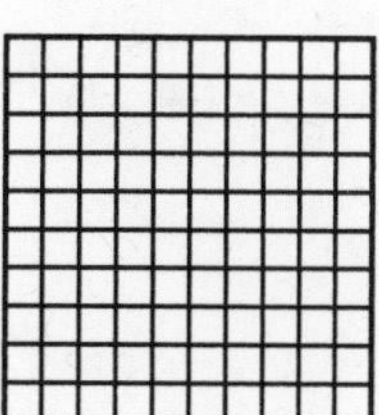

3. 0.5 × 1.7 = ____________

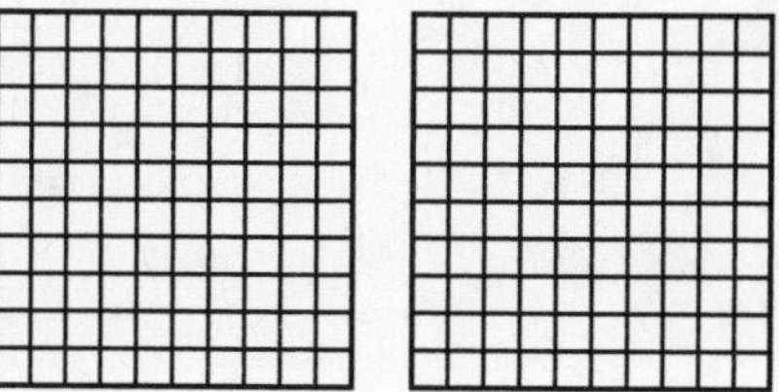

4. 0.6 × 0.7 = ____________

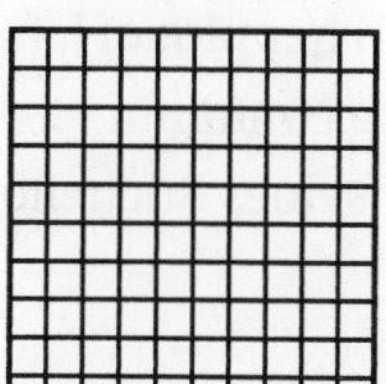

5. 0.8 × 0.5 = ____________

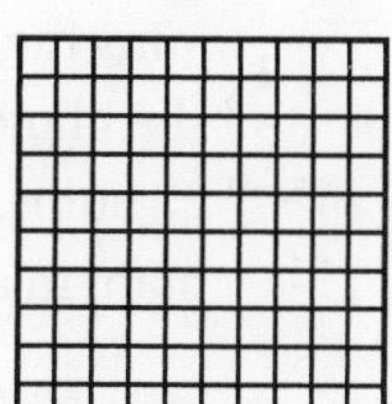

6. 0.4 × 1.9 = ____________

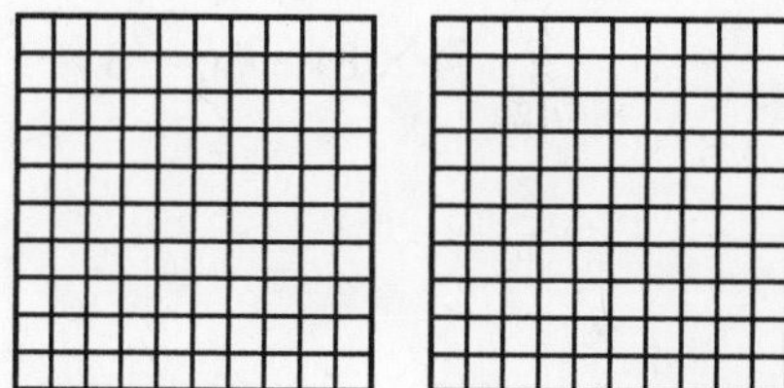

Problem Solving Real World

7. A certain type of bamboo plant grows 1.2 feet in 1 day. At that rate, how many feet could the plant grow in 0.5 day?

____

8. The distance from the park to the grocery store is 0.9 mile. Ezra runs 8 tenths of that distance and walks the rest of the way. How far does Ezra run from the park to the grocery store?

____

9. WRITE *Math* Write a story problem that involves multiplying a decimal less than 2 by a decimal less than 1. Include the solution and the work you did to find it.

____

____

____

Lesson Check (5.NBT.B.7)

1. Liz is hiking a trail that is 0.8 mile long. Liz hikes the first 2 tenths of the distance by herself. She hikes the rest of the way with her friends. How far does Liz hike by herself?

2. One cup of cooked zucchini has 1.9 grams of protein. How much protein is in 0.5 cup of zucchini?

Spiral Review (5.NBT.B.5, 5.NBT.B.6, 5.NBT.B.7)

3. What property does the statement show?

$$(4 \times 8) \times 3 = (8 \times 4) \times 3$$

4. At the beginning of the school year, Rochelle joins the school garden club. In her plot of land, she plants 4 rows of tulips, each containing 27 bulbs. How many tulip bulbs does Rochelle plant in all?

5. In which place is the first digit of the quotient?

$$3{,}589 \div 18$$

6. At a football game, Jasmine bought a soft pretzel for \$2.25 and a bottle of water for \$1.50. She paid with a \$5 bill. How much change should Jasmine get back?

FOR MORE PRACTICE GO TO THE **Personal Math Trainer**

Name ______________________________

Multiply Decimals

Essential Question What strategies can you use to place a decimal point in a product?

Number and Operations in Base Ten—5.NBT.B.7 *Also 5.NBT.A.2*

MATHEMATICAL PRACTICES
MP1, MP3, MP8

CONNECT You can use what you have learned about patterns and place value to place the decimal point in the product when you multiply two decimals.

$1 \times 0.1 = 0.1$

$0.1 \times 0.1 = 0.01$

$0.01 \times 0.1 = 0.001$

Remember

When a number is multiplied by a decimal, the decimal point moves one place to the left in the product for each decreasing place value being multiplied.

Unlock the Problem — Real World

A male leopard seal is measured and has a length of 2.8 meters. A male elephant seal is about 1.5 times as long. What length is the male elephant seal?

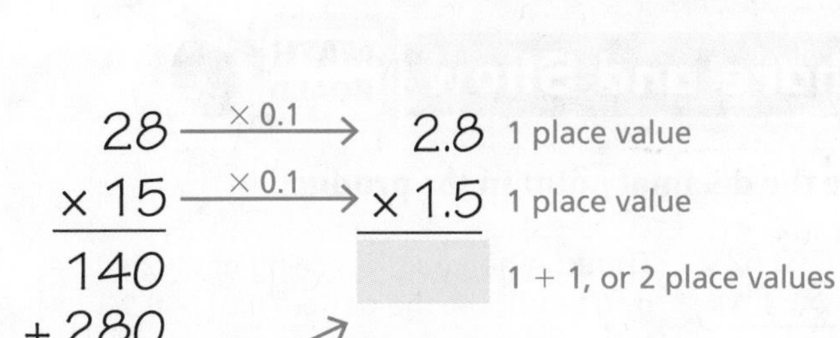

Multiply. 1.5 × 2.8

One Way Use place value.

STEP 1

Multiply as with whole numbers.

STEP 2

Place the decimal point.

Think: Tenths are being multiplied by tenths. Use the pattern 0.1 × 0.1.

Place the decimal point so the value of the decimal is ____________.

```
   28  --× 0.1-->   2.8   1 place value
 × 15  --× 0.1--> × 1.5   1 place value
  140              ____   1 + 1, or 2 place values
+ 280
  420  --× 0.01--^
```

So, the length of a male elephant seal is about ______ meters.

- MATHEMATICAL PRACTICE 1 **Analyze** What if you multiplied 2.8 by 1.74? What would be the place value of the product? Explain your answer.

____

____

Another Way Use estimation.

You can use an estimate to place the decimal point in a product.

Multiply. 7.8 × 3.12

STEP 1

Esimate by rounding each factor to the nearest whole number.

7.8 × 3.12
↓ ↓
____ × ____ = ____

$$\begin{array}{r} 312 \\ \times\ 78 \\ \hline \end{array}$$

STEP 2

Multiply as with whole numbers.

STEP 3

Use the estimate to place the decimal point.

Think: The product should be close to your estimate.

$$\begin{array}{r} 3.12 \\ \times\ 7.8 \\ \hline \end{array}$$

7.8 × 3.12 = ________

Share and Show MATH BOARD

Place the decimal point in the product.

1. $$\begin{array}{r} 3.62 \\ \times\ 1.4 \\ \hline 5068 \end{array}$$

Think: A hundredth is being multiplied by a tenth. Use the pattern 0.01 × 0.1.

2. $$\begin{array}{r} 6.8 \\ \times\ 1.2 \\ \hline 816 \end{array}$$

Estimate: 1 × 7 = ______

Find the product.

3. $$\begin{array}{r} 0.9 \\ \times\ 0.8 \\ \hline \end{array}$$

4. $$\begin{array}{r} 84.5 \\ \times\ 5.5 \\ \hline \end{array}$$

5. $$\begin{array}{r} 2.39 \\ \times\ 2.7 \\ \hline \end{array}$$

Math Talk MATHEMATICAL PRACTICES 8

Use Repeated Reasoning How can you know the place value of the product for Exercise 5 before you solve?

Name ___________________________

On Your Own

Find the product.

6. $\begin{array}{r} 7.9 \\ \times\ 3.4 \\ \hline \end{array}$

7. $\begin{array}{r} 9.2 \\ \times\ 5.6 \\ \hline \end{array}$

8. $\begin{array}{r} 3.45 \\ \times\ 9.7 \\ \hline \end{array}$

9. $\begin{array}{r} 45.3 \\ \times\ 0.8 \\ \hline \end{array}$

10. $\begin{array}{r} 6.98 \\ \times\ 2.5 \\ \hline \end{array}$

11. $\begin{array}{r} 7.02 \\ \times\ 3.4 \\ \hline \end{array}$

Practice: Copy and Solve **Find the product.**

12. 3.4×5.2
13. 0.9×2.46
14. 9.1×5.7
15. 4.8×6.01
16. 7.6×18.7
17. 1.5×9.34
18. 0.77×14.9
19. 3.3×58.14

20. Charlie has an adult Netherlands dwarf rabbit that weighs 1.2 kilograms. Cliff's adult Angora rabbit weighs 2.9 times as much as Charlie's rabbit. How much does Cliff's rabbit weigh?

____

21. GO DEEPER Gina bought 2.5 pounds of peaches that cost $1.38 per pound at the grocery store. Amy went to the local farmer's market and purchased 3.5 pounds of peaches at $0.98 per pound. Who spent more money, and how much more?

____

Problem Solving • Applications

22. GO DEEPER John has pet rabbits in an enclosure that has an area of 30.72 square feet. The enclosure Taylor is planning to build for his rabbits will be 2.2 times as large as John's. How many more square feet will Taylor's enclosure have than John's enclosure?

____

23. THINK SMARTER A zoo is planning a new building for the penguin exhibit. First, they made a model that was 1.3 meters tall. Then, they made a more detailed model that was 1.5 times as tall as the first model. The building will be 2.5 times as tall as the height of the detailed model. What will be the height of the building?

____

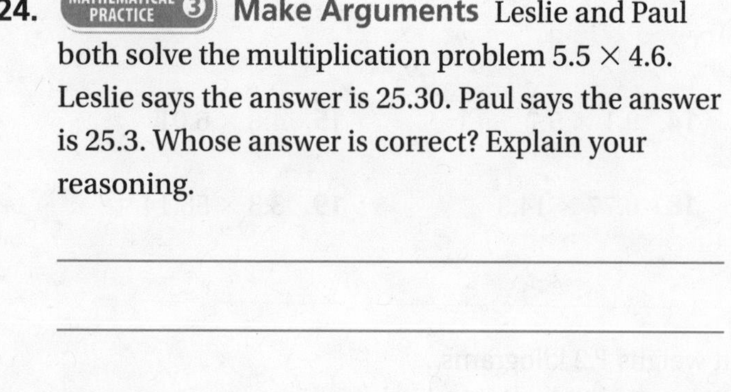

24. MATHEMATICAL PRACTICE 3 **Make Arguments** Leslie and Paul both solve the multiplication problem 5.5×4.6. Leslie says the answer is 25.30. Paul says the answer is 25.3. Whose answer is correct? Explain your reasoning.

____

____

____

____

25. THINK SMARTER For 25a–25d select True or False to indicate if the statement is correct.

25a. The product of 1.3 and 2.1 is 2.73. ○ True ○ False

25b. The product of 2.6 and 0.2 is 52. ○ True ○ False

25c. The product of 0.08 and 0.3 is 2.4. ○ True ○ False

25d. The product of 0.88 and 1.3 is 1.144. ○ True ○ False

Name ____________________

Multiply Decimals

COMMON CORE STANDARDS—5.NBT.B.7 *Perform operations with multi-digit whole numbers and with decimals to hundredths.*

Find the product.

1. 5.8 × 2.4 = 13.92

$$\begin{array}{r} 58 \\ \times\ 24 \\ \hline 232 \\ +\ 1{,}160 \\ \hline 1{,}392 \end{array}$$

2. $\begin{array}{r} 7.3 \\ \times\ 9.6 \\ \hline \end{array}$

3. $\begin{array}{r} 46.3 \\ \times\ 0.8 \\ \hline \end{array}$

4. $\begin{array}{r} 29.5 \\ \times\ 1.3 \\ \hline \end{array}$

5. $\begin{array}{r} 3.76 \\ \times\ 4.8 \\ \hline \end{array}$

6. $\begin{array}{r} 9.07 \\ \times\ 6.5 \\ \hline \end{array}$

7. 0.42 × 75.3

8. 5.6 × 61.84

9. 7.5 × 18.74

10. 0.9 × 53.8

Problem Solving

11. Aretha runs a marathon in 3.25 hours. Neal takes 1.6 times as long to run the same marathon. How many hours does it take Neal to run the marathon?

____

12. Tiffany catches a fish that weighs 12.3 pounds. Frank catches a fish that weighs 2.5 times as much as Tiffany's fish. How many pounds does Frank's fish weigh?

____

13. **WRITE** *Math* Write a problem that includes multiplying decimals. Explain how you know where to place the decimal in the product.

____

____

Lesson Check (5.NBT.A.2, 5.NBT.B.7)

1. Sue buys material to make a costume. She buys 1.75 yards of red material. She buys 1.2 times as many yards of blue material. How many yards of blue material does Sue buy?

2. Last week Juan worked 20.5 hours. This week he works 1.5 times as many hours as he did last week. How many hours does Juan work this week?

Spiral Review (5.NBT.A.2, 5.NBT.A.3a, 5.NBT.A.3b, 5.NBT.B.7)

3. The expression below shows a number in expanded form. What is the standard form of the number?

   $(2 \times 10) + (3 \times \frac{1}{10}) + (9 \times \frac{1}{100}) + (7 \times \frac{1}{1,000})$

4. Kelly buys a sweater for $16.79 and a pair of pants for $28.49. She pays with a $50 bill. How much change should Kelly get back?

5. Elvira is using a pattern to multiply $10^3 \times 37.2$.

   $10^0 \times 37.2 = 37.2$
   $10^1 \times 37.2 = 372$
   $10^2 \times 37.2 = 3,720$
   $10^3 \times 37.2 = \_\_\_\_\_\_$

   What is the product $10^3 \times 37.2$?

6. What digit should go in the box to make the following statement true?

   $63.749 < 63.\square2$

Name ______________________

Zeros in the Product

Essential Question How do you know you have the correct number of decimal places in your product?

Common Core **Number and Operations in Base Ten—5.NBT.B.7** *Also 5.NBT.A.2*

MATHEMATICAL PRACTICES
MP1, MP2, MP6, MP8

Unlock the Problem (Real World)

CONNECT When decimals are multiplied, the product may not have enough digits to place the decimal point. In these cases, you may need to write additional zeros as place holders.

Students are racing typical garden snails and measuring the distance the snails travel in 1 minute. Chris's snail travels a distance of 0.2 foot. Jamie's snail travels 0.4 times as far as Chris's snail. How far does Jamie's snail travel?

- Using the given information, describe what you are being asked to find.

____

____

____

Multiply. 0.4 × 0.2

STEP 1

Multiply as with whole numbers.

____

STEP 2

Determine the position of the decimal point in the product.

Since tenths are being multiplied by tenths,

the product will show __________.

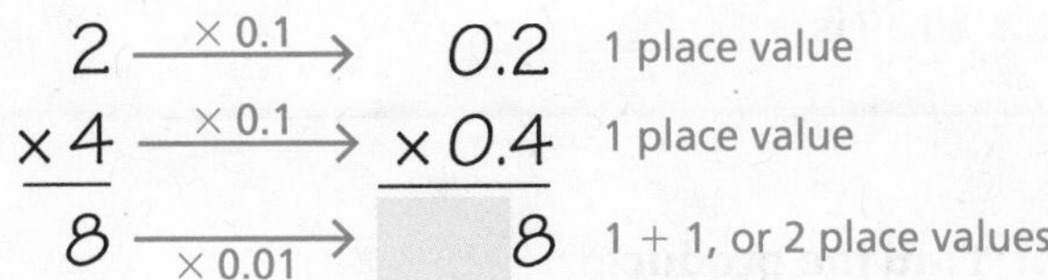

STEP 3

Place the decimal point.

Are there enough digits in the product

to place the decimal point? ______

Write zeros, as needed, to the left of the whole number product to place the decimal point.

MATHEMATICAL PRACTICES 8

Generalize Explain how you know when to write zeros in the product to place a decimal point.

So, Jamie's snail travels a distance of __________ foot.

Example Multiply money.

Multiply. 0.2 × \$0.30

STEP 1 Multiply as with whole numbers.

Think: The factors are 30 hundredths and 2 tenths.

What are the whole numbers you will multiply?

____

$$\begin{array}{r} \$0.30 \\ \times \quad 0.2 \\ \hline \end{array}$$

STEP 2 Determine the position of the decimal point in the product.

Since hundredths are being multiplied by tenths, the product will show ___________.

STEP 3 Place the decimal point. Write zeros to the left of the whole number product as needed.

Since the problem involves dollars and cents, what place value should you use to show cents?

____

So, 0.2 × \$0.30 is ___________.

Try This! Find the product.

0.2 × 0.05 = ___________

What steps did you take to find the product?

____

____

____

____

____

____

MATHEMATICAL PRACTICES 6

Explain why the answer to the Try This! can have a digit with a place value of hundredths or thousandths and still be correct.

Name ______________________________

Share and Show

Write zeros in the product.

1. $\begin{array}{r} 0.05 \\ \times\ 0.7 \\ \hline \square 35 \end{array}$

   Think: Hundredths are multiplied by tenths. What should be the place value of the product?

2. $\begin{array}{r} 0.2 \\ \times 0.3 \\ \hline \square 6 \end{array}$

3. $\begin{array}{r} 0.02 \\ \times 0.2 \\ \hline \square 4 \end{array}$

Find the product.

4. $\begin{array}{r} \$0.05 \\ \times\ \ 0.8 \\ \hline \end{array}$

5. $\begin{array}{r} 0.09 \\ \times\ 0.7 \\ \hline \end{array}$

6. $\begin{array}{r} 0.2 \\ \times 0.1 \\ \hline \end{array}$

Math Talk MATHEMATICAL PRACTICES 1

Analyze Relationships Why does 0.04×0.2 have the same product as 0.4×0.02?

On Your Own

Find the product.

7. $\begin{array}{r} 0.3 \\ \times 0.3 \\ \hline \end{array}$

8. $\begin{array}{r} 0.05 \\ \times\ 0.3 \\ \hline \end{array}$

9. $\begin{array}{r} 0.02 \\ \times\ 0.4 \\ \hline \end{array}$

10. $\begin{array}{r} \$0.40 \\ \times\ \ 0.1 \\ \hline \end{array}$

MATHEMATICAL PRACTICE 2 **Use Reasoning** **Algebra Find the value of n.**

11. $0.03 \times 0.6 = n$

    $n =$ ____________

12. $n \times 0.2 = 0.08$

    $n =$ ____________

13. $0.09 \times n = 0.063$

    $n =$ ____________

14. THINKSMARTER Michael multiplies 0.2 by a number. He records the product as 0.008. What number did Michael use?

____

Unlock the Problem 

15. GO DEEPER On an average day, a garden snail can travel about 0.05 mile. The snail travels 0.2 times as far as the average distance on Day 1. It travels 0.6 times as far as the average distance on Day 2. How far does it travel in two days?

a. What are you being asked to find? ______________________

b. What information will you use to solve the problem? ______________________

____

____

c. Which operations can you use to solve the problem? ______________________

____

____

d. Show how you will solve the problem.

e. Complete the sentence. A garden snail travels

__________ mile in 2 days.

16. In a science experiment, Tania uses 0.8 ounce of water to create a reaction. She wants the next reaction to be 0.1 times the size of the previous reaction. How much water should she use?

____

Personal Math Trainer

17. THINK SMARTER+ The library is 0.5 mile from Celine's house. The dog park is 0.3 times as far from Celine's house as the library. How far is the dog park from Celine's house? Write an equation and solve.

____

Name ______________________________

Zeros in the Product

Common Core **COMMON CORE STANDARDS—5.NBT.B.7**
Perform operations with multi-digit whole numbers and with decimals to hundredths.

Find the product.

1. $\begin{array}{r} 0.07 \\ \times\ 0.2 \\ \hline 0.014 \end{array}$ $\begin{array}{r} 7 \\ \times 2 \\ \hline 14 \end{array}$

2. $\begin{array}{r} 0.3 \\ \times\ 0.1 \\ \hline \end{array}$

3. $\begin{array}{r} 0.05 \\ \times\ 0.8 \\ \hline \end{array}$

4. $\begin{array}{r} 0.08 \\ \times\ 0.3 \\ \hline \end{array}$

5. $\begin{array}{r} 0.06 \\ \times\ 0.7 \\ \hline \end{array}$

6. $\begin{array}{r} 0.2 \\ \times\ 0.4 \\ \hline \end{array}$

7. $\begin{array}{r} 0.05 \\ \times\ 0.4 \\ \hline \end{array}$

8. $\begin{array}{r} 0.08 \\ \times\ 0.8 \\ \hline \end{array}$

9. $\begin{array}{r} \$0.90 \\ \times\ 0.1 \\ \hline \end{array}$

10. $\begin{array}{r} 0.02 \\ \times\ 0.3 \\ \hline \end{array}$

11. $\begin{array}{r} 0.09 \\ \times\ 0.5 \\ \hline \end{array}$

12. $\begin{array}{r} \$0.05 \\ \times\ 0.2 \\ \hline \end{array}$

Problem Solving

13. A beaker contains 0.5 liter of a solution. Jordan uses 0.08 of the solution for an experiment. How much of the solution does Jordan use?

____

14. A certain type of nuts are on sale at $0.35 per pound. Tamara buys 0.2 pound of nuts. How much will the nuts cost?

____

15. WRITE *Math* Explain how you write products when there are not enough digits in the product to place the decimal point.

____

____

Lesson Check (5.NBT.A.2, 5.NBT.B.7)

1. Cliff multiplies 0.06 and 0.5. What product should he record?

2. What is the product of 0.4 and 0.09?

Spiral Review (5.NBT.A.1, 5.NBT.A.4, 5.NBT.B.5, 5.NBT.B.6)

3. A florist makes 24 bouquets. She uses 16 flowers for each bouquet. Altogether, how many flowers does she use?

4. Mark has 312 books in his bookcases. He has 11 times as many fiction books as nonfiction books. How many fiction books does Mark have?

5. Dwayne buys a pumpkin that weighs 12.65 pounds. To the nearest tenth of a pound, how much does the pumpkin weigh?

6. What is the value of the digit 6 in the number 896,000?

Name ______________________

Chapter 4 Review/Test

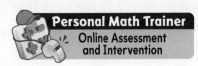

Personal Math Trainer
Online Assessment and Intervention

1. Omar is making a scale model of the Statue of Liberty for a report on New York City. The Statue of Liberty is 305 feet tall measuring from the ground to the tip of the torch. If the model is $\frac{1}{100}$ the actual size of the Statue of Liberty, how tall is the model?

______________ feet

2. For 2a–2d, choose Yes or No to indicate whether the product is correct.

2a. $0.62 \times 10 = 62$ ○ Yes ○ No

2b. $0.53 \times 10 = 5.3$ ○ Yes ○ No

2c. $0.09 \times 100 = 9$ ○ Yes ○ No

2d. $0.60 \times 1{,}000 = 60$ ○ Yes ○ No

3. Nicole is making 1,000 bows for people who donate to the library book sale. She needs a piece of ribbon that is 0.75 meter long for each bow. How many meters of ribbon does Nicole need to make the bows? Explain how to find the answer.

4. Fatima is shading this model to show 0.08×3. Shade the correct amount of boxes that will show the product.

Fatima should shade ☐ groups of ☐ small squares or ☐ small squares.

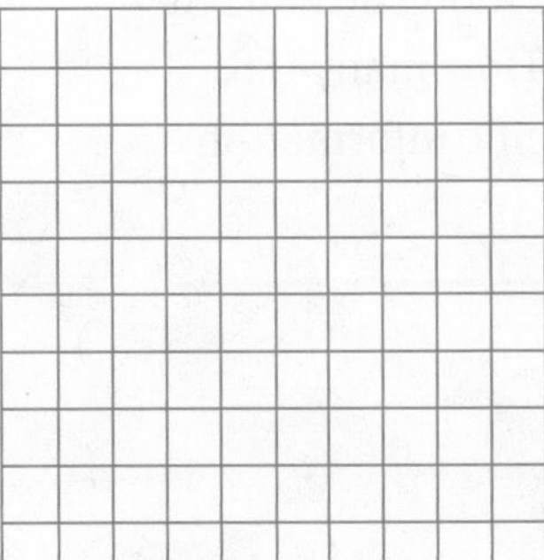

GO DIGITAL Assessment Options Chapter Test

5. Tenley is making a square frame for her painting. She is using 4 pieces of wood that are each 2.75 feet long. How much wood will Tenley use to make the frame?

______ feet

6. Which problems will have two decimal places in the product? Mark all that apply.

Ⓐ 5×0.89 Ⓑ 7.4×10 Ⓒ 5.31×10^0

Ⓓ 6.1×3 Ⓔ 3.2×4.3

Personal Math Trainer

7. THINK SMARTER + Ken and Leah are trying to solve a science homework question. They need to find out how much a rock that weighs 4 pounds on Earth would weigh on Venus. They know they can multiply the number of pounds the rock weighs on Earth by 0.91 to find its weight on Venus. Select the partial products Ken and Leah would need to add to find the product of 4 and 0.91. Mark all that apply.

Ⓐ 0.95 Ⓑ 0.04 Ⓒ 3.65 Ⓓ 3.6 Ⓔ 0.36

8. Sophia exchanged 1,000 U.S. dollars for the South African currency, which is called the rand. The exchange rate was 7.15 rand to $1.

Part A

How many South African rand did Sophia get? Explain how you know.

Part B

Sophia spent 6,274 rand on her trip. She exchanged the rand she had left for U.S. dollars. The exchange rate was 1 rand to $0.14. How many U.S. dollars did Sophia get? Support your answer using specific information from the problem.

Name ______________________________

9. Trevor is reading a book for a book report. Last week, he read 35 pages of the book. This week, he read 2.5 times as many pages as he read last week. How many pages of the book has Trevor read this week? Show your work.

10. Jonah drives his car to and from work. The total length of the trip to and from work is 19.2 miles. In August, Jonah worked 21 days. How many miles in all did Jonah drive to and from work that month? Show your work.

11. Use the numbers in the boxes to complete the number sentences. A number may be used more than once.

8.99	89.9	899

$29 \times 31 =$ ☐

$29 \times 3.1 =$ ☐

$0.29 \times 31 =$ ☐

$2.9 \times 31 =$ ☐

12. GO DEEPER Melinda, Zachary, and Heather went to the mall to shop for school supplies. Melinda spent $14.25 on her supplies. Zachary spent $2.30 more than Melinda spent. Heather spent 2 times as much money as Zachary spent. How much did Heather spend on school supplies?

$

13. The cost of admission to the Baytown Zoo is $10.50 for each senior citizen, $15.75 for each adult, and $8.25 for each child.

Part A

A family of 2 adults and 1 child plan to spend the day at the Baytown Zoo. How much does admission for the family cost? Explain how you found your answer.

Part B

Describe another way you could solve the problem.

Part C

What if 2 more tickets for admission are purchased? If the two additional tickets cost $16.50, determine what type of tickets the family purchases. Explain how you can determine the answer without calculating.

14. At a tailor shop, it costs $6.79 to shorten a pair of pants and 4 times as much to mend a dress. Choose the answer that correctly completes the statement.

It would cost Lisa [$19.47 | $27.16 | $33.95] to shorten one pair of pants and mend one dress.

Name ______________________________

15. Shade the model to show 0.5 × 0.3. Then find the product.

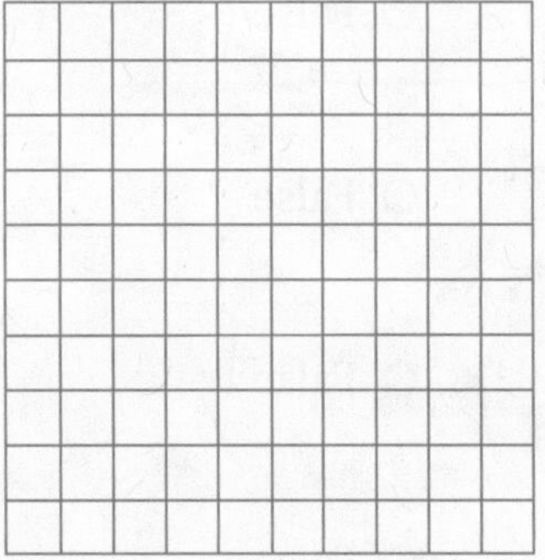

0.5 × 0.3 = ☐

16. Mr. Evans is paid $9.20 per hour for the first 40 hours he works in a week. He is paid 1.5 times that rate for each hour after that.

Last week, Mr. Evans worked 42.25 hours. He says he earned $388.70 last week. Do you agree? Support your answer.

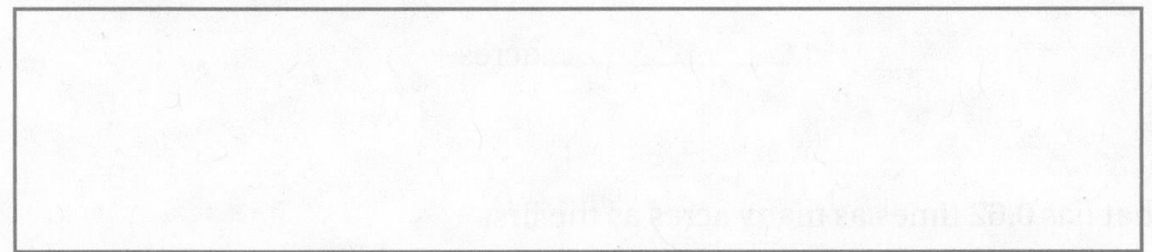

17. Explain how an estimate helps you to place the decimal point when multiplying 3.9 × 5.3.

18. On Saturday, Ahmed walks his dog 0.7 mile. On the same day, Latisha walks her dog 0.4 times as far as Ahmed walks his dog. How far does Latisha walk her dog on Saturday?

______ mile(s)

19. For 19a–19d select True or False for each statement.

19a. The product of 1.5 and 2.8 is 4.2. ○ True ○ False

19b. The product of 7.3 and 0.6 is 43.8. ○ True ○ False

19c. The product of 0.09 and 0.7 is 6.3. ○ True ○ False

19d. The product of 0.79 and 1.5 is 1.185. ○ True ○ False

20. A builder buys 24.5 acres of land to develop a new community of homes and parks.

Part A

The builder plans to use 0.25 of the land for a park. How many acres will he use for the park?

______ acres

Part B

He buys a second property that has 0.62 times as many acres as the first property. How many acres of land does the second property have? Show your work.

21. Joaquin lives 0.3 mile from Keith. Layla lives 0.4 times as far from Keith as Joaquin. How far does Layla live from Keith? Write an equation to solve.

______ mile

22. Brianna is getting materials for a chemistry experiment. Her teacher gives her a container that has 0.15 liter of a liquid in it. Brianna needs to use 0.4 of this liquid for the experiment. How much liquid will Brianna use?

______ liter

Divide Decimals

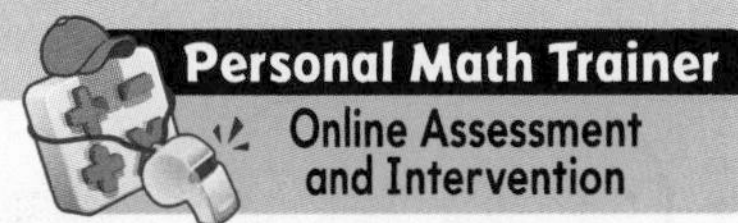

Check your understanding of important skills.

Name ______________________________

Division Facts **Find the quotient.** (3.OA.C.7)

1. $6\overline{)24}$ = ______
2. $7\overline{)56}$ = ______
3. 18 ÷ 9 = ______
4. 35 ÷ 5 = ______

Estimate with 1-Digit Divisors **Estimate the quotient.** (4.NBT.B.6)

5. $6\overline{)253}$ ______
6. $4\overline{)1,165}$ ______
7. $7\overline{)1,504}$ ______

Division **Divide.** (5.NBT.B.6)

8. $34\overline{)785}$
9. $27\overline{)1,581}$
10. $41\overline{)4,592}$

Instead of telling Carmen her age, Sora gave her this clue. Find Sora's age.

Clue

My age is 10 more than one-tenth of one-tenth of one-tenth of 3,000.

Vocabulary Builder

▶ Visualize It

Complete the bubble map using review words.

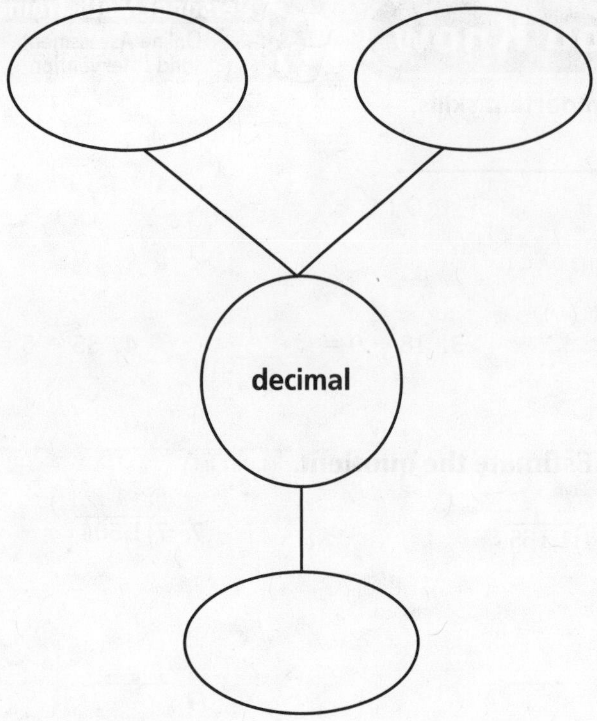

Review Words
compatible numbers
decimal
decimal point
dividend
divisor
equivalent fractions
estimate
exponent
hundredth
quotient
remainder
tenth

▶ Understand Vocabulary

Complete the sentences using the review words.

1. A ________________ is a symbol used to separate the ones place from the tenths place in decimal numbers.
2. Numbers that are easy to compute with mentally are called ________________.
3. A ________________ is one of ten equal parts.
4. A number with one or more digits to the right of the decimal point is called a ________________.
5. The ________________ is the number that is to be divided in a division problem.
6. A ________________ is one of one hundred equal parts.
7. You can ________________ to find a number that is close to the exact amount.

• Interactive Student Edition
• Multimedia eGlossary

Chapter 5 Vocabulary

decimal point (.)

punto decimal (.)

12

dividend

dividendo

18

divisor

divisor

19

equivalent fractions

fracciones equivalentes

22

estimate

estimación (s)
estimar (v)

23

exponent

exponente

26

quotient

cociente

57

remainder

residuo

59

The number that is to be divided in a division problem

Example: $36 \div 6$ or $6\overline{)36}$

dividend

A symbol used to separate dollars from cents in money, and to separate the ones place and tenths place in a decimal

\$1.65 4.324

decimal point

Fractions that name the same amount or part

Example: $\frac{1}{2}$ and $\frac{4}{8}$ are equivalent.

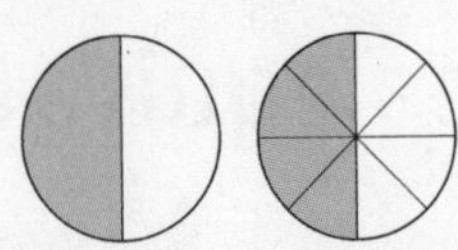

The number that divides the dividend

Example: $15 \div 3$ or $3\overline{)15}$.

divisor

A number that shows how many times the base is used as a factor

exponent

Example: $10^3 = 10 \times 10 \times 10$

noun: A number close to an exact amount

verb: To find a number that is close to an exact amount

The amount left over when a number cannot be divided equally

Example:

```
  102 r2 ← remainder
6)614
 -6
  01
  -0
   14
  -12
    2 ← remainder
```


The number that results from dividing

Example: $8 \div 4 = 2$

quotient

Picture It

Word Box
decimal point
dividend
divisor
equivalent fractions
estimate
exponent
quotient
remainder

For 3 to 4 players

Materials

- timer
- sketch pad

How to Play

1. Take turns to play.
2. To take a turn, choose a word from the Word Box. Do not say the word.
3. Set the timer for 1 minute.
4. Draw pictures and numbers to give clues about the word.
5. The first player to guess the word before time runs out gets 1 point. If he or she can use the word in a sentence, they get 1 more point. Then that player gets a turn choosing a word.
6. The first player to score 10 points wins.

The Write Way

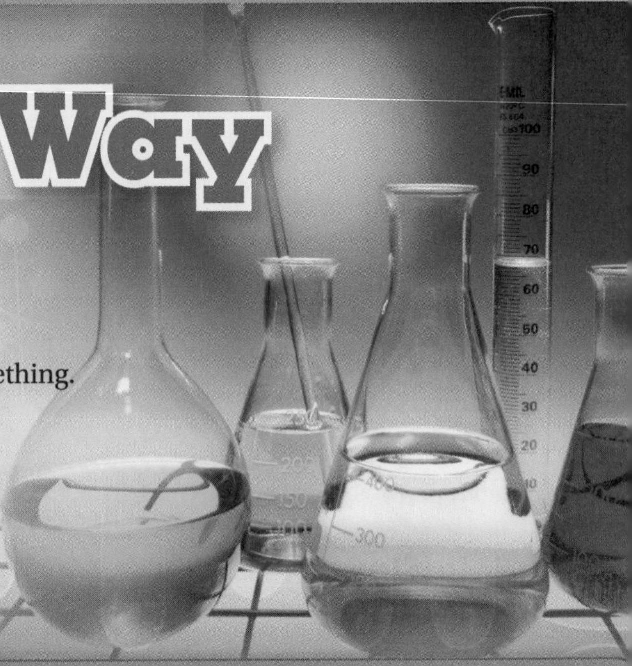

Reflect

Choose one idea. Write about it.

- Write a story about a person who needs to estimate something.
- Tell what happens to the decimal point in this pattern.
  $763 \div 10^1$ **$763 \div 10^2$** **$763 \div 10^3$**
- Explain equivalent fractions in your own words. Give an example.
- Tell how to solve this problem: $5\overline{)89.7}$ = _____.

Name ______________________________

Division Patterns with Decimals

Essential Question How can patterns help you place the decimal point in a quotient?

Number and Operations in Base Ten—5.NBT.A.2

MATHEMATICAL PRACTICES
MP5, MP6, MP7

Unlock the Problem

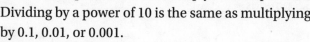

The Healthy Wheat Bakery uses 560 pounds of flour to make 1,000 loaves of bread. Each loaf contains the same amount of flour. How many pounds of flour does the bakery use in each loaf of bread?

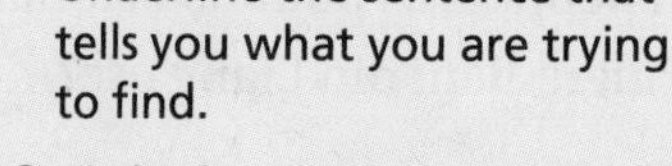

- Underline the sentence that tells you what you are trying to find.
- Circle the numbers you need to use.

You can use powers of ten to help you find quotients. Dividing by a power of 10 is the same as multiplying by 0.1, 0.01, or 0.001.

One Way Use place-value patterns.

Divide. $560 \div 1{,}000$

Look for a pattern in these products and quotients.

$560 \times 1 = 560$	$560 \div 1 = 560$
$560 \times 0.1 = 56.0$	$560 \div 10 = 56.0$
$560 \times 0.01 = 5.60$	$560 \div 100 = 5.60$
$560 \times 0.001 = 0.560$	$560 \div 1{,}000 = 0.560$

So, ______ pound of flour is used in each loaf of bread.

1. As you divide by increasing powers of 10, how does the position of the decimal point change in the quotients?

____

Another Way Use exponents.

Divide. $560 \div 10^3$

Look for a pattern.

$560 \div 10^0 = 560$

$560 \div 10^1 = 56.0$

$560 \div 10^2 = 5.60$

$560 \div 10^3 =$ ______

Remember

The zero power of 10 equals 1.

$10^0 = 1$

The first power of 10 equals 10.

$10^1 = 10$

2. Each divisor, or power of 10, is 10 times the divisor before it. How do the quotients compare?

____

CONNECT Dividing by 10 is the same as multiplying by 0.1 or finding $\frac{1}{10}$ of a number.

Example

Liang used 25.5 pounds of tomatoes to make a large batch of salsa. He used one-tenth as many pounds of onions as pounds of tomatoes. He used one-hundredth as many pounds of green peppers as pounds of tomatoes. How many pounds of each ingredient did Liang use?

Tomatoes: 25.5 pounds

Onions: 25.5 pounds ÷ ______

Think: 25.5 ÷ 1 = ______

25.5 ÷ 10 = ______

Green Peppers: 25.5 pounds ÷ ______

Think: ______ ÷ 1 = ______

______ ÷ 10 = ______

______ ÷ 100 = ______

So, Liang used 25.5 pounds of tomatoes, ______ pounds of onions,

and ______ pound of green peppers.

Try This! Complete the pattern.

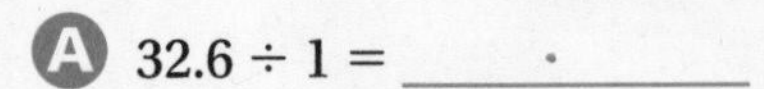

A 32.6 ÷ 1 = ____________

32.6 ÷ 10 = ____________

32.6 ÷ 100 = ____________

B $50.2 \div 10^0 =$ ____________

$50.2 \div 10^1 =$ ____________

$50.2 \div 10^2 =$ ____________

Share and Show

Math Talk MATHEMATICAL PRACTICES 5

Use Patterns How can you determine where to place the decimal point in the quotient $47.3 \div 10^2$?

Complete the pattern.

1. $456 \div 10^0 = 456$

   $456 \div 10^1 = 45.6$

   $456 \div 10^2 = 4.56$

   $456 \div 10^3 =$ ____________

Think: The dividend is being divided by an increasing power of 10, so the decimal point will move to the ______ one place for each increasing power of 10.

Name ______________________

Complete the pattern.

2. $225 \div 10^0 =$ ______

$225 \div 10^1 =$ ______

$225 \div 10^2 =$ ______

$225 \div 10^3 =$ ______

3. $605 \div 10^0 =$ ______

$605 \div 10^1 =$ ______

$605 \div 10^2 =$ ______

$605 \div 10^3 =$ ______

4. $74.3 \div 1 =$ ______

$74.3 \div 10 =$ ______

$74.3 \div 100 =$ ______

Math Talk — MATHEMATICAL PRACTICES 7

Look for a Pattern What happens to the value of a number when you divide by 10, 100, or 1,000?

On Your Own

Complete the pattern.

5. $156 \div 1 =$ ______

$156 \div 10 =$ ______

$156 \div 100 =$ ______

$156 \div 1{,}000 =$ ______

6. $32 \div 1 =$ ______

$32 \div 10 =$ ______

$32 \div 100 =$ ______

$32 \div 1{,}000 =$ ______

7. $23 \div 10^0 =$ ______

$23 \div 10^1 =$ ______

$23 \div 10^2 =$ ______

$23 \div 10^3 =$ ______

8. $12.7 \div 1 =$ ______

$12.7 \div 10 =$ ______

$12.7 \div 100 =$ ______

9. $92.5 \div 10^0 =$ ______

$92.5 \div 10^1 =$ ______

$92.5 \div 10^2 =$ ______

10. $86.3 \div 10^0 =$ ______

$86.3 \div 10^1 =$ ______

$86.3 \div 10^2 =$ ______

MATHEMATICAL PRACTICE 7 Look for a Pattern **Algebra** **Find the value of *n*.**

11. $268 \div n = 0.268$

$n =$ ______________

12. $n \div 10^2 = 0.123$

$n =$ ______________

13. $n \div 10^1 = 4.6$

$n =$ ______________

14. GO DEEPER Loretta is trying to build the largest taco in the world. She uses 2,000 pounds of ground beef, one-tenth as many pounds of cheese as beef, and one-hundredth as many pounds of lettuce as beef. How many pounds of lettuce and cheese combined did she use?

____

Problem Solving • Applications

Use the table to solve 15–17.

Dry Ingredients for 1,000 Corn Muffins

Ingredient	Number of Kilograms
Cornmeal	150
Flour	110
Sugar	66.7
Baking powder	10
Salt	4.17

15. GO DEEPER How much more cornmeal than flour does each muffin contain?

______

16. THINK SMARTER If each muffin contains the same amount of sugar, how many kilograms of sugar, to the nearest thousandth, are in each corn muffin?

______

17. MATHEMATICAL PRACTICE 5 **Use Patterns** The bakery decides to make only 100 corn muffins on Tuesday. How many kilograms of sugar will be needed?

______

18. WRITE Math Explain how you know that the quotient $47.3 \div 10^1$ is equal to the product 47.3×0.1.

______

______

______

______

______

19. THINK SMARTER Use the numbers on the tiles to complete each number sentence.

$62.4 \div 10^0 =$ ______

$62.4 \div 10^1 =$ ______

$62.4 \div 10^2 =$ ______

.	0	2
	4	6

Name ___

Division Patterns with Decimals

Common Core **COMMON CORE STANDARD—5.NBT.A.2**
Understand the place value system.

Complete the pattern.

1. $78.3 \div 1 =$ 78.3
$78.3 \div 10 =$ 7.83
$78.3 \div 100 =$ 0.783

2. $179 \div 10^0 =$ ___
$179 \div 10^1 =$ ___
$179 \div 10^2 =$ ___
$179 \div 10^3 =$ ___

3. $87.5 \div 10^0 =$ ___
$87.5 \div 10^1 =$ ___
$87.5 \div 10^2 =$ ___

4. $124 \div 1 =$ ___
$124 \div 10 =$ ___
$124 \div 100 =$ ___
$124 \div 1{,}000 =$ ___

5. $18 \div 1 =$ ___
$18 \div 10 =$ ___
$18 \div 100 =$ ___
$18 \div 1{,}000 =$ ___

6. $16 \div 10^0 =$ ___
$16 \div 10^1 =$ ___
$16 \div 10^2 =$ ___
$16 \div 10^3 =$ ___

7. $51.8 \div 1 =$ ___
$51.8 \div 10 =$ ___
$51.8 \div 100 =$ ___

8. $49.3 \div 10^0 =$ ___
$49.3 \div 10^1 =$ ___
$49.3 \div 10^2 =$ ___

9. $32.4 \div 10^0 =$ ___
$32.4 \div 10^1 =$ ___
$32.4 \div 10^2 =$ ___

Problem Solving Real World

10. The local café uses 510 cups of mixed vegetables to make 1,000 quarts of beef barley soup. Each quart of soup contains the same amount of vegetables. How many cups of vegetables are in each quart of soup?

___

11. The same café uses 18.5 cups of flour to make 100 servings of pancakes. How many cups of flour are in one serving of pancakes?

___

12. WRITE *Math* Explain how to use a pattern to find $35.6 \div 10^2$.

___

___

Lesson Check (5.NBT.A.2)

1. The Statue of Liberty is 305.5 feet tall from the foundation of its pedestal to the top of its torch. Isla is building a model of the statue. The model will be one-hundredth times as tall as the actual statue. How tall will the model be?

2. Sue's teacher asked her to find $42.6 \div 10^2$. How many places and in what direction should Sue move the decimal point to get the correct quotient?

Spiral Review (5.NBT.A.1, 5.NBT.B.6, 5.NBT.B.7)

3. In the number 956,783,529, how does the value of the digit 5 in the ten millions place compare to the digit 5 in the hundreds place?

4. Taylor has \$97.23 in her checking account. She uses her debit card to spend \$29.74 and then deposits \$118.08 into her account. What is Taylor's new balance?

5. At the bank, Brent exchanges \$50 in bills for 50 one-dollar coins. The total mass of the coins is 405 grams. Estimate the mass of 1 one-dollar coin.

6. A commercial jetliner has 245 passenger seats. The seats are arranged in 49 equal rows. How many seats are in each row?

FOR MORE PRACTICE GO TO THE **Personal Math Trainer**

Name ______________________________

Divide Decimals by Whole Numbers

Essential Question How can you use a model to divide a decimal by a whole number?

Common Core **Number and Operations in Base Ten—5.NBT.B.7**

MATHEMATICAL PRACTICES
MP1, MP2, MP5, MP6

Investigate

Materials ■ decimal models ■ color pencils

Angela has enough wood to make a picture frame with a perimeter of 2.4 meters. She wants the frame to be a square. What will be the length of each side of the frame?

A. Shade decimal models to show 2.4.

B. You need to share your model among ______ equal groups.

C. Since 2 wholes cannot be shared among 4 groups without regrouping, cut your model apart to show the tenths.

There are ______ tenths in 2.4.

Share the tenths equally among the 4 groups.

There are ______ ones and ______ tenths in each group.

Write a decimal for the amount in each group. ______

D. Use your model to complete the number sentence.

$2.4 \div 4 =$ ______

So, the length of each side of the frame will be ______ meter.

Draw Conclusions

1. MATHEMATICAL PRACTICE 5 **Use a Concrete Model** Explain why you needed to cut apart the model in Step C.

____

____

2. Explain how your model would be different if the perimeter were 4.8 meters.

____

____

Make Connections

You can also use base-ten blocks to model division of a decimal by a whole number.

Materials ■ base-ten blocks

Kyle has a roll of ribbon 3.21 yards long. He cuts the ribbon into 3 equal lengths. How long is each piece of ribbon?

Divide. 3.21 ÷ 3

STEP 1

Use base-ten blocks to show 3.21.

Remember that a flat represents one, a long represents one tenth, and a small cube represents one hundredth.

There are ______ one(s), ______ tenth(s), and ______ hundredth(s).

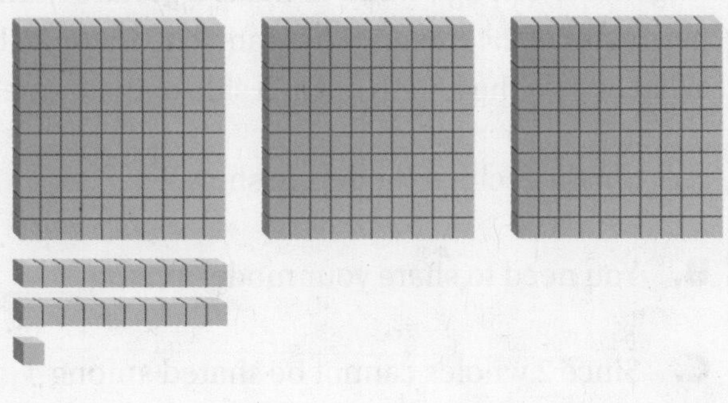

STEP 2 Share the ones.

Share the ones equally among 3 groups.

There is ______ one(s) shared in each group and ______ one(s) left over.

STEP 3 Share the tenths.

Two tenths cannot be shared among 3 groups without regrouping. Regroup the tenths by replacing them with hundredths.

There are ______ tenth(s) shared in each group and ______ tenth(s) left over.

There are now ______ hundredth(s).

STEP 4 Share the hundredths.

Share the 21 hundredths equally among the 3 groups.

There are ______ hundredth(s) shared in each group and ______ hundredth(s) left over.

So, each piece of ribbon is ____________ yards long.

Math Talk MATHEMATICAL PRACTICES 6

Explain why your answer makes sense.

Name ____________________

Share and Show

MATH BOARD

Use the model to complete the number sentence.

1. 1.6 ÷ 4 = ________

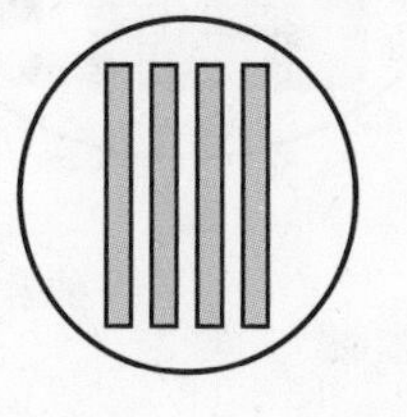
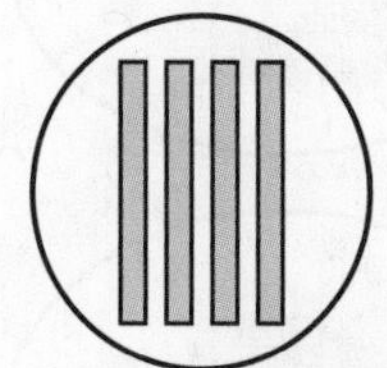
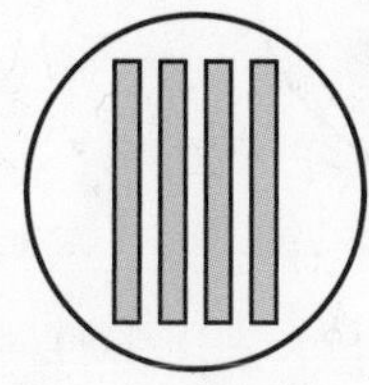
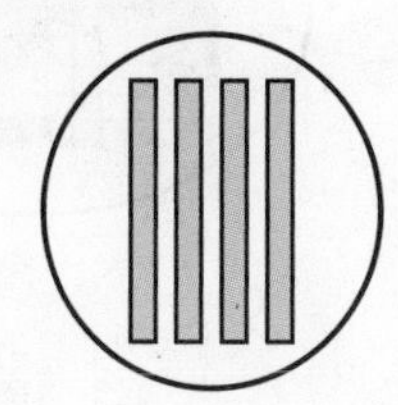

2. 3.42 ÷ 3 = ________

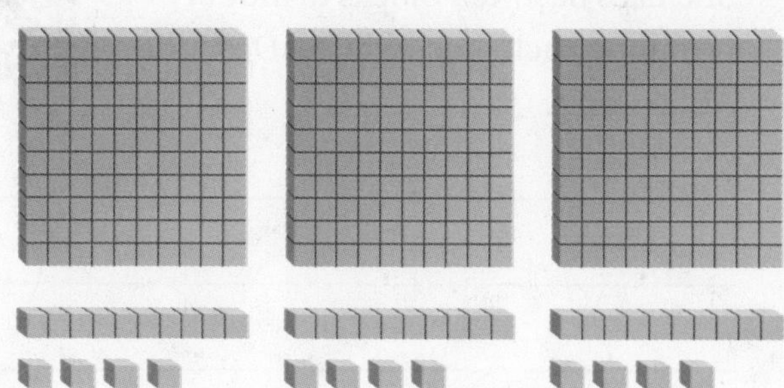

Divide. Use base-ten blocks.

3. 1.8 ÷ 3 = ________

4. 3.6 ÷ 4 = ________

5. 2.5 ÷ 5 = ________

6. 2.4 ÷ 8 = ________

7. 3.78 ÷ 3 = ________

8. 1.33 ÷ 7 = ________

9. 4.72 ÷ 4 = ________

10. 2.52 ÷ 9 = ________

11. 6.25 ÷ 5 = ________

Math Talk — MATHEMATICAL PRACTICES 1

Describe Relationships Explain how you can use inverse operations to find 2.4 ÷ 4.

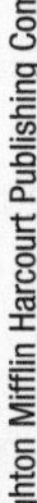

Problem Solving • Applications

12. THINK SMARTER **What's the Error?** Aida is making banners from a roll of paper that is 4.05 meters long. She will cut the paper into 3 equal lengths. She uses base-ten blocks to model how long each piece will be. Describe Aida's error.

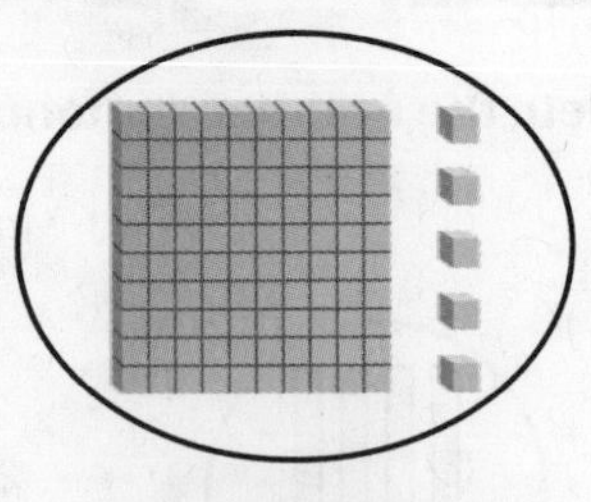

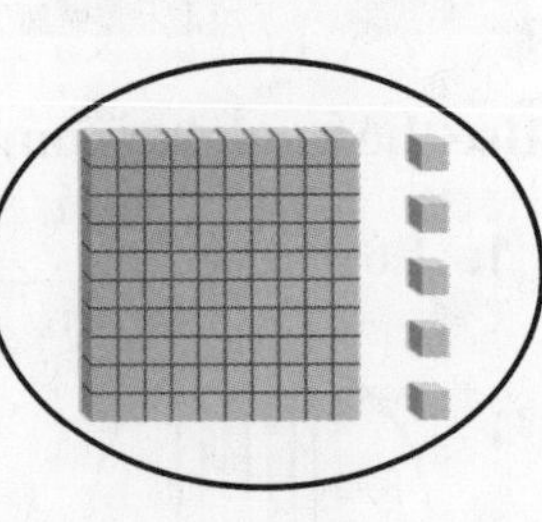

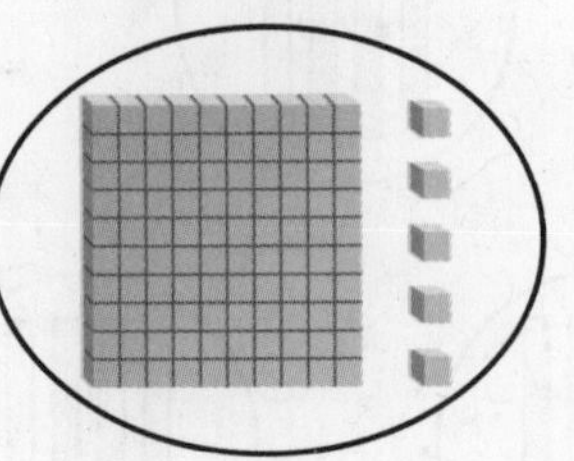

13. GO DEEPER Sam can ride his bike 4.5 kilometers in 9 minutes, and Amanda can ride her bike 3.6 kilometers in 6 minutes. Which rider might go farther in 1 minute?

14. MATHEMATICAL PRACTICE 2 **Use Reasoning** Explain how you can use inverse operations to find 1.8 ÷ 3.

15. THINK SMARTER Draw a model to show 4.8 ÷ 4 and solve.

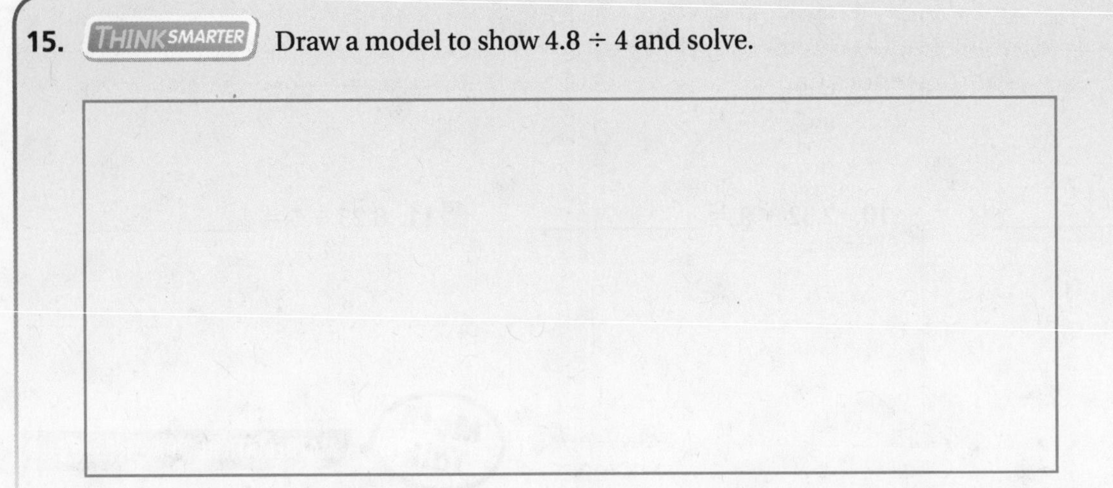

4.8 ÷ 4 = ________

Name ____________________

Divide Decimals by Whole Numbers

Common Core **COMMON CORE STANDARD—5.NBT.B.7** *Perform operations with multi-digit whole numbers and with decimals to hundredths.*

Use the model to complete the number sentence.

1. 1.2 ÷ 4 = 0.3

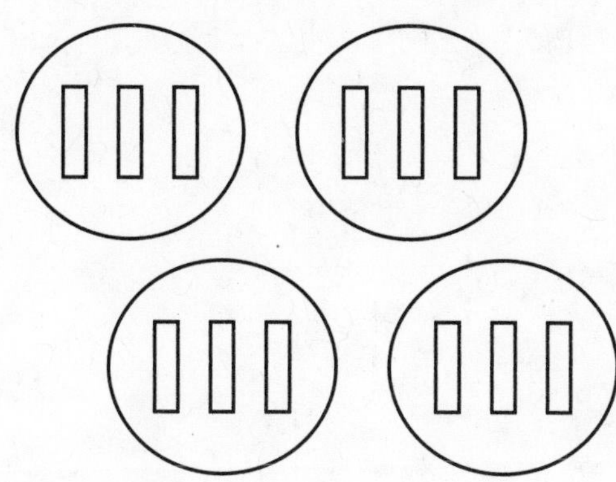

2. 3.69 ÷ 3 = ____________

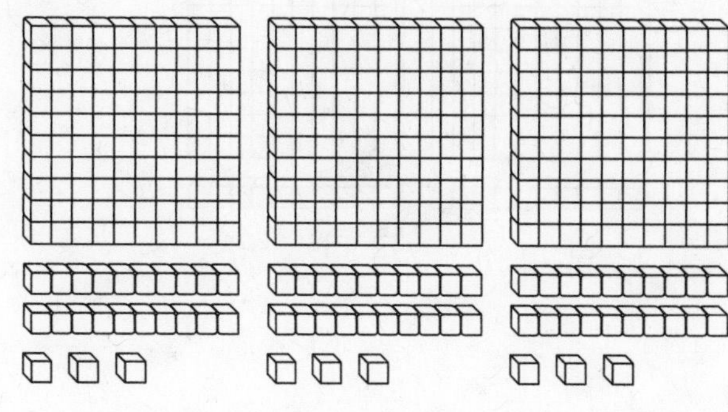

Divide. Use base-ten blocks.

3. 4.9 ÷ 7 = ____________

4. 3.6 ÷ 9 = ____________

5. 2.4 ÷ 8 = ____________

6. 6.48 ÷ 4 = ____________

7. 3.01 ÷ 7 = ____________

8. 4.26 ÷ 3 = ____________

Problem Solving Real World

9. In PE class, Carl runs a distance of 1.17 miles in 9 minutes. At that rate, how far does Carl run in one minute?

____

10. Marianne spends $9.45 on 5 greeting cards. Each card costs the same amount. What is the cost of one greeting card?

____

11. WRITE ▸ *Math* Explain how you can use base-ten blocks or other decimal models to find 3.15 ÷ 3. Include pictures to support your explanation.

____

____

Lesson Check (5.NBT.B.7)

1. Write a division sentence that tells what the model represents.

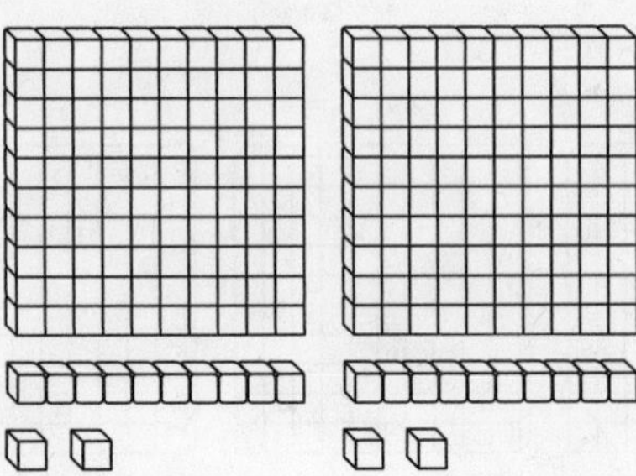

2. A bunch of 4 bananas contains a total of 5.92 grams of protein. Suppose each banana contains the same amount of protein. How much protein is in one banana?

Spiral Review (5.NBT.A.3b, 5.NBT.B.5, 5.NBT.B.6, 5.NBT.B.7)

3. At the deli, one pound of turkey costs $7.98. Mr. Epstein buys 3 pounds of turkey. How much will the turkey cost?

4. Mrs. Cho drives 45 miles in 1 hour. If her speed stays constant, how many hours will it take for her to drive 405 miles?

5. Write the following numbers in order from least to greatest.

   1.23; 1.2; 2.31; 3.2

6. Over the weekend, Aiden spent 15 minutes on his math homework. He spent three times as much time on his science homework. How much time did Aiden spend on his science homework?

FOR MORE PRACTICE GO TO THE Personal Math Trainer

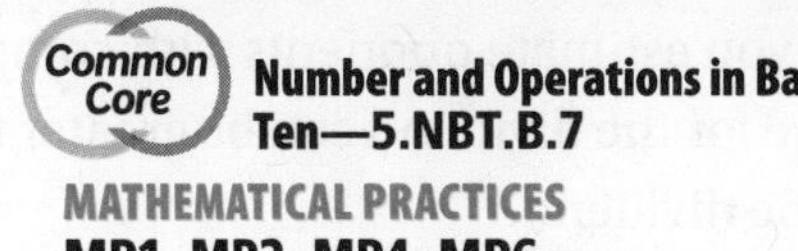

Name ______________________________

Estimate Quotients

Essential Question How can you estimate decimal quotients?

Number and Operations in Base Ten—5.NBT.B.7

MATHEMATICAL PRACTICES
MP1, MP2, MP4, MP6

Unlock the Problem Real World

Carmen likes to ski. The ski resort where she goes to ski got 3.2 feet of snow during a 5-day period. The *average* daily snowfall for a given number of days is the quotient of the total amount of snow and the number of days. Estimate the average daily snowfall.

You can estimate decimal quotients by using compatible numbers. When choosing compatible numbers, you can look at the whole-number part of a decimal dividend or rename the decimal dividend as tenths or hundredths.

Estimate. 3.2 ÷ 5

Carly and her friend Marco each find an estimate. Since the divisor is greater than the dividend, they both first rename 3.2 as tenths.

3.2 is ______ tenths.

CARLY'S ESTIMATE

30 tenths is close to 32 tenths and divides easily by 5. Use a basic fact to find 30 tenths ÷ 5.

30 tenths ÷ 5 is ______ tenths or ______.

So, the average daily snowfall is about

______ foot.

MARCO'S ESTIMATE

35 tenths is close to 32 tenths and divides easily by 5. Use a basic fact to find 35 tenths ÷ 5.

35 tenths ÷ 5 is ______ tenths or ______.

So, the average daily snowfall is about

______ foot.

1. MATHEMATICAL PRACTICE 1 **Interpret a Result** Whose estimate do you think is closer to the exact quotient?

   Explain your reasoning. ______________________________

   ____

2. Explain how you would rename the dividend in 29.7 ÷ 40 to choose compatible numbers and estimate the quotient.

   ____

   ____

Estimate with 2-Digit Divisors

When you estimate quotients with compatible numbers, the number you use for the dividend can be greater than the dividend or less than the dividend.

Example

A group of 31 students is going to visit the museum. The total cost for the tickets is $144.15. About how much money will each student need to pay for a ticket?

Estimate. $144.15 ÷ 31

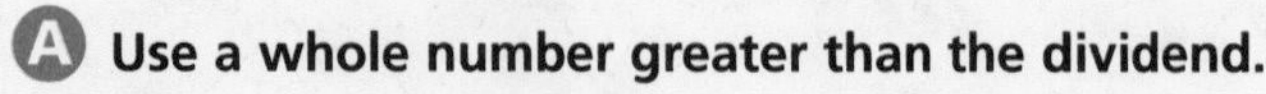

A Use a whole number greater than the dividend.

Use 30 for the divisor. Then find a number close to and greater than $144.15 that divides easily by 30.

$144.15 ÷ 31
↓ ↓
$150 ÷ 30 = $ ______

So, each student will pay about $ ______ for a ticket.

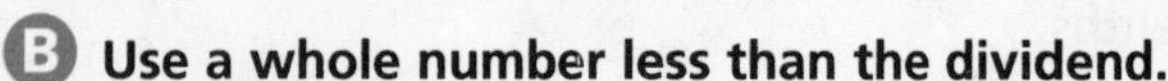

B Use a whole number less than the dividend.

Use 30 for the divisor. Then find a number close to and less than $144.15 that divides easily by 30.

$144.15 ÷ 31
↓ ↓
$120 ÷ 30 = $ ______

So, each student will pay about $ ______ for a ticket.

3. MATHEMATICAL PRACTICE 2 **Use Reasoning** Which estimate do you think will be a better estimate of the cost of a ticket? Explain your reasoning. ______

______

______

Share and Show

Use compatible numbers to estimate the quotient.

1. 28.8 ÷ 9

______ ÷ ______ = ______

2. 393.5 ÷ 41

______ ÷ ______ = ______

Name ______________________

Estimate the quotient.

3. 161.7 ÷ 7

4. 17.9 ÷ 9

5. 145.4 ÷ 21

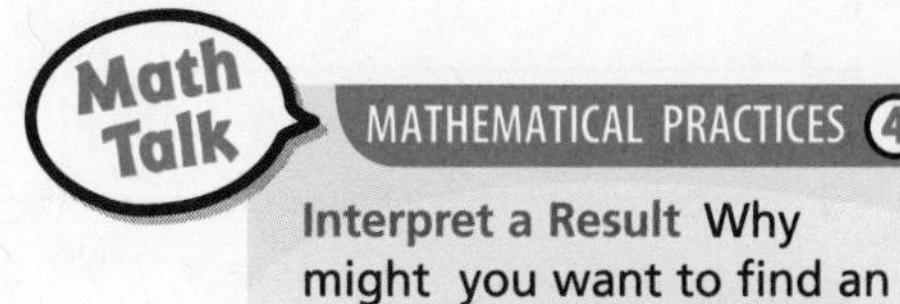

Math Talk
MATHEMATICAL PRACTICES 4
Interpret a Result Why might you want to find an estimate for a quotient?

On Your Own

Estimate the quotient.

6. 15.5 ÷ 4

7. 394.8 ÷ 7

8. 410.5 ÷ 18

9. 72.1 ÷ 7

10. 32.4 ÷ 52

11. $134.42 ÷ 28

12. MATHEMATICAL PRACTICE 6 Shayne has a total of $135.22 to spend on souvenirs at the zoo. He wants to buy 9 of the same souvenir for his friends. Choose a method of estimation to find about how much Shayne can spend on each souvenir. **Explain** how you used the method to reach your estimation.

____

____

____

13. GO DEEPER One week, Alaina ran 12 miles in 131.25 minutes. The next week, Alaina ran 12 miles in 119.5 minutes. If she ran a constant pace during each run, about how much faster did she run each mile in the second week than in the first week?

____

Problem Solving • Applications

Use the table to solve 14–15.

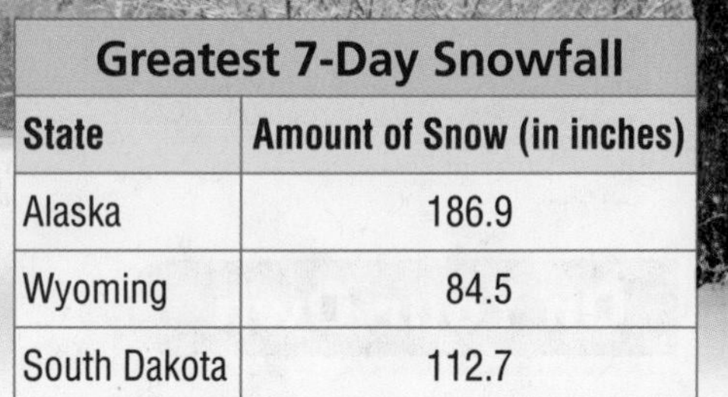

Greatest 7-Day Snowfall	
State	**Amount of Snow (in inches)**
Alaska	186.9
Wyoming	84.5
South Dakota	112.7

14. GO DEEPER How does the estimate of the average daily snowfall for Wyoming's greatest 7-day snowfall compare to the estimate of the average daily snowfall for South Dakota's greatest 7-day snowfall?

____

____

15. THINK SMARTER The greatest monthly snowfall total in Alaska is 297.9 inches. This happened in February, 1953. Compare the daily average snowfall for February, 1953, with the average daily snowfall for Alaska's greatest 7-day snowfall. Use estimation.

____

____

16. WRITE Math **What's the Error?** During a 3-hour storm, it snowed 2.5 inches. Jacob said that it snowed an average of about 8 inches per hour.

____

____

____

____

17. THINK SMARTER Juliette will cut a piece of string that is 45.1 feet long into 7 smaller pieces. Each of the 7 pieces will be the same length. Write a division sentence using compatible numbers to estimate the quotient.

____

WRITE Math • **Show Your Work**

Name ______________________

Estimate Quotients

Common Core **COMMON CORE STANDARD—5.NBT.B.7**
Perform operations with multi-digit whole numbers and with decimals to hundredths.

Use compatible numbers to estimate the quotient.

1. 19.7 ÷ 3

18 ÷ 3 = 6

2. 394.6 ÷ 9

3. 308.3 ÷ 15

Estimate the quotient.

4. 63.5 ÷ 5

5. 57.8 ÷ 81

6. 172.6 ÷ 39

7. 43.6 ÷ 8

8. 2.8 ÷ 6

9. 467.6 ÷ 8

10. 209.3 ÷ 48

11. 737.5 ÷ 9

12. 256.1 ÷ 82

Problem Solving Real World

13. Taylor uses 645.6 gallons of water in 7 days. Suppose he uses the same amount of water each day. About how much water does Taylor use each day?

____

14. On a road trip, Sandy drives 368.7 miles. Her car uses a total of 18 gallons of gas. About how many miles per gallon does Sandy's car get?

____

15. WRITE *Math* Explain how to find an estimate for the quotient 3.4 ÷ 6.

____

Lesson Check (5.NBT.B.7)

1. Terry bicycled 64.8 miles in 7 hours. What is the best estimate of the average number of miles she bicycled each hour?

2. What is the best estimate for the following quotient?

   891.3 ÷ 28

Spiral Review (5.NBT.A.2, 5.NBT.A.3b, 5.NBT.B.7, 5.NF.B.3)

3. An object that weighs 1 pound on Earth weighs 1.19 pounds on Neptune. Suppose a dog weighs 9 pounds on Earth. How much would the same dog weigh on Neptune?

4. A bookstore orders 200 books. The books are packaged in boxes that hold 24 books each. All the boxes the bookstore receives are full, except one. How many boxes does the bookstore receive?

5. Tara has $2,000 in her savings account. David has one-tenth as much as Tara in his savings account. How much does David have in his savings account?

6. Which symbol makes the statement true? Write >, <, or =.

   7.63 ◯ 7.629

FOR MORE PRACTICE GO TO THE **Personal Math Trainer**

Name ______________________

Division of Decimals by Whole Numbers

Essential Question How can you divide decimals by whole numbers?

Common Core **Number and Operations in Base Ten—5.NBT.B.7**

MATHEMATICAL PRACTICES
MP1, MP2, MP6

Unlock the Problem

In a swimming relay, each swimmer swims an equal part of the total distance. Brianna and 3 other swimmers won a relay in 5.68 minutes. What is the average time each relay team member swam?

- How many swimmers are part of the relay team?

______

One Way Use place value.

MODEL

THINK AND RECORD

STEP 1 Divide the ones.

$$\begin{array}{r} 1 \\ 4\overline{)5.68} \\ -4 \\ \square \end{array}$$

Divide. 5 ones ÷ 4

Multiply. 4 × 1 one

Subtract. 5 ones − 4 ones

Check. ______ one(s) cannot be shared among 4 groups without regrouping.

STEP 2 Divide the tenths.

$$\begin{array}{r} 1.\square \\ 4\overline{)5.68} \\ -4 \\ \square \\ -\square \\ \square \end{array}$$

Divide. ______ tenths ÷ 4

Multiply. 4 × ______ tenths

Subtract. ______ tenths − ______ tenths

Check. ______ tenth(s) cannot be shared among 4 groups.

STEP 3 Divide the hundredths.

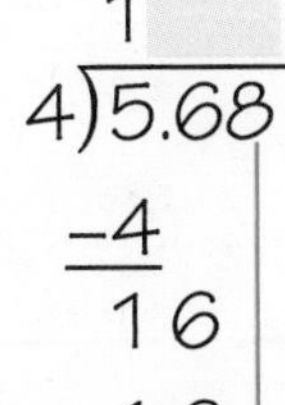

$$\begin{array}{r} 1\ \square\square \\ 4\overline{)5.68} \\ -4 \\ 16 \\ -16 \\ \square \\ -\square \\ \square \end{array}$$

Divide. 8 hundredths ÷ 4

Multiply. 4 × ______ hundredths

Subtract. ______ hundredths − ______ hundredths

Check. ______ hundredth(s) cannot be shared among 4 groups.

Place the decimal point in the quotient to separate the ones and the tenths.

So, each girl swam an average of ______ minutes.

Another Way Use an estimate.

Divide as you would with whole numbers.

Divide. $40.89 ÷ 47

- Estimate the quotient. 4,000 hundredths ÷ 50 = 80 hundredths, or $0.80
- Divide the tenths.
- Divide the hundredths. When the remainder is zero and there are no more digits in the dividend, the division is complete.
- Use your estimate to place the decimal point. Place a zero to show there are no ones.

$$47\overline{)40.89}$$

So, $40.89 ÷ 47 is ____________.

- MATHEMATICAL PRACTICE 6 **Explain** how you used the estimate to place the decimal point in the quotient.

____

____

Try This! Divide. Use multiplication to check your work.

$$23\overline{)79.35}$$

Check.

× 23

\+

Share and Show

Write the quotient with the decimal point placed correctly.

1. 4.92 ÷ 2 = 246 ____________

2. 50.16 ÷ 38 = 132 ____________

Name ___________________________

Divide.

3. $8\overline{)\$8.24}$

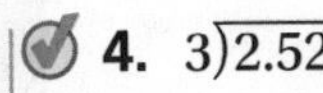
4. $3\overline{)2.52}$

5. $27\overline{)97.2}$

MATHEMATICAL PRACTICES 1

Evaluate Reasonableness How can you check that the decimal point is placed correctly in the quotient?

On Your Own

Practice: Copy and Solve Divide.

6. $3\overline{)\$7.71}$

7. $14\overline{)79.8}$

8. $33\overline{)25.41}$

9. $7\overline{)15.61}$

10. $14\overline{)137.2}$

11. $34\overline{)523.6}$

MATHEMATICAL PRACTICE 2 Use Reasoning **Algebra Write the unknown number for each ■.**

12. ■ $\div 5 = 1.21$

■ = ______

13. $46.8 \div 39 =$ ■

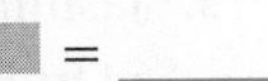

14. $34.1 \div$ ■ $= 22$

■ = ______

15. THINK SMARTER Mei runs 80.85 miles in 3 weeks. If she runs 5 days each week, what is the average distance she runs each day?

____

16. GO DEEPER Rob buys 6 tickets to the basketball game. He pays $8.50 for parking. His total cost is $40.54. What is the cost of each ticket?

____

Unlock the Problem 

17. MATHEMATICAL PRACTICE 1 **Make Sense of Problems** The standard width of 8 lanes in swimming pools used for competitions is 21.92 meters. The standard width of 9 lanes is 21.96 meters. How much wider is each lane when there are 8 lanes than when there are 9 lanes?

a. What are you asked to find? ______________________

____

b. What operations will you use to solve the problem? ______________________

____

c. Show the steps you used to solve the problem.

d. Complete the sentences.

Each lane is ______ meters wide when there are 8 lanes.

Each lane is ______ meters wide when there are 9 lanes.

Since ______ − ______ = ______, the lanes are ______ meter(s) wider when there are 8 lanes than when there are 9 lanes.

18. THINKSMARTER Simon cut a pipe that was 5.75 feet long. Then he cut the pipe into 5 equal pieces. What is the length of each piece?

____

19. Jasmine uses 14.24 pounds of fruit for 16 servings of fruit salad. If each serving contains the same amount of fruit, how much fruit is in each serving?

____

Name ______________________

Division of Decimals by Whole Numbers

COMMON CORE STANDARD—5.NBT.B.7
Perform operations with multi-digit whole numbers and with decimals to hundredths.

Divide.

1. $7\overline{)9.24}$

$$
\begin{array}{r}
1.32 \\
7\overline{)9.24} \\
-7 \\
\hline
22 \\
-21 \\
\hline
14 \\
-14 \\
\hline
0
\end{array}
$$

2. $6\overline{)5.04}$

3. $23\overline{)85.1}$

4. $36\overline{)86.4}$

5. $6\overline{)\$6.48}$

6. $8\overline{)59.2}$

7. $5\overline{)2.35}$

8. $41\overline{)278.8}$

9. $19\overline{)\$70.49}$

Problem Solving

10. On Saturday, 12 friends go ice skating. Altogether, they pay $83.40 for admission. They share the cost equally. How much does each person pay?

____

11. A team of 4 people participates in a 400-yard relay race. Each team member runs the same distance. The team completes the race in a total of 53.2 seconds. What is the average running time for each person?

____

12. **WRITE** *Math* Write a word problem involving money that requires dividing a decimal by a whole number. Include an estimate and a solution.

____

____

Lesson Check (5.NBT.A.2, 5.NBT.B.7)

1. Theresa pays $9.56 for 4 pounds of tomatoes. What is the cost of 1 pound of tomatoes?

2. Robert wrote the division problem below. What is the quotient?

$$13\overline{)83.2}$$

Spiral Review (5.OA.A.1, 5.NBT.A.2, 5.NBT.B.6, 5.NBT.B.7)

3. What is the value of the following expression?

$$2 \times \{6 + [12 \div (3 + 1)]\} - 1$$

4. Last month, Dory biked 11 times as many miles as Karly. Together they biked a total of 156 miles. How many miles did Dory bike last month?

5. Jin ran 15.2 miles over the weekend. He ran 6.75 miles on Saturday. How many miles did he run on Sunday?

6. A bakery used 475 pounds of apples to make 1,000 apple tarts. Each tart contains the same amount of apples. How many pounds of apples are used in each tart?

FOR MORE PRACTICE GO TO THE **Personal Math Trainer**

Name ___________________________

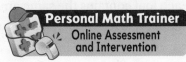

Personal Math Trainer
Online Assessment and Intervention

Concepts and Skills

1. **Explain** how the position of the decimal point changes in a quotient as you divide by increasing powers of 10. (5.NBT.A.2)

____

2. **Explain** how you can use base-ten blocks to find $2.16 \div 3$. (5.NBT.B.7)

____

____

____

____

Complete the pattern. (5.NBT.A.2)

3. $223 \div 1 =$ ______

$223 \div 10 =$ ______

$223 \div 100 =$ ______

$223 \div 1{,}000 =$ ______

4. $61 \div 1 =$ ______

$61 \div 10 =$ ______

$61 \div 100 =$ ______

$61 \div 1{,}000 =$ ______

5. $57.4 \div 10^0 =$ ______

$57.4 \div 10^1 =$ ______

$57.4 \div 10^2 =$ ______

Estimate the quotient. (5.NBT.B.7)

6. $31.9 \div 4$

7. $6.1 \div 8$

8. $492.6 \div 48$

Divide. (5.NBT.B.7)

9. $5\overline{)4.35}$

10. $8\overline{)9.92}$

11. $61\overline{)207.4}$

12. The Westside Bakery uses 440 pounds of flour to make 1,000 loaves of bread. Each loaf contains the same amount of flour. How many pounds of flour are used in each loaf of bread? (5.NBT.A.2)

____

13. Elise pays $21.75 for 5 student tickets to the fair. What is the cost of each student ticket? (5.NBT.B.7)

____

14. Jason has a piece of wire that is 62.4 inches long. He cuts the wire into 3 equal pieces. Estimate the length of 1 piece of wire. (5.NBT.B.7)

____

15. GO DEEPER Elizabeth uses 23.25 ounces of granola and 10.5 ounces of raisins for 15 servings of trail mix. If each serving contains the same amount of trail mix, how much trail mix is in each serving? (5.NBT.B.7)

____

Name ______________________

Decimal Division

Essential Question How can you use a model to divide by a decimal?

Common Core **Number and Operations in Base Ten—5.NBT.B.7**
MATHEMATICAL PRACTICES
MP2, MP4, MP5, MP6

Investigate

Materials ■ decimal models ■ color pencils

Lisa is making reusable shopping bags. She has 3.6 yards of fabric. She needs 0.3 yard of fabric for each bag. How many shopping bags can she make from the 3.6 yards of fabric?

A. Shade decimal models to show 3.6.

B. Cut apart your model to show the tenths. Separate the tenths into as many groups of 3 tenths as you can.

There are ______ groups of ______ tenths.

C. Use your model to complete the number sentence.

$3.6 \div 0.3 =$ ______

So, Lisa can make ______ shopping bags.

Draw Conclusions

1. Explain why you made each group equal to the divisor.

____

____

Remember

The divisor can tell the number of same-sized groups, or it can tell the number in each group.

2. MATHEMATICAL PRACTICE 2 **Represent a Problem** Identify the problem you would be modeling if each strip in the model represents 1.

____

3. MATHEMATICAL PRACTICE 5 **Communicate** Dennis has 2.7 yards of fabric to make bags that require 0.9 yard of fabric each. Describe a decimal model you can use to find how many bags he can make.

____

____

Make Connections

You can also use a model to divide by hundredths.

Materials ■ decimal models ■ color pencils

Julie has $1.75 in nickels. How many stacks of $0.25 can she make from $1.75?

STEP 1

Shade decimal models to show 1.75.

There are ______ one(s) and ______ hundredth(s).

STEP 2

Cut apart your model to show groups of 0.25.

There are ______ groups of ______ hundredths.

STEP 3

Use your model to complete the number sentence.

1.75 ÷ 0.25 = ______

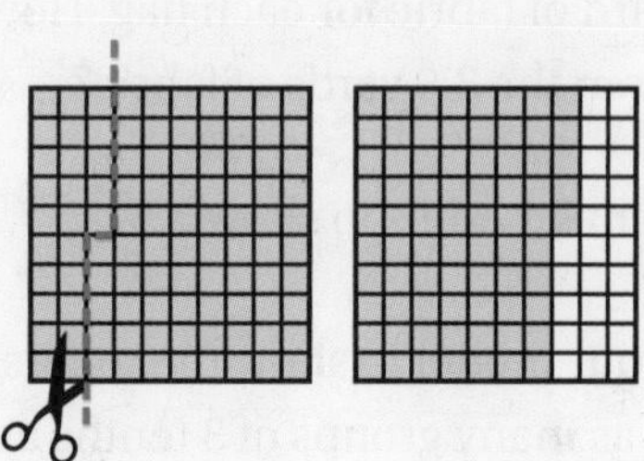

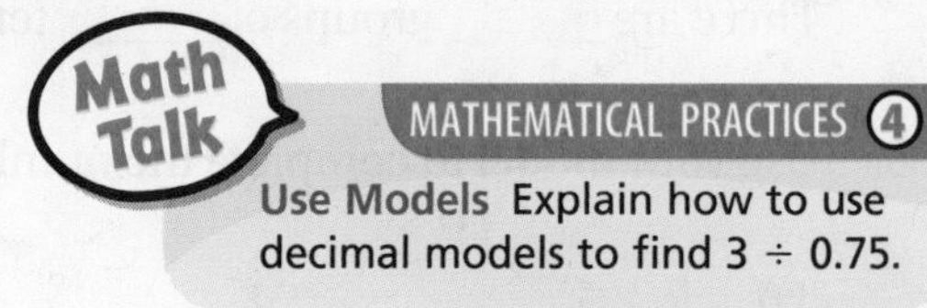

MATHEMATICAL PRACTICES 4

Use Models Explain how to use decimal models to find 3 ÷ 0.75.

So, Julie can make ______ stacks of $0.25 from $1.75.

Share and Show

Use the model to complete the number sentence.

1. 1.2 ÷ 0.3 = ______

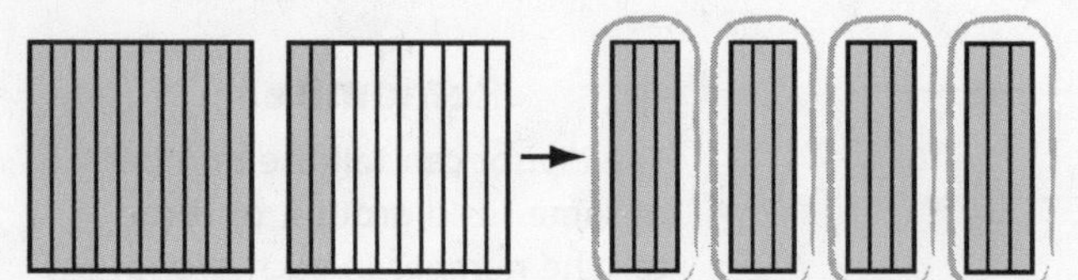

2. 0.45 ÷ 0.09 = ______

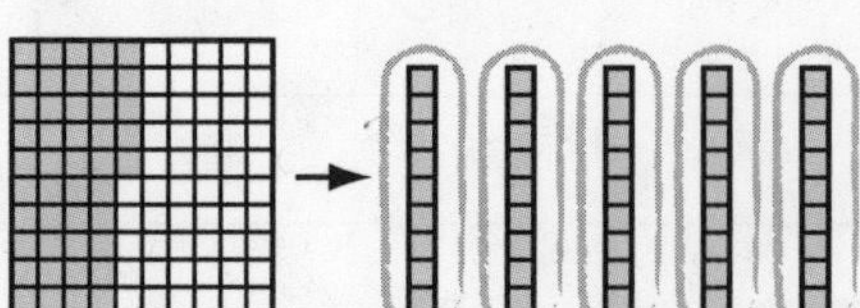

3. 0.96 ÷ 0.24 = ______

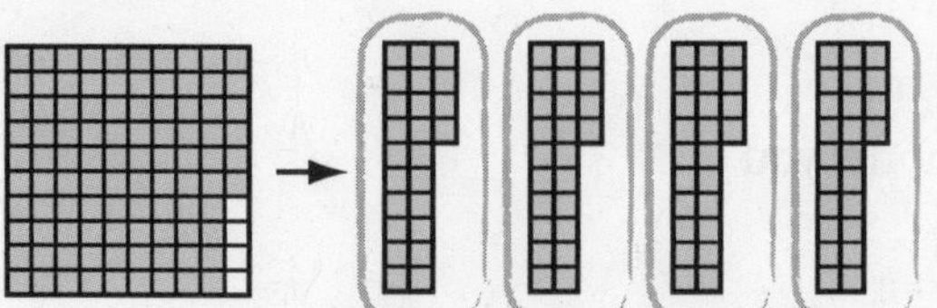

4. 1 ÷ 0.5 = ______

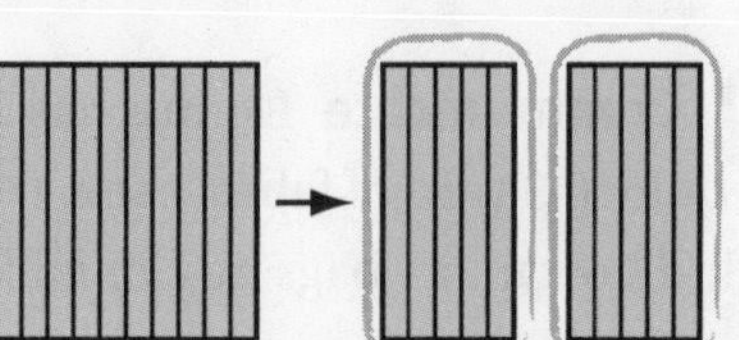

Name ______________________________

Divide. Use decimal models.

5. 1.24 ÷ 0.62 = ______

6. 0.84 ÷ 0.14 = ______

7. 1.6 ÷ 0.4 = ______

Problem Solving • Applications

MATHEMATICAL PRACTICE 5 Use Appropriate Tools **Use the model to find the unknown value.**

8. 2.4 ÷ ______ = 3

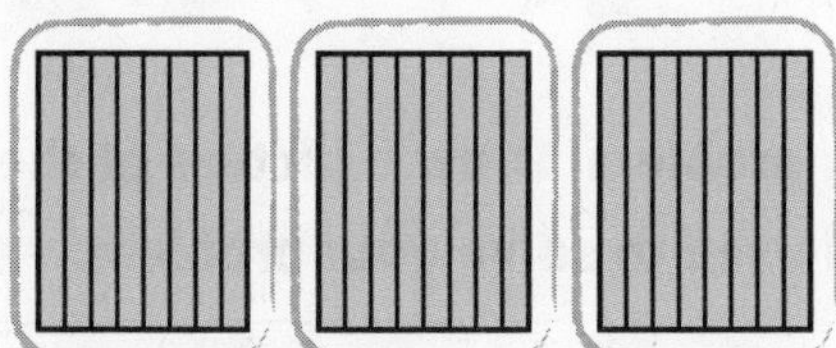

9. ______ ÷ 0.32 = 4

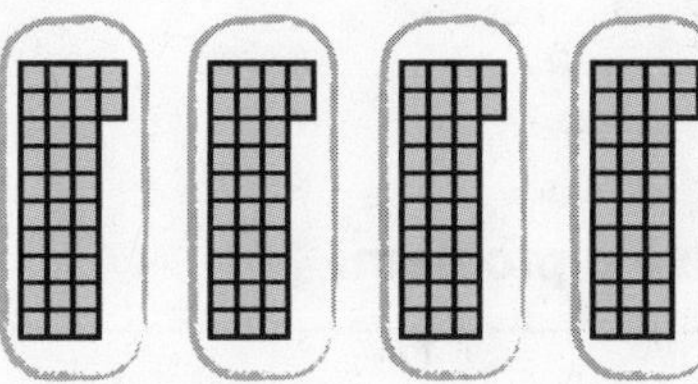

10. THINK SMARTER Make a model to find 0.6 ÷ 0.15. Describe your model.

____

____

11. MATHEMATICAL PRACTICE 6 **Explain** using the model, what the equation represents in Exercise 9.

____

____

Personal Math Trainer

12. 

Shade the model below and circle to show 1.8 ÷ 0.6.

1.8 ÷ 0.6 = 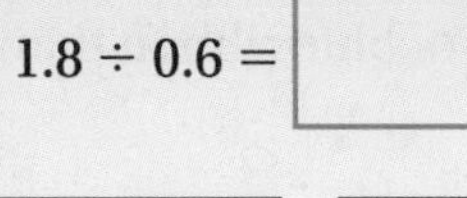

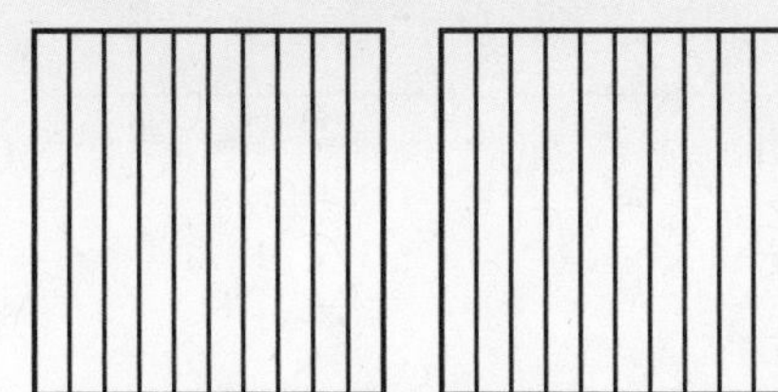

THINK SMARTER Pose a Problem

13. Emilio buys 1.2 kilograms of grapes. He separates the grapes into packages that contain 0.3 kilogram of grapes each. How many packages of grapes does Emilio make?

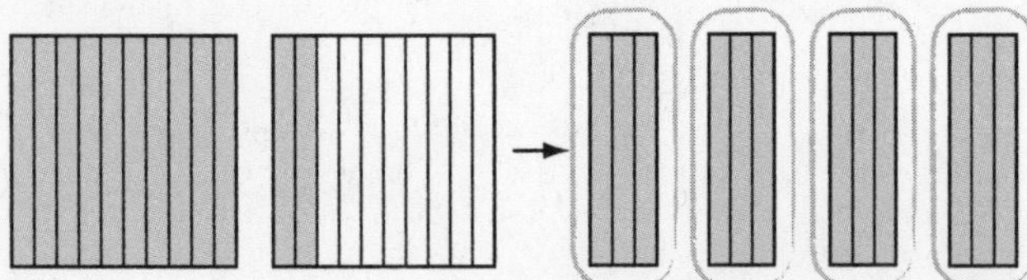

$1.2 \div 0.3 = 4$

Emilio made 4 packages of grapes.

Write a new problem using a different amount for the weight in each package. The amount should be a decimal with tenths. Use a total amount of 1.5 kilograms of grapes. Then use decimal models to solve your problem.

Pose a problem.

Solve your problem. Draw a picture of the model you used to solve your problem.

14. GO DEEPER Josie has 2.31 meters of blue ribbon that she wants to cut into 0.33-meter long pieces. She has 2.05 meters of red ribbon that she wants to cut into 0.41-meter long pieces. How many more pieces of blue ribbon than pieces of red ribbon will there be?

____

Name ______________________________

Decimal Division

Common Core **COMMON CORE STANDARD—5.NBT.B.7**
Perform operations with multi-digit whole numbers and with decimals to hundredths.

Use the model to complete the number sentence.

1. 1.6 ÷ 0.4 = 4

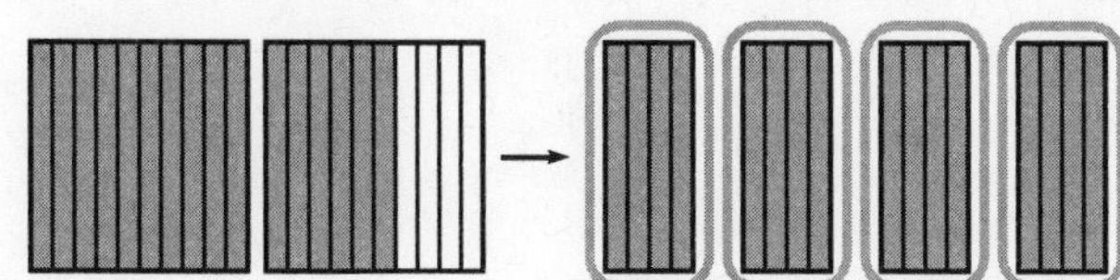

2. 0.36 ÷ 0.06 = __________

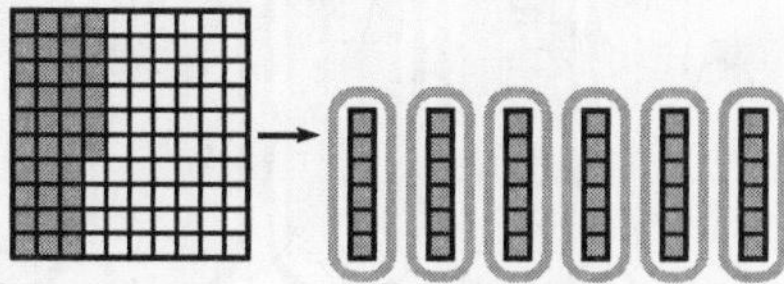

Divide. Use decimal models.

3. 2.8 ÷ 0.7 = __________

4. 0.40 ÷ 0.05 = __________

5. 0.45 ÷ 0.05 = __________

6. 1.62 ÷ 0.27 = __________

7. 0.56 ÷ 0.08 = __________

8. 1.8 ÷ 0.9 = __________

Problem Solving Real World

9. Keisha buys 2.4 kilograms of rice. She separates the rice into packages that contain 0.4 kilogram of rice each. How many packages of rice can Keisha make?

____

10. Leighton is making cloth headbands. She has 4.2 yards of cloth. She uses 0.2 yard of cloth for each headband. How many headbands can Leighton make from the length of cloth she has?

____

11. WRITE *Math* Write a word problem that involves dividing by a decimal. Include a picture of the solution using a model.

____

____

Lesson Check (5.NBT.B.7)

1. Write a number sentence that tells what the model represents.

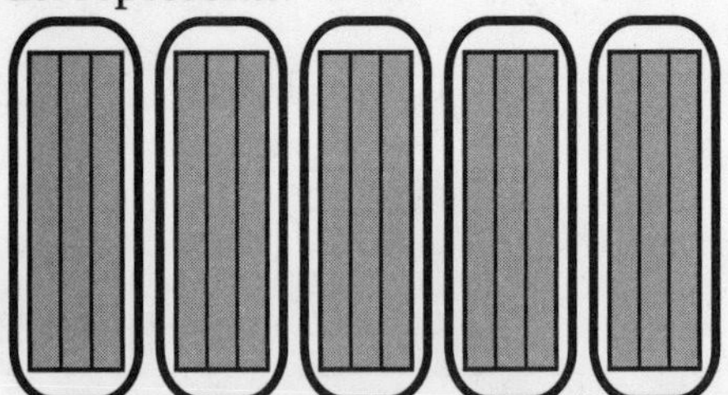

2. Morris has 1.25 pounds of strawberries. He uses 0.25 pound of strawberries to make one serving. How many servings can Morris make?

Spiral Review (5.NBT.B.5, 5.NBT.B.6, 5.NBT.B.7, 5.NF.B.3)

3. What property does the following equation show?

$$5 + 7 + 9 = 7 + 5 + 9$$

4. An auditorium has 25 rows with 45 seats in each row. How many seats are there in all?

5. Volunteers at an animal shelter divided 132 pounds of dry dog food equally into 16 bags. How many pounds of dog food did they put in each bag?

6. At the movies, Aaron buys popcorn for $5.25 and a bottle of water for $2.50. He pays with a $10 bill. How much change should Aaron receive?

FOR MORE PRACTICE GO TO THE Personal Math Trainer

Name ______________________________

Divide Decimals

Essential Question How can you place the decimal point in the quotient?

Common Core Number and Operations in Base Ten—5.NBT.B.7 *Also 5.NBT.A.2*

MATHEMATICAL PRACTICES MP1, MP2, MP8

When you multiply both the divisor and the dividend by the same power of 10, the quotient stays the same.

dividend		divisor		dividend		divisor
6	÷	3 = 2		120	÷	30 = 4
↓ × 10		↓ × 10		↓ × 0.1		↓ × 0.1
60	÷	30 = 2		12	÷	3 = 4
↓ × 10		↓ × 10		↓ × 0.1		↓ × 0.1
600	÷	300 = 2		1.2	÷	0.3 = 4

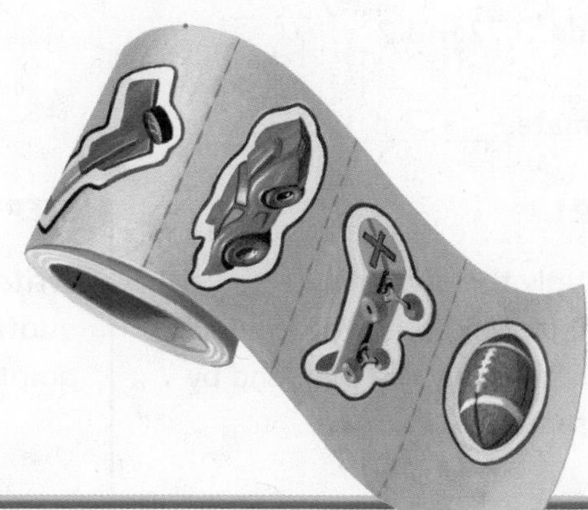

Unlock the Problem Real World

Matthew has \$0.72. He wants to buy stickers that cost \$0.08 each. How many stickers can he buy?

- What do you multiply hundredths by to get a whole number?

  ____

- Multiply both the dividend and the divisor by the power of 10 that makes the divisor a whole number. Then divide.

$0.72 \div 0.08 = \square$

↓ × 100 ↓ × 100

$72 \div 8 = \square$

So, Matthew can buy ______ stickers.

1. MATHEMATICAL PRACTICE 1 **Make Connections** Explain how you know that the quotient 0.72 ÷ 0.08 is equal to the quotient 72 ÷ 8.

____

____

Try This! Divide. 0.56 ÷ 0.7

- Multiply the divisor by a power of 10 to make it a whole number. Then multiply the dividend by the same power of 10.

  0.7 × ______ = ______

  0.56 × ______ = ______

- Divide.

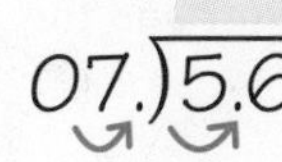

Example

Sherri hikes on the Pacific Coast trail. She plans to hike 3.72 miles. If she hikes at an average speed of 1.2 miles per hour, how long will she hike?

Divide. 3.72 ÷ 1.2

Estimate. ______

STEP 1

Multiply the divisor by a power of 10 to make it a whole number. Then, multiply the dividend by the same power of 10.

1.2 × ______ = ______

3.72 × ______ = ______

STEP 2

Write the decimal point in the quotient above the decimal point in the new dividend.

$12\overline{)37.2}$

STEP 3

Divide.

$12\overline{)37.2}$

−

−

So, Sherri will hike ______ hours.

2. MATHEMATICAL PRACTICE 8 **Generalize** Describe what happens to the decimal point in the divisor and in the dividend when you multiply by 10.

______

3. Explain how you could have used the estimate to place the decimal point.

______

______

Try This!

Divide. Check your answer.

$0.14\overline{)1.96}$

Multiply the divisor and the dividend by ______.

0.14
×

+

Name ______________________________

Share and Show MATH BOARD

Copy and complete the pattern.

1. 45 ÷ 9 = ______

4.5 ÷ ______ = 5

______ ÷ 0.09 = 5

2. 175 ÷ 25 = ______

17.5 ÷ ______ = 7

______ ÷ 0.25 = 7

3. 164 ÷ 2 = ______

16.4 ÷ ______ = 82

______ ÷ 0.02 = 82

Divide.

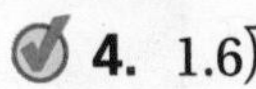

4. $1.6\overline{)9.6}$

5. $0.3\overline{)0.24}$

6. 3.45 ÷ 1.5

Math Talk

MATHEMATICAL PRACTICES 

Reason Quantitatively How do you know that your quotient for Exercise 5 will be less than 1?

On Your Own

Divide.

7. $0.6\overline{)13.2}$

8. $0.3\overline{)0.9}$

9. $0.26\overline{)1.56}$

10. MATHEMATICAL PRACTICE 1 Samuel has $0.96. He wants to buy erasers that cost $0.06 each. Describe how Samuel can find the number of erasers he can buy.

____

____

____

11. GO DEEPER Penny makes 6 liters of applesauce. She saves 0.56 liter for dinner and puts the rest in jars. If each jar holds 0.68 liter, how many jars can she fill?

____

____

Problem Solving • Applications

Use the table to solve 12–16.

Prices at School Store	
Item	**Price**
Eraser	$0.05
Marker	$0.36
Notepad	$0.65
Pencil	$0.12

12. Connie paid $1.08 for pencils. How many pencils did she buy?

13. Albert has $2.16. How many more pencils can he buy than markers?

14. GO DEEPER How many erasers can Ayita buy for the same amount that she would pay for two notepads?

15. THINK SMARTER Ramon paid $3.25 for notepads and $1.44 for markers. What is the total number of items he bought?

16. Keisha has $2.00. She wants to buy 4 notepads. Does she have enough money? Explain your reasoning.

17. WRITE Math **What's the Error?** Katie divided 4.25 by 0.25 and got a quotient of 0.17.

18. THINK SMARTER Tara has a large box of dog treats that weighs 8.4 pounds. She uses the large box of dog treats to make smaller bags, each containing 0.6 pound of treats. How many smaller bags of dog treats can Tara make?

WRITE Math • **Show Your Work**

Name ______________________

Divide Decimals

COMMON CORE STANDARD—5.NBT.B.7
Perform operations with multi-digit whole numbers and with decimals to hundredths.

Divide.

1. $0.4\overline{)8.4}$

Multiply both 0.4 and 8.4 by 10 to make the divisor a whole number. Then divide.

$$\begin{array}{r} 21 \\ 4\overline{)84} \\ -8 \\ \hline 04 \\ -4 \\ \hline 0 \end{array}$$

2. $0.2\overline{)0.4}$

3. $0.07\overline{)1.68}$

4. $0.37\overline{)5.18}$

5. $0.4\overline{)10.4}$

6. $6.3 \div 0.7$

7. $1.52 \div 1.9$

8. $12.24 \div 0.34$

9. $10.81 \div 2.3$

Problem Solving Real World

10. At the market, grapes cost $0.85 per pound. Clarissa buys grapes and pays a total of $2.55. How many pounds of grapes does she buy?

____

11. Damon kayaks on a river near his home. He plans to kayak a total of 6.4 miles. Damon kayaks at an average speed of 1.6 miles per hour. How many hours will it take Damon to kayak the 6.4 miles?

____

12. WRITE Math Write and solve a division problem involving decimals. Explain how you know where to place the decimal point in the quotient.

____

____

Lesson Check (5.NBT.A.2, 5.NBT.B.7)

1. Lee walked a total of 4.48 miles. He walks 1.4 miles each hour. How long did Lee walk?

2. Janelle has 3.6 yards of wire, which she wants to use to make bracelets. She needs 0.3 yard for each bracelet. Altogether, how many bracelets can Janelle make?

Spiral Review (5.NBT.A.2, 5.NBT.A.3b, 5.NBT.B.7)

3. Susie's teacher asks her to complete the multiplication problem below. What is the product?

$$\begin{array}{r} 0.3 \\ \times \ 3.7 \\ \hline \end{array}$$

4. At an Internet store, a laptop computer costs \$724.99. At a local store, the same computer costs \$879.95. What is the difference in prices?

5. Continue the pattern below. What is the quotient $75.8 \div 10^2$?

$75.8 \div 10^0 = 75.8$

$75.8 \div 10^1 = 7.58$

$75.8 \div 10^2 =$ ______

6. Which symbol will make the following statement true? Write >, <, or =.

58.827 ◯ 58.91

FOR MORE PRACTICE GO TO THE **Personal Math Trainer**

Name ______________________

Write Zeros in the Dividend

Essential Question When do you write a zero in the dividend to find a quotient?

Common Core **Number and Operations in Base Ten—5.NBT.B.7**
Also 5.NF.B.3

MATHEMATICAL PRACTICES
MP2, MP3, MP5, MP6, MP8

CONNECT When decimals are divided, the dividend may not have enough digits for you to complete the division. In these cases, you can write zeros to the right of the last digit.

Unlock the Problem (Real World)

The equivalent fractions show that writing zeros to the right of a decimal does not change the value.

$$90.8 = 90\frac{8 \times 10}{10 \times 10} = 90\frac{80}{100} = 90.80$$

During a fund-raising event, Adrian rode his bicycle 45.8 miles in 4 hours. Find his speed in miles per hour by dividing the distance by the time.

Divide. 45.8 ÷ 4 **Estimate.** 44 ÷ 4 = ______

STEP 1

Write the decimal point in the quotient above the decimal point in the dividend.

$4\overline{)45.8}$

STEP 2

Divide the tens, ones, and tenths.

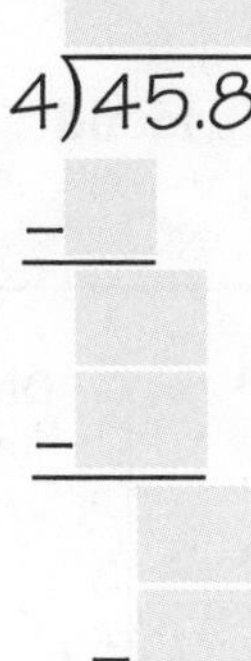

STEP 3

Write a zero in the dividend and continue dividing.

$4\overline{)45.80}$
−4
05
− 4
18
−16
−

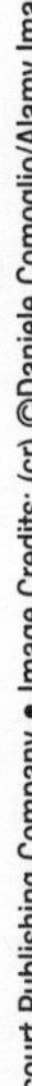

So, Adrian's speed was ____________ miles per hour.

MATHEMATICAL PRACTICES 5

Use a Concrete Model How would you model this problem using base-ten blocks?

CONNECT When you divide whole numbers, you can show the amount that is left over by writing a remainder or a fraction. By writing zeros in the dividend, you can also show that amount as a decimal.

Example Write zeros in the dividend.

Divide. 372 ÷ 15

- Divide until you have an amount less than the divisor left over.
- Insert a decimal point and a zero at the end of the dividend.
- Place a decimal point in the quotient above the decimal point in the dividend.
- Continue dividing.

So, 372 ÷ 15 = ______.

```
      24.
15)372.0
  −30
    72
   −60
```

- MATHEMATICAL PRACTICE 6 Sarah has 78 ounces of rice. She puts an equal amount of rice in each of 12 bags. What amount of rice does she put in each bag? **Explain** how you would write the answer using a decimal.

______

______

Try This! **Divide. Write a zero at the end of the dividend as needed.**

Divide. 1.23 ÷ 0.06

```
006.)123.        20.
               6)123.0
                 −12
                   03
                  − 0
                   30
                  −
```

Divide. 10 ÷ 0.8

```
08.)100.        8.)100.
```

Name ___________________________

Share and Show

MATH BOARD

Write the quotient with the decimal point placed correctly.

1. $5 \div 0.8 = 625$

2. $26.1 \div 6 = 435$

3. $0.42 \div 0.35 = 12$

4. $80 \div 50 = 16$

Divide.

5. $4\overline{)32.6}$

6. $1.2\overline{)9}$

7. $15\overline{)42}$

8. $0.14\overline{)0.91}$

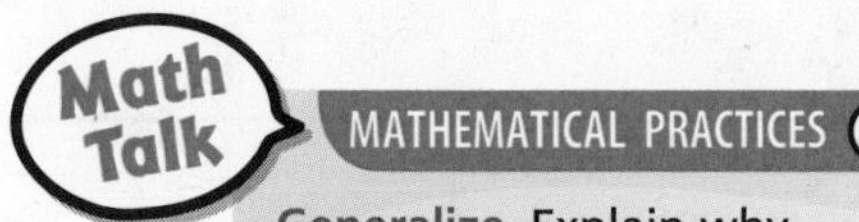

Generalize Explain why you would write a zero in the dividend when dividing decimals.

On Your Own

Practice: Copy and Solve **Divide.**

9. $1.6\overline{)20}$

10. $15\overline{)4.8}$

11. $0.54\overline{)2.43}$

12. $28\overline{)98}$

13. $1.8 \div 12$

14. $3.5 \div 2.5$

15. $40 \div 16$

16. $2.24 \div 0.35$

17. MATHEMATICAL PRACTICE 2 **Reason Quantitatively** Lana has a ribbon that is 2.2 meters long. She cuts the ribbon into 4 equal pieces to trim the edges of her bulletin board. What is the length of each piece of ribbon?

____

18. GO DEEPER Hiro's family lives 448 kilometers from the beach. Each of the 5 adults drove the family van an equal distance to get to and from the beach. How far did each adult drive?

____

Problem Solving • Applications

19. GO DEEPER Jerry takes trail mix on hikes. A package of dried apricots weighs 25.5 ounces. A package of sunflower seeds weighs 21 ounces. Jerry divides the apricots and seeds equally among 6 bags of trail mix. How many more ounces of apricots than seeds are in each bag?

20. THINK SMARTER Amy has 3 pounds of raisins. She divides the raisins equally into 12 bags. How many pounds of raisins are in each bag? Tell how many zeros you had to write at the end of the dividend to solve.

21. MATHEMATICAL PRACTICE 3 **Compare Representations** Find 65 ÷ 4. Write your answer using a remainder, a fraction, and a decimal. Then tell which form of the answer you prefer. Explain your choice.

22. THINK SMARTER For 22a–22d select Yes or No to indicate whether a zero must be written in the dividend to find the quotient.

22a.	5.2 ÷ 8	○ Yes	○ No
22b.	3.63 ÷ 3	○ Yes	○ No
22c.	71.1 ÷ 0.9	○ Yes	○ No
22d.	2.25 ÷ 0.6	○ Yes	○ No

Connect to Science

Rate of Speed Formula

The formula for velocity, or rate of speed, is $r = d \div t$, where r represents rate of speed, d represents distance, and t represents time. For example, if an object travels 12 feet in 10 seconds, you can find its rate of speed by using the formula.

$r = d \div t$

$r = 12 \div 10$

$r = 1.2$ feet per second

Use division and the formula for rate of speed to solve.

23. A car travels 168 miles in 3.2 hours. Find the car's rate of speed in miles per hour.

24. A submarine travels 90 kilometers in 4 hours. Find the submarine's rate of speed in kilometers per hour.

Name ______________________________

Write Zeros in the Dividend

Common Core **COMMON CORE STANDARD—5.NBT.B.7**
Perform operations with multi-digit whole numbers and with decimals to hundredths.

Divide.

1. $6\overline{)23.70}$

```
   3.95
6)23.70
 -18
   57
  -54
    30
   -30
     0
```

2. $25\overline{)405}$

3. $0.6\overline{)12.9}$

4. $0.8\overline{)30}$

5. $4\overline{)36.2}$

6. $35\overline{)97.3}$

7. $7.8 \div 15$

8. $49 \div 14$

9. $52.2 \div 12$

10. $5.16 \div 0.24$

11. $20.2 \div 4$

12. $138.4 \div 16$

Problem Solving

13. Mark has a board that is 12 feet long. He cuts the board into 8 pieces that are the same length. How long is each piece?

____

14. Josh pays $7.59 for 2.2 pounds of ground turkey. What is the price per pound of the ground turkey?

____

15. WRITE *Math* Solve $14.2 \div 0.5$. Show your work and explain how you knew where to place the decimal point.

____

____

Lesson Check (5.NBT.B.7)

1. Tina divides 21.4 ounces of trail mix equally into 5 bags. How many ounces of trail mix are in each bag?

2. A slug crawls 5.62 meters in 0.4 hours. What is the slug's speed in meters per hour?

Spiral Review (5.NBT.A.2, 5.NBT.B.6, 5.NBT.B.7)

3. Suzy buys 35 pounds of rice. She divides it equally into 100 bags. How many pounds of rice does Suzy put in each bag?

4. Juliette spends $6.12 at the store. Morgan spends 3 times as much as Juliette. Jonah spends $4.29 more than Morgan. How much money does Jonah spend?

5. A concert sold out for 12 performances. Altogether, 8,208 tickets were sold. How many tickets were sold for each performance?

6. Jared has two dogs, Spot and Rover. Spot weighs 75.25 pounds. Rover weighs 48.8 pounds more than Spot. How much does Rover weigh?

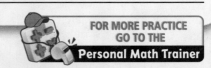

FOR MORE PRACTICE GO TO THE Personal Math Trainer

Name ______________________________

Problem Solving • Decimal Operations

Essential Question How do you use the strategy *work backward* to solve multistep decimal problems?

Number and Operations in Base Ten—5.NBT.B.7
MATHEMATICAL PRACTICES
MP2, MP6, MP7

Unlock the Problem

Carson spent $15.99 for 2 books and 3 pens. The books cost $4.95 each. The sales tax on the total purchase was $1.22. Carson also used a coupon for $0.50 off his purchase. If each pen had the same cost, how much did each pen cost?

Read the Problem

What do I need to find?	What information do I need to use?	How will I use the information?

Solve the Problem

- Make a flowchart to show the information. Then using inverse operations, work backward to solve.

Cost of 3 pens —plus→ Cost of 2 books —plus→ Amount of tax —minus→ Amount of Coupon —equals→ Total Spent

3 × cost of each pen + 2 × ______ + ______ − ______ = ______

Total Spent —plus→ Amount of Coupon —minus→ Amount of tax —minus→ Cost of 2 books —equals→ Cost of 3 pens

______ + ______ − ______ − ______ = ______

- Divide the cost of 3 pens by 3 to find the cost of each pen.

______ ÷ 3 = ______

So, the cost of each pen was ______.

Math Talk MATHEMATICAL PRACTICES 6

Explain why the amount of the coupon was added when you worked backward.

Try Another Problem

Last week, Vivian spent a total of $20.00. She spent $9.95 for tickets to the school fair, $5.95 for food, and the rest for 2 rings that were on sale at the school fair. If each ring had the same cost, how much did each ring cost?

Read the Problem

What do I need to find?	What information do I need to use?	How will I use the information?

Solve the Problem

So, the cost of each ring was ________.

MATHEMATICAL PRACTICES 2

Use Reasoning How can you check your answer?

Name ___________________________

Share and Show MATH BOARD

1. Hector spent $36.75 for 2 DVDs that cost the same amount. The sales tax on his purchase was $2.15. Hector also used a coupon for $1.00 off his purchase. How much did each DVD cost?

First, make a flowchart to show the information and show how you would work backward.

Then, work backward to find the cost of 2 DVDs.

____

Finally, find the cost of one DVD.

____

So, each DVD costs __________.

2. **What if** Hector spent $40.15 for the DVDs, the sales tax was $2.55, and he didn't have a coupon? How much would each DVD cost?

____

3. Sophia spent $7.30 for school supplies. She spent $3.00 for a notebook and $1.75 for a pen. She also bought 3 large erasers. If each eraser had the same cost, how much did she spend for each eraser?

____

WRITE *Math* • **Show Your Work**

On Your Own

WRITE Math • Show Your Work

4. The change from a gift purchase was $3.90. Each of 6 students donated an equal amount for the gift. How much change should each student receive?

____

5. GO DEEPER A mail truck picks up two boxes of mail from the post office. The total weight of the boxes is 32 pounds. One box is 8 pounds heavier than the other box. How much does each box weigh?

____

6. THINK SMARTER Stacy buys 3 CDs in a set for $29.98. She saved $6.44 by buying the set instead of buying the individual CDs. If each CD costs the same amount, how much does each of the 3 CDs cost when purchased individually?

____

7. MATHEMATICAL PRACTICE 7 **Look for a Pattern** A school cafeteria sold 1,280 slices of pizza the first week, 640 the second week, and 320 the third week. If this pattern continues, in what week will the cafeteria sell 40 slices? Explain how you got your answer.

____

____

____

Personal Math Trainer

8. THINK SMARTER+ Dawn spent $26.50, including sales tax on 4 books and 3 folders. The books cost $5.33 each and the total sales tax was $1.73. Fill in the table with the correct cost of each item.

Item	Cost
Cost of each book	
Cost of each folder	
Cost of sales tax	

Name ______________________________

Problem Solving • Decimal Operations

Common Core **COMMON CORE STANDARD—5.NBT.B.7**
Perform operations with multi-digit whole numbers and with decimals to hundredths.

1. Lily spent $30.00 on a T-shirt, a sandwich, and 2 books. The T-shirt cost $8.95, and the sandwich cost $7.25. The books each cost the same amount. How much did each book cost?

   (2 × cost of each book) + $8.95 + $7.25 = $30.00

   $30.00 − $8.95 − $7.25 = (2 × cost of each book)

   (2 × cost of each book) = $13.80
   $13.80 ÷ 2 = $6.90

   $6.90

2. Meryl spends a total of $68.82 for 2 pairs of sneakers with the same cost. The sales tax is $5.32. Meryl also uses a coupon for $3.00 off her purchase. How much does each pair of sneakers cost?

   ____

3. A 6-pack of undershirts costs $13.98. This is $3.96 less than the cost of buying 6 individual shirts. If each undershirt costs the same amount, how much does each undershirt cost when purchased individually?

   ____

4. **WRITE** *Math* Write a problem that can be solved using a flowchart and working backward. Then draw the flowchart and solve the problem.

____

____

____

Lesson Check (5.NBT.B.7)

1. Joe spends $8 on lunch and $6.50 on dry cleaning. He also buys 2 shirts that each cost the same amount. Joe spends a total of $52. What is the cost of each shirt?

2. Tina uses a $50 gift certificate to buy a pair of pajamas for $17.97, a necklace for $25.49, and 3 pairs of socks that each cost the same amount. Tina has to pay $0.33 because the gift certificate does not cover the total cost of all the items. How much does each pair of socks cost?

Spiral Review (5.NBT.A.2, 5.NBT.A.3b, 5.NBT.B.7)

3. List the following numbers in order from least to greatest.

   2.31, 2.13, 0.123, 3.12

4. Stephen wrote the problem 46.8 ÷ 0.5. What is the correct quotient?

5. Sarah, Juan, and Larry are on the track team. Last week, Sarah ran 8.25 miles, Juan ran 11.8 miles, and Larry ran 9.3 miles. How many miles did they run altogether?

6. On a fishing trip, Lucy and Ed caught one fish each. Ed's fish weighed 6.45 pounds. Lucy's fish weighed 1.6 times as much as Ed's fish. How much did Lucy's fish weigh?

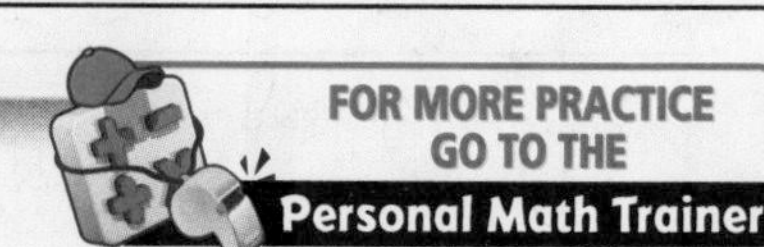

Name ________________________________

Chapter 5 Review/Test

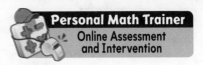

Personal Math Trainer
Online Assessment and Intervention

1. Rita is hiking along a trail that is 13.7 miles long. So far she has hiked along one-tenth of the trail. How far has Rita hiked?

_______ miles

2. Use the numbers on the tiles to complete each number sentence. You can use a tile more than once or not at all.

$35.5 \div 10^0$	=	
$35.5 \div 10$	=	
$35.5 \div 10^2$	=	

Tiles: . | 0 | 3 | 5

3. GO DEEPER Tom and his brothers caught 100 fish on a weeklong fishing trip. The total weight of the fish was 235 pounds.

Part A

Write an expression that will find the weight of one fish. Assume that the weight of each fish is the same.

Part B

What is the weight of one fish?

_______ pounds

Part C

Suppose the total weight of the fish caught stayed the same but instead of 100 fish caught during the weeklong fishing trip, only 10 fish were caught. How would the weight of each fish change? Explain.

GO DIGITAL Assessment Options Chapter Test

4. Draw a model to show 5.5 ÷ 5.

$5.5 \div 5 =$ ______

5. Emma, Brandy, and Damian will cut a rope that is 29.8 feet long into 3 jump ropes. Each of the 3 jump ropes will be the same length. Write a division sentence using compatible numbers to estimate the length of each rope.

6. Karl drove 617.3 miles. For each gallon of gas, the car can travel 41 miles. Select a reasonable estimate of the number of gallons of gas Karl used. Mark all that apply.

Ⓐ 1.5 gallons

Ⓑ 1.6 gallons

Ⓒ 15 gallons

Ⓓ 16 gallons

Ⓔ 150 gallons

7. Donald bought a box of golf balls for $9.54. There were 18 golf balls in the box. About how much did each golf ball cost?

8. Luke cut down a tree that was 28.8 feet tall. Then he cut the tree into 6 equal pieces to take it away. What is the length of each piece?

______ feet

Name ________________________________

9. Samantha is making some floral arrangements. The table shows the prices for one-half dozen of each type of flower.

Prices For $\frac{1}{2}$ Dozen Flowers	
Rose	\$5.29
Carnation	\$3.59
Tulip	\$4.79

Part A

Samantha wants to buy 6 roses, 4 carnations, and 8 tulips. She estimates that she will spend about \$14 on these flowers. Do you agree? Explain your answer.

Part B

Along with the flowers, Samantha bought 4 packages of glass beads and 2 vases. The vases cost \$3.59 each and the total sales tax was \$1.34. The total amount she paid was \$28.50, including sales tax. Explain a strategy she could use to find the cost of 1 package of glass beads.

10. Les is sending 8 identical catalogs to one of his customers. If the package with the catalogs weighs 6.72 pounds, how much does each catalog weigh?

______ pound(s)

11. Divide.

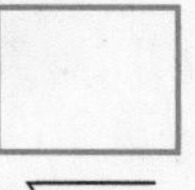

$5\overline{)6.55}$

12. Isabella is buying art supplies. The table shows the prices for the different items she buys.

Art Supplies	
Item	**Price**
Glass beads	$0.28 per ounce
Paint brush	$0.95
Poster board	$0.75
Jar of paint	$0.99

Part A

Isabella spends $2.25 on poster boards. How many poster boards does she buy?

______ poster boards

Part B

Isabella spends $4.87 on paintbrushes and paint. How many of each item does she buy? Explain how you found your answer.

13. Shade the model and circle to show 1.4 ÷ 0.7.

1.4 ÷ 0.7 = ☐

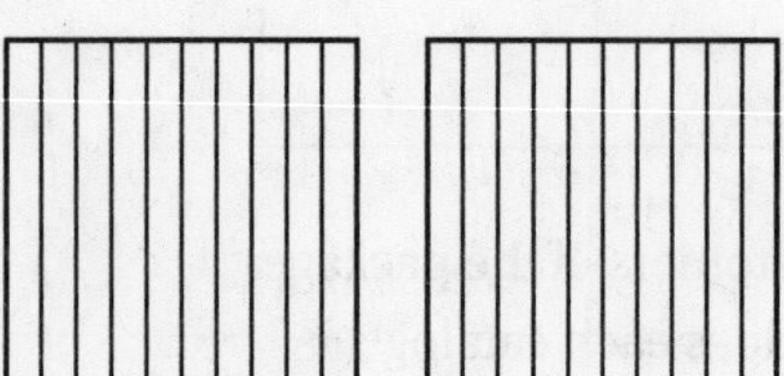

Name ___

14. Tabitha bought peppers that cost $0.79 per pound. She paid $3.95 for the peppers. How many pounds of peppers did she buy? Show your work.

15. Hank has a large bag of trail mix that weighs 7.8 pounds. He uses the mix in the large bag to make bags each containing 0.6 pound of mix. How many bags containing 0.6 pound can be made?

___ bags

16. Shareen walked a total of 9.52 miles in a walk-a-thon. If her average speed was 2.8 miles per hour, how long did it take Shareen to complete the walk?

___ hours

17. For 17a–17c, choose Yes or No to indicate whether a zero must be written in the dividend to find the quotient.

17a. $1.4 \div 0.05$ ○ Yes ○ No

17b. $2.52 \div 0.6$ ○ Yes ○ No

17c. $2.61 \div 0.3$ ○ Yes ○ No

18. Lisandra made 22.8 quarts of split pea soup for her restaurant. She wants to put the same amount of soup into each of 15 containers. How much soup should Lisandra put into each container?

___ quarts

19. Percy buys tomatoes that cost \$0.58 per pound. He pays \$2.03 for the tomatoes.

Part A

Percy estimates he bought 4 pounds of tomatoes. Is Percy's estimate reasonable? Explain.

Part B

How many pounds of tomatoes did Percy actually buy? Show your work.

20. Who drove the fastest? Select the correct answer.

(A) Harlin drove 363 miles in 6 hours.

(B) Kevin drove 435 miles in 7 hours.

(C) Shanna drove 500 miles in 8 hours.

(D) Hector drove 215 miles in 5 hours.

21. Maritza is buying a multipack of 3 pairs of socks for \$25.98. She will save \$6.39 by buying the multipack instead of buying 3 individual pairs of the same socks. If each pair of socks costs the same amount, how much does each pair of socks cost when bought individually? Show your work.

Personal Math Trainer

22. THINKSMARTER+ Eric spent \$22.00, including sales tax, on 2 jerseys and 3 pairs of socks. The jerseys cost \$6.75 each and the total sales tax was \$1.03. Fill in the table with the correct prices.

Item	Cost
Cost of each jersey	
Cost of each pair of socks	
Cost of sales tax	

Glossary

Pronunciation Key

a	add, map	ē	equal, tree	m	move, seem	o͞o	pool, food	ů	pull, book
ā	ace, rate	f	fit, half	n	nice, tin	p	pit, stop	û(r)	burn, term
â(r)	care, air	g	go, log	ng	ring, song	r	run, poor	yo͞o	fuse, few
ä	palm, father	h	hope, hate	o	odd, hot	s	see, pass	v	vain, eve
b	bat, rub	i	it, give	ō	open, so	sh	sure, rush	w	win, away
ch	check, catch	ī	ice, write	ô	order, jaw	t	talk, sit	y	yet, yearn
d	dog, rod	j	joy, ledge	oi	oil, boy	th	thin, both	z	zest, muse
e	end, pet	k	cool, take	ou	pout, now	th	this, bathe	zh	vision, pleasure
		l	look, rule	o͝o	took, full	u	up, done		

ə the schwa, an unstressed vowel representing the sound spelled a in above, e in sicken, i in possible, o in melon, u in circus

Other symbols:
- • separates words into syllables
- ʹ indicates stress on a syllable

acute angle [ə•kyo͞otʹ angʹgəl] **ángulo agudo** An angle that has a measure less than a right angle (less than 90° and greater than 0°)
Example:

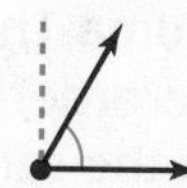

Word History

The Latin word for needle is *acus*. This means “pointed” or “sharp.” You will recognize the root in the words *acid* (sharp taste), *acumen* (mental sharpness), and *acute*, which describes a sharp or pointed angle.

acute triangle [ə•kyo͞otʹ trīʹang•gəl] **triángulo acutángulo** A triangle that has three acute angles

addend [adʹend] **sumando** A number that is added to another in an addition problem

addition [ə•dishʹən] **suma** The process of finding the total number of items when two or more groups of items are joined; the inverse operation of subtraction

algebraic expression [al•jə•brāʹik ek•sprehʹən] **expresión algebraica** An expression that includes at least one variable
Examples: $x + 5$, $3a - 4$

angle [angʹgəl] **ángulo** A shape formed by two rays that share the same endpoint
Example:

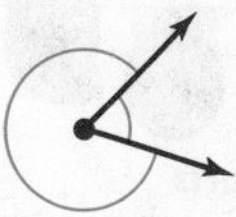

area [ârʹē•ə] **área** The measure of the number of unit squares needed to cover a surface

array [ə•rāʹ] **matriz** An arrangement of objects in rows and columns
Example:

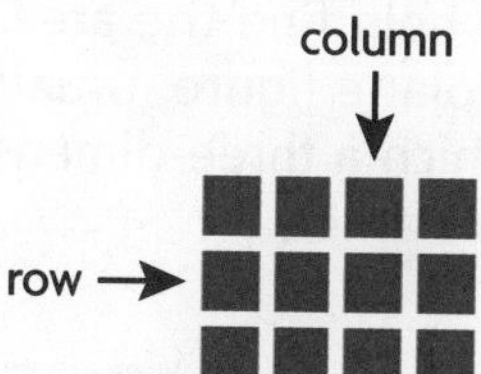

Associative Property of Addition [ə•sō′shē•āt•iv präp′ ər•tē əv ə•dish′ən] **propiedad asociativa de la suma** The property that states that when the grouping of addends is changed, the sum is the same
Example: (5 + 8) + 4 = 5 + (8 + 4)

Associative Property of Multiplication [ə•sō′shē•āt•iv präp′ər•tē əv mul•tə•pli•kā′shən] **propiedad asociativa de la multiplicación** The property that states that factors can be grouped in different ways and still get the same product
Example: (2 × 3) × 4 = 2 × (3 × 4)

balance [bal′əns] **equilibrar** To equalize in weight or number

bar graph [bär graf] **gráfica de barras** A graph that uses horizontal or vertical bars to display countable data
Example:

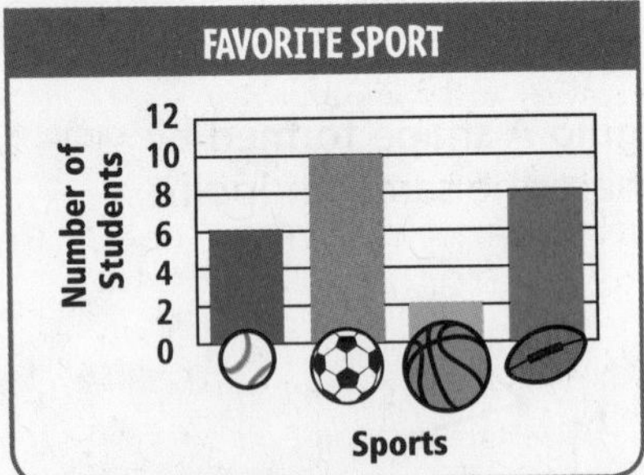

base (arithmetic) [bās] **base** A number used as a repeated factor
Example: $8^3 = 8 \times 8 \times 8$. The base is 8.

base (geometry) [bās] **base** In two dimensions, one side of a triangle or parallelogram that is used to help find the area. In three dimensions, a plane figure, usually a polygon or circle, by which a three-dimensional figure is measured or named
Examples:

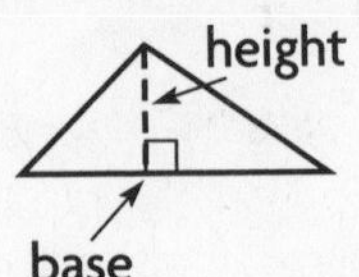

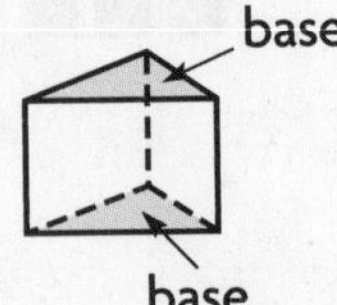

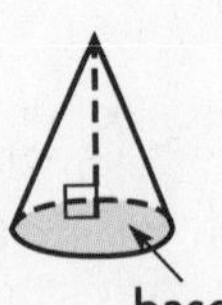

benchmark [bench′märk] **punto de referencia** A familiar number used as a point of reference

capacity [kə•pas′i•tē] **capacidad** The amount a container can hold when filled

Celsius (°C) [sel′sē•əs] **Celsius (°C)** A metric scale for measuring temperature

centimeter (cm) [sen′tə•mēt•ər] **centímetro (cm)** A metric unit used to measure length or distance; 0.01 meter = 1 centimeter

closed figure [klōzd fig′yər] **figura cerrada** A figure that begins and ends at the same point

common denominator [käm′ən dē•näm′ə•nāt•ər] **denominador común** A common multiple of two or more denominators
Example: Some common denominators for $\frac{1}{4}$ and $\frac{5}{6}$ are 12, 24, and 36.

common factor [käm′ən fak′tər] **factor común** A number that is a factor of two or more numbers

common multiple [käm′ən mul′tə•pəl] **múltiplo común** A number that is a multiple of two or more numbers

Commutative Property of Addition [kə•myoo͞t′ə•tiv präp′ər•tē əv ə•dish′ən] **propiedad conmutativa de la suma** The property that states that when the order of two addends is changed, the sum is the same
Example: 4 + 5 = 5 + 4

Commutative Property of Multiplication [kə•myoo͞t′ə•tiv präp′ər•tē əv mul•tə•pli•kā′shən] **propiedad conmutativa de la multiplicación** The property that states that when the order of two factors is changed, the product is the same
Example: 4 × 5 = 5 × 4

compatible numbers [kəm•pat′ə•bəl num′bərz] **números compatibles** Numbers that are easy to compute with mentally

composite number [kəm•päz′it num′bər] **número compuesto** A number having more than two factors
Example: 6 is a composite number, since its factors are 1, 2, 3, and 6.

cone [kōn] **cono** A solid figure that has a flat, circular base and one vertex
Example:

congruent [kən•grōō′ənt] **congruente** Having the same size and shape

coordinate grid [kō•ôrd′n•it grid] **cuadrícula de coordenadas** A grid formed by a horizontal line called the *x*-axis and a vertical line called the *y*-axis
Example:

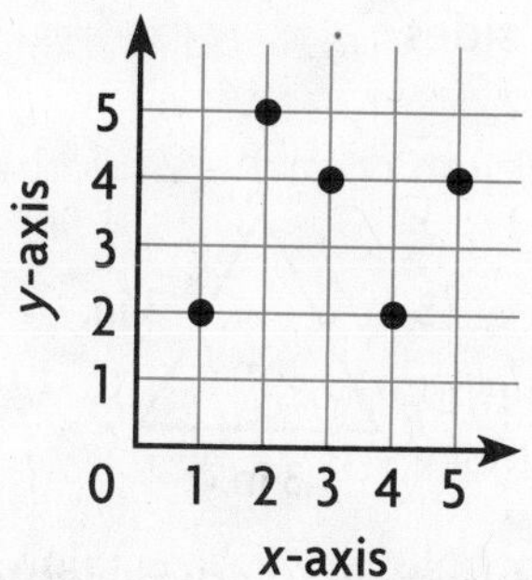

counting number [kount′ing num′bər] **número natural** A whole number that can be used to count a set of objects (1, 2, 3, 4, . . .)

cube [kyōōb] **cubo** A three-dimensional figure with six congruent square faces
Example:

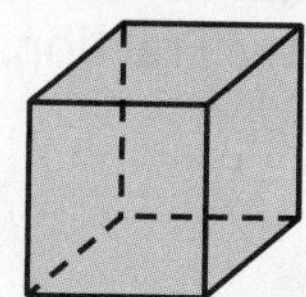

cubic unit [kyōō′bik yōō′nit] **unidad cúbica** A unit used to measure volume such as cubic foot (ft^3), cubic meter (m^3), and so on

cup (c) [kup] **taza (t)** A customary unit used to measure capacity; 8 ounces = 1 cup

cylinder [sil′ən•dər] **cilindro** A solid figure that has two parallel bases that are congruent circles
Example:

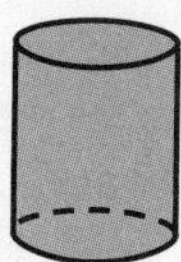

data [dāt′ə] **datos** Information collected about people or things, often to draw conclusions about them

decagon [dek′ə•gän] **decágono** A polygon with ten sides and ten angles
Examples:

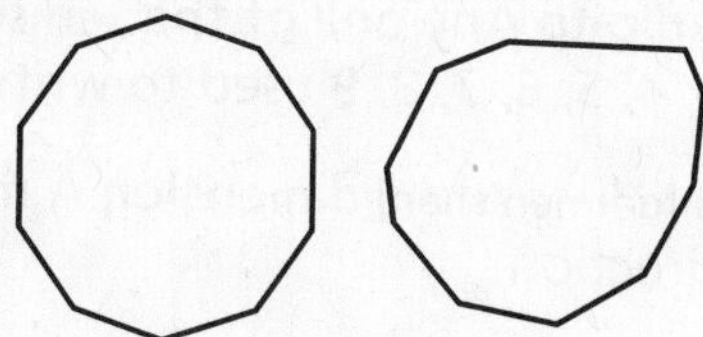

decagonal prism [dek•ag′ə•nəl priz′əm] **prisma decagonal** A three-dimensional figure with two decagonal bases and ten rectangular faces

decimal [des′ə•məl] **decimal** A number with one or more digits to the right of the decimal point

decimal point [des′ə•məl point] **punto decimal** A symbol used to separate dollars from cents in money, and to separate the ones place from the tenths place in a decimal

decimal system [des′ə•məl sis′təm] **sistema decimal** A system of computation based on the number 10

decimeter (dm) [des′i•mēt•ər] **decímetro (dm)** A metric unit used to measure length or distance; 10 decimeters = 1 meter

degree (°) [di•grē′] **grado (°)** A unit used for measuring angles and temperature

degree Celsius (°C) [di•grē′ sel′sē•əs] **grado Celsius** A metric unit for measuring temperature

degree Fahrenheit (°F) [di•grē′ fâr′ən•hīt] **grado Fahrenheit** A customary unit for measuring temperature

dekameter (dam) [dek′ə•mēt•ər] **decámetro** A metric unit used to measure length or distance; 10 meters = 1 dekameter

denominator [dē•näm′ə•nāt•ər] **denominador** The number below the bar in a fraction that tells how many equal parts are in the whole or in the group
Example: $\frac{3}{4}$ ← denominator

diagonal [dī•ag′ə•nəl] **diagonal** A line segment that connects two non-adjacent vertices of a polygon
Example:

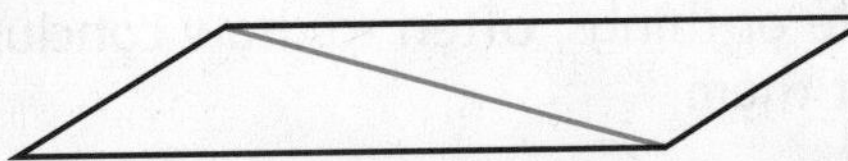

difference [dif′ər•əns] **diferencia** The answer to a subtraction problem

digit [dij′it] **dígito** Any one of the ten symbols 0, 1, 2, 3, 4, 5, 6, 7, 8, 9 used to write numbers

dimension [də•men′shən] **dimensión** A measure in one direction

Distributive Property [di•strib′yōō•tiv präp′ər•tē] **propiedad distributiva** The property that states that multiplying a sum by a number is the same as multiplying each addend in the sum by the number and then adding the products
Example: $3 \times (4 + 2) = (3 \times 4) + (3 \times 2)$
$3 \times 6 = 12 + 6$
$18 = 18$

divide [də•vīd′] **dividir** To separate into equal groups; the inverse operation of multiplication

dividend [div′ə•dend] **dividendo** The number that is to be divided in a division problem
Example: $36 \div 6$; $6\overline{)36}$ The dividend is 36.

division [də•vizh′ən] **división** The process of sharing a number of items to find how many equal groups can be made or how many items will be in each equal group; the inverse operation of multiplication

divisor [də•vī′zər] **divisor** The number that divides the dividend
Example: $15 \div 3$; $3\overline{)15}$ The divisor is 3.

edge [ej] **arista** The line segment made where two faces of a solid figure meet
Example:

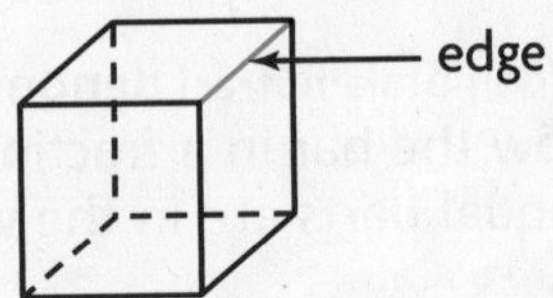

elapsed time [ē•lapst′ tīm] **tiempo transcurrido** The time that passes between the start of an activity and the end of that activity

endpoint [end′ point] **extremo** The point at either end of a line segment or the starting point of a ray

equal to (=) [ē′kwəl tōō] **igual a** Having the same value

equation [ē•kwā′zhən] **ecuación** An algebraic or numerical sentence that shows that two quantities are equal

equilateral triangle [ē•kwi•lat′ər•əl trī′ang•gəl] **triángulo equilátero** A triangle with three congruent sides
Example:

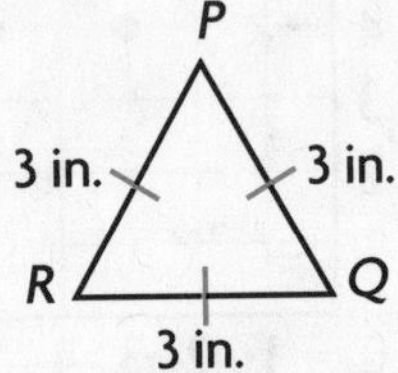

equivalent [ē•kwiv′ə•lənt] **equivalente** Having the same value

equivalent decimals [ē•kwiv′ə•lənt des′ə•məlz] **decimales equivalentes** Decimals that name the same amount
Example: $0.4 = 0.40 = 0.400$

equivalent fractions [ē•kwiv′ə•lənt frak′shənz] **fracciones equivalentes** Fractions that name the same amount or part
Example: $\frac{3}{4} = \frac{6}{8}$

estimate [es′tə•mit] *noun* **estimación (s)** A number close to an exact amount

estimate [es′tə•māt] *verb* **estimar (v)** To find a number that is close to an exact amount

evaluate [ē•val′yōō•āt] **evaluar** To find the value of a numerical or algebraic expression

even [ē′vən] **par** A whole number that has a 0, 2, 4, 6, or 8 in the ones place

expanded form [ek•span′did fôrm] **forma desarrollada** A way to write numbers by showing the value of each digit
Examples: $832 = 8 \times 100 + 3 \times 10 + 2 \times 1$
$3.25 = (3 \times 1) + (2 \times \frac{1}{10}) + (5 \times \frac{1}{100})$

exponent [eks′•pōn•ənt] **exponente** A number that shows how many times the base is used as a factor
Example: $10^3 = 10 \times 10 \times 10$.
3 is the exponent.

expression [ek•spresh′ən] **expresión** A mathematical phrase or the part of a number sentence that combines numbers, operation signs, and sometimes variables, but does not have an equal sign

face [fās] **cara** A polygon that is a flat surface of a solid figure
Example:

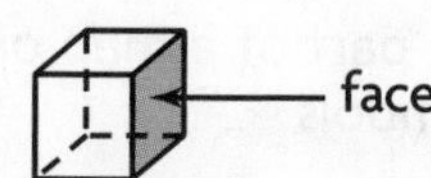

fact family [fakt fam′ə•lē] **familia de operaciones** A set of related multiplication and division, or addition and subtraction, equations
Examples: $7 \times 8 = 56$; $8 \times 7 = 56$;
$56 \div 7 = 8$; $56 \div 8 = 7$

factor [fak′tər] **factor** A number multiplied by another number to find a product

Fahrenheit (°F) [fâr′ən•hīt] **Fahrenheit (°F)** A customary scale for measuring temperature

fluid ounce (fl oz) [flo͞o′id ouns] **onza fluida** A customary unit used to measure liquid capacity; 1 cup = 8 fluid ounces

foot (ft) [fo͝ot] **pie (ft)** A customary unit used to measure length or distance; 1 foot = 12 inches

formula [fôr′myo͞o•lə] **fórmula** A set of symbols that expresses a mathematical rule
Example: $A = b \times h$

fraction [frak′shən] **fracción** A number that names a part of a whole or a part of a group

fraction greater than 1 [frak′shən grāt′ər <u>th</u>an wun] **fracción mayor que 1** A number which has a numerator that is greater than its denominator
Example:

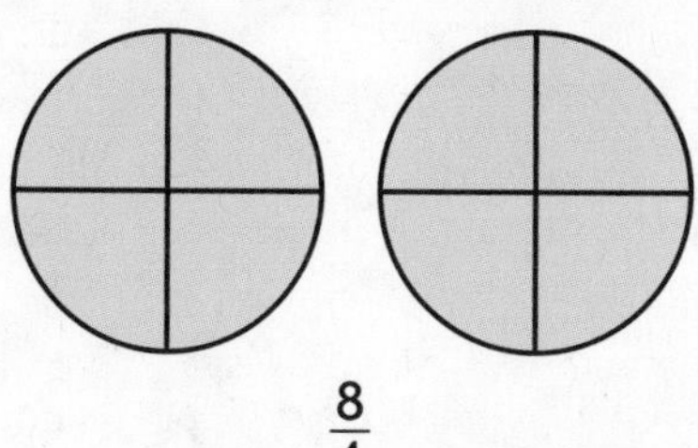

$\frac{8}{4}$

gallon (gal) [gal′ən] **galón (gal)** A customary unit used to measure capacity; 4 quarts = 1 gallon

general quadrilateral [jen′ər•əl kwä•dri•lat′ər•əl] **cuadrilátero en general** See *quadrilateral.*

gram (g) [gram] **gramo (g)** A metric unit used to measure mass; 1,000 grams = 1 kilogram

greater than (>) [grāt′ər <u>th</u>an] **mayor que (>)** A symbol used to compare two numbers or two quantities when the greater number or greater quantity is given first
Example: $6 > 4$

greater than or equal to (≥) [grāt′ər <u>th</u>an ôr ē′kwəl to͞o] **mayor que o igual a** A symbol used to compare two numbers or quantities when the first is greater than or equal to the second

greatest common factor [grāt′əst käm′ən fak′tər] **máximo común divisor** The greatest factor that two or more numbers have in common
Example: 6 is the greatest common factor of 18 and 30.

grid [grid] **cuadrícula** Evenly divided and equally spaced squares on a figure or flat surface

height [hīt] **altura** The length of a perpendicular from the base to the top of a two-dimensional or three-dimensional figure
Example:

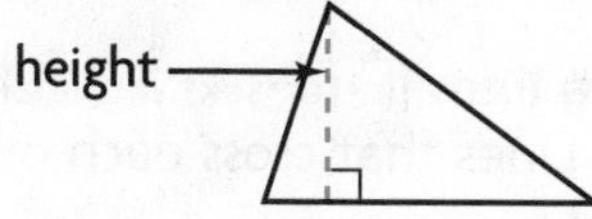

heptagon [hep′tə•gän] **heptágono** A polygon with seven sides and seven angles

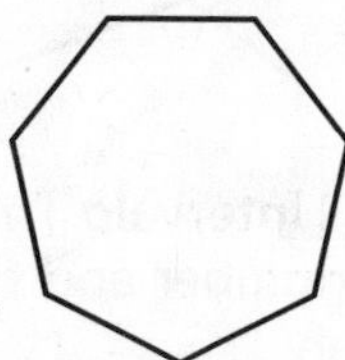

hexagon [hek′sə•gän] **hexágono** A polygon with six sides and six angles
Examples:

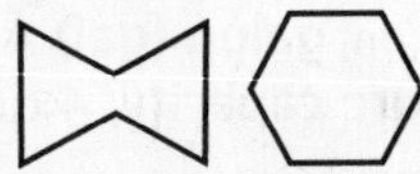

hexagonal prism [hek•sag′ə•nəl priz′əm] **prisma hexagonal** A three-dimensional figure with two hexagonal bases and six rectangular faces

horizontal [hôr•i•zänt′l] **horizontal** Extending left and right

hundredth [hun′drədth] **centésimo** One of 100 equal parts
Examples: 0.56, $\frac{56}{100}$, fifty-six hundredths

I

Identity Property of Addition [ī•den′tə•tē präp′ər•tē əv ə•dish′ən] **propiedad de identidad de la suma** The property that states that when you add zero to a number, the result is that number

Identity Property of Multiplication [ī•den′tə•tē präp′ər•tē əv mul•tə•pli•kā′shən] **propiedad de identidad de la multiplicación** The property that states that the product of any number and 1 is that number

inch (in.) [inch] **pulgada (pulg)** A customary unit used to measure length or distance; 12 inches = 1 foot

inequality [in•ē•kwôl′ə•tē] **desigualdad** A mathematical sentence that contains the symbol $<$, $>$, $\leq$, $\geq$, or $\neq$

intersecting lines [in•tər•sekt′ing līnz] **líneas secantes** Lines that cross each other at exactly one point
Example:

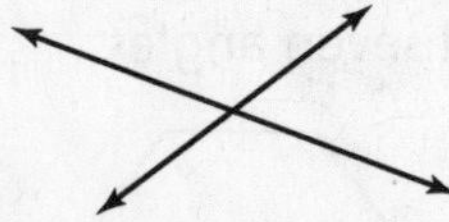

interval [in′tər•vəl] **intervalo** The difference between one number and the next on the scale of a graph

inverse operations [in′vûrs äp•ə•rā′shənz] **operaciones inversas** Opposite operations, or operations that undo each other, such as addition and subtraction or multiplication and division

isosceles triangle [ī•säs′ə•lēz trī′ang•gəl] **triángulo isósceles** A triangle with two congruent sides
Example:

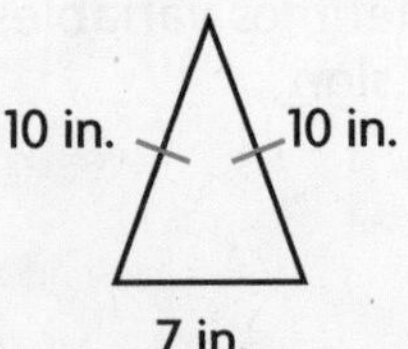

K

key [kē] **clave** The part of a map or graph that explains the symbols

kilogram (kg) [kil′ō•gram] **kilogramo (kg)** A metric unit used to measure mass; 1,000 grams = 1 kilogram

kilometer (km) [kə•läm′ət•ər] **kilómetro (km)** A metric unit used to measure length or distance; 1,000 meters = 1 kilometer

L

lateral face [lat′ər•əl fās] **cara lateral** Any surface of a polyhedron other than a base

least common denominator [lēst käm′ən dē•näm′ə•nāt•ər] **mínimo común denominador** The least common multiple of two or more denominators
Example: The least common denominator for $\frac{1}{4}$ and $\frac{5}{6}$ is 12.

least common multiple [lēst käm′ən mul′tə•pəl] **mínimo común múltiplo** The least number that is a common multiple of two or more numbers

less than (<) [les t͟hən] **menor que (<)** A symbol used to compare two numbers or two quantities, with the lesser number given first
Example: $4 < 6$

less than or equal to (≤) [les t͟han ôr ē′kwəl to͞o] **menor que o igual a** A symbol used to compare two numbers or two quantities, when the first is less than or equal to the second

line [līn] **línea** A straight path in a plane, extending in both directions with no endpoints
Example:

line graph [līn graf] **gráfica lineal** A graph that uses line segments to show how data change over time

line plot [līn plät] **diagrama de puntos** A graph that shows frequency of data along a number line
Example:

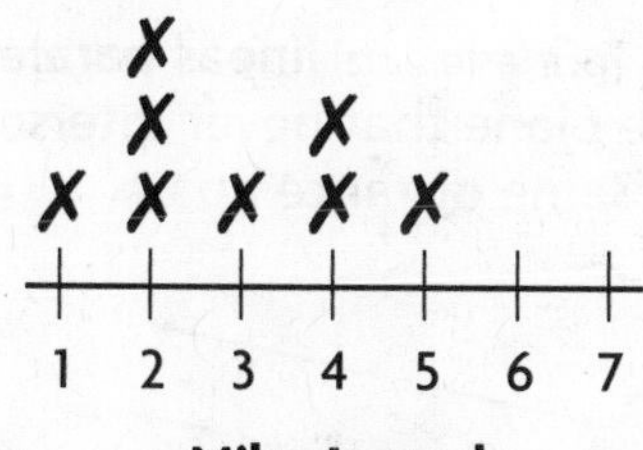

Miles Jogged

line segment [līn seg′mənt] **segmento** A part of a line that includes two points called endpoints and all the points between them

line symmetry [līn sim′ə•trē] **simetría axial** A figure has line symmetry if it can be folded about a line so that its two parts match exactly.

linear unit [lin′ē•ər yo͞o′nit] **unidad lineal** A measure of length, width, height, or distance

liquid volume [lik′wid väl′yo͞om] **volumen de un líquido** The amount of liquid in a container

liter (L) [lēt′ər] **litro (L)** A metric unit used to measure capacity; 1 liter = 1,000 milliliters

mass [mas] **masa** The amount of matter in an object

meter (m) [mēt′ər] **metro (m)** A metric unit used to measure length or distance; 1 meter = 100 centimeters

mile (mi) [mīl] **milla (mi)** A customary unit used to measure length or distance; 5,280 feet = 1 mile

milligram (mg) [mil′i•gram] **miligramo** A metric unit used to measure mass; 1,000 milligrams = 1 gram

milliliter (mL) [mil′i•lēt•ər] **mililitro (mL)** A metric unit used to measure capacity; 1,000 milliliters = 1 liter

millimeter (mm) [mil′i•mēt•ər] **milímetro (mm)** A metric unit used to measure length or distance; 1,000 millimeters = 1 meter

million [mil′yən] **millón** 1,000 thousands; written as 1,000,000

mixed number [mikst num′bər] **número mixto** A number that is made up of a whole number and a fraction
Example: $1\frac{5}{8}$

multiple [mul′tə•pəl] **múltiplo** The product of two counting numbers is a multiple of each of those numbers

multiplication [mul•tə•pli•kā′shən] **multiplicación** A process to find the total number of items made up of equal-sized groups, or to find the total number of items in a given number of groups. It is the inverse operation of division.

multiply [mul′tə•plī] **multiplicar** When you combine equal groups, you can multiply to find how many in all; the inverse operation of division

nonagon [nän′ə•gän] **eneágono** A polygon with nine sides and nine angles

not equal to (≠) [not ē′kwəl to͞o] **no igual a** A symbol that indicates one quantity is not equal to another

number line [num′bər līn] **recta numérica** A line on which numbers can be located
Example:

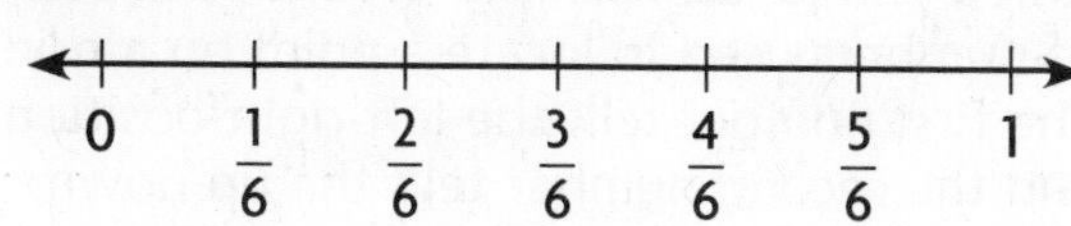

numerator [no͞o′mər•āt•ər] **numerador** The number above the bar in a fraction that tells how many equal parts of the whole or group are being considered

Example: $\frac{3}{4} \leftarrow$ numerator

numerical expression [no͞o•mer′i•kəl ek•spresh′ən] **expresión numérica** A mathematical phrase that uses only numbers and operation signs

obtuse angle [äb•to͞os′ ang′gəl] **ángulo obtuso** An angle whose measure is greater than 90° and less than 180°
Example:

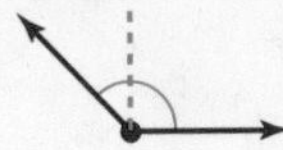

obtuse triangle [äb•to͞os′ trī′ang•gəl] **triángulo obtusángulo** A triangle that has one obtuse angle

octagon [äk′tə•gän] **octágono** A polygon with eight sides and eight angles
Examples:

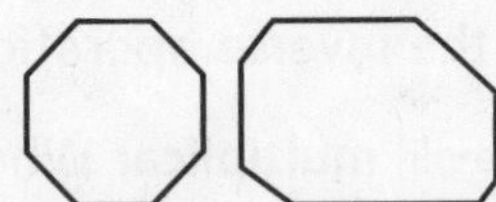

octagonal prism [äk•tag′ə•nəl priz′əm] **prisma octagonal** A three-dimensional figure with two octagonal bases and eight rectangular faces

odd [od] **impar** A whole number that has a 1, 3, 5, 7, or 9 in the ones place

open figure [ō′pən fig′yər] **figura abierta** A figure that does not begin and end at the same point

order of operations [ôr′dər əv äp•ə•rā′shənz] **orden de las operaciones** A special set of rules which gives the order in which calculations are done in an expression

ordered pair [ôr′dərd pâr] **par ordenado** A pair of numbers used to locate a point on a grid. The first number tells the left-right position and the second number tells the up-down position

origin [ôr′ə•jin] **origen** The point where the two axes of a coordinate grid intersect; (0, 0)

ounce (oz) [ouns] **onza (oz)** A customary unit used to measure weight; 16 ounces = 1 pound

overestimate [ō′vər•es•tə•mit] **sobrestimar** An estimate that is greater than the exact answer

pan balance [pan bal′əns] **balanza de platillos** An instrument used to weigh objects and to compare the weights of objects

parallel lines [pâr′ə•lel līnz] **líneas paralelas** Lines in the same plane that never intersect and are always the same distance apart
Example:

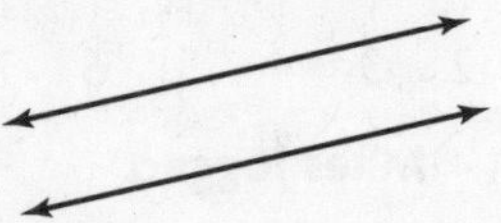

parallelogram [pâr•ə•lel′ə•gram] **paralelogramo** A quadrilateral whose opposite sides are parallel and have the same length, or are congruent
Example:

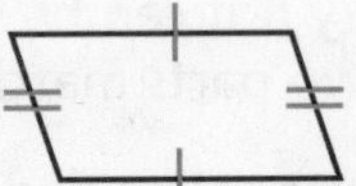

parentheses [pə•ren′thə•sēz] **paréntesis** The symbols used to show which operation or operations in an expression should be done first

partial product [pär′shəl präd′əkt] **producto parcial** A method of multiplying in which the ones, tens, hundreds, and so on are multiplied separately and then the products are added together

partial quotient [pär′shəl kwō′shənt] **cociente parcial** A method of dividing in which multiples of the divisor are subtracted from the dividend and then the quotients are added together

pattern [pat'ərn] **patrón** An ordered set of numbers or objects; the order helps you predict what will come next
Examples: 2, 4, 6, 8, 10

pentagon [pen'tə•gän] **pentágono** A polygon with five sides and five angles
Examples:

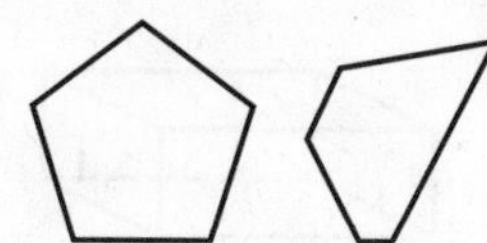

pentagonal prism [pen•tag'ə•nəl priz'əm] **prisma pentagonal** A three-dimensional figure with two pentagonal bases and five rectangular faces

pentagonal pyramid [pen•tag'ə•nəl pir'ə•mid] **pirámide pentagonal** A pyramid with a pentagonal base and five triangular faces

perimeter [pə•rim'ə•tər] **perímetro** The distance around a closed plane figure

period [pir'ē•əd] **período** Each group of three digits separated by commas in a multi-digit number
Example: 85,643,900 has three periods.

perpendicular lines [pər•pən•dik'yo͞o•lər līnz] **líneas perpendiculares** Two lines that intersect to form four right angles
Example:

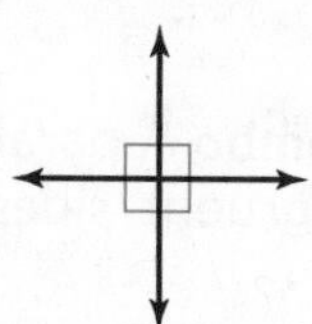

picture graph [pik'chər graf] **gráfica con dibujos** A graph that displays countable data with symbols or pictures
Example:

HOW WE GET TO SCHOOL

Walk	⊛ ⊛ ⊛
Ride a Bike	⊛ ⊛ ⊛ ⊛
Ride a Bus	⊛ ⊛ ⊛ ⊛ ⊛ ◐
Ride in a Car	⊛ ⊛

Key: Each ⊛ = 10 students.

pint (pt) [pīnt] **pinta** A customary unit used to measure capacity; 2 cups = 1 pint

place value [plās val'yo͞o] **valor posicional** The value of each digit in a number based on the location of the digit

plane [plān] **plano** A flat surface that extends without end in all directions
Example:

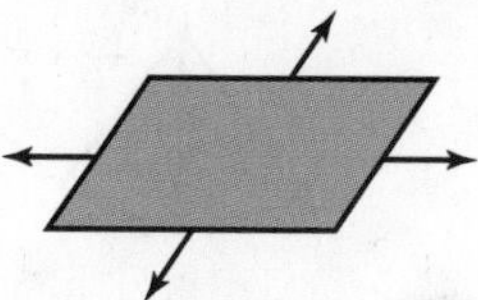

plane figure [plān fig'yər] **figura plana** See *two-dimensional figure*

point [point] **punto** An exact location in space

polygon [päl'i•gän] **polígono** A closed plane figure formed by three or more line segments
Examples:

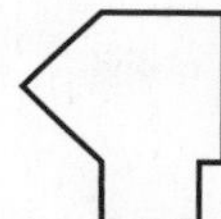

Polygons Not Polygons

polyhedron [päl•i•hē'drən] **poliedro** A solid figure with faces that are polygons
Examples:

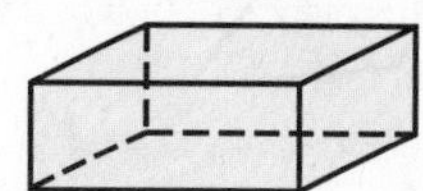
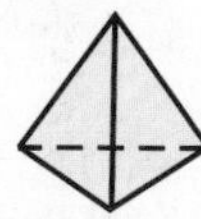

pound (lb) [pound] **libra (lb)** A customary unit used to measure weight;
1 pound = 16 ounces

prime number [prīm num'bər] **número primo** A number that has exactly two factors: 1 and itself
Examples: 2, 3, 5, 7, 11, 13, 17, and 19 are prime numbers. 1 is not a prime number.

prism [priz'əm] **prisma** A solid figure that has two congruent, polygon-shaped bases, and other faces that are all rectangles
Examples:

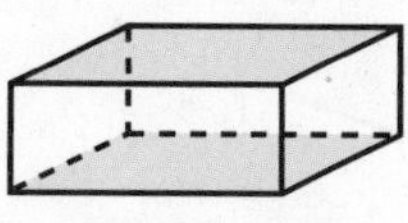
rectangular prism

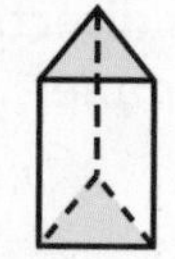
triangular prism

product [präd′əkt] **producto** The answer to a multiplication problem

protractor [prō′trak•tər] **transportador** A tool used for measuring or drawing angles

pyramid [pir′ə•mid] **pirámide** A solid figure with a polygon base and all other faces are triangles that meet at a common vertex
Example:

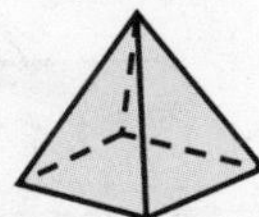

Word History

A fire is sometimes in the shape of a pyramid, with a point at the top and a wider base. This may be how *pyramid* got its name. The Greek word for fire was *pura,* which may have been combined with the Egyptian word for pyramid, *pimar.*

quadrilateral [kwä•dri•lat′ər•əl] **cuadrilátero** A polygon with four sides and four angles
Example:

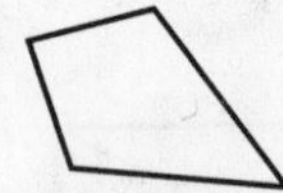

quart (qt) [kwôrt] **cuarto (ct)** A customary unit used to measure capacity; 2 pints = 1 quart

quotient [kwō′shənt] **cociente** The number that results from dividing
Example: 8 ÷ 4 = 2. The quotient is 2.

range [rānj] **rango** The difference between the greatest and least numbers in a data set

ray [rā] **semirrecta** A part of a line; it has one endpoint and continues without end in one direction
Example:

rectangle [rek′tang•gəl] **rectángulo** A parallelogram with four right angles
Example:

rectangular prism [rek•tang′gyə•lər priz′əm] **prisma rectangular** A three-dimensional figure in which all six faces are rectangles
Example:

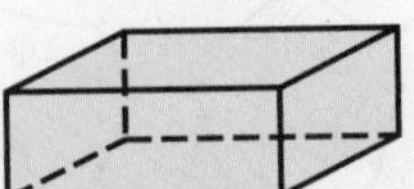

rectangular pyramid [rek•tang′gyə•lər pir′ə•mid] **pirámide rectangular** A pyramid with a rectangular base and four triangular faces

regroup [rē•grōōp′] **reagrupar** To exchange amounts of equal value to rename a number
Example: 5 + 8 = 13 ones or 1 ten 3 ones

regular polygon [reg′yə•lər päl′i•gän] **polígono regular** A polygon in which all sides are congruent and all angles are congruent

related facts [ri•lāt′id fakts] **operaciones relacionadas** A set of related addition and subtraction, or multiplication and division, number sentences

Examples: 4 × 7 = 28   28 ÷ 4 = 7
7 × 4 = 28   28 ÷ 7 = 4

remainder [ri•mān′dər] **residuo** The amount left over when a number cannot be divided equally

rhombus [räm′bəs] **rombo** A parallelogram with four equal, or congruent, sides
Example:

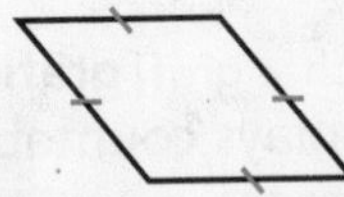

Word History

Rhombus is almost identical to its Greek origin, *rhombos.* The original meaning was "spinning top" or "magic wheel," which is easy to imagine when you look at a rhombus, an equilateral parallelogram.

right angle [rīt ang′gəl] **ángulo recto** An angle that forms a square corner and has a measure of 90°
Example:

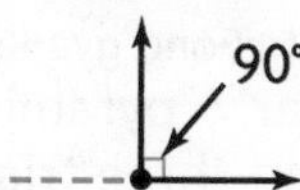

right triangle [rīt trī′ang•gəl] **triángulo rectángulo** A triangle that has a right angle
Example:

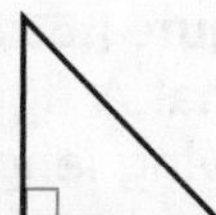

round [round] **redondear** To replace a number with one that is simpler and is approximately the same size as the original number
Example: 114.6 rounded to the nearest ten is 110 and to the nearest one is 115.

scale [skāl] **escala** A series of numbers placed at fixed distances on a graph to help label the graph

scalene triangle [skā′lēn trī′ang•gəl] **triángulo escaleno** A triangle with no congruent sides
Example:

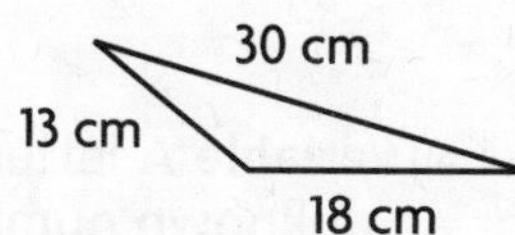

second (sec) [sek′ənd] **segundo (seg)** A small unit of time; 60 seconds = 1 minute

sequence [sē′kwəns] **sucesión** An ordered list of numbers

simplest form [sim′pləst fôrm] **mínima expresión** A fraction is in simplest form when the numerator and denominator have only 1 as a common factor.

skip count [skip kount] **contar salteado** A pattern of counting forward or backward
Example: 5, 10, 15, 20, 25, 30, . . .

solid figure [sä′lid fig′yər] **cuerpo geométrico** See *three-dimensional figure*

solution [sə•lo͞o′shən] **solución** A value that, when substituted for the variable, makes an equation true

sphere [sfir] **esfera** A solid figure whose curved surface is the same distance from the center to all its points
Example:

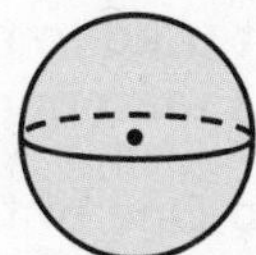

square [skwâr] **cuadrado** A polygon with four equal, or congruent, sides and four right angles

square pyramid [skwâr pir′ə•mid] **pirámide cuadrada** A solid figure with a square base and with four triangular faces that have a common vertex
Example:

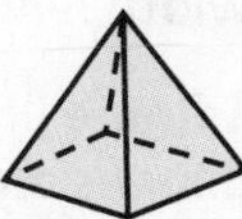

square unit [skwâr yo͞o′nit] **unidad cuadrada** A unit used to measure area such as square foot (ft^2), square meter (m^2), and so on

standard form [stan′dərd fôrm] **forma normal** A way to write numbers by using the digits 0–9, with each digit having a place value
Example: 456 ← standard form

straight angle [strāt ang′gəl] **ángulo llano** An angle whose measure is 180°
Example:

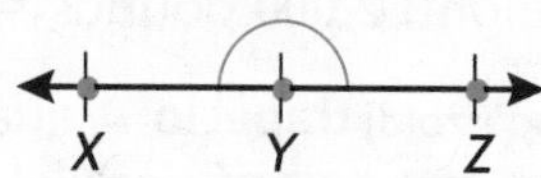

subtraction [səb•trak′shən] **resta** The process of finding how many are left when a number of items are taken away from a group of items; the process of finding the difference when two groups are compared; the inverse operation of addition

sum [sum] **suma o total** The answer to an addition problem

tablespoon (tbsp) [tā′bəl•spo͞on] **cucharada (cda)** A customary unit used to measure capacity; 3 teaspoons = 1 tablespoon

tally table [tal′ē tā′bəl] **tabla de conteo** A table that uses tally marks to record data

teaspoon (tsp) [tē′spo͞on] **cucharadita (cdta)** A customary unit used to measure capacity; 1 tablespoon = 3 teaspoons

tenth [tenth] **décimo** One of ten equal parts
Example: 0.7 = seven tenths

term [tûrm] **término** A number in a sequence

thousandth [thou′zəndth] **milésimo** One of one thousand equal parts
Example: 0.006 = six thousandths

three-dimensional [thrē də•men′shə•nəl] **tridimensional** Measured in three directions, such as length, width, and height

three-dimensional figure [thrē də•men′shə•nəl fig′yər] **figura tridimensional** A figure having length, width, and height
Example:

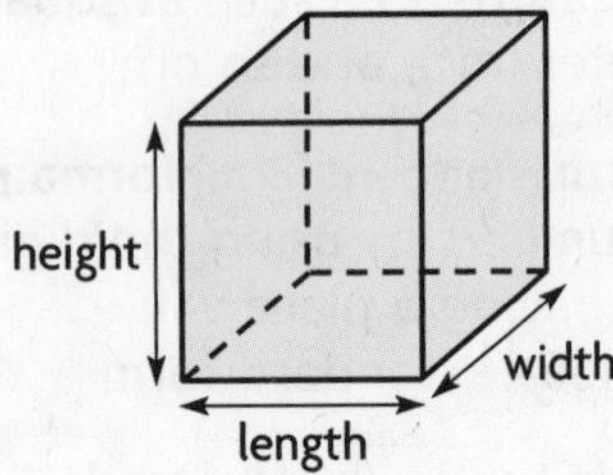

ton (T) [tun] **tonelada** A customary unit used to measure weight; 2,000 pounds = 1 ton

trapezoid [trap′i•zoid] **trapecio** A quadrilateral with at least one pair of parallel sides
Examples:

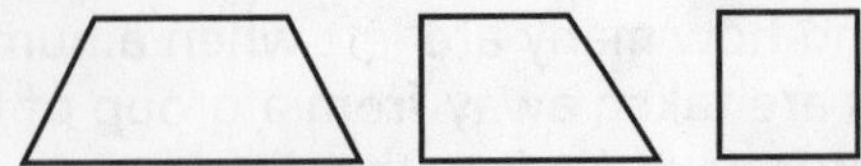

triangle [trī′ang•gəl] **triángulo** A polygon with three sides and three angles
Examples:

triangular prism [trī•ang′gyə•lər priz′əm] **prisma triangular** A solid figure that has two triangular bases and three rectangular faces

triangular pyramid [trī•ang′gyə•lər pir′ə•mid] **pirámide triangular** A pyramid that has a triangular base and three triangular faces

two-dimensional [to͞o də•men′shə•nəl] **bidimensional** Measured in two directions, such as length and width

two-dimensional figure [to͞o də•men′shə•nəl fig′yər] **figura bidimensional** A figure that lies in a plane; a figure having length and width

underestimate [un•dər•es′tə•mit] **subestimar** An estimate that is less than the exact answer

unit cube [yo͞o′nit kyo͞ob] **cubo unitaria** A cube that has a length, width, and height of 1 unit

unit fraction [yo͞o′nit frak′shən] **fracción unitaria** A fraction that has 1 as a numerator

unit square [yo͞o′nit skwâr] **cuadrado de una unidad** A square with a side length of 1 unit, used to measure area

variable [vâr′ē•ə•bəl] **variable** A letter or symbol that stands for an unknown number or numbers

Venn diagram [ven dī′ə•gram] **diagrama de Venn** A diagram that shows relationships among sets of things
Example:

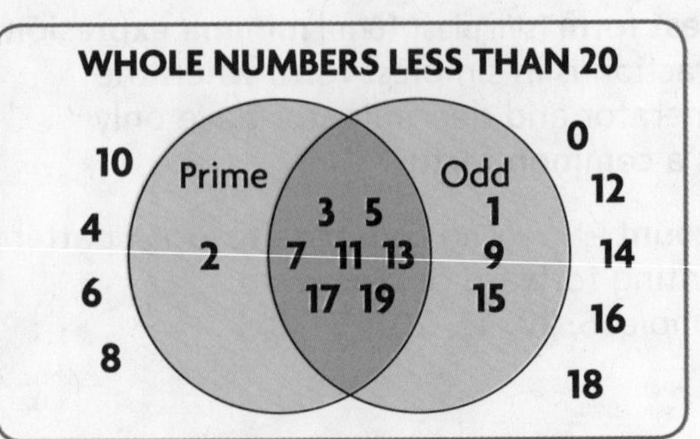

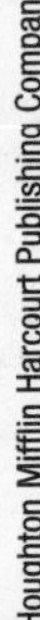

vertex [vûr′teks] **vértice** The point where two or more rays meet; the point of intersection of two sides of a polygon; the point of intersection of three (or more) edges of a solid figure; the top point of a cone; the plural of vertex is vertices
Examples:

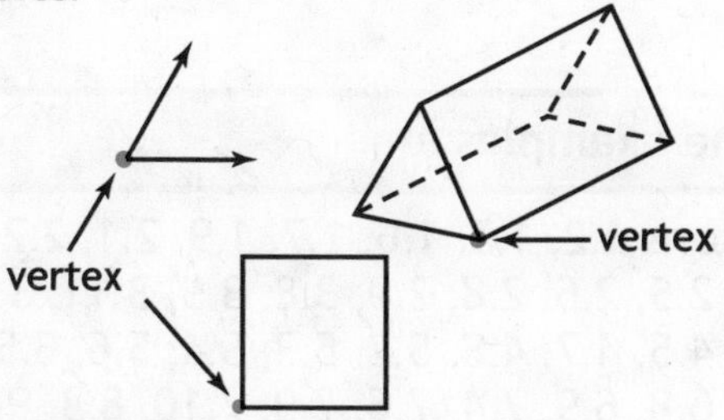

Word History

The Latin word *vertere* means "to turn" and also relates to "highest." You can turn a figure around a point, or *vertex*.

vertical [vûr′ti•kəl] **vertical** Extending up and down

volume [väl′yo͞om] **volumen** The measure of the space a solid figure occupies

weight [wāt] **peso** How heavy an object is

whole [hōl] **entero** All of the parts of a shape or group

whole number [hōl num′bər] **número entero** One of the numbers 0, 1, 2, 3, 4, . . . ; the set of whole numbers goes on without end

word form [wûrd fôrm] **en palabras** A way to write numbers in standard English
Example: 4,829 = four thousand, eight hundred twenty-nine

x*-axis** [eks ak′sis] **eje de la *x The horizontal number line on a coordinate plane

x*-coordinate** [eks kō•ôrd′n•it] **coordenada *x The first number in an ordered pair; tells the distance to move right or left from (0, 0)

yard (yd) [yärd] **yarda (yd)** A customary unit used to measure length or distance; 3 feet = 1 yard

y*-axis** [wī ak′sis] **eje de la *y The vertical number line on a coordinate plane

y*-coordinate** [wī kō•ôrd′n•it] **coordenada *y The second number in an ordered pair; tells the distance to move up or down from (0, 0)

Zero Property of Multiplication [zē′rō präp′ər•tē əv mul•tə•pli•kā′shən] **propiedad del cero de la multiplicación** The property that states that when you multiply by zero, the product is zero

Correlations

COMMON CORE STATE STANDARDS

Standards You Will Learn

Mathematical Practices		Some examples are:
MP1	Make sense of problems and persevere in solving them.	Lessons 1.2, 1.3, 1.6, 1.7, 1.9, 2.1, 2.2, 2.3, 2.4, 2.5, 2.6, 2.8, 2.9, 3.8, 3.9, 3.11, 3.12, 4.4, 4.5, 4.7, 4.8, 5.2, 5.3, 5.4, 5.6, 6.5, 6.6, 6.7, 6.8, 6.9, 7.4, 7.6, 7.9, 7.10, 8.3, 9.1, 10.1, 10.3, 10.4, 11.1, 11.4, 11.7, 11.8, 11.10
MP2	Reason abstractly and quantitatively.	Lessons 1.1, 1.2, 1.3, 1.4, 1.5, 1.6, 1.8, 1.9, 1.11, 1.12, 2.2, 2.5, 2.6, 2.7, 3.2, 3.3, 3.6, 3.7, 3.8, 3.9, 3.12, 4.1, 4.2, 4.3, 4.6, 4.8, 5.2, 5.3, 5.4, 5.5, 5.6, 5.7, 5.8, 6.2, 6.3, 6.4, 6.5, 6.6, 6.7, 6.9, 7.3, 7.5, 7.6, 7.7, 7.8, 7.9, 8.1, 8.3, 8.5, 9.1, 10.2, 10.3, 10.5, 10.6, 11.1, 11.2, 11.5, 11.7, 11.8, 11.9
MP3	Construct viable arguments and critique the reasoning of others.	Lessons 1.3, 1.5, 1.6, 1.8, 1.9, 1.10, 1.11, 2.3, 2.4, 2.5, 2.7, 2.9, 3.4, 4.1, 4.3, 4.4, 4.6, 4.7, 5.7, 6.2, 6.3, 6.5, 7.4, 7.5, 7.6, 7.8, 7.10, 8.4, 9.3, 10.6, 11.3, 11.6, 11.11
MP4	Model with mathematics.	Lessons 1.7, 1.10, 1.11, 1.12, 2.1, 2.3, 2.7, 2.9, 3.1, 4.2, 4.5, 5.3, 5.5, 6.1, 6.2, 6.4, 6.9, 6.10, 7.2, 7.7, 9.1, 9.2, 9.3, 9.4, 9.6, 9.7, 10.2, 10.4, 10.6
MP5	Use appropriate tools strategically.	Lessons 1.1, 3.1, 3.5, 3.6, 3.7, 3.9, 3.12, 5.1, 5.2, 5.5, 5.7, 6.1, 6.2, 6.7, 7.1, 7.2, 7.3, 7.4, 7.7, 7.8, 8.1, 8.4, 8.5, 11.1, 11.5, 11.6
MP6	Attend to precision.	Lessons 1.7, 1.8, 1.10, 2.1, 2.3, 2.8, 3.3, 3.4, 3.5, 3.7, 4.1, 4.2, 4.3, 4.4, 4.8, 5.1, 5.2, 5.3, 5.4, 5.5, 5.7, 5.8, 6.1, 6.3, 6.4, 6.6, 6.7, 6.9, 7.1, 7.2, 7.3, 7.5, 7.6, 7.8, 7.9, 7.10, 8.2, 8.3, 9.2, 9.4, 9.5, 9.6, 10.1, 10.2, 10.4, 10.5, 10.7, 11.1, 11.2, 11.4, 11.5, 11.6, 11.7, 11.8, 11.9, 11.10, 11.11
MP7	Look for and make use of structure.	Lessons 1.1, 1.2, 1.4, 1.8, 2.8, 3.1, 3.2, 3.10, 5.1, 5.8, 6.8, 6.10, 9.5, 9.6, 9.7, 10.1, 10.5, 10.6, 10.7, 11.2, 11.3, 11.4, 11.10
MP8	Look for and express regularity in repeated reasoning.	Lessons 1.3, 1.4, 1.5, 2.2, 2.4, 2.6, 3.4, 3.5, 3.6, 3.8, 3.10, 4.6, 4.7, 5.6, 5.7, 6.8, 6.10, 8.2, 9.3, 9.5, 11.2, 11.4

Standards You Will Learn

Student Edition Lessons

Domain: Operations and Algebraic Thinking		
Write and interpret numerical expressions.		
5.OA.A.1	Use parentheses, brackets, or braces in numerical expressions, and evaluate expressions with these symbols.	Lessons 1.3, 1.10, 1.11, 1.12
5.OA.A.2	Write simple expressions that record calculations with numbers, and interpret numerical expressions without evaluating them.	Lesson 1.10, 6.4
Analyze patterns and relationships.		
5.OA.B.3	Generate two numerical patterns using two given rules. Identify apparent relationships between corresponding terms. Form ordered pairs consisting of corresponding terms from the two patterns, and graph the ordered pairs on a coordinate plane.	Lessons 9.5, 9.6, 9.7

Standards You Will Learn

		Student Edition Lessons
Domain: Number and Operations in Base Ten		
Understand the place value system.		
5.NBT.A.1	Recognize that in a multi-digit number, a digit in one place represents 10 times as much as it represents in the place to its right and 1/10 of what it represents in the place to its left.	Lessons 1.1, 1.2, 3.1
5.NBT.A.2	Explain patterns in the number of zeros of the product when multiplying a number by powers of 10, and explain patterns in the placement of the decimal point when a decimal is multiplied or divided by a power of 10. Use whole-number exponents to denote powers of 10.	Lessons 1.4, 1.5, 4.1, 5.1
5.NBT.A.3	Read, write, and compare decimals to thousandths.	
5.NBT.A.3a	Read and write decimals to thousandths using base-ten numerals, number names, and expanded form, e.g., $347.392 = 3 \times 100 + 4 \times 10 + 7 \times 1 + 3 \times (1/10) + 9 \times (1/100) + 2 \times (1/1000)$.	Lesson 3.2
5.NBT.A.3b	Compare two decimals to thousandths based on meanings of the digits in each place, using >, =, and < symbols to record the results of comparisons.	Lesson 3.3
5.NBT.A.4	Use place value understanding to round decimals to any place.	Lesson 3.4

Standards You Will Learn

Standards You Will Learn		Student Edition Lessons
Perform operations with multi-digit whole numbers and with decimals to hundredths.		
5.NBT.B.5	Fluently multiply multi-digit whole numbers using the standard algorithm.	Lessons 1.6, 1.7
5.NBT.B.6	Find whole-number quotients of whole numbers with up to four-digit dividends and two-digit divisors, using strategies based on place value, the properties of operations, and/or the relationship between multiplication and division. Illustrate and explain the calculation by using equations, rectangular arrays, and/or area models.	Lessons 1.8, 1.9, 2.1, 2.2, 2.3, 2.4, 2.5, 2.6, 2.8, 2.9
5.NBT.B.7	Add, subtract, multiply, and divide decimals to hundredths, using concrete models or drawings and strategies based on place value, properties of operations, and/or the relationship between addition and subtraction; relate the strategy to a written method and explain the reasoning used.	Lessons 3.5, 3.6, 3.7, 3.8, 3.9, 3.10, 3.11, 3.12, 4.2, 4.3, 4.4, 4.5, 4.6, 4.7, 4.8, 5.2, 5.3, 5.4, 5.5, 5.6, 5.7, 5.8
Domain: Number and Operations—Fractions		
Use equivalent fractions as a strategy to add and subtract fractions.		
5.NF.A.1	Add and subtract fractions with unlike denominators (including mixed numbers) by replacing given fractions with equivalent fractions in such a way as to produce an equivalent sum or difference of fractions with like denominators.	Lessons 6.1, 6.4, 6.5, 6.6, 6.7, 6.8, 6.9, 6.10
5.NF.A.2	Solve word problems involving addition and subtraction of fractions referring to the same whole, including cases of unlike denominators, e.g., by using visual fraction models or equations to represent the problem. Use benchmark fractions and number sense of fractions to estimate mentally and assess the reasonableness of answers.	Lessons 6.1, 6.2, 6.3, 6.5, 6.6, 6.7, 6.9

Standards You Will Learn

Student Edition Lessons

	Apply and extend previous understandings of multiplication and division to multiply and divide fractions.	
5.NF.B.3	Interpret a fraction as division of the numerator by the denominator ($a/b = a \div b$). Solve word problems involving division of whole numbers leading to answers in the form of fractions or mixed numbers, e.g., by using visual fraction models or equations to represent the problem.	Lessons 2.7, 8.3
5.NF.B.4	Apply and extend previous understandings of multiplication to multiply a fraction or whole number by a fraction.	
5.NF.B.4a	Interpret the product $(a/b) \times q$ as a parts of a partition of q into b equal parts; equivalently, as the result of a sequence of operations $a \times q \div b$.	Lessons 7.1, 7.2, 7.3, 7.4, 7.6
5.NF.B.4b	Find the area of a rectangle with fractional side lengths by tiling it with unit squares of the appropriate unit fraction side lengths, and show that the area is the same as would be found by multiplying the side lengths. Multiply fractional side lengths to find areas of rectangles, and represent fraction products as rectangular areas.	Lessons 7.7, 7.10

Standards You Will Learn

	Standards You Will Learn	Student Edition Lessons
Apply and extend previous understandings of multiplication and division to multiply and divide fractions. *(Continued)*		
5.NF.B.5	Interpret multiplication as scaling (resizing), by:	
5.NF.B.5a	Comparing the size of a product to the size of one factor on the basis of the size of the other factor, without performing the indicated multiplication.	Lessons 7.5, 7.8
5.NF.B.5b	Explaining why multiplying a given number by a fraction greater than 1 results in a product greater than the given number (recognizing multiplication by whole numbers greater than 1 as a familiar case); explaining why multiplying a given number by a fraction less than 1 results in a product smaller than the given number; and relating the principle of fraction equivalence $a/b = (n \times a)/(n \times b)$ to the effect of multiplying a/b by 1.	Lessons 7.5, 7.6, 7.8
5.NF.B.6	Solve real world problems involving multiplication of fractions and mixed numbers, e.g., by using visual fraction models or equations to represent the problem.	Lessons 7.9, 7.10

Standards You Will Learn

Standards You Will Learn		Student Edition Lessons
Apply and extend previous understandings of multiplication and division to multiply and divide fractions. ***(Continued)***		
5.NF.B.7	Apply and extend previous understandings of division to divide unit fractions by whole numbers and whole numbers by unit fractions.	
5.NF.B.7a	Interpret division of a unit fraction by a non-zero whole number, and compute such quotients.	Lessons 8.1, 8.5
5.NF.B.7b	Interpret division of a whole number by a unit fraction, and compute such quotients.	Lessons 8.1, 8.2, 8.5
5.NF.B.7c	Solve real world problems involving division of unit fractions by non-zero whole numbers and division of whole numbers by unit fractions, e.g., by using visual fraction models and equations to represent the problem.	Lessons 8.1, 8.4
Domain: Measurement and Data		
Convert like measurement units within a given measurement system.		
5.MD.A.1	Convert among different-sized standard measurement units within a given measurement system (e.g., convert 5 cm to 0.05 m), and use these conversions in solving multi-step, real world problems.	Lessons 10.1, 10.2, 10.3, 10.4, 10.5, 10.6, 10.7

Standards You Will Learn

Student Edition Lessons

Represent and interpret data.		
5.MD.B.2	Make a line plot to display a data set of measurements in fractions of a unit (1/2, 1/4, 1/8). Use operations on fractions for this grade to solve problems involving information presented in line plots.	Lesson 9.1
Geometric measurement: understand concepts of volume and relate volume to multiplication and to addition.		
5.MD.C.3	Recognize volume as an attribute of solid figures and understand concepts of volume measurement.	Lesson 11.4
5.MD.C.3a	A cube with side length 1 unit, called a "unit cube," is said to have "one cubic unit" of volume, and can be used to measure volume.	Lesson 11.5
5.MD.C.3b	A solid figure which can be packed without gaps or overlaps using *n* unit cubes is said to have a volume of *n* cubic units.	Lesson 11.6
5.MD.C.4	Measure volumes by counting unit cubes, using cubic cm, cubic in, cubic ft, and improvised units.	Lessons 11.6, 11.7

Standards You Will Learn

Student Edition Lessons

Geometric measurement: understand concepts of volume and relate volume to multiplication and to addition. *(Continued)*		
5.MD.C.5	Relate volume to the operations of multiplication and addition and solve real world and mathematical problems involving volume.	
5.MD.C.5a	Find the volume of a right rectangular prism with whole-number side lengths by packing it with unit cubes, and show that the volume is the same as would be found by multiplying the edge lengths, equivalently by multiplying the height by the area of the base. Represent threefold whole-number products as volumes, e.g., to represent the associative property of multiplication.	Lessons 11.8, 11.9
5.MD.C.5b	Apply the formulas $V = l \times w \times h$ and $V = b \times h$ for rectangular prisms to find volumes of right rectangular prisms with whole-number edge lengths in the context of solving real world and mathematical problems.	Lessons 11.8, 11.9, 11.10
5.MD.C.5c	Recognize volume as additive. Find volumes of solid figures composed of two non-overlapping right rectangular prisms by adding the volumes of the non-overlapping parts, applying this technique to solve real world problems.	Lesson 11.11

Standards You Will Learn

	Standards You Will Learn	Student Edition Lessons
Domain: Geometry		
Graph points on the coordinate plane to solve real-world and mathematical problems.		
5.G.A.1	Use a pair of perpendicular number lines, called axes, to define a coordinate system, with the intersection of the lines (the origin) arranged to coincide with the 0 on each line and a given point in the plane located by using an ordered pair of numbers, called its coordinates. Understand that the first number indicates how far to travel from the origin in the direction of one axis, and the second number indicates how far to travel in the direction of the second axis, with the convention that the names of the two axes and the coordinates correspond (e.g., *x*-axis and *x*-coordinate, *y*-axis and *y*-coordinate).	Lesson 9.2
5.G.A.2	Represent real world and mathematical problems by graphing points in the first quadrant of the coordinate plane, and interpret coordinate values of points in the context of the situation.	Lessons 9.3, 9.4
Classify two-dimensional figures into categories based on their properties.		
5.G.B.3	Understand that attributes belonging to a category of two-dimensional figures also belong to all subcategories of that category.	Lessons 11.1, 11.2, 11.3
5.G.B.4	Classify two-dimensional figures in a hierarchy based on properties.	Lessons 11.1, 11.2, 11.3

Index

G

Table of Measures

METRIC	CUSTOMARY
Length	
1 centimeter (cm) = 10 millimeters (mm)	1 foot (ft) = 12 inches (in.)
1 meter (m) = 1,000 millimeters	1 yard (yd) = 3 feet, or 36 inches
1 meter = 100 centimeters	1 mile (mi) = 1,760 yards, or 5,280 feet
1 meter = 10 decimeters (dm)	
1 kilometer (km) = 1,000 meters	
Capacity	
1 liter (L) = 1,000 milliliters (mL)	1 cup (c) = 8 fluid ounces (fl oz)
1 metric cup = 250 milliliters	1 pint (pt) = 2 cups
1 liter = 4 metric cups	1 quart (qt) = 2 pints, or 4 cups
1 kiloliter (kL) = 1,000 liters	1 gallon (gal) = 4 quarts
Mass/Weight	
1 gram (g) = 1,000 milligrams (mg)	1 pound (lb) = 16 ounces (oz)
1 gram = 100 centigrams (cg)	1 ton (T) = 2,000 pounds
1 kilogram (kg) = 1,000 grams	

TIME
1 minute (min) = 60 seconds (sec)
1 half hour = 30 minutes
1 hour (hr) = 60 minutes
1 day = 24 hours
1 week (wk) = 7 days
1 year (yr) = 12 months (mo), or about 52 weeks
1 year = 365 days
1 leap year = 366 days
1 decade = 10 years
1 century = 100 years
1 millennium = 1,000 years

SYMBOLS

$=$	is equal to	$\overleftrightarrow{AB}$	line *AB*
$\neq$	is not equal to	$\overrightarrow{AB}$	ray *AB*
$>$	is greater than	$\overline{AB}$	line segment *AB*
$<$	is less than	$\angle ABC$	angle *ABC*, or angle *B*
(2, 3)	ordered pair (x, y)	$\triangle ABC$	triangle *ABC*
$\perp$	is perpendicular to	$^\circ$	degree
$\parallel$	is parallel to	$^\circ$C	degrees Celsius
		$^\circ$F	degrees Fahrenheit

FORMULAS

Perimeter		Area	
Polygon	P = sum of the lengths of sides	Rectangle	$A = b \times h$, or $A = bh$
Rectangle	$P = (2 \times l) + (2 \times w)$, or $P = 2l + 2w$		
Square	$P = 4 \times s$, or $P = 4s$		

Volume

Rectangular prism $V = B \times h$, or $V = l \times w \times h$

B = area of base shape, h = height of prism